DIVORCE AND NEW BEGINNINGS

DIVORCE AND NEW BEGINNINGS

An Authoritative Guide To Recovery and Growth, Solo Parenting, and Stepfamilies

Genevieve Clapp, Ph.D.

JOHN WILEY & SONS, INC.
New York • Chichester • Brisbane • Toronto • Singapore

This publication is designed to provide accurate and
authoritative information in regard to the subject matter
covered. It is sold with the understanding that the publisher is
not engaged in rendering legal, accounting, psychotherapeutic,
or other professional service. If legal advice or other expert
assistance is required, the services of a competent professional
person should be sought. *Adapted from a Declaration of
Principles jointly adopted by a Committee of the American
Bar Association and a Committee of Publishers.*

Library of Congress Cataloging-in-Publication Data:

Clapp, Genevieve.
    Divorce and new beginnings : an authoritative guide to recovery and
growth, solo parenting, and stepfamilies / Genevieve Clapp.
        p.   cm.
    Includes bibliographical references (p.   ) and index.
    ISBN 0-471-52631-2 (cloth)
    1. Divorce—United States. 2. Divorced people—United States—
Psychology. 3. Children of divorced parents—United States. 4. Single
parents—United States. 5. Stepfamilies—United States. I. Title.
HQ834.C58 1992
306.89—dc20   91-27824

To Jerry,
This is almost as much
your book as it is mine.

I withdrew to a higher vantage
to start anew . . .
The anger has passed,
now only remains a calm.
Confusion replaced with conviction
that transitions are made
. . . pain with memories
. . . fear with understanding
. . . loneliness with vision
old joys with new beginnings.

anonymous

Acknowledgments

My sincere thanks go to the hundreds of researchers and mental health professionals throughout the country whose work forms the basis of this book, especially those who were kind enough to send me copies of their studies. I sincerely apologize for not including each and every source that made a contribution to these pages. I could include only the relatively few that contributed most heavily to the content.

I also thank the library staffs at San Diego State University and the University of California at San Diego for their enormous help during my two years of research. The San Diego County Library System was immensely helpful in obtaining material from libraries throughout the state.

This book would have been a very different product had it not been for some very special people. Foremost is my husband Jerry, who spent long hours discussing ideas with me and reading and rereading every page of the manuscript. His critiques and suggestions were invaluable. So was his bottomless reserve of support and humor, which has kept me afloat more than a few times over the years. I especially thank Dr. Barbara Jean Shea, who strengthened many chapters with her keen clinical mind and expertise. My editor, Herb Reich, maintained an active interest throughout, contributing significantly with his suggestions. My appreciation goes to Ray McKinley and other people at New Beginnings—if only this wonderful divorce support group were nationwide. A thanks to Diane Murdoch, who is always ready to conduct her own personal survey for me with her extensive contacts. And thanks to my children, Gary and Karen, for their unfailing support—with a special thanks to Karen, who stepped in, unasked, and took over for me at home during the last three weeks of rewriting.

G.C.

Preface

*I*f you are reading this book, you are doing so probably not for academic interest but because divorce or a stepfamily has touched you personally. You may be looking for some insight: "Is what I'm going through common?" "How typical are my children's problems?" "Why do I feel *this* bad?" Or you may be searching for specific help: "Can I avoid some of the problems I see in so many others?" "What is the best way I can prepare myself and my children for what lies ahead?" "How can I best cope with the seemingly endless problems that are being hurled my way?" "What can I do to help my children bounce back without scars?"

The good news: Over the past decade and a half, there has been an explosion of research studying divorcing men and women, children of divorce, single parents and their children, and stepfamilies. From it, a wealth of new and practical information has emerged that can be of enormous help to you. Thanks to what has been learned, you need not be surprised, as so many others have been, by what lies ahead of you, and you need not be unprepared for it, either. This book fully capitalizes on the flood of new findings. It is based on more than 400 studies, reports, and books published by experts in each of these areas. Don't misunderstand; this is not an academic report. It is a one-hundred-percent practical guide geared directly to your needs.

Within these pages, you will gain access to the experiences of thousands who have weathered the rupture of their marriages and families and have started over again. If you know what to expect and understand why it happens, the upcoming months and years will be considerably less stressful. But more importantly, you will learn what actions you can take to deal with the feelings, problems, and challenges that you and your children, if you have any, will encounter.

Whether you are a parent or childless, a man or a woman, a parent with or without custody, a stepparent, or a parent creating a stepfamily for your children, you will be armed with a road map of what lies ahead and a repertoire of good coping skills. With them, you can avoid many of the problems that face so many people in your situation, and you can build successful new beginnings.

Why combine divorce, solo parenting, and stepfamilies in a single book? Because even years after their legal divorces, many people have not resolved divorce-related issues. And, unfortunately, their unfinished business creates stumbling blocks to building either rewarding single lives or good remarriages and stepfamilies. If you have some unfinished business related to your divorce, you can take care of it now so you can finally complete your transition to new beginnings. Maybe you still need to deal with your anger (Chapter 5). Perhaps you still need to end your conflict with your ex-spouse and build a different kind of relationship so you can cooperate in the parenting of your children (Chapter 11). Maybe you still need to rebuild your self-esteem (Chapter 12) or build a new identity separate from your married one (Chapter 12). You may need to finally let go of your former marriage (Chapter 6) or help your children with divorce-related issues (Chapters 8 and 10).

This is a true self-help book that will take you, and your children, if you have any, step by step through each stage of divorce and rebuilding. If you take the route of the majority of divorcing men and women by remarrying, this book will guide you in creating a successful stepfamily, whether children live with you full-time or part-time. To help you handle your daily problems and long-term concerns, there are hundreds of practical suggestions and effective coping strategies based on the findings and collective insights of hundreds of experts. These are just a few examples of what you will learn: How to manage your stress, anxiety, and turbulent emotions; how to take charge of your life, move in positive directions, and prevent yourself from drifting back into old patterns; and how to ease your children's distress and best handle common problems. The book will show you specific steps you can take to create the conditions that will enable your children to thrive despite the divorce. You will also see how to deal with discipline, with children playing one parent against the other, with holidays and guilt, and with dating and intimacy. If you are a noncustodial parent, you will learn how to meet the special challenges of visitation and how to build and maintain good relationships with your children. If you are starting a stepfamily, you will learn about the paths stepfamilies often take that lead to spiraling problems and the alternative paths you can take that usually lead to successful stepfamilies.

Throughout the book, case studies illustrate points made or coping strategies discussed. Some are composites of several people, some have had identifying characteristics altered to assure anonymity, and some have been cited from other sources.

GENEVIEVE CLAPP
SAN DIEGO, CALIFORNIA

Contents

PART I

LAYING THE FOUNDATION:
Coping Successfully with Divorce

1

THE AFTERMATH OF MARRIAGE

Barbara, an attractive 40-year-old brunette, sat mesmerized at a divorce workshop. It was the first time she had heard about the feelings and problems that people encounter as they go through divorce. "My God," she blurted out, "you're describing my life for the past five months. I didn't know everyone felt like that." There was an immediate restlessness in the room—some nervous laughter, some mumbled comments, one or two heads nodding. "God," Barbara's voice seemed to boom, "what a relief, it's not just me!"

Over the past decade and a half, there has been an explosion of studies on divorce and its aftermath, providing us access to the experience of thousands who have weathered the rupture of their marriages and families. Thanks to those who have gone before you, the course of divorce is no longer unmapped, and you can be prepared for what lies ahead. If you understand the psychological process of divorce and know what to expect, the upcoming months and years will be considerably less stressful.

This book is more than a road map of the coming years, however. It is a survival guide as well. Drawing from the work of hundreds of researchers and therapists, it provides a rich array of information and coping tools to help you handle and sometimes avoid the difficulties divorce so often generates. Among the things you will learn are the following:

- What to expect as you progress through "the divorce experience"
- How to manage your stress, anxiety, and turbulent emotions
- How to get over feeling defeated and immobilized
- What to do about your anger
- How to communicate and negotiate effectively with your ex-spouse in an anger-laden atmosphere
- How to let go of your marriage and get on with your life
- How children experience divorce at different ages

- The answer to the question, "Is it better to stay together for the children's sake?"
- How to help your children through divorce step by step
- What circumstances have been identified as *critical* in determining whether children adjust well or poorly to divorce
- Specific steps you can take to avoid any long-term negative repercussions in your children
- Specific steps you can take to create the kind of environment after divorce that will enable your children to thrive
- Whether one form of custody is better than another
- How to establish a different kind of relationship with your ex-spouse after divorce so you can co-parent your children without destructive conflict
- How to rebuild your self-esteem and new social networks
- How to overcome loneliness and your identity crisis
- How to take control of your life and move in a positive direction
- How to make changes in your life and stick to them

Armed with this road map and a repertoire of good coping skills, you can more easily clear the hurdles that divorce presents and avoid many of the difficulties that complicate the lives of so many divorcing people. Your divorce may remain a significant event in your life, but it does not have to remain the dominant one.

THE IMPACT OF SEPARATION AND DIVORCE

In the 1970s, two northern California researcher/psychotherapists, Judith Wallerstein and Joan Kelly, began what was to be an intensive year-long study of divorcing couples and their children. The researchers wished to learn both how families are affected by divorce and how they resolve the disruptions to their lives. Wallerstein and Kelly had fully expected families to have recovered by the end of the study, since parents would have been separated eighteen months by that time. But the researchers had been mistaken: The majority of adults and children had not yet resolved their divorce-generated difficulties. Wallerstein and Kelly were stunned to find that most families were still in crisis and had not gotten their lives back together yet. More disturbing, a large number of children were doing worse rather than better.

Were the findings of this ground-breaking study a fluke? Since that time, many other studies have been published that have confirmed that adjustment to divorce is neither quick nor easy. On the average, people need two years before they regain their equilibrium. They usually need additional time to become emotionally detached from an ex-spouse and to establish a stable and satisfying new life-style.

You are probably wondering why divorce adjustment should take so long. After all, divorce is the solution to so many problems, isn't it? It may be easy to see why divorce is difficult for someone who had fought against it, or for someone whose partner suddenly walked out. But is divorce also difficult for the person who walks out? Is it also difficult for couples who bitterly argue for years and finally call it quits? Usually yes. It appears that relatively few people escape the effects of divorce easily. In general, divorce is difficult for both the "leaver" and the "left," for men and for women, for those who bickered and fought and for those who lived in indifferent silence, for those married 25 years and for those married five years (although breakups of short-lived marriages tend to be less distressing). Of course, it is more difficult for some people than for others. And it takes some people longer to adjust than it does others; two years is only an *average*.

Once you learn more about divorce, you will see why it has such an impact on each member of the family and why such a long adjustment period is commonly needed. Undoubtedly, the best way to understand the nature of divorce is to look at the experiences that most people encounter.

Loss and Turbulent Emotions

Divorcing men and women are often astounded by the extent of their losses. The marriage that had been an important part of life at one time is now gone. So is a life-style, future plans, a chunk of one's identity, and perhaps a home, financial security, free access to children, and shared friendships. The list goes on. For many, the massive losses create a feeling of rootlessness—a need to feel connected. For many, the feelings of loss and unconnectedness are entangled with a gnawing sense of failure and dwindling feelings of self-worth.

Lives are further complicated by turbulent and conflicting emotions. Men and women who are filled with bitterness, resentment, and anger may suddenly feel stunned by surges of love and yearning for their exs. Their predominant feelings of self-pity, sadness, and depression are suddenly displaced by intoxicating feelings of euphoria, well-being, and freedom. Then, as suddenly as it appeared, the euphoria is snatched away. The pendulum swings back and forth, leading people to feel as if they are in a tiny raft being tossed around on a stormy sea or as if they are on an emotional roller coaster.

The Upheavals

We tend to think of divorce as a single event in people's lives. Nothing could be further from the truth. Separation and divorce set into motion a chain of events that spans an extended period of time. Each link in the chain represents upheaval and change, and each change must be dealt with—changes in routine, finances, personal and social lives, family life, identity, and even changes in expectations and life goals. Studies suggest that divorce requires more readjustment and reorganization than any other stressful life event in our society, except for the death of a spouse.

Few divorcing men and women are prepared for the extent to which their lives are disrupted. Of course, most know there will be major changes, but they usually underestimate them. They also do not anticipate how unsettling the changes in daily routines and comfortably entrenched habits will be. The magnitude of change in day-to-day living causes a good deal of disorientation. This phenomenon has been called "the tyranny of habit."

One woman, Sue, wrote about some of the changes she encountered after she separated from her husband:

> I'm surprised at how many changes there are, considering I'm in the same house, I have no dire money problems, and Jim and I weren't that close to begin with. Some things are small, of course—like staggering in to get a cup of coffee in the morning and finding none made. Some are depressing—like coming home to a half-furnished house and knowing that it will have to be sold at some point to divide our assets. Some come from having to take over the things Jim used to do. These are more troublesome because sometimes I forget about them, like checking the transmission fluid in my old car and paying bills.
>
> Of course, I initiated some changes myself, like a new hairstyle and getting into jogging. Other things *need* to change, but I can't seem to break old habits—I still shop for too much food, still say "we" instead of "I," and still don't think of myself as a single person.
>
> Of course, things have been very different socially. The usual Wednesday night bridge game is off, since I don't have a partner. I've been avoiding parties because they are couples parties and I've begun to feel like an outsider in conversations. I also avoid casual acquaintances because I hate their obvious discomfort. Thank God I have some supportive friends who invite me over. But things are even different with them. My private life has become an open book. A lot of it is my own fault because I'm feeling bad and talk too much. But I'm also getting so many questions and so much well-meaning advice that I feel like a dependent little girl who can't take care of herself. Then there are my in-laws. I seem to have stopped existing for them. That hurts. I've had a few dates, but I wouldn't call them rousing successes. Dating is going to take *a lot* of getting used to. So are the new rules (or should I say lack of rules) in the singles scene. I just haven't faced all that yet. And yes, my sex life is *very* changed.
>
> But I think evenings and weekends are the hardest changes to get used to. I never imagined how lonely and empty I could feel. I've learned what the phrase "deafening silence" means. There isn't anyone handy to tell when I have a rotten day or to commiserate with about the nasty neighbor. I even miss the fights. At least they were *something*. But the worst thing about nights and weekends is the lack of things to keep my mind off Jim and the divorce. I love to entertain and go out to dinners and plays. But doing them alone doesn't appeal to me. Sometimes I feel

plain lost. I literally don't know what to do with myself! Sometimes I wander from room to room and cry. I try reading or watching TV but can't seem to concentrate. I've always been a together person and very much in control, so this is a little scary.

As many changes as Sue felt, her changes are minimal compared to those of a parent who moves out of the family home, sets up a new household, loses daily contact with family life, and becomes a weekend visitor to his or her children. Sue's changes are also minimal compared to those of a new single parent who must shoulder total responsibility for distraught children, find and tackle a full-time job, and sort out a confusing array of day care options. They're minimal compared to the changes experienced by a "corporate wife" whose life has revolved around her husband's career. And they're minimal compared to those of a family whose finances were already tight and now must spread its limited income to pay for two substandard residences.

Besides the upheavals, most divorcing men and women encounter a host of practical problems that would tax anyone's resources, even under the best circumstances.

The Practical Hurdles

With the divorce process comes time-consuming paperwork, the necessity of dealing with an unfamiliar legal system, new loneliness, difficulties concentrating, countless questions from relatives and friends, and the endless list of decisions (about custody, visitation, how to handle holidays, who should go to the children's school play, how every material possession collected over a lifetime together should be divided, and so on).

Divorcing women must suddenly assume the household tasks that may have been formerly in their husbands' domain. Home and car maintenance and repairs, tax returns, and financial planning often top their list of practical problems. Women with primary physical custody of children have a particularly difficult time. Their problems multiply exponentially with the responsibility for dealing with hurt, baffled children who may develop any number of transient problems in response to their family's rupture. Typically, divorcing mothers' lives and homes are in a state of disorganization. Financial worries, caused by their inevitably reduced resources, are a major source of stress. Mothers often must return to full-time employment, turning an overloaded schedule into an exhausting one. Many report having to stay up past midnight just to get the bare essentials done. Yet those who remain at home often complain of being locked into a child's world. Many mothers report that their stress is overwhelming.

Divorcing men have their own set of problems. Many wind up in small or furnished apartments, bitter that they have lost so much of what they had spent years building. A surprising number are lost when it comes to the mechanics of cooking, shopping for food, cleaning, and doing laundry. Fathers without custody report feeling rootless, shut out, guilty, and anxious. The great majority miss daily contact with their children, some desperately so. One 25-year-old man, divorced for a year and a half, complains:

> Their mother claims she has no time to herself and tells me about all my freedom. Freedom? No! It has another name; it's called loneliness.[1]

Many men, in fact, are astonished at the intensity with which they miss being involved in their children's daily lives. They never would have predicted it. Even men who have not been involved fathers miss their children, becoming aware for the first time of all the things they never did when they had the chance. Nor do most fathers predict the practical problems involved in becoming a weekend parent. Visits seem strange and strained. Where do you go? What do you do? How do you relate to your own kids in these strange new circumstances?

Reflecting their stress, fathers tend to sleep less, eat erratically, develop physical symptoms, and bury themselves in work during that first year after separation. It is also common for them to engage in a frenzied social life, not because it is satisfying or pleasurable, but because it helps ward off feelings of being shut out and rootless.

The Uncoupling Hurdle

In their study of almost a thousand divorced men and women, Morton and Bernice Hunt discovered that few people had realized before they were separated how totally bound they were to their former partners—because of children, the years spent together, emotional commitments to each other, shared experiences, entrenched habits developed to accommodate one another, shared friends and relatives, mutual obligations, and joint possessions. Essentially the strands of spouses' lives are woven together into a single fabric. The task of disentangling the threads of their lives is an enormous one that may extend over a period of years.

Completely uncoupling yourself from your spouse could be the most difficult struggle you have after divorce. The disentangling process includes some difficult tasks, including coming to terms with the end of your marriage and becoming *emotionally* detached from your ex. (Chapter 6 will help you with these tough jobs.)

In the process of uncoupling, you may find that a large chunk of your identity is also entangled with your ex-partner's, and with your role as a "husband" or "wife." Talk of an "identity crisis" is a common theme among divorcing men and women, and the question "Who *am* I?" is asked over and over again.

So along with everything else you have to do after divorce, you must forge a new identity for yourself and establish a new life-style that is satisfying to you. You will no longer be tied to the life goals you formulated with your spouse, to the kind of person your spouse accepted (or expected) you to be, or to the life-style you developed together. You can now determine what things you enjoy, what kind of life-style you wish to have, what kind of person you want to be, and what you want to do with the rest of your life. Some people find this prospect exhilarating, as did Ted, a 31-year-old father of an eight-year-old son.

> I felt such exuberant freedom. I had a second chance at life. I no longer had to make the "sensible" and "responsible" choices as Phyllis had always insisted. I decided I would leave my dead-end job and take a chance at starting my own business. I didn't care if I had to work 16-hour days, seven days a week to make it work.

Others, however, find the prospect terrifying, as did Helen, a 48-year-old Michigan mother of a 17-year-old son.

> I would sit by the window in a trance for long hours watching the world go by, feeling my life was over. I would keep coming back to the same question, "What will I do with the rest of my life?" Sometimes I would become so afraid I'd go into a panic. My heart would race, my hands would sweat, I'd shake all over. At first I was afraid I was cracking up. Then I began to wish that I would so Ralph would feel some guilt about what he had done to me.

By now there may be no skeptics left. Adjusting to divorce *is* hard work. It requires learning how to cope with extensive loss, pervasive change, endless practical problems, and intense emotions that may play havoc with your life. It motivates reappraisal, soul searching, and self-exploration. It necessitates breaking with the past, reorganizing your life, and restructuring family relationships. It is no wonder that it so often takes a person a number of years to adjust to a divorce.

Progression through divorce can be divided into three broad stages: *preseparation, transition–restructuring,* and *recovery–rebuilding.* Looking at these three stages can provide you with a road map of what may lie ahead. The road map is only a rough one, however. It sketches the types of experiences and feelings that are common during these stages. You will probably have many of the same feelings and experiences, but you may not experience all of them, and you may not experience them as intensely as many others have.

PRESEPARATION

People's experiences are most varied *before* they make the decision to separate and file for divorce. For some the long months, and perhaps years, before the decisive separation is a volatile period of acrimony and anger. For some it is a period of mutual indifference, whereas for others it is a period of sinking disillusionment and hopelessness. Some engage in endless discussions and negotiations in an attempt to save their marriages, while others are taken by complete surprise when a spouse leaves, as was Jenny:

> To this day I still don't understand it. Some sort of midlife crisis, I suppose. We were considered the ideal family in the community—the ones everyone assumed would be together forever. He kept up the charade of the loving husband right up till the end. Oh, he was having more than his share of troubled moods, but he always passed them off as trouble at work. I never suspected a thing. We went out to dinner for his birthday—a celebration, I thought. That's the moment he chose to drop the bomb. I guess it symbolized his independence day or something. No discussion, no nothing. He just wanted out. He had already rented himself a condo.

In a well-known Pennsylvania study, 29 percent of the people who had been left by a spouse reported that they were either very or completely surprised by their spouses' decision to divorce.

Women often experience the preseparation stage as more stressful than do men. Women are more likely to report having been depressed, pessimistic, and lonely during this period. Their greater distress may reflect a greater sensitivity to a poor marriage or more awareness of the difficulties divorce may create. Or, because women are the ones who suggest divorce far more often than men do (and actually initiate divorce twice as frequently as do men, according to the National Center for Health Statistics), their greater distress during this period may reflect the turmoil they experience while trying to reach a decision about divorce. For some, the preseparation period is the most traumatic period of their divorce. This was certainly true for Jean.

> The year before Jean first left Michael was like a progressive, downhill spiral. She was so depressed that there were days she never made it out of bed. And when she did, she was virtually immobilized. She cried uncontrollably and suffered from migraine headaches for days at a time without relief. A friend helped her make the decision to leave and, using connections, got her a job. Although life still was not easy, Jean found that she liked working and that people in her large office liked and respected her. Eventually, she formed several good friendships, got a promotion, and began to feel good about herself. Then Michael talked her into coming back to him, promising he would change. He tried for a short while but then drifted back to his old destructive patterns. Finally accepting the futility of the marriage and realizing she was well on her way to establishing an independent and satisfying life for herself, Jean left him for the second and final time.

TRANSITION–RESTRUCTURING

The period of transition and restructuring after a divorce begins with the separation and lasts, on the *average*, two years. It is during this period that the majority of divorcing men and women seem to encounter the most similar experiences and feelings—sometimes referred to as the "divorce experience," although with differing intensity.

During this stage, divorcing partners usually experience far more trauma and disorientation than they had anticipated. Sure, the continuous battles are ended. So is the constant criticism and uncomfortable indecision. But this is the time of turbulent and conflicting emotions, when people are literally assaulted with loss, change, and practical problems. It is a time when the familiar past is traded for the unknown future.

People express their anxiety and distress in different ways. Some withdraw into the sanctuary of their homes, while others engage in a frenzy of activity to escape. Some sleep the days away, while others feel fortunate to sleep a few uninterrupted hours each night. Some people bury themselves in work; others can't concentrate. Some barely eat enough for subsistence, while others can't seem to stop eating. Some are apathetic, others irritable. Some cry uncontrollably; others stoically hold in everything. Some turn to friends, some to alcohol, tranquilizers, violence, religion, or professional therapy. Journalist Abigail Trafford graphically refers to this period as "Crazy Time."

Transitions: The Divorce Experience

In her book *Crazy Time*, Trafford interviewed hundreds of men and women across the country who had been married at least ten years and were now divorced. Capturing the disorientation and turbulent emotions so typical during this period, she writes:

> The world is turned upside down; you've lost your center of gravity. You can't get your feet back on the ground. Instead you flip-flop in slow motion like astronauts in space. You don't seem to go in any particular direction; not forward, not backward. You just float and sink, float and sink again. . . .
>
> This is Crazy Time. It starts when you separate and usually lasts about two years. It's a time when your emotions take on a life of their own and you swing back and forth between wild euphoria and violent anger, ambivalence and deep depression, extreme timidity and rash actions. You are not yourself. Who are you? . . .
>
> You can't believe how bad your life is, how terrible you feel, how overwhelming daily tasks become, how frightened you are. . . . You can't believe that life is worse now than when you broke up.[2]

Other research study groups have echoed the gist of Trafford's description— in varying intensities, of course. Early in the stage of transition and restructuring, the decision to divorce can turn into a nightmare. Many men and women become tense, listless, painfully lonely, and overwhelmed with feelings of failure, inadequacy, poor self-esteem, and "not belonging" anywhere. Too often, they feel out of control, victims of intense emotions previously unknown to them. Self-pity and depression leave many wondering if they will ever return to normal.

Bitterness, anger, and resentment fuel fantasies of revenge. Guilt, fear, and panic cause some to question their sanity.

Barbara, a high-level manager in a profitable company, was baffled by her reactions.

> Why am I acting like this? I'm a competent professional, in charge of million-dollar contracts and 200 people, and here I am, feeling like a frightened, helpless little girl! I thought I wanted this divorce. What's wrong with me?

But it is the intensity of their anger that frightens many people the most. Twenty-five-year-old Wendy, married for five years, entered divorce counseling because she was so alarmed at the intensity of her rage.

> At first I was okay. I had no anger at all. It had always disgusted me to see divorcing people acting so vindictively toward one another. I swore it would never happen to me. Then, just when I was patting myself on the back for behaving so rationally, it was like a dam broke. Right now, I'm so angry at the bastard, I just want to see him suffer, and I'll do anything I can to hurt him. It's almost become an obsession— I sit and plot my next moves. It's beginning to scare me. I've never been a vindictive person. I don't know what's happening to me.

For a minority, rage is so intense that it incites disturbed and sometimes bizarre behavior toward a former spouse. A New Orleans man shredded his ex-wife's favorite clothes. A New York man held his former wife hostage and shot up her living room. In San Diego, a man left bloody hunting knives in his ex's mailbox, and a Dallas woman dumped her estranged husband's $500 suits out a second-story window into the muddy backyard. One northern California woman had the family dog destroyed, telling her sobbing youngsters that their father didn't give them enough money to feed it, and a southern California woman rammed her car into her ex-husband's house while he and their children were inside. Breaking down doors, obscene phone calls, physical violence, and hysterical rages are not unusual. In a northern California study, about one-fourth of the men and women displayed such behavior.

During the transition period, divorcing men and women usually become obsessed with thoughts about the ex-spouse and the broken marriage. The history of the marriage is relived time and time again—the fights, the accusations, the significant events, the trivial occurrences that may have contributed to the breakup. When did the trouble start? Who is to blame? Was it inevitable? For some, the obsessive thoughts become maddening.

Although a minority of couples report that they get along better once they no longer have daily contact, the majority report having primarily explosive and conflict-laden interactions after separation. Yet despite the conflict, the majority of divorcing men and women are haunted by memories of the good times and many fall victim to impulses to call, to initiate dates, to seek out information about their exs' new lives, or just to drive past their exs' home or office. The majority of divorced people studied have questioned, at some time, whether they made the right decision to end the relationship. People vacillate between feelings of love and hate, of longing and anger.

In euphoric moods, people insist the divorce was the best thing that ever happened to them. They talk of feeling intoxicated by their newfound freedom and independence, and they report feeling more alive than ever. Life is seen as an adventure, and they feel as if they can attain any goal they set their minds to. Most people swing back and forth between these exhilarating periods of bliss and periods of sadness, anxiety, and anger. For some, euphoric periods last for several months; for others it may be only days until the pendulum swings back again.

During this first half of the transition-restructuring phase, many people report feeling "split," "on the edge," or "not themselves" anymore. Many report that their major goal is making it through till tomorrow without cracking up. People who are asked to recall this period of their divorce frequently offer comments like "I couldn't believe how awful I felt" and "I felt I couldn't go on." When interviewed on "Saturday Night with Connie Chung," Jane Fonda remarked about her own divorce, "All I can say is that I experienced pain unlike anything I've ever felt in my life."

Not everyone encounters the "divorce experience" or Trafford's "crazy time." Some feel primarily relief, hope, and positive feelings at the end of their marriage; function fairly well; and quickly begin to rebuild their lives. Morton and Bernice Hunt found that 20 percent of their very large study group seemed to fit into this category, and the Pennsylvania study found that an unusually high percentage of their smaller study group did so: 35 percent of the men and 41 percent of the women.

Positive emotions are very intense for some people, who may talk of being released from prison or bondage, of new beginnings, of a chance for a better life. Sometimes there are celebrations and self-indulgences like massages, facials, new wardrobes, and new cars. Unless they have another partner already waiting, these people usually immerse themselves into the dating and "singles scene" immediately, sometimes at a hectic pace, as if making up for lost time.

Although this initial positive outlook and functioning may continue, people sometimes prove to be fragile. Many a divorcing person is stunned to find his or her initial enthusiasm and aplomb shattered after a few months, often when the first personal failure is encountered. It is almost as if a bubble bursts: spirits, once high, take a nosedive and the divorce experience, heretofore unknown, becomes familiar.

Though it is tempting to assume that it is the "leavers" who breeze through separation and divorce and their reluctant partners who suffer through the divorce experience, reality is not so simple. Those who are left usually *do* have more to overcome immediately after separation and frequently do have more problems at this time. They are more likely to feel helpless and pessimistic and to have difficulty accepting the breakup. Their self-esteem is more likely to plummet, and they report more intense feelings of anger, love, and/or hate toward their mates.

But the picture is not a rosy one for "leavers" either. Although they are more likely to feel relief, leavers still have high levels of stress, which is the natural consequence of a major life change. It appears that leavers are more likely than those who are left to experience high levels of stress *before* separation and feelings of guilt *after* separation. In their book, *The Divorce Experience*, the Hunts reported that approximately one-third of the leavers in their large study group felt bad "all or almost all of the time" after separation, complaining of general depression, sleeplessness, and loss of appetite. They didn't want to go back, but they didn't expect to feel as bad as they did. A University of Tennessee study reported that leavers, as a group, felt similar levels of emotional trauma to those who were left, but the *timing* of their peak stress levels was different.

Contrary to conventional wisdom, whether one leaves or is left may not affect how rapidly he or she recovers from divorce. Although reluctant partners have more problems immediately after separation, studies report that these differences diminish. Some leavers have surprisingly slow recoveries, whereas some who were left are found to recover surprising quickly, even when the separation had been unexpected. Some people who had been adamantly opposed to the divorce admit later that it was the best thing that could have happened to them.

Incidentally, in the lion's share of cases, divorce is not mutually desired. It appears that one spouse wants the divorce far more than the other in 75 to 90 percent of divorces.

Restructuring

Usually, sometime during the first postseparation year most people begin to achieve a more even keel emotionally. As less energy is needed for survival, more can be devoted to the task of restructuring their lives and attending more closely to the needs of children. Nothing will mark the onset of this time for you, and your progress is not likely to be smooth. For a long time, you will likely have one foot in each world. You will probably experience a lot of hills and valleys, starts and stops in which your productive periods of restructuring will be followed by setbacks, periods of discouragement, and apathy.

The uneven course that progress usually takes was clearly illustrated in a well-known study conducted at the University of Virginia by E. Mavis Hetherington and her research team. Within the first year following their legal divorces, people in this study group as a whole were immersed in a flurry of self-improvement activities (changed physical appearance, physical fitness programs, new social activities, classes, and so forth). Yet at the end of that year, the majority felt that they were at an all-time *low*. Perhaps they were merely discouraged that their life-styles were not yet satisfactory, but the majority of the study group reported that they were functioning poorly, that the divorce had been a mistake, and that they should have worked harder to save their marriages. Other study groups confirm that things usually get worse before they get better.

In the process of restructuring, most people at some time enter a phase of experimentation and do things they had always wanted to do by trying out new activities, interests, and relationships. Trafford humorously refers to this as the hummingbird phase, because of their tendency to flit from plan to plan, from interest to interest, and from relationship to relationship. The frenetic pace that is often evident in this phase is easily detected in this man's plans:

> My plan right now is to enroll in graduate school, which will be a big switch. And I think I've got to learn to play tennis, because I need exercise bad. And I have bought a ten-speed bike, and I am going to start doing the bicycle trails. And I really want to get back into sailing. I used to play golf, too, and I want to get back. . . . I plan to go to Europe . . . and I could take my oldest son with me.[3]

People enter this phase at widely varying times, some dashing into it rapidly, others waiting until they gain some semblance of equilibrium in both their own and their children's lives. It is only a phase. Gradually the frenetic pace calms down and people become more selective in their activities and plans.

When Judith Wallerstein and Joan Kelly reinterviewed their study group 18 months after separation, they found that most people were still grappling with restructuring their lives and coming to terms with their divorce. However, three-fifths of the men and slightly more than half of the women were pleased with the direction their lives were taking. Although Bill and Lynne, the couple in the following example, were not part of this study group, they seem to be fairly typical of the divorced people in the study group a year and a half into the transition–restructuring period:

> When Lynne pressed for a divorce, Bill moved into a new singles condo, determined to "show her" by living the life of a swinging bachelor. Eighteen months later, life was not quite what he had expected. He was tired of the frenetic social activity and one-night stands and longed for some stability and intimacy in his life. He had recently traded nightly forays to singles bars for a membership in a health club and had joined a singles support and social group called "New Beginnings." "Much calmer" was how he described his life. "I don't feel like I'm on a roller coaster anymore. But I still get depressed, and I still feel like I'm drifting without an anchor."
>
> Bill thought that he was making progress toward coming to terms with the end of his marriage. He was beginning to realize that his immaturity had played a big role in the breakup, and due to this insight, he felt less anger and hostility toward Lynne. Things were still hard when he picked up the kids. At least he and Lynne had stopped their open warfare and snide comments, but things were still very tense.

He hoped, for the kids' sake, that someday they could find some kind of comfortable way of relating.

Things hadn't gone as Lynne had anticipated either. Bill had so seldom been there for her during their marriage that she hadn't believed that life as a single parent could be much worse, but it had been. The kids hadn't done well after the split—Jenny had become withdrawn, and Jeff had become abusive at home and a bully at school. For the first year, Lynne had barely kept afloat, trying to give the children some extra time, to deal with their anger and hurt, to keep the house going by herself, to deal with Bill's hostility, and to cope with her own wildly fluctuating emotions—all while she had to return to school to learn some marketable skills. She didn't have a minute to herself. She resented Bill's freedom and was jealous of his women.

Now, a year and a half after they separated, things were much better. She and the kids had made it through the worst and had established a close-knit little family. Surviving had helped her reach a new level of self-assurance, and she very much liked this new, competent person she was becoming. She had finished up her year in school and had landed a job she liked. She was also getting out a little now, beginning to meet some new people and try some new things. For the most part, she had put her feelings of hopelessness behind her and now felt that life would be better one day, although she still had a long way to go. She still felt overwhelmed much of the time with the problems of daily living, still felt lonely, and still had spells of depression, although not nearly as often. She realized things had gotten better with Bill, but she still harbored a lot of anger and resentment toward him because of his immaturity and irresponsibility.

Although Bill and Lynne seem to be typical of the "average" man and woman at this point in the divorce process, some are not this far along, while others have already moved on to the recovery–rebuilding stage.

RECOVERY–REBUILDING

The recovery and rebuilding period is sometimes humorously referred to as the "Phoenix stage," when people rise from the ashes of divorce. Whereas the period of transition–restructuring was a time of reacting to divorce and surviving it, this is a period of personal growth. The former may have been a time of frenetic experimentation; this is one of self-discovery and carving a new identity. On the average, people enter the recovery–rebuilding phase roughly two years after separation, and it lasts two to three years. However, some people get stalled in this stage for many years.

Those who successfully complete this stage have learned to accept the end of their marriages and the role they played in the breakup. They have disentangled themselves from their former spouses and created separate identities. They have achieved some detachment from their exs so there is no longer a need for either hostility or dependence. And they have clarified their priorities, set realistic goals, and found a satisfying life-style.

As in the transition–restructuring period, progress during this phase does not follow a smooth course but has starts and stops. It may reassure you to know that success at this stage is not related to the circumstances of the breakup. A devastating breakup does not predict a poor recovery, just as early feelings of relief, hope, and optimism do not necessarily predict a good recovery. Carl is an example.

> Carl and Elizabeth had been married 12 years and had three children. He was a guy who loved family life and could have played the dad in *Father Knows Best*. But Elizabeth returned to work after the children were all in school, and within two years had fallen in love with Ted, a co-worker with eclectic interests that excited her. The two kept the affair secret for a year before Elizabeth made the difficult decision to leave Carl and marry Ted.
>
> Carl was devastated. He felt betrayed, deceived, and abandoned and went into a period of deep depression in which he was suicidal. Eventually his rage surfaced, and he blamed Elizabeth for destroying their family. Carl and Elizabeth had joint custody of the children, none of whom had fared well since the breakup. Two of the children had been referred for counseling. Fortunately, Carl remained a sensitive and caring father and was able to see, with a therapist's help, how his erratic behavior and conflict with Elizabeth was escalating his children's problems. He then sought help for himself.
>
> As of this writing, three years later, Carl has picked up the pieces of his life. He has his children much of the time, and they've discovered bicycling, hiking, and camping together. He's developed a passion for cooking, photography, and making stained glass windows, and he reports that he is "involved with a wonderful and caring woman." He says that he is happy, feels whole again, and is finding that life is surprisingly good. Meanwhile, Elizabeth's second marriage is in trouble. A few years ago, Carl confides, he would have taken great satisfaction in this, but at this point he feels a tinge of compassion for her.

As Carl's story shows, a successful recovery from your divorce will depend not so much on the amount of stress you encounter but on how well you can cope with that stress, how thoroughly you can put the past behind you, and how successfully you can rebuild your life. Chapters 3 through 6, 12, and 13 will guide you each step of the way so that you can emerge from divorce a stronger person.

ECONOMIC RAMIFICATIONS: WHAT FEW PEOPLE REALIZE

Money can be a major issue of conflict, not only during divorce but in the ensuing years. Some couples relitigate over child support for more than a decade. Other couples continue to argue between themselves about the fuzzy details of their divorce agreement, such as who pays for children's college educations.

Morton and Bernice Hunt reported that one-third of the women in their large study group claimed their ex-husbands denied them money as a means of retaliation, while some women demanded money more out of resentment than need. Sometimes children join in the economic battlefield, as they accuse Dad of not providing enough money or Mom of spending it on herself. In their book *Games Divorced People Play*, Melvyn Berke and Joanne Grant point out that the poor, the middle class, and the wealthy play money games equally ferociously.

Economic concerns are real. Most often, financial cutbacks go hand in hand with divorce because of the need to maintain two households, make new purchases for the second household, and, of course, pay legal costs. Sometimes therapy and full-time child care become added expenses as well. Judith Wallerstein and Joan Kelly reported that virtually every parent in their middle class study group became preoccupied with family finances after divorce.

Study after study conducted since the late seventies reveals that women generally suffer greater economic consequences than men do. New liberalized divorce laws and present trends in divorce judgments have in practice worked against women and have increased the economic inequality between former husbands and wives. Generally, women now receive lower child support payments and either no or limited spousal support payments. Not only are women expected to become self-supporting, but there is an assumption of their economic equality with men. The reality, of course, is that men receive higher wages than women. Gathering recent statistics from a number of sources, Daniel Evan Weiss, in his book *The Great Divide*, reports just how wide the gender gap still is in the 1990s. Weiss reports that the median full-time earnings for women is $16,900, compared to $26,000 for men. Compared to men in the same jobs, women computer analysts earn 27 percent less, female secretaries 33 percent less, and female attorneys 37 percent less. The statistics go on. Not only are women more poorly paid, but their husbands are more likely to have advanced to higher positions. (Studies find that it is usually women who sacrifice career goals for family needs.) Women are also more likely to have custody of children, narrowing their opportunities for career advancement, which frequently requires overtime or travel. Particularly hard hit are stay-at-home moms who often must enter the job market on the bottom rung with few or rusty skills, while their former partners enjoy seniority and its economic benefits. To make matters worse, a large percentage of fathers do not make their child support payments, forcing the entire family to exist on the mothers' lower salaries. What these fathers perhaps fail to realize is that their absence does not significantly reduce many family expenses. Mothers still must pay for housing that is large enough to accommodate children. Utility bills do not decrease appreciably. Youngsters still need health and dental care and, with the passing years, they need larger clothes and greater amounts of food to accommodate their growing bodies. Additionally, there are school- and activity-related expenses and, of course, that money guzzler—child care. New York University sociologist Richard Peterson estimates that women's standard of living decreases 30 to 40 percent after divorce. Over time, many manage to recover at least *some* of their economic well-being, although it is often a struggle. Peterson based his estimates on an analysis of a number of nationally conducted studies.

Although women share in the division of joint assets, many women do not benefit significantly. Many couples have limited assets, and those they do have are often tied up in the family home. In the past, the home traditionally was awarded to women and their children and helped to compensate for their economic losses in divorce. Now the home often must be sold, which adds to the hardships women face.

Although divorce is often an economic hardship on both spouses, men usually recover economically. In a large national study, South Dakota State University researcher Randal Day and Brigham Young University researcher Stephen Bahr found that the mean per capita income for men after divorce was approximately twice the mean per capita income for women. For women who had dependent children, the discrepancy did not dwindle with time and sometimes grew wider. Every "rule" has exceptions, of course, and the financial inequality in divorce is no exception. In some cases, it is husbands who are financially strapped while wives live in relative luxury, and if these men remarry, their financial situation can border on the impossible. Statistically speaking, however, these cases constitute a small minority.

SOCIAL RAMIFICATIONS: EXPECTED CHANGES

If you are a typical divorcing person, most of your friendships are with married people, and most of them will be affected by your divorce in some way. Well-known sociologist Robert Weiss reports there are three phases through which relationships with married friends generally progress after separation and divorce.

In the first, friends are likely to rally around you, listening sympathetically and offering support. In the second, they no longer see you as a friend in need but as someone moving on in a new direction. Here, their reactions will be idiosyncratic. Some may remain supportive, others may feel threatened or uncomfortable, and some may ally themselves with either you or with your spouse. Some may withdraw because your separation is painful to them, and some of the opposite sex may become attracted to you. Your most vulnerable friendships are likely to be those based on your being part of a married couple, whereas the least vulnerable will be those based on intimacy, interests, and your qualities as an individual.

In the third phase, you are likely to sense that you are growing apart from most of your married friends (though not all) because your lives, interests, and concerns have taken such divergent paths that the friendships are no longer rewarding to either of you. Gradually you will probably shift toward friends with whom you have more in common. About these new friendships, one woman in her late 50's reported:

> I've found that once you're divorced, you get different friends. They're better friends, though. They've helped me cope. In fact, I have more friends now than when I was married.[4]

Until you have built up a new network of friendships, however, you may have a period in which you feel somewhat alone and isolated. Dealing with loneliness and reestablishing social support networks are discussed in chapters 12 and 13.

THE VERDICT, PLEASE: IS DIVORCE WORTH IT?

Although the specific figures differ from study to study and from poll to poll, the majority of divorced men and women maintain that yes, the divorce was worth the trauma and the difficult years they experienced afterward. Following are some examples of reported statistics.

In the northern California study reported by Judith Wallerstein and Joan Kelly, about two-thirds of the men and slightly more than half the women reported five years after their decisive separation that the divorce had been beneficial and had improved the quality of their lives. Slightly less than 20 percent considered the divorce to be an unqualified failure, while the remainder had mixed feelings. Morton and Bernice Hunt reported that the majority of their large sample claimed to be both happier and more successful human beings because of the divorce that had occurred earlier in their lives.

In a national survey reported in the January 1987 issue of *Parents Magazine*, 72 percent of the divorced population said that they were happier now than they had been before their divorces. And in 1989, a Gallup poll asked divorced men and women this question: "Looking back, do you think you made the right decision by separating, or would things be better if your marriage stayed together?" Eighty-two percent believed the decision had been a good one.

Speaking retrospectively about their divorces, many people conclude that their marriages and divorces played an integral part in their growth as human beings. They are not necessarily people who initiated the divorce or who sailed through it relatively smoothly. Many were considerably traumatized at the time and experienced a great deal of pain in the aftermath of their marriages. Thirty-two-year-old Louisa is an example. Looking back on a difficult divorce, she concluded:

> It was a hard lesson to learn but I'm so glad I learned it. I'm a competent, well-liked, talented human being in my own right. I can survive alone and will never fear it again. ... Looking back now I'm almost glad it all happened. I'm a far better person, more understanding of myself and others—and isn't that what living is all about?[5]

2

LEGAL FUNDAMENTALS:
What Everyone Should Know

Divorce law and divorce procedures are the subjects of entire books written by attorneys and are beyond the scope of this book. What we will take a look at in this chapter are some very basic ABCs of current legal trends, and we'll discuss the psychological implications of some of your alternatives.

Each state has its own divorce laws, and frequently each county within a state follows somewhat different procedures. For this reason, you would do well to get some straight legal information from an attorney about how your state laws and county procedures may affect you personally. Go to a specialist—one whose practice has an emphasis in family law. The visit will not obligate you to hire the attorney further. In fact, it is important that you shop around for a lawyer to represent you, but more on that later.

A PRIMER ON CURRENT DIVORCE TRENDS

In January 1970, California became the first state in the nation to put into effect a "no-fault" divorce law. The concept of no-fault removed the traditional notion that one party is guilty and the other innocent in divorce. Either spouse could obtain a divorce without the consent of the other and without having to prove marital wrongdoing; irreconcilable differences became satisfactory grounds. Since that time, virtually every state has passed some form of no-fault laws.

In general, continuing alimony (now called spousal support or maintenance) is also a thing of the past. The most common exceptions are in cases involving older women who have poor employment prospects because of age, health, or inexperience. Currently spousal support, when awarded, is usually done so temporarily to give a spouse time and an opportunity to get on her (or his) feet and become self-supporting. Each state has its own guidelines.

On the issue of child support, generally the courts make both parents responsible for partial support of their children. As the press has made everyone aware, a court order for child support does not insure that the support will actually be paid. However, there are now in place legal measures that can be taken that may help enforce child support court orders. There is more on this in Chapter 17.

How marital property is divided varies once again from state to state. Some states have community property laws, but the majority have equitable distribution laws. Generally, in community property states each spouse is entitled to an equal share of the marriage assets. However, a few states take marital wrongdoing into consideration when property is divided, according to attorney Elliot Samuelson in *The Divorce Law Handbook*. In contrast, equitable distribution laws, theoretically, at least, emphasize fairness rather than equality. Although these laws vary from state to state, common factors that are supposed to be taken into consideration, according to Samuelson, are the duration of the marriage, respective contributions to it, support awards, likely financial circumstances in the future, minor children, health, age, and so forth. In some states, marital misdeeds are also allowed to be considered. However, judges in equitable distribution states have a great deal of discretion in interpreting state guidelines. Most sources agree that women generally receive less than 50 percent of the marital assets in equitable distribution states.

In most states, marital property includes assets acquired during the marriage up until the date of separation, regardless of who has legal title to the property. Business interests, furs, jewelry, and pensions are considered marital property, along with the couple's real estate, bank accounts, furniture, and so forth. Some property is considered separate: usually inheritances, gifts to one party, and property owned before the marriage (although some states, according to Samuelson, include *appreciation* of separate property as a marital asset).

DIVORCE SETTLEMENT AGREEMENTS

Usually, before your divorce is granted, the issues of custody, visitation, support, and property distribution will have to be settled in some manner and set down in legal language in a divorce settlement agreement. The settlement may also include other provisions, such as life and health insurance, payment of legal fees, and the use of a jointly owned home. (In some states, an attorney can get some of these issues set aside for future decision to expedite the divorce.)

Many couples arrive at a settlement through their respective attorneys, although Justice Joseph Steinberg, a superior court judge in the state of Connecticut, warns that attorneys' values too often creep into such negotiations and replace clients' values.

You and your spouse may be able to reach an agreement on these issues yourselves. However, domestic law can be very complicated. In his book, *The Divorce Decision*, West Virginia Supreme Court of Appeals Judge Richard Neely compares "do-it-yourself lawyering" with "do-it-yourself brain surgery." If you have children, assets, or obligations, have your agreement reviewed and written by an attorney. It can be far more costly in the long run if the agreement is written incorrectly or if you have not considered a myriad of tax implications, your children's college educations, health insurance, or a number of other issues with which professionals are familiar. A word of caution: It is never advisable to rely on your spouse's personal lawyer, since attorneys must represent their clients' interests, which may be at odds with yours. Some couples are now reaching their own agreements with the help of a divorce mediator; this alternative to an adversarial divorce will be discussed shortly.

If a settlement is reached, the divorce is considered uncontested, and the court basically rubber-stamps the agreed-upon terms. Kenneth Kressel, a psychology professor at Rutgers University, documents that the average court hearing in an uncontested case without children or assets takes three-and-one-half minutes. With children or assets, it is longer—an average of five minutes!

The terms of child support usually can be modified at a future date if there are substantial changes in circumstances. Custody can also be modified, although in practice, the longer children are in the custody of one parent, the less likely judges are to remove them from their home because of their need for stability. Whether spousal support is modifiable depends upon the wording of the settlement agreement—another reason to seek the expertise of an attorney. The terms of a property settlement are unlikely to be changed unless fraud can be shown.

LITIGATION

If no agreement can be reached, the divorce remains a contested one and is settled in court. The number of divorces that go to litigation is relatively small. Attorneys traditionally estimate 10 percent, but studies suggest it is higher, particularly when children are involved. Litigation has a number of serious financial and emotional pitfalls about which you should be aware.

Your legal fees may escalate out of proportion to your assets. Bob and Debbie Jameson, a middle class couple with relatively modest assets, found this out the hard way, as Bob relates:

> Debbie and I were so bitter, we both wanted blood and neither would budge an inch. I understand her lawyer tried to talk some sense into her, but mine just said, "If you want to go for the jugular, we'll go for it." By the time we were done, the only ones who won were the lawyers—$65,000 worth! That was more than either of us got. What a stupid waste. It will take me years to recover financially.

When you take your case to court, your life is scrutinized in public and you are robbed of the right to have a say in your future and that of your children.

Instead, your future is turned over to a judge who neither knows your family nor has the time to tailor a decision to your unique case. His or her judgment is determined by some combination of "formulas," the opinions of experts (mental health professionals, accountants, and appraisers called in for your case), and the judge's own biases. Justice Richard Neely warns that litigation is chancy and courts unpredictable. He points out that every trial lawyer has had the experience of turning down settlement offers because they were too low, only to obtain far lower settlements in court.

In their book *The Dynamics of Divorce*, Psychologist Florence Kaslow, director of the Florida Couples and Family Institute, and Pennsylvania State University psychologist Lita Schwartz reported that divorcing partners who go the adversarial route are more likely to feel helpless, pessimistic, depressed, and detached. If the point of contention is custody, both parents and children usually hang in an extended state of limbo and anxiety. (The adverse repercussions of custody battles are further discussed in Chapter 11.)

Not every case that goes to court gets nasty, but many do. And for the many divorcing men and women who fall into the pattern of deception and game playing, point out Kaslow and Schwartz, the usual consequence is a plummet in their own self-esteem as well as an escalation in their ex-partner's anger, resistance to settlement, and vindictiveness in the future. For example, studies suggest that when disputes have been bitter, court-ordered support payments are less likely to be complied with, and the parties are more likely to be back in court in the future. More legal costs! But the children are the greatest losers. Studies consistently find that children who are exposed to long-term parental conflict are more likely to be emotionally troubled, to be depressed, to have low self-esteem, to do poorly in school, and to have behavior problems such as tantrums, aggressiveness, and rebelliousness.

Avoid litigation if you can, especially over custody. However, if your former spouse is determined to litigate and mediation hasn't helped, don't feel you have to sign away your future to avoid conflict.

SELECTING AN ATTORNEY

Before selecting an attorney, do some research. Start by getting referrals from others. Singles support groups and the organization Parents Without Partners are good sources. You would be wise to visit several recommended attorneys before making your decision; the initial consultation is usually free or inexpensive.

Law is a highly specialized profession, and one attorney is *not* necessarily as good as another. Justice Neely points out that many highly paid attorneys who are proficient in their own specialty may have no better idea of how to draft a divorce settlement agreement or try a divorce case than they have of building an atomic bomb. Begin by restricting yourself to attorneys who specialize in family law, but this is only a start. Attorneys will still have different amounts of experience in complicated negotiations and in litigation. They will differ in their awareness of individual judges' thinking and biases, in how thoroughly they will prepare your case, and in cost. Some attorneys will handle your case themselves, whereas others will turn it over to an associate—perhaps an inexperienced one.

Attorneys also differ philosophically, both in the way they deal with clients and in the way they approach cases. In a study of attorneys, social psychologist Kenneth Kressel found that attorneys seem to fall primarily within two broad groups, which he labeled the "advocates" and the "counselors." Advocates, he reported, enjoy the legal challenge of divorce cases, endorse the adversarial approach, emphasize "winning," and do not feel responsible for their clients' emotional welfare. Psychologists Janet Johnston and Linda Campbell, who conducted an extensive study of couples in intense conflict, warn that some of the tactical maneuvers advocates commonly use generally escalate conflict between divorcing couples. Examples are instructing clients to cease communication with their former spouses, advising them to take extreme positions so there will be more negotiating room, and submitting motions to the court that characterize the ex-spouse unfavorably. (Essentially, this publicly shames the former spouse and tends to incite his or her fury and desire to retaliate.) Most couples fail to realize that it is the other spouse's attorney rather than the spouse who is orchestrating these moves. Even when a spouse does realize it, the end result is often destructive, as one woman relates:

> The lawyers got involved, and we had that situation where we were told not to talk to each other. . . . And it just got to be impossible. . . . There was so much bitterness and so much anger and so much mistrust.[1]

At the extreme end of the advocate continuum are lawyers who are cynical about human nature, doubt the feasibility of a *constructive* divorce, and even disparage their clients. (Kressel calls this extreme subgroup the "undertakers.")

In contrast, the second group of attorneys, the counselors, are concerned with the emotional climate of divorce. They provide clients with support and practical advice, they watch out for the welfare of the children, and they emphasize finding a cooperative solution that will be fair to all.

Connecticut Superior Court Judge Joseph Steinberg refers to these two approaches as the "Rambo" and the "Mother Theresa" approaches. Following are some comments from an advocate and from a counselor, respectively.

> It is neither my responsibility nor my prerogative to attempt reconciliation or emotional counseling. Psychological counseling, whether done by myself or professionally, is of little or no value during the divorce process.[2]

People are usually "tender" and upset when they seek a divorce attorney. . . . The legal method is not necessarily the best and I try to add some counseling into my work.[3]

Justice Neely advises that the best attorney is one who has a good deal of experience in contested divorces and who is well versed in the "tricky procedural rules." He warns against the attorney who *never* goes to court because his reputation is known by other attorneys who may demand higher terms in exchange for an out-of-court settlement. He also warns against the "mindless litigator" who does not encourage good-faith negotiations.

Appendix C contains sources, written by attorneys for the lay person, that offer guidance on a wide variety of legal issues that may concern you.

DIVORCE MEDIATION: AN ALTERNATIVE TO AN ADVERSARIAL DIVORCE

Mediation is an alternative to the traditional adversarial path to divorce and is being used by increasing numbers of people as they learn about it. The rationale behind mediation is that divorcing partners, not attorneys or judges, should be the ones to make the decisions about their own futures and those of their children. The problem is, of course, that emotions run high during divorce, and many couples are unable to talk constructively with one another and arrive at mutually acceptable decisions. This is where a mediator comes in.

A mediator is an impartial professional who helps divorcing spouses reach out-of-court agreements about divorce-related issues (custody, parenting schedules and concerns, child support, spousal support, and property division). Some couples use mediation to negotiate all issues. Some use it only for decisions related to the children. Some use mediation to negotiate child-related issues and support issues, while their attorneys handle their property settlements. Mediators never take sides. Their goal is to hammer out agreements that are fair, informed, workable, and acceptable to *both* spouses. In mediation, there is no winner and loser, as there is so often in an adversarial divorce. Mediators take a win-win approach.

Some people confuse mediation with arbitration, which also involves a dispute and a neutral third party. However, in arbitration, parties accept the decision of the arbitrator. A mediator, on the other hand, never makes a decision and doesn't force a decision on either party. He or she helps disputing parties arrive at their *own* decisions about each separate issue. If they cannot reach a decision on one or more issues, they are free to resolve those issues through attorneys and the courts. Settlements in mediation are completely voluntary.

Don't confuse mediation with counseling or therapy, either. A mediator's job is not to help people decide whether to get divorced or to help them work through their emotions and losses. It is to help people reach mutually acceptable divorce-related decisions once they have *decided* to divorce.

Mediation can be used at any time. Some couples use it before one moves out of the home, others after they have met with an attorney. Some try it as a last attempt to avoid litigation, although by this time conflict has often escalated out of control. Some couples seek out family mediation *after* divorces are final to settle new disputes that have arisen over children. Some use it after remarriage to work out a detailed parenting agreement in which everyone's roles and responsibilities are spelled out when one or more stepparents are involved.

How Mediation Works

In mediation, the mediator helps the parties identify all the issues that need to be considered, clarify and prioritize each party's needs and goals, work out and evaluate a variety of options, and reach decisions that are acceptable to both parties. He or she also helps the parties compile information needed to make informed decisions, such as financial records, their separate living expenses, pension valuations, and property and business appraisals.

In mediation, couples can begin with any immediate problems they have not worked out on their own—a parenting schedule; how bills will be paid; how children will be supported; how medical and dental expenses, bank accounts, and charge cards will be handled; and so on. Once these stopgap decisions are made, long-term agreements can be hammered out when the couple is ready.

How do mediators guide emotional and angry spouses to reach decisions? Part of their job is to keep spouses focused, and they do this on a number of levels. They focus attention *on* each spouse's interests and needs and *away* from "positions." They do this because taking positions can lead people to become intractable. (For example, rather than allowing a couple to get bogged down over *who* will "get the children," a mediator is likely to focus on developing a parenting agreement that will enable each parent to continue parenting the children in a meaningful way. A label for the agreed-upon parenting arrangement can then be determined.) Mediators also keep the couple focused on the issues at hand and on attacking the *problems* rather than each other. Finally, they keep the focus on the future rather than the past. The past cannot be changed, and past grievances and discussions of who is at fault are not a part of the mediation process.

To facilitate reaching agreements, mediators break down issues into small, manageable pieces and help parties tackle them one at a time. When a spouse uses angry language that is likely to hurt or anger the other, a mediator will reframe the angry statements in more neutral language. An important strategy that facilitates agreements is drawing out information from both parties. The more information that is shared and available, the greater the number of alternatives and options that can be generated. Sometimes the intensity of disputes even diminishes once the facts and each party's perspectives are understood. Mediators will also ask probing questions and clarify points made by each spouse to make sure that each party *really* hears what the other is saying and understands the other's perspective. Many mediators also look for ways to narrow the gap between couples and hunt for trade-offs, concessions, and areas of compromise. Suppose a spouse rigidly clings to unrealistic demands. Mediators challenge faulty assumptions so that parties become more in tune with reality.

Very importantly, mediators control the parties' conflict. They are also sensitive to one party having more controlling power in the relationship than the other, and they work to strengthen the negotiating ability and assertiveness of the weaker party. Since the couple make their own decisions, it is important that each person is on an equal footing.

Mediation has ground rules on which couples must agree before they begin. For example, couples who are mediating property settlements must agree to full disclosure of all assets and liabilities and to provide supporting documentation. They must also agree not to change the status of their assets except by mutual consent. Usually mediation sessions are conducted with both spouses present, although some mediators meet with spouses separately on occasion. After mediation is completed, the mediator drafts a "memorandum of understanding," detailing the agreements reached. Usually the memorandum is reviewed by the spouses' attorneys to assure that the rights of each were protected, tax consequences were considered, and so forth. Typically, an attorney adds the legal language to the memorandum, and it is incorporated into the divorce settlement agreement. If any issues were not resolved in mediation they can be resolved in whatever way the couple and their respective attorneys see fit.

Why Mediation?

Your divorce may not be the end of your relationship with your spouse as much as it may be a milestone in that relationship, especially if you have children. Mediation gets spouses communicating in a constructive way and demonstrates that cooperation can be more to your advantage than confrontation. It also models skills that can be used to resolve future disagreements. This is quite a contrast from the escalating bitterness and conflict that are often by-products of adversarial divorces and that inevitably color future interactions.

Through mediation you have the chance to take control of your life and determine your own future, even though you were not successful in reaching agreements with your spouse on your own. You are not at the mercy of your attorney's negotiating skills, a mental health professional's evaluations of you, or a judge's current dispositions. Couples in mediation generally feel like they are constructively moving ahead to shape their own futures rather than like they are victims of a callous system. Children can benefit enormously, too. You will see over and over within these pages how destructive parental conflict is to children's well-being and divorce adjustment. Whereas a traditional adversarial divorce usually escalates conflict, a mediated divorce often reduces conflict and increases cooperation. Not only that, a great deal of care is given in mediation to creating a detailed parenting agreement that is tailored to the specific needs of the couple's children.

Couples usually consider it a major benefit that mediation is a less time-consuming process than the adversarial path to divorce. On the average, mediation usually takes between four to eight sessions to cover all divorce issues. If only one or two issues are involved (for example, a parenting agreement), the time, of course, is significantly less. This means that the period of uncertainty and its accompanying stress does not drag on as in an adversarial divorce, and divorcing partners are better able to get on with their lives.

Comprehensive mediation costs, including costs for attorneys and other professionals when needed (tax consultants, appraisers, etc.), are usually considerably less than for an adversarial divorce. In a recently reported study, Dr. Joan Kelly, a former president of the Academy of Family Mediators, found that average costs for couples using the traditional adversarial route were 134 percent higher than were average comprehensive costs for couples using mediation.

Studies have pointed out some other impressive benefits of this approach. Generally people are more satisfied with the mediation process and with mediated agreements than with adversarial procedures and their resultant settlements. People are also more willing to adhere to mediated agreements. For this reason, couples who go through mediation are found to be far less likely to drag one another back to court. In fact, presently some states have mandatory mediation for couples involved in custody disputes.

The Drawbacks of Mediation

Mediation is not a panacea, and for some couples it is an inappropriate choice. If one or both partners are currently fixated on revenge or "winning," mediation is unlikely to be successful at this time. Mediation would be a poor choice if one partner is determined to hide assets, even though bound by mediation rules to full disclosure. If a spouse cannot let go of the marriage, all issues may not be resolved in mediation because an agreement to do so would result in exactly what the spouse is fighting—the end of the marriage. If one spouse has clearly dominated the relationship or if there has been ongoing physical abuse in the family, it takes a very highly skilled and astute mediator to guide the couple to a fair agreement. Mediation is also not a good alternative if a party's functioning is seriously impaired because of very low intelligence, severe psychopathology, or serious and chronic substance abuse.

As with all professionals, some mediators are more experienced and skilled than others. Additional caution must be taken when you choose a mediator, however, since as of this writing there is no set educational or experience requirements for professionals in this field. One approach to finding a trained and experienced mediator is writing to the Academy of Family Mediators, the primary professional organization for family and divorce mediators, asking for a list of mediators in your area. Before a mediator is placed on the Academy's referral list, he or she has had to meet the Academy's educational and experience requirements. The address is P.O. Box 10501, Eugene, OR 97440; phone, (503) 345-1205. However, there are skilled and experienced mediators who are not on this referral list.

Before choosing a mediator, learn about his or her background and how he or she conducts mediation. Most mediators are either mental health professionals (the majority) or attorneys. A small percentage have a financial, ministry, or different type of background. Some mediators co-mediate with a professional from a different background. Mediation is used in many circumstances other than divorce, so find out if the mediator specializes in divorce and family mediation. Ask what *specific* training he or she had in mediation, and how many divorce cases he or she has mediated. Ask about his or her financial expertise and how he or she uses outside financial experts such as tax experts and professional appraisers. Also find out a mediator's position on consulting an attorney while you are in mediation. You should be aware that when attorneys act as mediators, they cannot give you legal advice (although they can provide legal information). Many attorney-mediators advise their clients to seek independent legal advice. You will also want to make sure that the mediator seems fair and impartial. Does he or she show empathy? Is he or she someone you can have confidence in and work with?

Successful mediation may mean you can avoid years of bitterness, hard feelings court battles, and relitigations. It is a process far better suited to families than is the adversarial process, particularly for issues concerning children. If all issues are not resolved in mediation, you can always fall back on adversarial means to resolve those issues. Mediation is an option well worth considering at any time during the divorce process.

STRESS AND THE EMOTIONAL ROLLER COASTER:
Tools To Cope

Amy and Jake had mutually decided to separate because, as they put it, they couldn't be in the same room for more than an hour without being at each other's throats. Amy had the children with her most of the time and had been able to change her part-time receptionist job at a large medical clinic to a full-time position. Three months later, she reported that her life was a shambles and that she was barely able to keep her head above water. Ten-year-old Jake Junior was angry about the pending divorce. It seemed to Amy that at least once a day he screamed at her that he hated her—for the divorce, for his father not being there, for not having enough money anymore to buy all the things the other kids had. He was sullen, surly, and rebellious. Five-year-old Max had become whiny and clinging, had begun to wet his bed again, and had come down with three illnesses in the past three months. Some mornings he clung to her so tightly when she tried to leave him at the day care center that she arrived at work wrinkled and disheveled.

As hectic as her job at the clinic sometimes got, it was the best part of her days. Each night she returned home with a sinking feeling in her stomach and felt as if she were going back into battle. Besides the kids to deal with, it seemed like the house was always a mess, the laundry was never done, and there was never enough food in the refrigerator. They lived on sandwiches because she had so little energy left over after work to shop and cook. There just weren't enough hours in the day.

She was always worried. How would they make it financially? There wasn't enough money to go around now that they needed two places, full-time day care, another car, and additional furniture for Jake's apartment. She was lonely living alone and her future looked bleak. She had no idea what lay ahead. Would her life ever get any better? Sometimes she was overwhelmed with anxiety or even panic. At other times she was "just plain angry," as she put it—at Jake for being so difficult to live with, at herself for failing to make her marriage work, at the kids for making it so hard, at fate for being so cruel. When they'd gotten married, they'd had such hopeful plans for the future together.

Jake was angry, too. He hated his cramped, barren apartment. He hated living

31

alone. He missed his own home, familiar surroundings, a fireplace, his neighbors, hot dinners that didn't come out of a box. And he resented Amy having all those things while he had nothing.

But most of all he hated being away from his kids, especially Jake Junior. The limited time they spent together wasn't even good time, he reported. He never knew what to do with the boys when he saw them. The apartment was so small and empty that he had to take them somewhere—on nice days, to the park. On rainy days, they usually went to McDonald's and a movie. He was filling up the time, but they all seemed to have lost their rapport and naturalness with each other. To make matters worse, young Jake was angry so much of the time. He didn't understand why his parents had to get a divorce, and Jake himself sometimes wondered if they had made the right decision.

Jake went through periods when he was sure the decision had been a good one. It felt good to be free of the fighting and of a wife he no longer loved. He felt as if he could start over again and make up for all his past mistakes. Sometimes he felt almost light-headed with joy. But his black moods always returned. Suddenly one morning, his sense of freedom and adventure would be gone, replaced by the emptiness of his current reality. He didn't know who he was anymore or where in life he was going. If he had made such a mess of the past, what made him think he would do any better with the future? He would chastise himself for not trying hard enough, and he wondered if he still loved Amy after all. Sometimes he questioned his own sanity.

COPING WITH STRESS

Divorce has an inevitable fallout. It causes profound disruption—both internally and externally in almost all areas of life. With divorce comes pervasive losses, an overload of major and minor life changes, a seemingly endless array of unfamiliar practical problems, and intense and wildly fluctuating emotions. Divorce demands the restructuring of relationships with former partners, with friends, and even with children, as a single parent. It necessitates the forging of a new identity and the building of a new life-style, and it motivates self-exploration and reappraisal. Divorce is synonymous with disruption, change, readjustment, and reorganization—and consequently with stress.

Stress is generally worse for spouses who are left, particularly if they are unprepared for separation. Believing they have lost control over their lives, they often feel as if they are pawns at the mercy of their former partners. However, divorce is inevitably stressful for both spouses. With the exception of the death of a spouse, divorce has been identified as the most broadly disruptive and stressful event that people face in our society.

There is convincing evidence that the stress caused by separation and divorce can have a number of negative repercussions for you. Researchers Bernard Bloom, Stephen White, and Shirley Asher conducted a very thorough and now well-known examination of the large number of existing studies on the topic of stress and divorce. They discovered the following disconcerting findings:

- Divorced people are more frequent users of mental health services, most commonly for problems of anxiety, depression, anger, and feelings of rejection.
- Separated people have an increased susceptibility to viruses and other illnesses.
- Automobile accident rates *double* for people during the six months before and after separation.
- Separated and divorced people have higher rates of alcoholism, suicide, and involvements in homicides.

I tell you this not to scare you but to emphasize the importance of learning some effective methods to deal with your stress. Effective coping will minimize the negative repercussions this stressful period will have on you, whereas ineffective coping will complicate your life even further. In fact, *how* you cope with your stress may be more important to your morale and functioning than is the severity of your stress.

To many people, coping with stress is equated with taking tranquilizers, drinking, smoking, or abusing other drugs—methods that create further stress on their bodies. Fortunately, other stress-reducing methods have been found that are far more effective and will not further complicate your life as these old standards will.

First, we'll look at methods that will help you cope with stress. Then we'll look at the more common feelings and emotions people experience during and after divorce and how to best cope with them. These feelings and emotions are often called the "emotional roller coaster" because they so often come in turbulent waves of ups and downs.

If you have trouble motivating yourself to begin using any of the coping tools discussed throughout the book or if you find yourself reverting to old patterns, turn to Appendix A, "How to Make Changes in Your Life and Stick to Them." It contains a five-step method to help you get started with and stick to self-change programs. The method is not difficult, and it *is* effective.

You will find that the coping strategies used to reduce stress are a deviation from the coping tools discussed throughout the remainder of the book. This is because stress causes physiological changes in your body. Therefore, some of the most effective strategies to combat it are physiological in nature. Don't minimize their importance or underestimate what they can do for you. They are well worth learning and incorporating into your life. Not only will they be helpful now, but they will help you through *any* period of stress in the future.

Deep Relaxation

One effective way to combat the physiological and psychological effects of stress is learning a deep relaxation technique. This does not mean indulging in a drink to unwind. It is a method of creating beneficial physiological changes in your body, such as decreasing the activity of your sympathetic nervous system (for example, your heart rate), decreasing your muscle tension, and decreasing your blood lactate level (a substance associated with anxiety). Subjectively, deep relaxation allows you to feel calm, relaxed, and refreshed. It is difficult to feel tense when your entire body feels relaxed!

Learning a deep relaxation technique is not difficult, and once you have learned the technique, you will be able to relax with little effort, even in situations that are stressful, anxiety-arousing, or anger-provoking. Think of the tool you will have if you can relax, at will, during times of high tension!

Appendix B, "Learning a Deep Relaxation Technique," will teach you the steps to an easy and effective deep relaxation method. Don't put off learning it because you "don't have the time." You will be trading 20 minutes a day for a less stressful life. It may prove to be the most productive 20 minutes you spend each day.

Physical Exercise

There is a second highly effective method to counteract the physiological and psychological toll that stress can take: a regular program of aerobic exercise (any activity that will increase your heart rate for a continuous period of 20 minutes or longer, such as jogging, fast walking, bicycling, swimming, aerobics, or rowing).

Exercise relaxes your tensed muscles and increases your energy level. It clears your mind and helps you sort out problems. It improves your self-image. And, as an added bonus, it's been found to improve your immune system. Believe it or not, if you make exercise a regular part of your routine, you will find that you miss it if you skip it.

Limiting the Amount of Change in Your Life

The more change you are bombarded with at once, the more stress you will experience. Most people adjust better to separation if they can maintain a sense of continuity in other aspects of their lives. This is one reason why the divorcing spouse who leaves home and children generally finds the period immediately after separation more stressful than does his or her ex-partner, despite the hassles that the remaining partner has with parenting solo. Be sensitive to the number of changes you introduce into your life, and try to keep them at a tolerable level.

Taking Good Physical Care of Yourself

It is now generally accepted that stress negatively affects the immune system and makes people more susceptible to illness. Stress places *extra* demands on your body, which *increases* your need for *good nutrition* and *sleep*. Both are so important, in fact, that scientists now consider them to be good coping strategies for combatting some of the negative effects that stress can have. Paying attention to your diet and sleep needs will not only reduce the likelihood that you will fall prey to viruses, but will also help you feel better both physically and mentally. Especially during the two-year period following separation, be sure to take good physical care of yourself and your children.

Let's turn now to the confusing array of emotions and feelings people commonly experience after separation and divorce and how best to cope with them. In this chapter we'll look at anxiety, denial, sadness and grief; attachment, ambivalence, and obsessive thoughts about your ex; feelings of rejection, worthlessness, and failure; and finally, euphoria. Chapter 4 will look at depression and Chapter 5 at anger, two important components of the turbulent emotional roller coaster.

If you adopt some of the coping tools given for each of these, you will feel more in control of your life, and the period after separation and divorce will be considerably less turbulent. Many of these coping tools are ones that you can use in times of trouble throughout life.

Although the coping tools discussed are ones that you can use on your own, no discussion about coping with divorce should fail to mention counseling or psychotherapy. It is invaluable at this time to have at least one objective person to provide you strength and support, act as a sounding board, give perspective, and help you sort out your feelings and future options. If money is tight, some mental health professionals will adjust their fees to your ability to pay. You may also find a divorce support group an enormous help and source of support. These groups are becoming more common and are often offered through community or family service organizations.

DEALING WITH ANXIETY

There were times that I was so overwhelmed, I thought I'd go crazy. My whole world had collapsed. I had spent five years putting Tony through school and we spent the next seven building—his career, an expensive house, some money to invest. I thought we had finally made it to the point where I could comfortably quit my job and raise a family. Then wham. Everything was gone—Tony, the house, the chance to have kids, all our plans, the bright future.

I didn't know what to do or where to turn. What would I do with the rest of my life? I wasn't even sure who I was now that I was no longer Mrs. Tony Simpson. I was a single person living in a rented condo who had a job I never did care about. But inside I screamed, "Is this all? Is this really me?" I would flit wildly from one idea to another. Should I go back to college? Maybe I could find a more satisfying job. I could adopt an older child and become a single parent. What about marrying again? But did I ever want to take the chance of getting hurt this much again? I was so scared.

There were periods when I would keep a frenetic pace—doing anything to keep myself busy so I wouldn't have to think or spend time alone. I would go to bed well after midnight, drained and exhausted, but then a few hours later I would wake up in sheer terror, shaking and sweating. I just couldn't escape, no matter what I did.

Anxiety such as this woman described is a familiar companion to most people after separation, and not surprisingly. Anxiety is almost inevitable at a time of such major disruption, when the familiar past is replaced with an unknown future, emotions are turbulent, decisions are pressing, and new day-to-day problems demand solutions. At times, anxiety may become so overwhelming that a person reaches a point of sheer panic, accompanied by a racing pulse, a tightened chest, shortness of breath, and sweaty hands.

At first, all your emotions are likely to be intense, overwhelming, and so jumbled that you may not be able to identify what it is that you are feeling. Many find it tempting to bury their confusing feelings and emotions and push their problems out of their minds. They bury themselves in work, keep themselves frenetically busy, or ignore their feelings. They deny their losses. But trying to bury emotions and problems usually doesn't work very well. Notice how in the previous example the woman was able to bury her emotions during the day by keeping a frenetic pace but would awaken during the night in a panic.

Try to sort out your jumbled emotions and feelings. If you don't, you are likely to have residual emotion tied to your marriage and former spouse, which may interfere with your ability to close the doors on your marriage. The first step in sorting out your emotions is to allow yourself to *feel* them—the full range of them. This chapter and the next two should help you identify and cope with these feelings. Besides sorting them out, you need to address your new problems, acknowledge your losses, deal with your children's pain, and plan for your future. As you begin to make progress with each of these tasks, your anxiety will gradually subside.

However, there is a catch here. You can't tackle problems constructively if you are too overwhelmed to function. You need to reduce your anxiety to a manageable level *now*. Here are some coping tools that will help you handle those anxiety attacks.

- Do you see threats assaulting you at every turn? Every crisis situation is like a two-sided coin, with threats on one side and challenges on the other. Try to do a tune-up on your thinking so you focus more on the challenging side of the coin. Focusing on the threats will encourage you to feel helpless and victimized, whereas focusing on the challenges will encourage you to mobilize your resources. Potential traumas *can* be converted to strengthening experiences.

- Identify a small number of problems that are critical *at this point in time.* Focus on solving these, and table the rest for a later time. Once these immediate concerns are dealt with, you can choose a few more. Continue to prioritize your problems in this way, focusing on the few that are *most* important at the time.

- Keep in mind that *all* your decisions right now do not have to be permanent ones. Making some stopgap decisions will help you feel calmer and more in control of your life. (*Do*, however, try to reach decisions about where the children will live and a parenting schedule that will allow them to see *both* parents *regularly* and *frequently*. Your children should be able to rely on this. If you cannot reach an agreement about your children, consider going to a family mediator who will help you hammer out a mutually acceptable agreement. (Mediation was discussed in Chapter 2.)

- If you can't control your worrying about low-priority problems, ask yourself what's the worst thing that could happen. If it is something drastic, you may want to reorder your priorities. If not, it will help put these problems in perspective.

- Set aside a specified time slot each day (half an hour to an hour) for the sole purpose of worrying. Devote the entire time to worrying about your problems and trying to solve them. You will find that it is much easier to control your worrying for the rest of the day.

- Write in a journal during your worry time. It will help you sort out your thoughts and options. It is also better to get your thoughts on paper than to keep them locked in your head where they are more likely to intrude during the day.

- At times, a new concern or solution to a problem may pop into your head when you least expect it. Write it down immediately and set it aside until your scheduled "worry time." This will get it off your mind and free you to go on to something else. (Carry a small notebook with you to jot down your thoughts so they will all be in one place.)

- If worries continue to intrude during the day, an effective method to stop them is called *thought stoppage.* Wear a wide rubber band around your wrist and snap it every time you begin to worry outside your scheduled time. If you use this technique consistently (along with a worry time), you should find that worry and anxiety invade the remainder of your day less and less frequently. Some people find it is effective to simply command themselves to stop worrying by firmly saying "STOP" out loud. (This sometimes takes several repetitions.) Once they condition themselves this

Checklist for Dealing with Your Anxiety

✓ Shift your focus from the threats to the challenges.

✓ Prioritize problems, focusing on a few at a time.

✓ Make stopgap decisions.

✓ If low-priority problems worry you, ask yourself, "What's the worst thing that could happen?"

✓ Schedule a "worry time."

✓ Use a journal to sort out your concerns and solutions.

✓ If solutions pop into your head during the day, write them down and set aside for your worry time.

✓ Use thought stoppage or distraction when worries intrude.

✓ If anxiety continues to be a problem, set smaller goals for worry-free periods. Seek professional help.

✓ Use a deep relaxation technique every day.

✓ Follow a regular exercise program.

way, they can stop their thoughts by commanding themselves in a whisper or even silently.

- *Distraction* is another effective way to control your anxiety. You may find it useful to carry a small, challenging puzzle with you to distract yourself, or you may prefer word or other games that you can play in your head. Some people find it effective to have some fun or interesting things ready to think about when their anxiety begins to rise.

- If after trying these techniques you are still not making satisfactory progress, set a smaller goal for yourself. Try to go just a few hours without worrying. Each time you are successful, praise yourself lavishly. When you are not successful, encourage yourself not to worry for the next few hours. You may need to schedule two shorter worry periods at different times of the day, but as soon as you can manage, cut back to one. Remind yourself that the most effective way to deal with your problems is step by step, just as you are doing.

If your anxiety is this pervasive, don't hesitate to get some professional help to deal with it.

FEELING LIKE A ROBOT: IS THERE A PERSON IN THERE?

When Meg told Hank their marriage was finally over after years of fighting and months of counseling, he was incredulous. "It will be okay, Meg," he kept saying. "We'll work it out." Meg had her things already packed and was booked on a 5 P.M. plane to Chicago where she hoped to start a new life close to her family.

When Hank came home that evening, he almost expected to find Meg there. For the next two weeks, he stayed close to the phone whenever he could, expecting her to call and say she was coming back. Hank finally called Meg's parents to locate her. "She wants me to make the first move," he reasoned. Instead, Meg held firmly to her decision. The marriage was over; there was no chance for reconciliation.

Hank continued with his daily schedule, telling people Meg was visiting her folks. "This can't be happening," he would say to himself over and over again. "She'll come back. She's got to come back." He tried calling but got only an answering machine and received no return calls. He wrote but his letters were returned unopened.

Finally Hank had to accept that Meg was serious. But what was he feeling? Why wasn't he upset? He wasn't angry. He wasn't panicked. He wasn't depressed. He wasn't anything! "A robot," he thought. "I'm just like a robot. I go to work. I do what needs to be done. I go through all the motions. And I don't seem to feel anything at all. A robot."

Hank's reactions are not unique, though they lasted longer than many people's. Frequently the first response to the end of a marriage is denial. This is true not only for those who are left; leavers can also go through a period of denial. ("I can't believe I would walk out on 20 years. I can't believe after all this time that there is just nothing left.") Emotionally, many are in a state of shock. They are simply numb, feeling very much like robots, just as Hank did.

Denial and emotional numbness are not only common, they serve a useful purpose, *if* they do not continue for too long. Denial allows you to stall, so to speak, providing you with time to gain your strength so that you can face the inevitable turmoil ahead. To *continue* to deny the end of your marriage, however, is self-defeating. Many an ex-spouse becomes stalled indefinitely, unable to get on with his or her life because to do so would be an acknowledgement that the marriage *is* indeed ended.

In his book *Rebuilding*, therapist Bruce Fisher suggests you take a deep breath, say out loud that your marriage is indeed ended, and allow yourself a good long cry. If you find that you cannot get past the denial stage, get some professional help from a divorce therapist. You cannot let go of your marriage and get on with your life until you accept that your marriage is over.

SADNESS AND GRIEF:
THE IMPORTANCE OF MOURNING

Sadness is a normal and expected emotion in divorce. Even when a relationship has seriously deteriorated in recent years, there is plenty to be sad about at its end. At one time the relationship had been good, the partner had been cherished, and hopeful plans had been made for a lifetime together. These past good memories are mixed with the recent bad ones, and usually there is at least a tinge of wistfulness about what was and what might have been. Besides this, a past and a whole way of life is left behind, as well as a good chunk of each partner's identity. A home, possessions, continuous contact with children, and other relationships may be left behind as well.

When any marriage ends, there are losses that require good-byes so you can close the door permanently behind you. As with any death, the death of a relationship needs to be mourned. In fact, many therapists and theorists maintain that the divorcing person needs to go through the same mourning process as do the widow and widower to completely free themselves of the relationship.

For many divorcing men and women, the sadness is overwhelming. They feel out of control. They can't eat, sleep, or concentrate. They feel drained and helpless, and fear that they will never stop crying. This is normal. The worst of your pain is likely to peak during the first several months. By the end of the first year it will probably have leveled off.

Many people shut out their feelings of sadness and loss. "Why should I be sad? I'm happy to be out of a bad marriage." They dismiss their losses as insignificant, bury their sorrow, and assume an air of nonchalance. Allowing yourself to mourn the end of your relationship and your losses does not mean that you have to be sad that the marriage is over. It will help you close the doors on your marriage and get on with your life. Your tears and feelings of sadness and grief are not only appropriate, they will help release you from the marriage.

However, you do not have to be a victim of out-of-control emotions. There are ways that you can cope with your overwhelming feelings while you still mourn your losses. Try the following.

- Set aside a time period each day (no more than an hour) to focus on your sorrow and shed your tears, much as I suggested with "worry time." Use this time to fully experience all your losses, sadness, and self-pity. If you have trouble getting started, try writing a letter (but do not mail it) to your former spouse, relating how you are feeling and anything else you would like your former mate to know. Setting aside this time will help you control your emotions for the rest of the day and help you through the mourning process as well.
- Keep a journal and write in it during your scheduled sadness time. Write about the way you feel, the things you are struggling with, and the things you have learned. Your journal will not only help you with the mourning process, but it will also help you track your progress.
- When sadness overwhelms you outside your scheduled sadness time, use the same techniques discussed to control your anxiety. Of course, you can talk your feelings out with friends, but don't overdo it so they begin avoiding you. Overindulge yourself during your sadness time.
- Another way to stop sad feelings that occur outside your scheduled time

is to force yourself to think instead of an unpleasant memory about your former spouse.

- In his book *Rebuilding*, Bruce Fisher suggests that you write letters of good-bye to each loss in your life—to your ex-spouse, to the relationship, to your home, to your way of life, and so forth. Include all the things you will miss as well as the things you will be glad to leave behind. Dr. Fisher's research suggests that this method is not only an effective way to express your sadness, but will move you closer to letting go of your marriage and getting on with your life. These are not easy letters to write, warns Fisher. Begin with a superficial loss and gradually work your way up to more important losses. This is a good activity to do during your sadness time.

- If you find yourself getting hooked on feeling sorry for yourself and wallowing in self-pity during your sadness time, begin to schedule it at an inconvenient time and in an uncomfortable setting, suggests psychologist Zev Wanderer, who is associated with the Center for Behavior Therapy in Beverly Hills, California. (You might try a hard chair or uncomfortable clothing.) Why? If you are uncomfortable, you will be able to shorten and eventually give up your "sadness time" a lot easier.

THOUGHTS ABOUT YOUR EX: AM I GOING CRAZY?

For months after we split I drove myself and everyone else crazy. I was completely obsessed with thoughts of my marriage. I went through each year, each fight, over and over again. Why did it go so wrong? When did things start going sour? First I blamed myself for everything. Then I would go through it all again and blame him for everything. People would tell me to put it all behind me. But I couldn't. I couldn't concentrate on anything else. I couldn't talk about anything else. I thought I'd go mad!—Jessica

I couldn't understand what was going on. I didn't love Peggy anymore. I wanted the divorce. Yet I missed her! I would call her on the phone and her voice would sound so damn comforting. I would drive past the house and become uneasy if she wasn't home.—Frank

Here we were, supposed to be getting divorced, and we were sneaking around sleeping with each other about once a month. I was too embarrassed to let anyone know. I was so confused. One day I would forgive him all the past hurts and want to try again. The next I would be in a rage. I just couldn't seem to make up my mind. —Cara

Sound familiar? If so, you are in good company. The majority of people who are divorcing are plagued with obsessive thoughts of their marriages, with lingering attachments to their former spouses, and with the strong vacillating feelings of ambivalence. All three contribute to the ups and downs and the confusing turbulence of the emotional roller coaster.

Obsessive Thoughts of Your Ex: The "Account"

After marriages end, divorcing men and women usually have an urgent need to think and talk about their marriages. They go through the same events over and over again. What each partner said and did. What triggered each significant event and fight. What each partner could have done differently. Where it may have gone wrong. Who was to blame. Often it becomes such a consuming obsession that people question their sanity, as did Jessica.

This kind of obsessive thinking is not only natural and expected, it is an important step in the process of coming to terms with the end of your marriage and laying it to rest. It is your search for an explanation. Retrospectively you can put events in perspective, search for missed clues, and make sense out of events that you did not understand at the time. Each time you go through the events of your marriage, more of the pieces fall into place. Constructing *an account* of your marriage's collapse will help you achieve closure on that chapter of your life. Without it, you are likely to continue to wonder years down the road what went wrong.

Of course, the account you construct is not necessarily an accurate one. In fact, some husbands and wives construct such different accounts that it is difficult to believe they were in the same marriage. However, it is far better for your own adjustment and for your future relationships if you try to gain a balanced perspective. You should neither take all the blame nor assign all the blame. It would be a rare marriage if one person were entirely at fault and the other entirely faultless. More about accounts in Chapter 6.

It may take several months before you no longer have the urgent need to ruminate about your marriage all the time. Until then, there are ways to gain control of your thoughts so your ruminations will not consume your waking hours.

- One way is to restrict your ruminations to a scheduled time, using thought stoppage and distraction techniques during the rest of the day.
- Psychologists at the Center for Behavior Therapy in Beverly Hills have come up with a different and ingenious solution. You can ruminate all you want, but at a price. You must write down *each* thought you have *every* time you ruminate about your marriage. Keep your notes together in a journal. Why is this method effective? Your natural inclination will be to rehash the same events over and over again. However, if you have to write down the same things repeatedly, it will be boring, and a hassle,

too. Pretty soon you will be less tempted to rehash the same old events, and you will be quite satisfied to fill in the missing details of your account as they occur to you.

Attachments and Ambivalence

To many divorcing men and women, one of the most incomprehensible and frustrating feelings they experience is the continued pull toward an ex-spouse. Ex-partners think and wonder about one another and seek news about the other's activities. Some make excuses to call or stop by, some actively miss their exs, some even pine for them. It is not only those who are left who experience this pull. Leavers experience it too, and many find it incomprehensible.

University of Massachusetts sociologist Robert Weiss first identified this phenomenon more than a decade and a half ago. He called it attachment. Research suggests that lingering attachment is somewhat more common among those who are left and somewhat more common among men than women.

Just what is attachment? It is a sort of emotional bonding and a feeling of connectedness, a feeling of ease in the other's presence and restlessness when the other is inaccessible. One woman, who had left her husband after years of unhappiness, describes her feelings of attachment that were aroused by their meeting in her lawyer's office.

> I felt that as long as my husband was in the room I felt protected, and that it was just the two of us, not the lawyers. . . . [Later] I wanted to call him and say, what a colossal mistake we've made. I only feel together when I'm with you.[1]

Attachment can paralyze a spouse with fear when he or she even thinks about leaving the unhappy marriage. It can cause a spouse to fight any and all settlement agreements in order to delay the final divorce. It can prevent a spouse from taking steps toward starting a new life.

Attachment persists far longer than do love, liking, admiration, respect, or the marriage. It persists despite conflict and antagonism. It appears that proximity alone is enough to sustain it. And it seems to fade only gradually, without contact and sometimes with the help of a new love.

Given the widespread feelings of attachment, it is not surprising that divorcing partners so often have intensely ambivalent feelings about one another. They vacillate between longing and anger, between love and hate. What does it all mean, they wonder. Are they doing the right thing by divorcing? Some go through periods of dating each other again. Some resume sexual relations. (In a University of California study reported by Dr. Terry Arendell, one-third of the study group had had sexual relations with their ex-spouse during the first year following their legal divorce.) People tell the couple to make up their minds, but this advice is easier said than followed. It is a difficult time to get through, but it's easier when you know it is normal.

FEELINGS OF REJECTION, WORTHLESSNESS, AND FAILURE

This trio of feelings is such a common component of the emotional roller coaster that divorced members in singles groups often refer to themselves as the "walking wounded."

It is common for at least one and sometimes both members of a divorcing couple to feel rejected. Frequently, however, the leaver is not rejecting the *person left* as much as *the person he or she once was* and no longer wishes to be. A leaver frequently has moved in a new direction that may be incompatible with the direction the spouse desires. There can be any number of reasons why someone moves in new directions, ranging from personal growth to a reaction to some life event such as a trauma, a new job, a religious experience, or relocation. Whatever the reason, the leaver may feel that the only two choices are to sacrifice his or her new direction or to leave the relationship. Whereas at one time society clearly pressed people into the first option, it now openly accepts the second. Words like self-fulfillment, self-actualization, growth, being true to oneself, and irreconcilable differences have become familiar. However, society sends out a double-edged message. On the one hand, it pays lip service to the acceptability of divorce On the other, it tenaciously clings to the tenet "till death do us part." It also refers to "failed" marriages and extends very little support to the divorcing, who so often feel as if they have been deserted in a world full of quicksand. It is no wonder that so many divorcing men and women, caught in the middle of these double-edged messages, feel like failures.

How do you deal with feelings of rejection, worthlessness, and failure? Try the following.

- Find some comfort in the knowledge that you are not alone. Your feelings are common among divorcing men and women.
- Work on rebuilding your self-esteem using the strategies in Chapter 12. Divorce is usually very hard on people's self-esteem, and as you rebuild yours, your feelings of rejection, worthlessness, and/or failure will diminish.
- Look at the broader picture. What are the *many* causes contributing to your divorce? Don't put all the blame on yourself. Also think about the two-million-plus people who divorce each *year* in this country alone. Do you really think all those millions of people are worthless? Do you really think they all are failures in life? Then why are you?

- Don't write off your *entire* marriage as a failure because it ended in divorce. Look for the successes over the years.
- Ask yourself, "Because my marriage ended, does it negate my worth as a *person*? How does the end of my marriage make me into a different person than I was before? Does it detract from my other successes?" Now evaluate again how worthless you are and how much of a failure you are.

EUPHORIA: WHY CAN'T IT ALWAYS BE LIKE THIS?

You do not need special coping tools to deal with your periods of euphoria, but no coverage of the emotional roller coaster would be complete without a discussion of the highs as well as the lows. Euphoric periods are the sunshine between the storms, when you may be delirious with feelings of freedom, brimming with self-confidence, and certain that your world abounds with unlimited opportunities. However, as suddenly as your euphoria appeared, it can be cruelly whisked away—often at the first hint of personal failure—leaving you feeling like you are drowning in quicksand once again. It is all part of the emotional roller coaster. As you progress through the transition–restructuring period and become more confident in your new state of life, you will be less susceptible to these emotional ups and downs.

Learning that euphoria is probably only temporary is enough to throw some people back into a downward spiral. Don't let this happen to you. Take full advantage of the extra energy you have during your euphoric periods to start a new self-change program (or two) that you may not otherwise have the energy or motivation to start. (This book is full of ideas for self-change programs.) Follow the steps in Appendix A, but don't get carried away because you are feeling good. *Always* set your goals in small steps so you will be successful. (If you choose to do more, it will be icing on the cake.) If you can get a self-change program going when you are feeling good, the momentum can help you continue it through the low times. And the more successful you are with self-change programs, the fewer low times you will have!

The following chapter focuses on these low times, when you are feeling defeated and immobilized. It discusses depression and how to get yourself out of it.

4

FEELING DEFEATED AND IMMOBILIZED: How To Combat Depression

*S*ometimes overwhelming sadness and grief drag on week after week, or even month after month. It may be so intense that it is a struggle to carry on with your job or care for your children. You may feel worthless and hold little hope for your future. The activities you once loved may no longer give you any pleasure. Your world may seem joyless, and you may spend your time in passive solitary activities such as watching television. Your appetite may be poor and you may be chronically fatigued, perhaps unable to sleep. Sometimes even the most mundane tasks—getting out of bed, brushing your teeth, and getting dressed—may seem like insurmountable obstacles and require supreme effort. This is depression.

In one major study, roughly 30 percent of the men and 30 percent of the women were seriously depressed after separation. Another one-third of the men and three-fifths of the women were mildly to moderately depressed. Depression hits both leavers and those who are left.

Depression usually peaks early in the separation period. A short-lived depression is nothing to be concerned about; some people need a period of withdrawal before they can begin to face the new demands of separation. However, it is never too soon to learn some tools to cope with it. Depression can become a long-term problem that does not get better with time. In fact, the longer depression continues, the more likely it is to perpetuate itself.

If your depression has gone on for days, begin today to use some coping tools. You *can* turn your depression around, and you *can* begin to get on with your life. However, if you do not feel that you can handle your depression by yourself, if your depression continues week after week, and certainly if you feel suicidal, please get professional help immediately. Do not try to cope alone with depression at this level.

Many people have a second period of depression much later in the transition–restructuring phase of divorce. In fact, in a carefully conducted University of Virginia study, the majority of men and women in the study group reported that they were at an all-time low one year after their divorces were final. If you have this second period of depression, don't be discouraged. You are not going backward after so many months of hard work. In fact, this second depression has been called the "darkness before the dawn."

The coping methods discussed here can be used effectively at any time you are depressed. In fact, if you continue to follow their principles, they are likely to *prevent* periods of depression in the future. Many of these methods have been developed by either psychiatrist David Burns or Dr. Peter Lewinsohn and his associates, who have devoted years to the study of depression. The methods have had a lot of success.

TAKING POSITIVE ACTION

One of the most effective cures for depression is so deceptively simple that you may be skeptical that it will work. It is *activity*. The more you get yourself going, the less depressed you will feel.

You see, your feelings and your behavior are intimately bound together: Feelings affect behavior and behavior affects feelings. When you are depressed you don't feel like doing anything. (Your feelings affect your behavior.) But the less you do, the more depressed you become. (Your behavior affects your feelings.) You are in a vicious circle!

Increasing Your Pleasurable Activity

Increasing your *pleasurable* activity is more effective in combatting depression than increasing activity at random. Dr. Lewinsohn finds that compared with most people, depressed people engage in very little pleasurable activity from day to day. Most depressed people put off doing pleasurable things until they "feel better." What they don't realize is that taking the opposite approach is a much quicker way out of depression. Usually, when depressed people start increasing the pleasant activities in their lives, they begin to feel better, their mood begins to improve, and their depression begins to lift. The vicious cycle is broken. Their better mood enables them to do more, which boosts their mood and morale still higher. Instead of a downward vicious cycle in which their depression worsens, they begin an upward spiraling cycle in which their depression lifts.

The trick is to get yourself started. Lewinsohn and his associates have developed many effective methods to help you do this. Try the following.

1. Sit down *right away* and start making a list of activities that you might find pleasant. If you have a handy list, you can refer to it each day and

choose some activities that appeal to you at the time. In Lewinsohn's book *Control Your Depression*, he lists over 300 widely varied activities that might give you pleasure. It is a great source of ideas. I'll give you some examples here to get you going on your own list: reading, solving puzzles, listening to music; building or watching a fire, bicycling; enjoying nature; hiking; painting; sculpting; making crafts; restoring antiques; gardening; sitting in the sun; going to a health club; having coffee with a friend; repairing something; going to discussion groups or club or church functions; doing volunteer work; participating in or watching sports; attending concerts; doing photography, meditation, or yoga; or getting facials or massages. There are also some very simple activities that make most people feel good, which you may not think of on your own. Examples are praising or complimenting someone, smiling at people, thinking about people you like, doing a job well, breathing clean air, taking in some beautiful scenery, becoming involved in a project, planning a trip, and learning to do something new. You may find that these give you pleasure, too. Notice that a pleasant activity does not have to be time-consuming.

Don't worry about making a complete list right away. You can keep adding to it as new things come to mind. Start tuning into the small things that give you pleasure, and start allowing your imagination to roam. Lewinsohn's book is a good source of ideas. Eventually you will want a long and varied list of about 100 pleasant activities from which to choose.

2. Rate your mood *right now* on a scale of 1 (the pits) to 9 (feeling great). Keep track of your mood each day and record it daily on a "daily mood chart." Graphing your mood like this will allow you to track it visually and notice small improvements. Starting immediately will give you a baseline measure of your mood *before* you increase your daily pleasant activities. Then you can enjoy watching it rise.

3. How do you know how many pleasant activities to do each day? Keep track for a few typical days of the number of activities you usually do that give you pleasure. (The small number may surprise you.) Then start by increasing that number by three to five each day. (Remember, pleasant activities do not need to be time-consuming.) By keeping a daily mood chart, you will be able to tell how many pleasant activities you need to do each day in order to feel better. It varies from person to person.

4. Because it is so difficult to motivate yourself when you are depressed, you may wish to follow the self-change method discussed in Appendix A. With it you will be able to successfully break your do-nothing pattern. Without it, you may continue to take the path of least resistance— nothing! The program is simple. Here is a quick summary of its five steps.

a. Set a goal that is short-term, modest, and achievable.
b. Write and sign a contract to commit yourself to your goal.
c. Keep track each day of whether you met your goal for the day and how close you came if you didn't.
d. Reward yourself for sticking to your contract or penalize yourself for breaking it.
e. Evaluate your success. If you met your goal, set a new one, perhaps *slightly* higher. If you didn't, either try a shorter-term goal, a less ambitious goal, or a more motivating reward.

Harry Pennfield is a 40-year-old divorcing father who had been moderately depressed for four months. Although he functioned at his job as an accountant, he buried himself in numbers and overtime work and had withdrawn from all social contacts. When he wasn't at the office, he sat in his apartment amidst the boxes he had yet to unpack, watching television and drinking scotch. He finally sought therapy.

At the urging of his therapist, Harry kept track of the number of activities he did each day that gave him pleasure; he averaged four a day. He also kept a daily mood chart; his average mood was 2.5. Then using Lewinsohn's book, *Control Your Depression*, he made up a personal list of 100 activities that he thought might be pleasurable.

Harry did not think much of the approach but was willing to try it. He wrote the following contract for himself and signed it.

"During the next week, I will increase my pleasant activities by four each day. I will not allow myself any television or scotch in the evening until I have reached my goal for that day. If I stick to my goal for the week, I will treat myself to a dinner at Mario's. If I do not, I will take the 20 dollars I would have spent on dinner and send it to my wife.—Harry Pennfield"

Harry's self-imposed penalty made him very motivated to stick to his contract. Each night he checked his list of potentially pleasant activities and decided which he would do the next day. He also included some extras as backups. Some of the easiest were his favorites: going into the employees' lounge for a coffee break, smiling at people and saying hello (he determined that greeting five people should equal one activity), stopping at the nursery and buying a plant to brighten up his stark apartment, calling his sons in the evening and hearing about their day, finally getting his stereo hooked up, buying a new best-seller and reading a chapter or two every night.

Each night, Harry recorded how many pleasant activities he had engaged in that day and rated and graphed his mood. Some days he exceeded his goal, and he was pleased to note an improvement in his mood that the graph made quite obvious. Maybe this approach wasn't so bad after all.

Over the next weeks he gradually increased his goal to include more daily pleasant activities. Then he decided to make it a goal to try at least one completely *new* pleasant activity on his list each week. This motivated him to initiate a number of social activities with other single people in his firm, to take his kids on a camping trip, to learn how to cook several gourmet dishes, and to fix up his apartment step by step to make it look and feel like a home.

Do you already feel so overwhelmed with things you *must* do that you cannot find time in your schedule to increase your pleasant activities? Try two things. First, keep in mind that pleasurable activities do not *have* to be time-consuming. Focus on the activities on your list that require only a small amount of time (for example, smiling and saying hello to people, taking a hot bath, listening to music while you're doing something else, taking more care with your appearance, taking the kids for an ice cream cone). Second, try keeping track for a few days of how you typically spend your time, and record it on a chart broken into 30-minute segments. Then look at it with a critical eye. Is there any waste you can trim? Can you delegate some activities to someone else? Can you lower your standards so you can do some things quicker than you do them now? This might help you find the time for some pleasure in your life.

Combatting Depression Via Other Kinds of Action

Increasing your pleasurable activities isn't the only way you can lift your depression through action. Try the following.

- Regular aerobic exercise is a great antidote to depression. You don't believe it? According to a University of Kansas study of people who were confronted with serious life change (divorce, death of a loved one, and so forth), those who were physically fit experienced less depression than did their less physically fit counterparts. You say you don't have the energy to exercise? Force yourself to go for a brisk 20-minute walk. If you record your mood on your mood chart before and again after your walk, I think you will be surprised at the improvement. Set a goal for yourself each day and reward yourself for achieving it.
- Work on building your self-esteem using the methods in chapter 12. As you begin to feel better about yourself, it will automatically lift your mood.
- Reach out to other people. Social support can be a real boost to your morale. People who have gone through divorce can be particularly helpful. Join Parents Without Partners or a small divorce support group. Either is likely to provide you with willing volunteers to support you through this troubling time.
- Make a special effort to do some nice things for yourself and for someone else, too. Take more care with your appearance, get a new outfit, do a favor for someone. It will make you feel good, and it's difficult to feel good and depressed at the same time.
- Some of your depression may come from feeling deprived of many things that you routinely enjoyed in your marriage—for example, a primary relationship, companionship, home-cooked meals, reliable financial plan-

ning, a relief babysitter, a sounding board, continuous contact with your children, a reliable sex life, and so forth. Make a list of all the things your ex provided you that you now miss. Then try to figure out if there is some other way that you can fill at least some of those voids. Could a close friend or a therapist fill your need for the time being for a primary relationship? Could a pet and/or a number of different friends fill the companionship void? Could you arrange with another single parent to exchange relief babysitting? Could you learn to cook a few meals you really enjoy? Could you call your children every night to keep abreast of their lives and activities?

- Think of one thing that would make you feel good to accomplish—writing a long-owed letter, spending some quality time with your child, getting your desk organized, making a good meal for a change. Then get started doing it. If it is a big task, break it down into small steps, such as spending 15 minutes organizing your desk each day. Write a contract if needed, and by all means reward yourself for sticking to your goals each day. Notice how much better you feel with each small accomplishment.
- Keep a journal of your feelings, and reread it frequently. It's often an eye-opener and a morale-booster to realize how much you have improved over time.

DOING A TUNE-UP ON YOUR THINKING

If you cannot combat your depression sufficiently by taking action, you may have to do a tune-up on your thinking. There is a very logical reason for this. You see, not only are your *feelings* and your *behavior* intimately bound together, your *feelings* and your *thinking* are intimately bound together, too. How you think influences the way you feel, and how you feel influences the way you think. Let me give you a hypothetical example. Two couples, Phil and Maureen and Andy and Sheila, had been in marital counseling for several months, trying to save their rocky marriages. Both women were committed to trying indefinitely, but Phil and Andy gave up and told their wives they wanted a divorce. How did Maureen and Sheila feel? Maureen chastised herself. "I should have tried harder. I should have been a better wife. I was too involved doing my own thing. Now it's too late. He's gone. I'm such a failure. What will I do? Life will be so meaningless and empty. I'll never find someone to love me again." Maureen felt depressed, guilty, unlovable, and like a failure. She went through a period in which she withdrew from life, continuing to chastise herself and sinking further into depression.

Sheila, on the other hand, blamed Andy. "He never even gave the counseling a chance. That self-centered, inconsiderate creep. Well, I'll be damned if I'm going to wither up and die. I'll show him." Sheila was angry and bitter. In a rage, she threw his belongings in the backyard, working herself into a frenzy. For the next two months she went to singles bars three or four times a week, determined to show Andy that she didn't need him. Maureen and Sheila reacted very differently to their husbands' divorce plans. How they felt (depressed and guilty, or angry and bitter) was profoundly influenced by how they thought. How they thought was also influenced by how they felt (depressed or angry).

Dr. Aaron Beck, a leading expert in the area of depression, has focused his attention on how depression and thinking affect each other. He discovered that when people are depressed, they lose their ability to think clearly and put things into perspective. They magnify their mistakes and imperfections and the negative events in their lives. Negatives clearly dominate their reality. This is evident in some of the typical thoughts people have when they are depressed: "I'm such a loser." "I'm so worthless." "What's the use?" "It's all my fault." "Life is so unfair." "Why does everything bad happen to me?" Dr. Beck describes depressive thinking as the four Ds: defeated, defective, deserted, and deprived. Who wouldn't be depressed if such thoughts filled their minds all the time?

This is why you may not be able to combat your depression effectively by *only* taking positive action (although many people can). You may also need to do a tune-up on the self-defeating thoughts that fill your mind. Let me guess what you are thinking: "That's okay for other people, but *my* thoughts aren't self-defeating. *I'm* just being realistic!" *All* depressed people feel this way *when they are depressed*; they are convinced that they are thinking objectively. However, when they are not depressed, their thinking is not nearly so negative. Negative thinking is both caused by depression and causes further depression.

Combatting Your Depression by Reprogramming Your Thinking

One way to combat your depression is to break your negative thinking pattern. To break it, you must be aware of it. So a first step is to tune into your *self-talk* for a day or two and write down the negative things you say to yourself. You will find that you say some things over and over again. Mark the thoughts that seem to be most important in contributing to your depression.

Jamie Anderson kept track of his self-talk for two days and felt that these thoughts were having the most impact on his mood:

> "You're such a loser, Anderson."
> "No wonder she dumped you. Who wouldn't?"
> "What a screw-up I am. I'll never be able to get anywhere in life."
> "Why bother? It's all so pointless."
> "God, this is awful. I can't cope with losing her."
> "I'll never find anyone else who could love a jerk like me."

Jamie Anderson sounds like a real loser and would probably be able to convince a stranger that he was, too. But anyone who knew him would have been shocked at his self-talk. Jamie is a well-liked and respected associate in a prestigious law firm. For eight of the past ten years, his marriage had been fairly successful. He is a good father, and his children adore him. Jamie's thinking had become his own worst enemy.

Here are some ways to break your negative thinking pattern. Choose the ones that make the most sense to you.

- Use thought stoppage (Chapter 3) to stop your negative thinking.
- When you catch yourself in negative self-talk, replace it with some positive self-talk. The following technique will give you a ready supply of positive self-talk to use.
- Make a list of your good points, and write each one on a small index card. Post a few someplace where you will see them frequently, such as on a bathroom mirror. Rotate your cards from week to week. When you read the card, take some time to think about it. In this way, you can *systematically* implant some positive thoughts in your mind and break the continuous pattern of negative thoughts.

Jamie had a difficult time with this assignment. He had been down on himself for so long, he couldn't think of *anything* positive about himself. He began writing down the compliments people gave him, rather than ignoring them as he usually did. He toyed with the idea of asking his good friend to tell him some of his strong points, but decided it would be embarrassing. One day when he was berating himself, his friend lectured him on all he had going for him. Jamie later wrote each point down, although some he discarded because they seemed far too flattering to be accurate. He finally came up with a list of ten positive statements he could accept. Over the next few weeks, he was able to expand his list. The original ten were these: "I'm a respected member of the firm. My clients find me sensitive. I'm a good father. My kids are great. I'm dependable. I'm organized and efficient. I'm attractive. I'm in good physical shape. My friends say I'm a caring person. I have a good sense of humor (when I'm not depressed)."

- Use the "pat-on-the-back" technique. Get into the habit of giving yourself a pat on the back throughout the day at every opportunity you can. ("That was a good report I wrote." "I'm getting better at remembering my positive self-talk." "I'm doing a good job sticking to my contract." "That was a good meal I fixed." "I organized my time well today." "I was really patient with the kids today.")
- Focus on what you *do* accomplish rather than what you fail to accomplish. Make a list each day of all your successes, however small.
- Keep a daily journal in which you focus on the *positives* in your life. Include everything positive that occurred that day, no matter how small.

And don't forget the big things—your health, children, friends, family, job. Your journal will counteract your tendency to focus only on the negatives.

Combatting Your Illogical Thinking

Some people find they can fight depression better by combatting their illogical thinking. Remember that when people are depressed, they lose their ability to think clearly and put things in perspective. Invariably, their self-talk is not only negative, it is *illogical or distorted* as well. Let me give you two examples.

One of the most common types of distorted thinking used by divorcing people who are depressed is what Dr. Albert Ellis, the father of Rational-Emotive Therapy, calls catastrophizing. Catastrophizing means interpreting a very unfortunate event as the end of the world. ("This is horrible!" "I can't stand it anymore!" "I can't live without him (her)!") When you use words like "awful," "terrible," "I can't stand it," and "I can't live without _____ ," you are probably catastrophizing. Why is catastrophizing a distorted kind of thinking? Because you are confusing what you would like *very much* with what you *need to survive*. You may hate what is happening to you. But it is not the end of the world, as more than two million people who divorce each year learn. Catastrophizing is not only distorted thinking, it is self-defeating as well because it tends to immobilize you. It makes you feel the situation is too difficult to do anything about. If you stop catastrophizing and start using some good coping tools, you will survive quite well.

All-or-nothing thinking is a second type of distorted thinking commonly used by divorcing people who are depressed. In all-or-nothing thinking, you use blanket labels to define yourself. ("I'm such a jerk." "I'm a loser." "I'm worthless." "I'm a complete failure." "I never do anything right.") Why is this distorted thinking? Because people fail in *some* areas, not in *all* areas of their lives. And they make mistakes at *some* times and in *some* situations. Defining yourself with a blanket negative label ignores everything in your life that is positive and everything you do well. It is unrealistic and will always make you feel bad.

How can you attack your distorted or illogical thinking? A number of general changes you can make in the way that you think will help you combat your depression. Following are a few of Dr. David Burns' methods.

- *Think in shades of gray.* This is an antidote for much of your distorted thinking. Avoid slapping *any* negative labels on yourself or your problems ("I'm a failure." "I'm a loser." "I'm so stupid." "All the bad things happen to me." "I've ruined my life."). Instead, Dr. Burns recommends that you evaluate your shortcomings, mistakes, and problems on a scale from 0 to 100. Be as honest as you can. Before you use the scale, consider *all* the evidence. What evidence is there to confirm the label you've given yourself (loser, failure, worthless, jerk)? What evidence is there to refute the label? Spend time thinking about each area of your life, and write down everything you think of that counteracts the label so you can't forget about them. Then use the 0 to 100 scale.

> When Jamie did this exercise, he had to admit that he was far from being a loser. He had had many successes professionally. He was a good father and his kids loved him. He had friends. He kept himself in shape. This realization made him feel so much better that he vowed he would never again tell himself that he was a loser. And once he stopped telling himself that, he began to feel better!

- *Look for partial successes.* Remember the old dilemma: Is the glass half empty, or is it half full? The optimist is happy because he perceives his glass as half full; the pessimist is sad because his is half empty. When you are depressed, you are bound to be a pessimist. Rather than looking at situations as failures, start looking for the partial successes. For example, if you have been married for ten years and you get divorced, does that make your *entire* marriage a failure? What about the good times? What about the things you brought away from the marriage? In what ways are you different now than you were before you married?
- *Watch those emotionally loaded words.* This is a good antidote for catastrophizing. Replace your catastrophizing language with language that is *less emotional*. Here are some examples:

Instead of: "My life has been *terrible* since we split up!"
Try: "My life has been *difficult* since we split up."
Instead of: "It's just *awful* that Mary left."
Try: "It's *unfortunate* for me that Mary left."
Instead of: "I just *can't* cope with my divorce."
Try: "I *don't like* having to cope with my divorce."
Instead of: "I *can't stand* Ted living with someone else."
Try: "I *really wish* Ted weren't living with someone else."
Instead of: "It *shouldn't* have turned out this way."
Try: "I'd *certainly prefer* that things had turned out differently."

You might be thinking, "Okay, this sounds better, but isn't it just a game of words?" No, it isn't. When a situation is difficult, unfortunate, and not what you prefer, you tend to try to do something to improve your circumstances. But when a situation is disastrous, you tend to feel that it is out of your control and that you *cannot* help yourself. You become frozen in self-pity, misery, and despair. Spending your time catastrophizing saps initiative, time, and energy that would be better used getting on with your life.

Dr. Burns' two books, *Feeling Good* and *The Feeling Good Workbook*, offer many ways besides these to identify and correct your distorted and illogical thinking. Either is an excellent source if you would like to work on changing your distorted thinking in greater depth. The books are listed in Appendix C.

While you are trying to combat depression, do not try to do everything at once. You will set yourself up for failure and disappointment and, consequently, feel even more depressed. Make your goals small ones and increase them very gradually, step by step. Start with increasing the number of pleasant activities in your life or with other positive action. This is probably the easiest way to get quick results. If this doesn't do the trick, then work on giving your thinking a tune-up. Don't forget to use the self-change program in Appendix A to keep you on track. Dr. Burns' and Dr. Lewinsohn's books, listed in Appendix C, offer even more methods for relieving depression.

Sometimes, depression saps your motivation and energy to such an extent that it is difficult to get yourself going without some external support. If you find this to be the case, see a counselor or therapist. He or she can provide you with the support, strength, and primary relationship that you need right now.

The emotional roller coaster does not end here. Missing is the emotion of anger. It is one of the biggies in divorce and is the subject of the following chapter.

WHAT DO I DO WITH ALL THIS ANGER?

Early on a Sunday morning in November 1989, a prominent San Diego attorney and his newlywed wife were found shot to death in their beds. Later that day the attorney's distraught ex-wife called a friend and admitted to the shooting. As the story unfolded, it told of bitter acrimony between the formerly married pair since their divorce several years earlier. In fact, the attorney had been quoted as saying, "It is not going to end until one of us is gone."

One of the interesting things about the incident was the compassion that many in the community seemed to feel for the ex-wife, despite their horror at what she had done. What had happened to this once well-functioning woman whose smile had frequently graced the local paper's society pages and who had entertained the city's finest? How could her anger have gotten so far out of control?

As you come to accept that your marriage is truly over, a dam may seem to break inside you, spilling out a torrent of anger—or perhaps even rage, more intense than you had thought yourself capable of. Unfamiliar feelings of bitterness and vindictiveness may become your new companions, consuming a greater share of your thoughts each day. You may become obsessed with old hurts you had almost forgotten, reliving each as vividly as if it had occurred yesterday, each memory pouring fuel on your seething anger. Your friends may notice that you have added some very graphic language to your vocabulary, and you may find that you are unable to have a conversation with your ex-spouse without the anger erupting into a full-blown battle.

Judith Wallerstein and Joan Kelly found that 80 percent of the men and a somewhat higher percentage of the women they studied experienced such anger and bitterness after separation. Both leavers and those they left became victims of their own rage. Frightened children heard their dads called disgusting, crazy, liars, and bastards, while they heard their moms called whores, drunken bitches, greedy, and grasping.

WHERE DOES IT ALL COME FROM?

Where does all this anger come from? From frustration and resentments that have been bottled up over the years. From unfulfilled expectations. From the losses and disappointments. From thwarted needs for love and affection. From uncertainty about the future. From feelings of being exploited and betrayed. From hurt and humiliation. From wounded self-esteem. From feelings of helplessness. And, of course, from genuine conflicts of interest over property settlements, support payments, and custody. It may be little comfort to know that the intensity of your rage is likely to reflect the importance the relationship had in your life. If it did not matter to you, there would be little reason to get so angry when the relationship ended.

Anger and divorce go together about the same as do love and marriage. Anger is not only understandable, it is to be expected. Potentially, there is a good side to your anger. It can make it easier to distance yourself from your former spouse so that you can get on with your life, but only under one condition: that you get beyond your anger and *let it go*. As long as you hold onto your anger, you will be bound to your ex as surely as if you were still in love; the only difference is that the bonds will be negative rather than positive. For your own sake, you need to eliminate both the positive *and* the negative bonds with your former mate. You have the potential to create a future in which your former spouse will no longer have power over you and will no longer trigger an emotional reaction within you. Your anger and resentment can be exchanged for indifference and perhaps even concern. This is a goal toward which many of you will be motivated to work.

Many divorced men and women *do* hold onto their anger, however. In their large-scale study, Morton and Bernice Hunt found that for one-third of their study group, anger had been the *predominant* feeling toward the ex-spouse months after divorces had been finalized. But far more surprising was Judith Wallerstein's report that one-half of the women in her study group and one-third of the men were still intensely angry at their former mates *10 years after* they had divorced. Shocked by how little effect the passage of time had had, she reported that she sometimes felt as if she had wandered into a play with the same characters relating the same story, with the same script delivered with the same fervor.

Who is hurt when a spouse holds onto anger? The spouse who will not let the anger go, as well as his or her children. Investing emotional energy into anger and revenge saps away the energy needed to build a new life. The still-angry spouse can become stalled in the past, bound to the dead relationship. He or she may become one of the embittered divorced who are unable to have a meaningful present or hopeful future, who go into a tirade at each new encounter with their former partners, who attempt new court actions year after year, who sometimes resort to physical violence, and who draw their children into a quicksand of emotional turmoil.

Letting go of your anger is critical to your divorce adjustment. This chapter will discuss a number of methods to help you deal with your anger and finally let it go. But before we begin, it may be helpful to take a brief diversion and note some important distinctions about your anger that you may otherwise find confusing.

WHEN ANGER IS SELF-DEFEATING

All anger is not necessarily self-defeating. In addition to making it easier for spouses to distance themselves from one another so they can get on with their lives, anger can also be a strong *motivator*, propelling people to take constructive action to improve a situation. Let me give you an example.

George Frieze had never been able to assert himself with his wife, Eugenia. She always seemed to have the upper hand, and he had always given in to her demands. Now that they were divorcing, nothing was different. She still called him constantly— demanding more money, demanding most of their joint possessions, dictating how he spent his time with the children. Would it always continue like this, he wondered. He still had no idea about how to deal with her, but the resentments of the past 15 years were erupting, and George felt ready to kill. Fortunately, members of George's divorce support group encouraged him to take an assertiveness training class. The class gave George a new feeling of confidence, and he diligently worked on using his new skills to communicate and negotiate effectively with Eugenia. "Maybe if I had taken this class earlier, I wouldn't be getting divorced," mused George. "Funny, I knew about assertiveness training for years and never did anything about it. I guess I just wasn't angry enough before to get myself off my duff."

To determine whether your anger is useful or self-defeating, ask yourself these questions: Can your anger be useful in improving the upsetting situation? Can you channel it constructively in some way to achieve a positive end? George's anger motivated him to learn effective ways to deal with his ex-wife. Some people who have been angered by the legal system during their divorces have channeled their anger into activist activities that help others avoid similar problems.

But what about situations that you cannot change or influence? Anger about these situations is self-defeating. You are investing emotional energy into making yourself miserable! It is far better for you to gracefully and realistically accept situations you cannot change, points out well-known psychologist and anger expert Dr. Albert Ellis. Take your emotional energy and invest it in rebuilding a new life instead of in self-defeating anger. This is what Betty Johnson did.

Betty Johnson was devastated when her husband of 30 years left her for his young assistant. For six months she was in a deep depression, unable to function. She had no idea what she would do now that he was gone, and she didn't care. Then her anger surfaced, and Betty was filled with destructive energy. She yelled, screamed, swore, and threw things. She'd never before realized that she had the capacity for such anger or violence. Then gradually she came to a conclusion: "I'll be damned if I'll let him ruin my life. Who the hell needs him? I'll show him I can get along just fine without him." That was the beginning of a new life for Betty. She took her anger and channeled it constructively; it provided her with the motivation to reconstruct her life. Once she had successfully launched herself in school, she let go of her anger; it no longer served a useful purpose.

Your anger probably has two sources right now. The first is what Judith Wallerstein calls "old anger," left over from the relationship you are no longer in (all the injustices, hurts, frustrations, betrayals, and losses in your marriage). Your old anger is about situations you clearly cannot change. You can never change the past hurts, and since the relationship is over, there is no purpose in bringing up all the past resentments, injustices, frustrations, and betrayals. To do so would in all probability incite your spouse to retaliate and may set into motion a spiraling cycle of angry accusations that would refuel your anger and escalate your conflict. Before you can adjust successfully to your divorce, you will need to let go of your old anger. The methods discussed in this chapter will help you to do this.

What is the other source of your anger? Wallerstein calls it "new anger," and it is caused by definable situations in the here and now (such as your ex-wife making it difficult to see the kids, your ex-husband not making his child support payments, your ex going on your dream vacation with a new love while you sit at home and stew). Some of this new anger is likely to stem from situations in which your rights are being disregarded (for example, missed child support payments or barriers that prevent you from seeing your kids). These are situations that you *may* be able to influence, and later we'll take a look at how to use your anger constructively to help bring about desired change.

But some of your new anger may be about situations that do not affect you directly and are clearly out of your sphere of influence (like that upcoming vacation with the new love, who your ex dates, how he or she conducts life from now on). The only thing that anger about these situations will accomplish is making you miserable. It is self-defeating anger, and the best way to deal with it is to treat it like your old anger—*let it go* by using the methods discussed in this chapter. It is self-defeating to hang onto anger over situations that you cannot change, whether they are past *or* present situations.

HOW TO DEAL WITH SELF-DEFEATING ANGER AND LET IT GO

How do you let go of your self-defeating anger? First, be sure you recognize your anger and acknowledge it. This may sound like a joke to those of you who are *very greatly* aware of your anger. But some among the divorcing do not recognize anger as part of the turmoil they are feeling. This is especially true about their old anger.

In their book *Letting Go*, psychologist Zev Wanderer and co-author Tracy Cabot suggest a useful technique for those of you who feel only sadness and depression rather than any anger. Compile a "crime sheet," listing every specific incident you can think of throughout your marriage in which your ex was guilty of lies, hurts, humiliations, coldness, thoughtlessness, selfishness, or cruelty. Write each incident on a three-by-five-inch index card so you can easily carry your crime sheet with you. Include not only the incident but how you felt at the time. Then, when your sadness begins to erupt, block it by dwelling on some of the incidents on your crime sheet, and especially on your feelings at the time.

If you do not acknowledge your old anger, you are likely to find it popping up in all sorts of ways—snide comments, overreacting to your ex's behavior or mannerisms, resenting your child because of a resemblance to your ex, "forgetting" to mail child support payments, lashing out at your children, heightened anxiety, and so forth. Your unacknowledged anger could stand in the way of your freeing yourself completely from your former spouse and from your marriage. As Morton and Bernice Hunt point out in their book *The Divorce Experience*, expressed anger tends to *break* the bonds between former spouses, whereas suppressed anger tends to *maintain* the bonds.

Effective Methods of Diffusing Self-Defeating Anger

Once you acknowledge your anger, there are a number of safe and constructive ways to diffuse your pent-up anger so that you can let it go. (Punching your ex or slashing his or her tires is not on the list.) Try some of the following:

- Tell your former partner off in a letter. This is your time to let him or her have it about all your past hurts and the injustices inflicted on you. Go ahead and use the meanest, nastiest language you can think of, and be as critical as you like. BUT DO NOT MAIL IT! The unmailed letter technique will not only help you ventilate and diffuse some of your anger, it will also help you sort out your feelings in your own mind and acknowledge them. You may also have some fun writing it.
- Exercise is an excellent way to drain the emotional energy created by your anger. Take up fast walking, jogging, bicycling, swimming, racketball, or some other aerobic activity, and do it *regularly*. Most people who exercise fairly strenuously when they are angry feel invigorated afterward rather than angry. Activities such as strenuous housework and chopping wood can also dissipate some of the extra adrenaline your anger pumps into your body.

- Rechannel your emotional energy into constructive activities that will help you rebuild your new life.
- Talk out your feelings with a supportive friend or therapist. This will allow you to vent some of your anger and will also help you to sort out some of your feelings and acknowledge them, such as the pain that underlies your anger. A word of caution, however: Though talking is good, unlimited talking is not necessarily better. Ranting and raving about the same list of grievances over and over again is likely to have negative repercussions. Why? In her well-documented book *Anger: The Misunderstood Emotion*, social psychologist Carol Tavris reports that with each new recitation of your grievances, your emotional arousal tends to *increase*. You experience your anger all over again, often right down to a flood of adrenaline, a rise in blood pressure, tightened muscles, and quickened pulse. Instead of reducing your anger, you increase it! Find a compromise between holding your anger in and talking about it to death. If you begin to find yourself feeling angrier *after* talking than you felt before, try a different anger-releasing method. At a later date, you may want to talk again, but for the purpose of either gaining perspective or acknowledging your pain rather than rehashing old injustices one more time.
- Keep a journal in which you can release your feelings.
- Some people, men as well as women, find that some good, hard crying is an effective emotional release from their anger.
- Some find they get an emotional release from screaming or from pounding something. Some scream in their cars with their windows rolled up. Some scream into a pillow. Some pound the pillow as well. The screaming and/ or pounding method is not for everyone, however. Studies find that these methods can escalate rather than diminish feelings of anger in some people. Watch your own response. It's probably best to use these methods strictly as a release. For example, if you punch a pillow strictly to release your pent-up rage, you may very well feel better afterward. If you punch a pillow while pretending it is your ex-spouse, you may wind up feeling angrier afterward.
- If you are certain that you can never be happy until you tell your ex off in person, psychologist Zev Wanderer, who is associated with the Center for Behavior Therapy in Beverly Hills, California, suggests you call your ex, have your say, and hang up immediately. Do not get involved in arguments, discussions, and/or excuses.
- Do you have an *uncontrollable* urge for revenge? You say there is *no* way that you can resist mailing a letter about your ex to the IRS or calling his or her new love? If so, Dr. Wanderer suggests you play out this vindictive behavior in fantasy. Vividly create the whole sequence of events that you would like to have happen. Studies find that fantasizing gives you almost as much gratification as does the actual act. And you will not have to

worry about retaliation, legal repercussions, or feelings of regret or guilt. However, Wanderer wisely points out, the sweetest revenge you can have on your ex is to build a good life and be happy.

Finishing the Job: Rearrange Your Thinking

The preceeding methods will help you to ventilate your anger, but they may not do the whole job. If you want to let go of your anger, you must do more than lower your pulse rate, points out social psychologist Carol Tavris. You must also "rearrange your thinking."

How can you let go of your anger by rearranging your thinking? People, including your ex-spouse, do not *make* you angry. What makes you angry is the interpretation or meaning that you give to their behavior. Let me give you an example. Suppose a superior tells you, in a not very kindly way, that something you did was really stupid, and then storms off, leaving you red-faced. Think for a minute how you would feel if you believed the criticism was justified. If you are like most people, you would feel humbled. But how would you feel if you believed the criticism was *unjustified*? Now, if you are like most people, you would probably get rather hot under the collar. But who is making you feel humbled or angry? Your superior, who has said exactly the same thing in each case? Or is it you, because of the way you appraise the situation and evaluate what is said? In reality, *your interpretation of the situation influenced your feelings*.

Dr. Albert Ellis, the father of Rational-Emotive Therapy, refers to this phenomenon as the A-B-C of emotions. Think of it like this: The A is the actual event (your superior calls you stupid). The C represents your feelings of being upset. Most people assume that the event (A) causes the feelings (C). But in fact, something intervenes between A and C, and this is the real culprit that causes anger. That culprit is B, your *beliefs* or *interpretation* of the event. After your superior storms off, you may think further about the criticism and hold a conversation in your head ("God, how could I have been so stupid? I'm such a jerk!" or "The more I think about it, the more I'd like to tell that SOB off!"). As you are talking to yourself, your feelings may become even more intense. Who is escalating your upset? Your superior? He has already left the scene. Or is it yourself via your thoughts?

Now try something else. Vividly imagine the times you really get angry with your ex, and allow yourself to get as upset as you can. If you need to recall a single situation that angered you, go ahead. Let yourself go with your vivid imagery for five minutes before you continue reading.

If you did this exercise, you probably had a rather elaborate conversation running through your mind. Get a pencil and paper and write down the things you were saying to yourself. Rick did this exercise. These were the thoughts he wrote down.

> She shouldn't have just walked out. What right did she have? I didn't deserve this. She should have told me she was unhappy. But no, what does she do? Walks out! On ten years! No discussion. No nothing! Oh, there was something, all right. She had it all planned down to the last detail. Apartment all lined up. I wouldn't be surprised if she had a boyfriend all lined up too! Conniving! Says she can't take it anymore. Can't take *what* anymore? She should have said something. What ever happened to "till death do us part"? It isn't fair! She had no right to just unilaterally walk out like that. This isn't the way marriages should end!

After Rick worked through this exercise, he reported that he was very angry, that his muscles were tense, and that he had a tightness in his chest and a lump in his throat. If you completed this exercise, take a brief audit of how *you* are feeling right now. Had Rick been hooked up to some monitors, they probably would have indicated that his blood pressure was elevated and his pulse rate was faster than normal. Was it Rick's ex-wife that made him this angry? How could she have? She wasn't even there!

In his best-seller *Feeling Good*, psychiatrist David Burns points out that we create our *own* anger, and we create it by our belief that either an incident was unjustified or someone behaved unfairly toward us. This was certainly indicated in the thoughts running through Rick's mind, that is, in his *self-talk*. Were these beliefs evident in your self-talk as well?

When people are angry, usually their self-talk has been full of *should* and *should not* statements. ("Marriages *shouldn't* end this way. She *shouldn't* have walked out. She *should have* said something.") Sometimes, of course, the "shoulds" and "should nots" are implicit. For example, "I don't deserve to be treated like this" really means "She *should not* have treated me this way." "She had no right" means "She *should not* have acted in this way."

The trouble with using "should" statements is that they give you the illusion that your *personal* standards of behavior are *absolute* standards. What you really are saying is, "My ex-spouse *should* behave the way that I think is right." Then, if you are like most people, you go one step further: When your ex violates your personal "rules," you think of him or her in derogatory terms ("The creep!" "The SOB!" "What a louse!" "Can you believe that conniving bitch?" "Only an inconsiderate, self-centered jerk would have done that."). Of course, you would *prefer* your ex (and everyone, for that matter) to behave the way that you think is right, and it would be a better world if everything were fair. But unfortunately, there are no universal laws dictating either fairness in human relationships or fairness in the world. Using "should" statements only sets you up to become angry, frustrated, resentful, and blaming. They are what Dr. Burns calls "hot thoughts." The more you use them, the angrier you become. The angrier you become, the more you get carried away with hot thoughts ("I could kill her!" "Just let me at the bastard!"). Emotions and thoughts form a two-way street.

Giving Your Angry Thoughts a Tune-up

Watch your anger further dissipate when you use these methods to change the way you think about your former spouse.

- Become aware of your self-talk when you are angry. When you start to become emotionally aroused, tune into the sentences that are running through your mind, and jot them down. Once you are aware of the "hot thoughts" that are keeping your resentments alive, you can more easily change them. Probably the easiest way to do this is by eliminating your "should" statements. Dr. Ellis suggests that you replace the "shoulds" with statements about your preferences and dislikes ("I wish . . . I would have preferred . . . I'm disappointed . . . I do not like the fact that . . ."). This is not a simple exercise in semantics. Avoiding "shoulds" will help you keep in mind that your personal rules are just that—they are personal, *not* unbreakable laws. Avoiding "shoulds" also markedly changes the emotional tone of an event. Suppose we give Rick's thinking a tune-up and replace his hot thoughts, which were full of stated and implied shoulds, with preferences and dislikes. His self-talk might then go something like this:

  > I don't like it one bit that she just walked out like that. I certainly would have preferred that she give me a chance to correct our problems. I wish she had just told me she was unhappy. We could have discussed things. Worked on some changes. I'm certainly disappointed that she arranged for an apartment the way she did. I would have preferred some semblance of honesty from her. This isn't my idea of how marriage should work.

  How would you rate Rick's emotional state now? Perhaps very annoyed, disappointed, hurt. But do you suppose extra adrenaline is pumping through his system? Are his pulse and breathing becoming faster as he is talking to himself? Are his muscles tightening? There are many other approaches to changing your self-talk in addition to eliminating your "shoulds." Two books listed in Appendix C will be especially helpful: *Feeling Good* by David Burns and *How to Live With—and Without—Anger* by Albert Ellis.
- Humor is a great way to dissipate anger. Here is a technique that Dr. Burns suggests. When you feel yourself getting angry at your ex, imagine that he or she is walking around a crowded department store in baby diapers and nothing more. Visualize all the details vividly—a pot belly hanging

out, hairy legs, and so forth. If your ex would look great in diapers, then imagine wet, sagging diapers. Sucking on a baby bottle and wailing loudly might complete your fantasy.

- This technique is the "ultimate anger antidote," says Dr. Burns. Try to put yourself in your ex's shoes and see the world through his or her eyes. Try to think of as many varied reasons as you can to explain your ex's behavior. If you do, you may find that his or her behavior is not as unreasonable as it once seemed. This technique very frequently dissipates anger, as Dan discovered.

> Dan had recently received what he believed to be very unreasonable demands for a property settlement from Mary Beth's lawyer. Dan saw red. He immediately called her to tell her off, but she had bought an answering machine and wouldn't return his calls. After several days of phoning, he went over to her house, but Mary Beth wouldn't answer the door and had changed the locks as well. Dan was livid. He pulled up the new flowers she had planted and stomped over all her prized plants. "Who the hell does she think she is? I don't deserve this kind of treatment. Live with someone for 15 years and you think you know them. Hah! Now her true colors come out. I won't stand for being treated like this. She doesn't want to play fair. OKAY. She'll be sorry she ever started this game."
>
> After talking to his lawyer, Dan learned that Mary Beth's lawyer instructed all his clients not to talk to their spouses and to change the locks on their doors. Furthermore, he had a reputation for demanding high property settlements so he would have more negotiating room. With some help from a close friend, Dan realized that Mary Beth had always depended on him to make all the decisions and had never questioned them. It was one of the things he had found so infuriating about her. Perhaps she had become just as dependent on her lawyer and was accepting his instructions blindly. It would be just like her. Dan was surprised that his anger drained away when he finally was able to look at the situation through Mary Beth's eyes.

- Some anger will dissipate on its own if you refrain from making an issue of each new annoyance. For example, if your ex makes a snide comment, refrain from responding, and learn to occupy yourself with some pleasant activity rather than thinking about it. Dr. Tavris points out that the age-old advice of counting to 10 has survived for centuries because it *is* effective.
- You say you just *can't* seem to stop rehashing all the old grievances over and over again. You just *can't* seem to stop yourself from using all those "should" statements. This may mean that you have upset yourself to such an extent that your autonomic nervous system has "temporarily gone out of kilter," says Dr. Ellis. Try one of the following.
  a. Start tuning into the signs of tension and upset within yourself. When you feel your tension rising, take a few minutes to focus on the deep relaxation technique that I hope you have already learned (see Appendix

B). This will benefit you in two ways: It will interrupt your negative self-talk, and it will obstruct the physiological arousal that accompanies anger.

   b. If you haven't yet learned deep relaxation, you can derail your negative self-talk by using the thought stoppage and distraction techniques discussed in chapter 3.

- Remember that *you* are the only person who can make *you* angry. Your emotions are yours. Don't let someone else control them!

If, after you have worked on the anger-reducing methods described, your "old anger" continues to consume you month after month, preventing you from getting on with your life, please see a divorce therapist. Don't let yourself and your children become casualties of divorce.

"NEW ANGER" AND DEALING WITH IT CONSTRUCTIVELY

If you ask a divorced person, he or she is likely to have a list of gripes about an ex-spouse's behavior ("His checks are always late." "She bad-mouths me to my son." "He doesn't show up when he's supposed to, and it screws up my

---

Techniques for Letting Go of Your Self-Defeating Anger*

Diffusion Techniques
✓ Unmailed letter technique
✓ Physical exercise
✓ Rechanneling emotional energy into constructive activities
✓ Talking out your feelings
✓ Releasing your feelings in a journal
✓ Having a good cry
✓ Screaming; pounding a pillow**
✓ Carrying out *uncontrollable* urges for revenge in fantasy, *not* reality

Finishing Up the Job: Giving Your Thinking a Tune-Up
✓ Eliminate "shoulds"; replace with your preferences and dislikes
✓ Use humor
✓ Examine situations from your ex's perspective
✓ Use distraction rather than making big issues over minor events
✓ Use deep relaxation, thought stoppage, and distraction to interrupt obsessive negative self-talk
✓ Remember, *you* are the only one who can make *you* angry

---

* Anger that cannot be channeled into changing an upsetting situation for the better.
** Can sometimes increase angry feelings. If you feel angrier afterward, use another technique.

plans." "She plans other activities for the kids when I'm suppose to see them." "The kids are never ready when I come, and she uses the time to needle me.").

If you have gripes like these, they are probably accompanied by frustration and anger. Since your anger is about definable situations in the here and now, we'll call it "new anger." How do you deal with new anger? You could, of course, diffuse it by employing one of the methods discussed previously. If your new anger is about situations that do not directly affect you and that you cannot change, this is exactly what you should do. (Examples include whom your ex dates and what your ex does with his or her life from now on.) However, if your new anger stems from situations in which your ex is infringing on your rights (such as the examples in the preceding paragraph), why not try to do something about them? Your anger can be a great motivator for you to take positive action to find a solution to an upsetting situation.

You say you've tried everything? Yelled? Threw tantrums? Threatened? Called your lawyer? *Nothing* worked? Perhaps you are using the wrong approach. The best way to change these upsetting situations is to enlist your former spouse's *cooperation*. Impossible, you say? Maybe not, if you learn how to express your new anger directly and constructively and learn some good negotiating strategies.

First, let's look at the way most former partners express their anger at one another. Many do not express it directly. Instead, they hang up each other, slam doors, bad-mouth each other, "forget" to send support payments, needle one another, and so forth. Many others do express their anger directly, but in destructive ways, such as physical violence or verbal attacks ("You bitch! Why did you tell Johnny I wasn't sending you enough money?" "You irresponsible SOB! Where the hell is the check?").

How do you suppose tactics such as these affect former partners' interactions with one another? Rarely do they inspire goodwill or cooperation. Listen to some typical reactions when these methods are used by an ex-spouse: "I give it right back to him." "It gives me pleasure to make her so mad." "I really get ticked off." "I become pretty defensive and strike back." "I ignore the jerk."

There is, however, a way to express anger that is more likely to encourage cooperation and less likely to invite retaliation or scorn. What you do is state your feelings openly in the form of what mental health professionals call "I statements" or "I messages." The idea of I statements is simple. You start a sentence with "I" and complete it by stating the way you feel. "I'm very angry." "I'm really annoyed." "I'm feeling very put upon." "I feel like I'm being personally attacked." "I feel so frustrated."

What is so good about these simple I statements? They allow you to get your feelings out in the open in a nonaggressive, nonthreatening way. You are not using sarcasm. You are not blaming. You are not using put-downs. Furthermore, you are taking the responsibility for your own feelings, which is where the responsibility should lie ("I get very angry when you do that" instead of "You make me so angry.")

Usually when people verbally express their anger, they use "you statements" ("You make me so damn angry." "You make me so furious I could scream!"). You statements blame other people for your anger. Even worse, they put people on the defensive, rile them up, and encourage them to strike back. I statements, on the other hand, set the tone for a constructive solution to be found. Some examples might make this clearer. Imagine how you would react if your former partner told you each of the following.

- "Who do you think you are? You have no right to say those things to the kids about me!" (you statement). Or, "I get so angry when you say those things to the kids about me; I feel it's undermining my relationship with them" (I statement).
- "Your irresponsibility is infuriating! The judge ordered those child support payments and you'd better pay them!" (you statement). Or, "I get so furious when I don't receive the child support payments. I count on them to help pay the kids' share of the rent, utilities, and food bill each month. I'm in a real bind without them" (I statement).
- "You inconsiderate creep! Where the hell were you Sunday? Your kids were in tears when you didn't show. And you made me miss my plans!" (you statement). Or, "I'm really annoyed that you didn't come or call on Sunday. The kids were in tears and I had to cancel my own plans" (I statement).
- "You knew damn well I was supposed to have the kids this weekend. You planned something else so I couldn't see them" (you statement). Or, "I get really upset when the kids have other plans on my weekend with them. How can I keep a relationship with them if I don't see them regularly?" (I statement).
- "You are such an intrusive person!" (you statement). Or, "I feel like you're intruding in my life" (I statement).

When using I statements, use them assertively. Don't grovel. If you whine, "I get so upset when you do these things," it is not a statement of your anger as much as it is a plea for pity. As such, it may provoke a different response from your ex than will an assertive statement about your feelings of anger and upset. If assertiveness is not your strong suit, a good source for help in expressing your feelings assertively is the book *Your Perfect Right* by Robert Alberti and Michael Emmons. It is listed in Appendix C.

If you keep a lid on your anger (by tuning up your thinking beforehand) and express it with nonthreatening I statements, you will create an atmosphere that is conducive to cooperation rather than hostility ("I get really upset when you come several hours late to pick up Jenny. My plans for the day get fouled up, and she becomes very anxious that you won't come. Can we see if we can find a way to solve the problem?").

Chapter 11 will be a further help. It discusses how to reduce your conflict with your former partner, and it takes you step by step through specific strategies that will help you negotiate with your ex-spouse in an emotionally charged atmosphere.

If a situation in the present is having a negative impact on your rights, don't become a helpless victim of either your former spouse or your own anger. Express your anger directly and constructively, and channel it into trying to bring about a change for the better. What if, after all your efforts, it seems certain that the situation will never change? Then use the techniques discussed here to diffuse your anger. There is no sense in hanging onto anger about situations that you cannot change. In the long run, you will be the loser.

LETTING GO OF YOUR MARRIAGE

On the evening of January 10, 1986, James Faller came home to a house devoid of half its furniture and found a note on the kitchen table from his wife, saying she had left him. Now, years later, he is still very bitter. He continues to tell his story to willing listeners and does so with such detail and anger that the unsuspecting person is inevitably shocked to learn that the incident occurred years ago. James defends his feelings as most appropriate, however. "I did NOTHING to deserve this. She ruined our lives, and I didn't even have a part in it. Why shouldn't I be bitter?" James and his two college-age sons still live in the home that he had shared with his wife. Little has changed over the years, other than the purchase of some new items to replace what she had taken. James' life now consists of his job, his sons, and his preoccupation with the past. He refers to his former wife as "that woman." His sons are concerned about what will happen to him when they leave and have never told him that they have started to see their mother on a regular basis.

Ann is an attractive, vibrant, 48-year-old successful businesswoman. Six years ago her husband left her to marry his secretary, 15 years his junior. Ann shakes her head at the memory of the shocked, angry, depressed, and suicidal homemaker she had been at that time. "It was only six years ago, but it seems like a lifetime ago," she says. "There is so little left of that Ann now. After a year of hell and four months of therapy, I worked up the energy and nerve to go back to school to take some business courses. It was the best thing I could have done. I found a wonderful support group in a reentry women's organization on campus. In fact, that's where I met my partner Phyllis. After we finished our course work, we took the money from our respective divorce settlements and invested it in this franchise. I suppose it was risky, but it's been a wonderful success. I found I have a real head for business, and she is wonderful on the PR end. I love being out in the world and feeling competent and successful. I've made a number of very dear friends, both men and women. I've developed so many new interests. My children are doing well now and freely float back and forth between their father's house and mine. After several years of bitterness and conflict, we now have a quite civilized relationship. In fact, about two years ago I actually thanked him for leaving. It was the best thing that ever happened to me!"

Letting go is accepting the end of your marriage, saying goodbye to your past, and getting on with a future of your own design. It is being able to think about or see your former spouse without feeling bad. It is feeling only indifference, concern, or tenderness for your former mate rather than anger, hatred, resentment, regret, sorrow, longing, or dependency. It is feeling like a single person rather than a married one.

People let go of their marriages to different degrees; not everyone is a glaring failure like James or a dazzling success like Ann. Those with moderate success may still harbor strong feelings but may be able to compartmentalize them so they do not interfere with their day-to-day lives. Others may successfully co-parent their children but not without a constant struggle to avoid conflict.

There is no widely accepted "formula" for letting go of a marriage. Many people rely entirely on the passage of time, and time will most likely ease the intensity of your emotions. However, circumstances that help or hinder people in the letting-go process have been identified. The guidelines in this chapter will help you through the letting-go process so that you can more quickly get on with your life and more completely let go of your marriage.

SETTING THE STAGE: SEPARATION

In the ground-breaking studies they conducted at the Child and Family Divorce Counseling Service at Children's Hospital of San Francisco, psychologists Janet Johnston and Linda Campbell discovered that the events at separation can play a critical role in the futures of divorcing couples. Specifically, a traumatic separation (such as discovering a humiliating affair, being left unexpectedly without explanation, or uncharacteristic violence) tends to set the stage for prolonged conflict between former mates and thwarts their attempts to let go of their marriages. What often happens is that the hurt spouse *redefines* the character of the leaver at the time of separation, based on the traumatic events (he or she is obviously untrustworthy, irresponsible, dangerous, crazy, or no good). If this were just a temporary reaction, no harm would be done. But because of intense emotional distress, the hurt spouse's thinking often becomes distorted and polarized, and he or she concludes that the *true* nature of the leaver has been discovered for the first time ("I guess I really didn't know her at all." "His true colors certainly came out." "Now I know just what she *really* is." "How could I have been so blind all these years?"). This is what happened with one couple. Talking about the decisive separation, the husband, who is a physician, reported the following:

> I was stressed by work at the hospital. When I came home she was always nagging me, demanding this and that. I restrained myself, was very depressed and morose. One night I couldn't take it any longer. She was bugging me about some stupid

thing. ... I hit her ... hard. It was awful. I felt so bad. That has never happened before or since.

But his wife now defines her ex-husband based on the events at separation. Referring to him, she reported this much later:

He is violent and dangerous. He has homicidal tendencies. The children are not safe with him.[1]

Third parties (friends or relatives) usually play a significant role, too. Usually they spend hours with the hurt spouse, offering comfort and support, rehashing the traumatic separation, and trying to make sense of the unexpected events, although they know only half the information. During this process, third parties often *validate* the new perception of the leaver's character ("How terrible. I never realized (s)he was like that."). The hurt spouse's redefinition of the leaver's character then becomes more firmly accepted.

The situation can turn from bad to worse. The events of the separation often destroy the hurt partner's belief that the leaver had *ever* valued the marriage. Now, all the years and energy that the spouse had invested in caring for the leaver seem wasted. Feeling enraged and exploited, the hurt spouse frequently sets out either to retaliate, to seek "justice," or to capture *some* power in a situation that is clearly in the leaver's control (like snatching bank accounts, making threats, refusing to cooperate, turning the children against the leaver, destroying the leaver's clothing, and so forth). Unfortunately, this tends to begin a vicious circle of attack and counterattack. The hurt spouse's new perceptions of the leaver are further confirmed by the leaver's counterattack. Meanwhile, the leaver, also under emotional distress, undergoes a similar process of negatively redefining the hurt spouse in light of this new unexpected behavior.

Each spouse tends to conclude that the current actions of the other reflect the other's *true* character. In reality, they are usually the unfortunate outcome of stress and an emotionally charged situation gone out of control. If former partners were to talk with each other rationally, they might discover that their new perceptions are inaccurate. But few can carry this off in such an emotionally charged environment. Instead, the new negative perceptions each has about the other become frozen for years to come. One or both partners sometimes dehumanize the other as well (he or she is thought of *only* as a bastard, a bitch, a whore, and so forth, rather than as the once-loved mate). This finally opens the door for the wild accusations divorcing spouses so often hurl at each other without a shred of evidence ("He sexually abused our daughter." "She's a morally unfit mother.").

Obviously, the best way to avoid this scenario is with preparation, discussion, and sensitivity before separation. If you are already enmeshed in such a situation, understanding the dynamics underlying it may help you to extricate yourself from it. Could there be explanations for your former spouse's behavior other than those you have assumed are fact? You may need help in sorting out your feelings and in gaining some perspective of your spouse and your situation. A good divorce therapist could be an invaluable help to you. As long as you cling to very unrealistic perceptions of your spouse and the end of your marriage, you are likely to feel victimized. And as long as you feel victimized, it will be more difficult for you to put the marriage behind you. Your efforts to separate yourself from your spouse will be further thwarted if you become enmeshed in an escalating cycle of anger and retaliation.

EARLY STEPS

Immediately after separation, you can begin to take the first steps to help your adjustment and to eventually let go of your marriage.

Balancing Change and Continuity

Studies find that people seem to adjust better if they create *some* changes in their environment, yet maintain some continuity and stability in their lives as well. If you remain in the home you shared with your spouse, you might make an effort to put your own stamp of individuality on it. You might make it more feminine or masculine and get some new plants or pictures to give it a fresh look. You might rearrange some furniture, particularly the bedroom furniture. However, if you have children living with you, do not make the changes too drastic. Their need for continuity is much stronger than yours.

If you are the spouse who leaves, you will have plenty of change, perhaps too much. You need to guard against feelings of rootlessness and a loss of identity, which are common for spouses who leave home and children. Most people do better when they take some favorite things from their home with them. Also take time to find a place you like and begin right away to make it look and feel like a home.

What the great majority of departing parents miss most is daily contact with their children. If you have children, either call them or ask them to call you on a daily basis so that you can keep abreast of their lives. (If you call them, arrange a specific time so they can answer the phone themselves.) As much as daily contact with them will help you, it will help them even more.

Painful Memorabilia

You may have enough sorrow in your life after separation without being surrounded by things that automatically trigger sadness because of their strong association with your spouse. Collect them all—photos, gifts, clothes, wedding ring, mementos, special records, or whatever causes you particular sadness—and put them away where you will not see them for the time being. However, *do not* throw them away.

The Announcement

Telling people about your separation or pending divorce is a difficult step that many people delay. However, Stephen Johnson, a clinical psychologist at the University of Oregon who has developed treatment programs for divorcing people, has found that announcing the separation is an important contributor to early adjustment. Tell each family member, friend, and associate directly, says Johnson. Your explanation does not have to be extensive, particularly with acquaintances. Plan in advance what you will say.

Announcing your separation or pending divorce serves two purposes. First, it opens the door to your receiving a good deal of social support when you need it the most. People, particularly family and friends, usually rally around a newly separated person. However, most people are very hesitant to intrude and will not make an overture unless they know it will be welcome. Johnson suggests that you tell friends that you hope your relationship with them can continue. He also suggests that you have some suggestions ready should people ask how they can help. You might ask them to be available to talk or to go out for an evening. You may prefer that they invite you to their homes or introduce you to some single people. Or perhaps you would like help with some new skills you will need to learn (cooking, child care, car and home maintenance, financial advice, and so on).

Second, making your new status public will help you to start feeling and acting like a single person rather than a married one. It serves as a sort of ritual to mark the end of your marriage and the beginning of your single life. There will be more later about the potential importance to you of some type of divorce ritual.

Be Attentive To Yourself

You may have so many negative things going on in your life right now that it may be easy to slip into the twin modes of lethargy and feeling bad about yourself. It is important to do some things for yourself that will make you feel good, boost your feelings of self-worth and self-confidence, and symbolize your new beginning. This will help you get started on the right foot in your single life. Pamper yourself—get a facial, a massage, or a new haircut; buy yourself some new clothes; take a trip; develop some new interests.

DISENGAGING FROM YOUR SPOUSE

Johnson and other therapists have concluded that once the decision to divorce has been made, noninvolvement between divorcing partners is a *must*. The following steps are recommended:

- If you are a departing spouse, take everything with you and change your mailing address. Do not keep keys to the family home.
- Limit all contact and discussions with each other to *necessary* matters only (children, property division, and so forth).
- Formalize how you will initiate contact with each other, or set prearranged meetings.
- Establish a set schedule for the children to see the departing spouse and stick to it. This avoids unnecessary contact with your spouse. It also provides your children with some of the stability and continuity they need.
- Send support payments through the mail.
- If your former partner persistently tries to make unnecessary contact, make it difficult to reach you (for example, get an answering machine).
- Do not rely on your ex-spouse for any of the functions (other than parenting) that he or she took responsibility for in the marriage (cooking, laundry, car or house repairs, bill paying, financial planning, and so forth). Although arrangements such as exchanging home-cooked meals for home repairs may appear to be very efficient, they are self-defeating. They force you into a state of limbo, where you are no longer a part of your old world but you are unable to enter a new one. This is likely to impede your progress toward letting go of your marriage and getting on with your life.

Many people balk at the idea of disengagement, feeling that it is unnecessary. However, in the long run, relatively few people find they were correct in their assessment, Johnson reports. Disengagement usually is necessary.

Don't misunderstand. Disengagement does not mean permanently terminating your relationship with your ex-spouse. A good relationship or even a friendship with your ex can be a real asset in the future, particularly if you have children. And a conflict-free relationship is critical when children are involved. However, to have a good relationship in the future, your present relationship must change; it must be *redefined* and *restructured*. You need to stop interacting in your old ways and find mutually acceptable new ways of relating. It is a rare couple who can manage this in the emotionally charged atmosphere of separation. A period of noninvolvement is usually necessary before a new and different relationship can develop successfully. Specific steps to take to restructure your relationship with your spouse are discussed in Chapter 11, "How to End Conflict with Your Ex-Spouse."

DISLODGING YOUR SPOUSE FROM YOUR MIND

Disengaging from your spouse physically will be far easier than dislodging him or her from your mind. If you have read the preceding chapters, you are aware that intense sorrow, bitter anger, and obsessive thoughts about your former spouse are likely to be familiar companions for a while. But sometimes former mates influence one's behavior long after divorces are final. Some people continue to buy clothes their former partners would have liked, some continue to act in ways their ex-spouses would have expected, some continue to frequent places because of their association with happier times in the marriage. Many cannot "move on" because of their hopes of reconciliation. Many others are so consumed with anger at their ex-spouses that it dominates their postdivorce lives. For your own future happiness, it is essential to dislodge your former mate from your mind. Return to Chapters 3, 4, and 5 and use some of the coping techniques to deal with overwhelming sadness, anger, and obsessive thoughts.

As tempting as it will be, don't seek out or listen to information about your spouse or his or her activities. It is only likely to upset you anyway. You may need to tell well-meaning friends that you don't want to hear any information or news about what he or she is doing. If you have an uncontrollable urge to call your former partner, *don't*. Distract yourself instead, either with some activity or by going somewhere. When you think of something that you *must* discuss with your former partner, write it down and save it for your scheduled discussions. Writing it down will get it off your mind so you can go on to something else. Keep all your notes together in a special book so you can take care of all these loose ends during your next meeting.

A critical step in dislodging your spouse from your mind is to get rid of your hopes of reconciliation. In their book *Letting Go*, psychologist Zev Wanderer and co-author Tracy Cabot call hopes of reconciliation the "hope trap," because they keep you hooked to the past and prevent you from moving on to the future. Many divorcing men and women refuse to give up their hope trap because they believe that doing so would ruin their chances of reconciliation. Nothing could be further from the truth. In fact, many leavers decide they want a reconciliation only *after* they notice dramatic changes in their former mates and see how well their exs are doing without them. Giving up the hope trap is a necessary prerequisite to getting on with your new life as a single person. And it will not destroy the possibility of reconciliation in the future, unless you yourself decide your new life is preferable to your old one, as many left spouses do eventually decide.

Equally critical in dislodging your spouse from your mind is letting go of your anger. Anger keeps you emotionally bound to your former partner just as much as love does. The only difference is that the bonds are negative rather than positive. Chapter 5 provided strategies to help you let go of your self-defeating anger.

YOUR "ACCOUNT"

If you recall from Chapter 3, most divorcing men and women are obsessed with thoughts of their spouses and their marriages. What went wrong? What was the sequence of events that led to the breakup? Who was to blame? What could have been done differently? Each potentially significant event and fight is replayed and examined over and over again. Very gradually, most people construct a subjective account of the history of their marriages and their breakups.

Constructing this account is important to your ability to let go. Without understanding what went wrong in your marriage, it is difficult to lay the marriage to rest. Many men and women who have not worked through the confusion of marital events and have not found an explanation for the breakup seem unable to put the marriage behind them, and they continue to lament years later, "If only I knew what happened."

Since accounts are subjective, the accounts that two divorcing spouses construct sometimes bear little resemblance to one another. However, the account that you construct can have important implications for your future. It is important to achieve a *balanced* version. Usually, collapsed marriages are not the fault of a single partner, although many former spouses place the entire blame on their exs' nagging, drinking, affairs, neglectfulness, gambling, dependence, frigidity, sloppy housekeeping, and so forth. It is also rare for a single factor outside the marriage to be completely at fault, although some place all the blame on a third party—a spouse's job, women's lib, or in-laws.

What difference does it make if you place all the blame elsewhere and fail to recognize your role in your marriage's collapse? Such an unbalanced account may affect your future in three ways. Failing to recognize the role you played increases your chances of repeating the same patterns in future relationships. It may also affect your ability to let go of your marriage. People who continue to place all the blame outside themselves usually continue to feel victimized and are more likely to remain bound to their former spouses in some way, whether it be a lingering attachment, hate, anger, or conflict. As this suggests, future relationships with spouses are also impacted by an unbalanced account. If you are a parent, it is particularly important to construct a balanced view of your children's other parent and acknowledge his or her strengths and weaknesses. Why? Because it will increase your chances of being able to co-parent your children successfully with each other.

When constructing your account, try out all the possible reasons for your marriage's end. Although you may go through periods when it appears to be all your spouse's fault, all someone else's fault, or even all your fault, do not get stalled at this point. Work toward a balanced view of both your marriage and your ex. Try to identify the following:

- Why you married
- What difficulties contributed to your marital problems

- What sequence of events led to the divorce
- How each of you contributed to the problems

After much struggling, the woman in the following example came to terms with the role she played in her husband's affair and the end of their marriage.

Who could ever imagine anything like that happening to my marriage? My husband was the squarest, straightest of men—a deacon in the church, a Little League Dad, a Cub Scoutmaster, a non-drinking, crew-cut junior executive. But I let it happen. Our marriage had become nothing but a kind of corporate enterprise without my ever taking time to wonder about it. How it got that way I don't know. It seemed as if we were so busy with children, the house, and local activities, that we never paid any attention to each other; we never said anything real to each other. As for sex, I was bored by it. I felt I could live nicely forever without it, and tried to avoid it as much as possible. I hardly ever thought about any of this, but when I did, I told myself that every marriage goes through phases of this sort and there was nothing to worry about. I was living in never-never land, refusing to see the truth or do anything about it.[2]

If you have trouble identifying why your marriage ended, you may find it helpful to learn about unhealthy love relationships that frequently end in divorce. Yours may have fallen into one of these patterns. Read Bruce Fisher's book *Rebuilding*, listed in Appendix C.

SOCIAL SUPPORT CAN MAKE ALL THE DIFFERENCE

Social support can play a critical role in your divorce adjustment. Many divorcing men and women are convinced that they never would have made it without the support of friends and family. The caring, warmth, and reassurance of others seems to serve as a cushion that softens the impact of divorce-related stress. When friends and social support are lacking, depression and anxiety commonly soar.

Reach out to others. Don't make the mistake of withdrawing into a shell because you do not want to "bother" people. Family and friends usually rally around a newly divorcing person, providing moral support and sometimes financial support and services as well (baby-sitting, errands, home repairs). If you remember to give something of yourself back to those who offer their support, you will not feel like a burden.

When you are with others, don't fall into the trap of always dwelling on your divorce and your former partner. Some talking is healthy; but *continually* talking about your ex can become addictive and can fuel your anger. It can also frustrate and alienate friends who otherwise would be supportive. Instead, push yourself to engage in social activities. A recent study, conducted by researchers at the Center for the Family in Transition in Corte Madera, California, found that social involvement helps to diminish attachment to a former spouse. It also offers temporary distractions, something to anticipate, a relief from loneliness, a lift from depression, and perhaps encourages some new friendships as well.

If you do not already have a support group, it's important to develop one. Accept the overtures of others. Many people report that their best source of support during divorce came from an unlikely person, such as a co-worker, acquaintance, or attorney who had also gone through a divorce. A wonderful source of support now available in most communities are divorce support groups, often available through community colleges, YMCAs and YWCAs, churches, mental health centers, marriage counseling centers, and singles groups such as Parents Without Partners. How to build new social support networks is discussed in Chapter 13.

A word of caution, however. Sometimes social support, particularly from family, can be a double-edged sword. In addition to the many benefits families can offer, they are sometimes a source of difficulties. Families are more likely than friends to openly voice their opinions, including displeasure, about the divorce and each partner's behavior. But more important, family members are sometimes drawn into the dispute in full force. Family outrage has been known to fuel conflict between divorced couples for years. And prolonged family sympathy encourages a divorced person to feel victimized, which may impede his or her progress toward closing the doors on the divorce and getting on with life. Although it may be very comforting to hear that you really were married to a no-good so-and-so, be aware that you may be the one to suffer in the long run if your family's outrage and sympathy do not temper with time. Whether or not you have this type of family involvement, studies suggest that you will do better if you have a social support network that includes friends in addition to your family.

MOURNING

When you divorce, you not only part with a spouse, you also leave behind your past, your whole way of life, the future plans and expectations you once had, and a good chunk of your identity. Part of the letting-go process is mourning your losses and the death of your marriage, just as you mourn the death of a person who has been an important part of your life. Once a death is mourned, the pain eases, memories of the departed person lose their power to provoke tears and sorrow, and the mourner feels that he or she can let go of the past and get on with life once again. This is what happens when people mourn the death of their marriage and the inevitable losses it entails. Psychotherapists strongly maintain that mourning your marriage and losses is necessary in order to completely let go and get on with your life, free of your ex-spouse. Even if you are happy to be out of the marriage, you still need to mourn your inevitable losses. Chapter 3 discussed the importance of mourning in greater detail, as well as a number of ways to deal with your sadness and mourn those losses.

Mourning Through Implosion

In their book *Letting Go*, Wanderer and Cabot describe a method that may help some people considerably with the mourning process. The reason that so many people carry around sorrow about their marriages for many years, say Wanderer and Cabot, is that they have never grieved *thoroughly* enough to get past their grief. They recommend mourning through *implosion* because it allows thorough grieving, and their research at the Center for Behavior Therapy in Beverly Hills, California, appears to support its effectiveness. The idea of implosion is to literally flood yourself with all your painful memories until they lose their power over you. If you use implosion, I suggest that you wait until you have had the time to release a good deal of your sadness through the methods discussed in Chapter 3. This is likely to be quite a while after separation. Mourning through implosion is extremely intense and is likely to be too intense for many people. It's best to know yourself before you try this.

Here is how Wanderer and Cabot's implosion method works. Set aside a day that evokes nostalgia, such as an anniversary, your ex's birthday (or yours), a holiday, or even a day of the week that you and your former mate consistently spent together. This can be your implosion day. Arrange to have at least six hours with no distractions or interruptions; have your children cared for elsewhere, and do not answer the phone or doorbell. However, if you are shaky about trying implosion and have a good friend who could be available somewhere in your home to be called on if needed, it would be a good idea. Have some food prepared in advance—nothing elaborate or comforting. Wanderer and Cabot suggest some protein for nourishment, some of your ex's favorite snacks for nostalgia, and *no* alcohol. Then take out *everything* that evokes sadness because of its association with your former partner—love letters, photos, home movies, gifts, all the memorabilia you put away earlier, your wedding ring, your ex's clothes and favorite cologne, and so forth. For the next six hours or longer, surround yourself with all your memories while you listen to the songs that remind you of the good times in your relationship. You may want to begin by reading the love letters. Let them stir up all kinds of memories, and dwell on each one. This is the day to think of all the *good* memories, the time you will no longer have together, and the future plans you will no longer keep together. Take each of the gifts, photos, and mementos one by one and vividly replay in your mind every good memory associated with each. Allow yourself to cry and grieve over each memory and each item until there are no more tears or feelings left and you actually get *bored* doing it. Then go for an overkill.

Continue to handle the item and think about the memories associated with it so your boredom will be reinforced. Then go on to the next item.

Remember that implosion is intense. Don't feel that you *have* to stick it out for the entire six hours once you start. You may not be ready for it yet, and you can always return to it at a later date if you so choose. If you do stick it out, your implosion day will be over when nothing has the power to affect you any longer. All those things that used to be associated with sorrow will be associated with boredom instead. If you find afterward that some things continue to trigger sorrow, set them aside for a booster implosion day sometime in the future (which can be much shorter), suggest Wanderer and Cabot. Meanwhile, continue with other methods to help you mourn (Chapter 3), as you feel you need them.

Incidentally, in their book *Letting Go*, Wanderer and Cabot provide a 12-week program, based on the principles of behavior therapy, that is designed to erase most of the painful memories of your relationship. The book is listed in Appendix C.

Ceremonies and Rituals

More and more mental health professionals are now recommending that you participate in some type of ceremony or ritual to mark the end of your marriage to help you close the door on it permanently. Every major event in our lives has some type of ritual to mark it, with the exception of divorce. The impact such a ceremony can have was vividly described by Kathryn Hallett, who watched one several years after her own divorce.

> I clearly remember the day of my divorce and my anger that this "letting go" process had none of the elements of my marriage ceremony. . . . I remembered thinking that had one of us died, we would have at least received support in our grief. . . . Years later, when I watched . . . a divorce ritual, my children and I cried our tears and relived our own situation. I envied that couple and their children, for they had a chance to participate in the letting go process. I watched the woman remove her ring and give back the obligations that he had given to her. I listened to her tell what she would remember that was good and what she would forgive and forget. . . . The couple cried, their children cried, and we all mourned the passing of an important event in their lives.[3]

The couple she described had already been divorced for two years but had continued in bitter conflict with one another, refusing to let go until that day.

Some therapists are now conducting divorce ceremonies. This is a route you might wish to explore. Well-known divorce therapist Florence Kaslow, Director of the Florida Couples and Family Institute in West Palm Beach, suggests that you write your own divorce decree as a sort of divorce ritual. In the decree, she suggests that you include what went wrong with your marriage in some detail, what is likely to lie ahead for you in the next two years, and what your future goals are. Dr. Kaslow says that such a written decree, which you can reread often, will help you accept the finality of your marriage's end and help you move forward to restructure your life.

The letters of goodbye, which were discussed in Chapter 3, might also serve as a sort of divorce ritual. Therapist Bruce Fisher suggests you write letters of goodbye to each of the losses in your life—your spouse, your marriage, your home, your past, your way of life, the future you had planned together, and so forth. In each, you should include all the things you will miss, as well as the things you will be relieved to leave behind. These letters are difficult to write. Begin with the easier ones first.

DEVELOPING THE RESOURCES TO LIVE AUTONOMOUSLY

In his book *First Person Singular*, University of Oregon psychologist Stephen Johnson reports that people who are able to function autonomously are more successful in letting go of their marriages. The principle is a simple one: It is easier to let go of your married life when you can live a satisfying single life. However, to do this, you must find other ways to fulfill the needs formerly fulfilled by your former spouse and marriage. Once you have found other ways to fill the glaring voids in your life, you will find that you miss your former partner and your marriage less.

Make a list of all the things your ex used to do for you that you miss. Then try to figure out some other way to satisfy as many of them as possible. Learning survival skills is a good first step. Depending on the division of labor you had in your marriage, you may have to learn how to cook, do laundry, shop for groceries, care for children, decorate your home, budget or invest money, maintain and repair your home and car, and so forth. Of course, if you have enough money to hire people, there will be no problem. However, if you are like most others who are divorcing, you may be in a financial crunch. Check out classes in survival skills, which are frequently available either through local community colleges or as extension courses at your local high school. These classes will be a good source for making new contacts as well. "How-to" books and friends are also good sources of help. Single friends are likely to be particularly helpful in guiding you through tasks that they have already mastered. In some cases, you may be able to swap skills with friends and provide help to one another. Divorce-adjustment groups and Parents Without Partners are good places to meet new single friends who are likely to be very supportive. By the way, when learning new skills, you are far more likely to succeed if you follow the five-step method found in Appendix A.

Undoubtedly, your former spouse fulfilled more than basic survival needs. List these as well. Can friends and/or a pet fill your ex's companionship role? Will a cooperative arrangement with other single parents satisfy the relief child care your ex provided? Will initiating more physical contact with friends (hugs, touching people when talking to them) satisfy your needs for affection? Can masturbation satisfy your sexual needs until you find a new partner? Can your parents lend you money until you can get back on your feet financially?

It is likely that your divorce left another glaring void in your life. It probably severely wounded your self-esteem. Self-esteem is one of the most important resources you can have if you are to live successfully on your own. With high self-esteem, your happiness can come from inside of you, rather than your depending on a spouse, a marriage, or some other external source. Begin to rebuild your feelings of self-worth right away, using the strategies in Chapter 12.

REINVOLVING YOURSELF

Many divorcing men and women make a common mistake: They put off reinvolving themselves with life until they can rid themselves of their sorrow, depression, and anger. "There's no point in doing anything when I feel this bad," they say. However common this approach is, it is tantamount to putting the cart before the horse. Here is something many people do not realize: Once you reinvolve yourself, you will feel better! The woman in the following example tells how she floundered in misery until she finally reinvolved herself.

> I hated him. Yet I couldn't ignore him. I could see his face in my son's eyes; I saw him in the house, remembering the rooms he painted. For a while I tried to suppress every nice remembrance. This hurt more than it helped. It was only after I went back to school and stopped pitying myself that I could face the good memories and accept what was.[4]

The importance of reinvolving yourself was clearly illustrated in a well-known study conducted by Dr. Graham Spanier, of the State University of New York at Stony Brook, and his research team. These researchers found that creating a new life-style was *more crucial* to adjustment after divorce than was successful coping with the divorce itself—that is, dealing with the legal process, emotions, feelings about the ex-spouse and marriage, and so forth. Perhaps the best example of this surprising finding is offered by the story of one woman, Grace:

> Grace was 65 when her husband uprooted her and moved to the Southwest, supposedly for the climate, but in reality for the liberal divorce laws. Within several weeks of their move, he shocked her by moving out of their rented apartment. Within days, a uniformed marshal banged loudly on her door and handed divorce papers to the stunned woman. Grace had nowhere to turn. She had not yet made

friends since her move and was too embarrassed and ashamed to talk to her friends back home. She sat in her apartment for weeks, depressed and bewildered; fortunately for her, her religion precluded suicide. The divorce became final too quickly for her to assimilate all that was happening. She was given a share of her husband's Social Security allowance, but the couple had few assets and little savings for her to fall back on. Grace's situation had all the makings of a disastrous divorce and a bitter lifetime ahead, except for one thing. She met a woman at church who worked in a program for abused children. One day the woman convinced Grace to come along for a few hours, and Grace discovered that, for the first time in many months, she was able to take her mind off the nightmare she had been living. She signed up as a volunteer that day, and within several months was receiving a modest stipend for her dedicated work. One year later, Grace was a smiling, cheerful woman. She had met several good friends and was congenially sharing an apartment with one. She loved the children and experienced a new sense of fulfillment working with them. "Never have I felt so needed, so loved, or so productive," she beamed. Grace never sees or talks about her husband and seems to have completely closed the door on her marriage.

Steps To Help You "Let Go"

- Some Early Steps:
    - ✓ Strive for sensitivity and discussion at the time of separation.
    - ✓ Achieve a balance between change and continuity.
    - ✓ Remove painful memorabilia temporarily.
    - ✓ Make your separation public.
    - ✓ Do something to symbolize your new beginning.
- Disengage from your partner in all but parenting roles.
    - ✓ Develop a firm parenting schedule and stick to it.
    - ✓ Avoid all unnecessary contact, including phone calls.
    - ✓ Resolve problems and decisions at scheduled meetings.
- Move toward dislodging your spouse from your mind.
    - ✓ Avoid information about his or her activities.
    - ✓ Avoid the "hope trap."
    - ✓ Work on letting go of your anger.
- Construct a *balanced* "account" of why your marriage ended, acknowledging your role.
- Seek out social support.
- Thoroughly mourn your marriage and losses.
- Mark the end of your marriage with a ritual or ceremony.
- Start developing the resources you need to live autonomously.
- Start rebuilding your self-esteem.
- Reinvolve yourself; don't wait to feel better.
- Start to build a new identity separate from that of your spouse.

The principle of reinvolvement is simple. It is easier to give up the past and your old identity when there is something to replace them with in the present. So quit investing your emotional energy in a dead relationship, and begin investing it in yourself. Begin today to reinvolve yourself with life and to forge a fresh identity separate from that of your spouse and your marriage. You will get plenty of help with this in Chapters 12 and 13. Remember that it will be easier to get yourself going and keep on track if you follow the five-step self-change program in Appendix A.

FINAL RESOLUTION

The advice to resolve the relationship with their former partners and the end of their marriages is commonly given to divorcing men and women. You have probably heard it a number of times. What exactly does it mean to resolve your relationship? Basically, it is synonymous with letting go. It means truly accepting both the end of your marriage and the role that you played in its collapse. It means laying your past to rest and being free of the pain and grief. It means being able to distance yourself from your ex so that you can see him or her *objectively*, recognizing your former mate's weaknesses *and* strengths. It means being able to distance yourself from your divorce so that you can objectively recognize your hurts and disappointments without them triggering the emotional turmoil they once did. It means feeling and acting like a single person and getting on with a future of your own design. It means that you have identified your feelings of loss, sadness, anger, and resentment and let them go, so that you no longer harbor them. Don't misunderstand. Resolving your relationship does not mean that you should never get angry with your ex. If your former spouse is failing to pay child support, arranging other activities for the kids on your weekend, or bad-mouthing you to your kids, of course you will be frustrated, irritated, and probably angry, too. But your anger will be tied to *current* situations. (Chapter 5 suggested ways to help you handle these.) It is only when anger is left over from the past that your relationship is not yet resolved.

Chapters 3 through 5, and of course this one, were designed to help guide you to this final resolution. Chapters 12 and 13 are devoted to the rebuilding of your life. In reality, there are no such arbitrary boundaries as there must be in books. You will start to rebuild your life while you are still trying to resolve the end of your marriage. So please go on to read Chapters 12 and 13.

In her book *Coming Apart: Why Relationships End and How to Live Through the Ending of Yours*, therapist Daphne Kingma suggests one last thing to do in the letting-go process, and I think it is a good thought to leave you with. It is to acknowledge the "gifts" you took away from your marriage. Kingma is not referring to material gifts, but rather to the changes in yourself, the lessons you learned, the needs that were fulfilled, and the accomplishments that your marriage made possible. Even if you feel as if you were the one who did all the giving, spend some time analyzing your marriage and comparing the person you are now with the person you were before. Every relationship is enriching in some way.

Kingma suggests that you actually write a letter to your former mate (it never needs to be mailed) thanking him or her for all the gifts you received from your marriage. Having a written record of the benefits you derived from your marriage and an acknowledgment of your former spouse's contribution to them is not a bad idea. It will not only dissipate your resentments, but in the future it will allow you to view your marriage from a fresh and positive perspective.

PART II

HELPING CHILDREN THROUGH DIVORCE

THE CHILD'S PERSPECTIVE

During the London blitz of World War II, the British carried out mass evacuations of their children to safe rural areas. An estimated 25 to 50 percent of the evacuated children, separated from their families during this stressful time, developed emotional problems. The children who had good relationships with their parents from whom they were now separated generally handled their exile well. Children who had poor relationships with their parents generally fared poorly. However, the children who fared the best of all emotionally were those who remained with their parents right through the terror of the German bombings! Apparently, the security provided by their parents offset the trauma of the air raids, the bombs, and the rubble surrounding them.

The point of this anecdote is to illustrate the powerful role that parents can play in buffering their children from severe and prolonged stress. If you understand this very significant function that mothers and fathers play in children's lives, you will be better able to fully understand children's divorce experience.

It is easy for parents to downplay their importance to their children on a day-to-day basis, particularly if their youngsters are already involved with peers, school, and their own activities. But to children of all ages, parents are very much like a reserve bank account. When all is well with the world, a reserve bank account may go unnoticed and have no apparent influence on day-to-day activities. However, it provides a safety net that allows its owner to explore and enjoy new horizons without the threat of peril hanging overhead. If a disaster does strike, the reserve account can take on enormous significance; it could mean the difference between the survival or the demise of the person's way of life.

Parents are usually concerned about how their divorce may affect their children. To give you a straight answer, parental divorce is very painful to children, and most do experience problems for a while. Does divorce cause *long-term* problems? A significant number of kids also develop long-term problems, even some who appeared to be doing well during the crisis itself. However, the majority are not troubled with lasting problems, and some even develop greater psychological strength because of the divorce. Which path will your children take?

The last decade and a half of research has taken much of the guesswork and uncertainty out of why some children emerge from their parents' divorce unscathed while others develop long-term problems. As yet, research has not provided *all* the pieces to this complex puzzle, but it has provided enough critical pieces to allow you to engineer a situation that is likely to enable your children to thrive despite your divorce. The following chapters will guide you in doing this.

Right now, we are going to take a look at divorce through a child's eyes. You may find the chapter discouraging in spots, but this and the following chapters will help you to avoid many mistakes that other parents have made. Many problems can be short-lived when handled well. While reading the chapter, try to keep in mind the experience of the British children who remained with their parents through the wartime bombing and the protective role parents can play in buffering their children from stress.

CHILDREN'S DIVORCE EXPERIENCE

To children, divorce does *not* mean the second chance that it so often means to one or both parents. To children it is the loss of their family—the entity that provides them with support, stability, security, and continuity in an often unpredictable world. Children assume that their family is a given and that their parents are permanent; after all, their family and parents are what provide for their needs. In their eyes, they are intricately woven with survival.

Studies uniformly find that divorce is a jolt to most children. Even youngsters who have lived in tense, conflict-ridden homes for many years seldom think of divorce as a remedy for unhappiness; the remedy would be for parents to stop fighting. And among children for whom verbalized threats of divorce have loomed for many years, the actual happening most often is perceived not as an expected event but as a nightmare that becomes a waking reality. Suddenly the assumptions children have accepted as givens and the structure they have relied on fall apart. They feel not only vulnerable but powerless to have any influence on a situation that profoundly impacts their lives.

The inevitable anxiety children feel is intensified when they are given little information—a situation that occurs with alarming frequency. "What will happen to me?" "Who will take care of me?" "If my parents don't love each other anymore, will they continue to love me?" "Where will I live?" "Who will I live with?" "Will I have to give up my school, my friends, my activities?" "What will my life be like now?" "Will I still see my other parent? How? How often?" "What will that parent do now?" "Will we have enough money to live?" "Can

I still go to camp?" "Can I still go to college?" Children's unanswered questions are endless and their worry intense. It feels more precarious having only one parent to rely on. Can that parent manage? What will happen if something happens to that parent too? Will that parent find someone else and get remarried? Will the child get lost in the shuffle?

Children's Confusing Feelings

Many children feel intensely rejected, perceiving that the parent is leaving them as well as the spouse. "(S)he wouldn't have left if (s)he cared about me." Intense fears of abandonment are not uncommon. In the widely cited California Children of Divorce study, Judith Wallerstein and Joan Kelly found that one-half of the children they studied (who ranged from preschoolers to adolescents) were intensely afraid of being abandoned by their fathers, while one-third feared abandonment by their mothers. A few children even feared they would be placed in foster homes. Not surprisingly, children's self-esteem frequently takes a plunge after divorce.

The majority of children are intensely sad and feel a deep sense of loss— of their family, their security, even their daily routines and family traditions. Even most of those who never had a close relationship with their departing parent long for that parent now. Many children have little control over their tears. Fourteen-year-old Meredith described how she felt when her parents were divorcing:

> The divorce really affected me emotionally. I just felt bad all the time. I used to cry a lot, and when I wasn't crying, I would feel like crying. . . . it was just a terrible time in my life.[1]

Anger is a fairly common reaction among children. Many feel betrayed by the very people they have trusted to protect and care for them. They feel no one is considering their needs, and they feel powerless to alter the situation that is completely disrupting their worlds. Some angry children hide their anger, fearing it will further upset or alienate their parents. Others have explosive outbursts. Some act out their anger in temper tantrums, noncompliance, aggressiveness, destructiveness, rebelliousness, or sexual promiscuity.

Some youngsters, especially younger ones, are haunted by gnawing feelings that they are responsible for the divorce. Some will remember parental fights they overheard about child-rearing differences. Others will remember their parents' exasperation over sibling quarrels. Some turn into model children, hoping they can undo the damage they think they have done. One child confessed the following to her mother years later:

I felt I was being punished by God for being really bad, so I tried being really good so God would change His mind . . . and let Dad come home.[2]

Some youngsters feel relief when parents divorce, although it appears that this happens to only a relative few. One widely cited study found fewer than 10 percent felt this way—most often older children who lived in fear that the violence in their homes would end in physical injury. Several studies have reported that initial feelings of relief are sometimes temporary and are later replaced by sadness and anger.

If children have *only* their parents' divorce to contend with, their situation is not so bleak, and their poor functioning is usually short-lived. But for most children, the divorce is only the beginning of what they must contend with.

Will the Fighting Ever Stop?

From children's perspectives, the one positive aspect divorce may have is putting an end to the fighting and tension they have been living with. But studies find that conflict between parents usually increases after separation as details about custody, visitation, support, and property settlements must be worked out between hurt and embittered ex-spouses, and also as new dating partners enter the picture. Distressed and bewildered children hear their mothers called whores, drunken bitches, and inept mothers, and their fathers called terrible parents, liars, and bastards who sleep around with cheap women. In the California Children of Divorce Study, over one-half the children studied had been witness to at least one incident of physical violence between their parents, many of whom had never had such incidents before being separated. Even worse, some children found themselves blatantly used as weapons by one parent to punish the other.

Children who are caught in this parental cross fire become frightened and angry at the incomprehensible behavior of their parents and wonder if the conflict will ever stop. Many feel unremitting pressure created by conflicting loyalties; a move toward one battling parent is a move away from the other. If they remain loyal to one, will their relationship with the other be jeopardized? Some children offer themselves as mediators or even scapegoats, some withdraw from both parents, some align themselves with one parent. Children can feel as if they are being torn apart or split in two.

Is Anything the Same Anymore?

When parents separate, the world as the child knows it begins to change and sometimes ends. There are abrupt changes in daily life. Children lose daily contact with one parent, and the great majority long for that parent, whether the relationship had been close or not. Often early visits are infrequent and follow no predictable schedule that children can count on, increasing their fears of abandonment. Will they see the parent again? Will this visit be the last?

At the same time, many youngsters also experience a sharp drop in contact with busy and overwhelmed custodial parents, leaving children feeling isolated and intensely lonely at the very time they most need reassurance and support. Many children find themselves for the first time spending long hours in day care or alone after school. Even some very young children must get themselves off to school, prepare their own meals, or put themselves to bed. One six-year-old who had to put himself to bed each night tried to cope with his fears by writing a note to himself and taping it to his bed. It said, "Go to sleep Jimmy. Don't be afraid."

Studies find that in most postseparation homes, established rules and routines fall by the wayside, discipline becomes inconsistent, family meals become infrequent and erratic, and general disorganization prevails. Many children could take these disruptions in stride at another point in their lives. But when so many disruptions coincide with their family's collapse, their insecurity is compounded, and they become more convinced that life is in complete chaos. They wonder if it will ever become normal again.

Money also becomes tighter, now that two homes must be maintained, and often becomes a source of conflict between parents. Anxiety over money is easily transmitted to children, whose vigilance alerts them to each new problem in their lives. Things once taken for granted can no longer be afforded. What will the future hold? What plans will no longer be possible? It is not uncommon for families to move and for children to be forced to find a way to cope with losing their home, school, and friends at a time when every aspect of their lives is already in flux.

Each of these changes requires children to adapt anew at a time when many of them are already taxed near the limits of their capacities. However, the worst changes from children's perspectives are the dramatic changes in their mothers and fathers and in their relationships with them.

Will My Old Parents Please Return?

For many children, the parents they experience after separation do not seem to be the same people they have known all their lives. Many parents' behavior becomes unfamiliar and unpredictable; bewildered youngsters commonly observe rage, tirades, wide mood swings, lethargy, new pursuits, changed appearances, and increased drinking, smoking, and drug use. Some become painfully aware for the first time of their parents' sexuality, as a number of new "friends" begin to share their parents' beds. Some keep a vigilant watch on a parent who they fear may commit suicide.

The rapid and dramatic changes in parents, occurring at the same time that children's lives are in flux and in chaos, is often incomprehensible and frightening to children—younger and older alike. Ordinarily when children are in crises, they can rely on the security, stability, and support that is offered by their families, and these provide a cushion that softens the blows of stress. This is what happened with the British children who stayed with their parents throughout the wartime bombings. The children looked to that reserve account of theirs—their parents—to help them through the turmoil so that they could emerge from it unscathed.

During the stressful postseparation period, however, a large percentage of parents are so overwhelmed with their own stress, emotions, and new demands for rebuilding their lives that either they do not recognize their children's neediness and distress, or they simply do not have the emotional resources to tend to them. In one study, only 10 percent of the children felt that their fathers were very sensitive to and in tune with their feelings, and only 15 percent felt that their mothers were. Over one-half felt that their fathers were *completely* unaware of their distress, while over one-third found their mothers to be completely unaware. Studies report that a significant percentage of parents, custodial and noncustodial alike, become markedly less available, less supportive, less nurturant, and less sensitive to their children's needs. They communicate with their youngsters less, enjoy them less, and are less affectionate. They are inconsistent in their discipline and provide fewer rules and guidelines, often because they fear children's rejection and preference for their ex-partners. At the same time, parents' stress makes them more negative and volatile with their children. Said one parent,

> Detached, I'd go through periods of ignoring Hank. Then I'd spank him and holler. Real extremes.[3]

Explaining her situation, another reported,

> I felt as if I had to build a new life for myself instantly. I got a job, enrolled in school, and started dating, all within three months of my separation. When the school called me to tell me Jan was withdrawing in class, I realized that I had forgotten that her life was also important.[4]

A third woman, who worked 60-hour weeks while trying to maintain an active social life, tells this story:

> I was too needy myself and too self-involved. . . . I have a great sadness about the kids and my relationship with them, even though they're nearly grown now. In many ways, they were emotionally neglected. I was under a lot of stress, and they added to it. So they became targets for my outbursts and my anger. That's the worst part of all this, and I wish I could do it over again.[5]

Generally, younger children, who are obviously more needy, tend to receive more attention than do their siblings who are eight or older, but many of these younger children also experience what Judith Wallerstein and Joan Kelly labeled "diminished parenting." Whatever children's ages, if they lose their parents' support at this critical time in their lives, they usually feel rejected, abandoned, and profoundly hurt. They lose their most powerful buffer from the severe stress they are experiencing and must face it alone, feeling exposed and vulnerable. When asked what he would like to tell his parents, one teen responded that he would like to physically shake them to make sure they were really listening. Then he would say, "I'm here, too! Why do you always forget about me? Why can't you see what you're doing to me?"

As you might suspect from all this, children's relationships with their parents also change. In fact, studies find that frequently a parent-child relationship before separation bears little resemblance to the relationship after it. Sometimes these dramatic changes are temporary, but sometimes they are permanent. Eleven-year-old Amy is an example.

Three years ago Amy basked in the warmth of her parents' attention, feeling loved, protected, and treasured. Unhappy with one another, both parents showered their only daughter with all their time and affection. But once they divorced, Amy's storybook life came to a screeching halt. Her dad embraced his new single life with the same devotion he had once shown his daughter. Her mom, who had not worked since Amy's birth, now juggled a full-time job and classes. Amy went from coming home to a stay-at-home mom and home-baked cookies to spending every afternoon and evening alone. She did her homework, cleaned up the house, made dinner, which she kept warm for her mother, and went to bed before her mother got home several nights a week. Now, three years later, Amy's parents' lives have changed for the better, but Amy is still a very lonely child. Her dad has remarried and has a new family. She sees him alternate weekends, which generally means four days each month. They have never regained the closeness they once had. Usually he and her stepmother take her someplace with her stepsiblings. "It's okay, I guess," she says sadly when asked about her relationship with her father. "It's just that I wish I could spend more time with him, and I wish we could spend some time alone so we could talk. It feels like he's just some man who lets me tag along when he takes his *real* family places." When asked about her mother, Amy reports in a flat voice, "Mom has a job she likes and lots of new friends. She always talks about how close we are. I guess we are. She tells me all about her friends and dates and all the things she does. She even asks my advice sometimes. But she's pretty busy with her life and I'm more like someone on the outside looking in than a real part of it. I guess we're more like roommates than a family."

Changes in relationships are frequently in the form of increasing distance between parent and child, although not always. Some parents suddenly become overly protective and possessive. Some enlist their children in an angry and bitter alliance against the other parent. Some parents and children develop a close and companionate relationship, sharing a high degree of empathy and affection for each other as well as sharing responsibilities and decision making. In contrast, some parents draft their children as stand-ins, assigning them excessive responsibility for their years—for housework, cooking, and the care of younger siblings. Still other parents become emotionally dependent on their youngsters, clinging to them for their own emotional survival and the fulfillment of their needs. Their children become their caretakers, companions, and confidants and basically parent their parents. Frequently these youngsters become emotionally overburdened themselves and are at risk for developing serious problems. (This is discussed in more depth in Chapter 14, "About Single-Parent Homes".)

How Can Anyone Expect Me to Act the Same?

Very often, children's behavior is an expression of their feelings. With all this turmoil and disruption in their lives, it is hardly surprising that children's behavior is usually affected, at least for a while. Some become more withdrawn. Some do less well socially. Others do poorly academically or become more difficult to manage.

The children of divorce studied by British researcher Yvette Walczak reported, in retrospect, that they had been unhappy, insecure, and apathetic at the time of their parents' divorces. They were no longer able to appreciate or look forward to things they had once enjoyed. They lost their appetites, had difficulty falling asleep, and were restless throughout the night as well. Tears, withdrawal, and bad tempers were common ways to express the misery they felt.

A significant percentage of children have a hard time maintaining friendships and a social life. They become tense, irritable, demanding, and bossy. They smile less and scowl more. They seek attention, pick fights, antagonize people, and drive friends away. Said one teen,

> I'd go around and I was a real bitch all day. I was depressed. I couldn't talk to anybody, or when I did all I did was talk about the divorce and what it was doing. I lost quite a few friends without realizing it.[6]

Declining academic performance is another frequent fallout. Children's preoccupation with difficulties at home makes it difficult if not impossible for them to concentrate. Some children report being so distracted that they are unable to make sense out of what teachers say. Children's anxiety and restlessness compound their learning difficulties, as does the disruptive behavior that some develop in the classroom.

Many parents have new difficulties in managing their children after separation. Children tend to be angry, irritable, cranky, unruly, and rebellious. Younger children are likely to become aggressive, noncompliant, demanding, clinging, or whiny. They are also likely to have temper tantrums. Older children are more likely to become rebellious about rules and discipline or to verbally attack others. A relatively small subgroup turn to truancy, delinquent activities, or precocious sexual activity.

It is often difficult to separate children's behavior from that of their custodial parents, for they are intimately woven together. Children's and parents' behavior during the postseparation months actually exacerbates each other's stress. Many parents and children find themselves in vicious cycles, fueling the very behavior in one another that each is trying to avoid. One mother of a four-year-old described her interactions with her son this way:

> The more I feel trapped, the more desperate Mike becomes. The more he clings, the more desperate I am to escape.[7]

In their well-known study of preschoolers after their parents' divorces, E. Mavis Hetherington of the University of Virginia and her colleagues reported that although divorced mothers gave their children a hard time, they received "tough treatment" from their children in return, particularly from their sons. Distraught preschoolers became demanding and whiny and clung to fatigued mothers whom they ignored and disobeyed. Mothers, in return, became increasingly more restrictive and negative while offering less nurturance and support. One mother described her relationship with her preschooler as "declared war."

Twelve-year-old Sarah describes what happened to her relationship with her mom.

> After my father packed his bags and moved out, I was really upset and my mother was all depressed. It had a big effect on my life and for about two months I was fighting all the time with my mom—about anything. About taking vitamins in the morning, eating my breakfast, making my bed, keeping my room clean, doing my homework—dumb stuff like that. I used to scream at her, which was something I'd never done before. I'd never heard her yell at me, either. It was because she was miserable and I was, too, but I didn't realize it at the time.[8]

There is another slightly different and also common variation of the vicious cycle: Anxious, angry children become increasingly demanding, rebellious, and accusatory, using every opportunity to arouse their mothers' guilt about the divorce. Custodial mothers, who are emotionally overwhelmed and fatigued, are unresponsive to their children's outbursts to a point. However, once their limit is reached, mothers resort to yelling, nagging, and becoming less nurturant. These are all reactions that make children even more anxious, angry, and doubtful of their mothers' love. And so the cycle begins anew. (Effective methods of discipline are discussed in Chapter 16.) Research conducted at the University of Michigan helped to clarify the dynamics of this vicious cycle. The study's author, Tracy Barr Grossman, analyzed and compared the perceptions of parents and children in postseparation homes. Dr. Grossman found that mothers do not understand that their children's angry outbursts stem from the stress of the divorce. They also do not understand that what their children need is understanding. Instead, they misinterpret their children's outbursts as a series of isolated incidents that deserve disciplinary action (although the mothers may not use it). At the same time, children do not recognize their mothers' fatigue but misinterpret it as disinterest or anger, which of course fuels youngsters' feelings of hurt and isolation. The University of Michigan study found that mothers who reported feeling the most overwhelmed typically had children who felt unloved and angry at their mothers' perceived "indifference."

Which children have the most *intense* reactions to their parents' divorce?

- Children who are already poorly adjusted or who already have doubts about their parents' love and acceptance. The stress of the divorce exacerbates their problems.
- Children from close-knit families for whom the divorce is particularly bewildering.
- Children with a parent in considerable turmoil because he or she bitterly opposes the divorce.
- Children who experience very chaotic homes and very poor care after divorce.

DO CHILDREN REACT DIFFERENTLY AT DIFFERENT AGES?

Is it better for parents to divorce when their children are one age rather than another? Do older children have an easier time than younger ones? Some feel that divorce is easier on older children because they have more sources of support outside the family. However, divorce causes a unique set of problems for older children that do not concern their younger siblings. There is no clear-cut evidence that divorce is markedly easier on one age group than on another. Children of all ages experience intense sadness, anger, anxiety, fear, rejection, and loneliness. However, studies find that age *does* affect children's initial reaction to divorce: It appears that each age group has its own *unique set of problems*.

Infants and Toddlers

Even infants are affected by divorce because of the upset and tension transmitted to them by their parents, disruptions in their routines, and lapses in their care due to their parents' distress. It is common for infants to become fretful and have eating and digestive problems.

In response to the stress in their homes and the sudden disappearance of a parent, toddlers tend to become irritable and aggressive, have temper tantrums, and regress to earlier forms of behavior.

Preschoolers

Children between the ages of three and five-and-a-half are the youngest children to be studied in any detail and show the most dramatic changes in behavior. Having a poor grasp of what is happening, they are bewildered and frightened. Preschoolers perceive their parents as a single unit; therefore, once one leaves, they become terrified that the other will abandon them, too. Routine separations become traumatic. So do bedtimes, because these panic-stricken little ones are sure they will wake up to an empty house. For the same reason, they wake up fretful and crying throughout the night. Because of their intellectual stage of development, preschoolers perceive that the world revolves around them. This explains why they so often believe that the divorce is, in some way, their fault and that the departing parent is rejecting them personally. "My mommy and daddy are getting divorced because I was bad." "My daddy left because I was too noisy." "My mommy left because she didn't love me anymore." Consider the following interchange between a three-year-old and a researcher. The child is obviously confused about his father's absence and believes that, somehow, the confusing events revolve around him.

> *Researcher*: Will you tell me your story?
> *Child*: Somebody stole the daddy.
> *Researcher*: Somebody stole the daddy?
> *Child*: Yeah, someone took him away.
> *Researcher*: Why did they do that?
> *Child*: So the little boy would feel bad. The daddy doesn't love the little boy.
> *Researcher*: Why doesn't the daddy love the little boy?
> *Child*: 'Cause he went away.[9]

Preschoolers are overwhelmed with anxiety, and it is expressed in ways most parents find aversive: irritability, clinging, whining, increased aggressiveness, and temper tantrums. Due to their insecurity, these youngsters also generally lose their most recently acquired skills and regress to younger behavior. A return to lapses in toilet training, security blankets, old toys, thumb sucking, and masturbation are common. Regressions to younger behavior are transient and generally last from a few weeks to a few months.

> Four-year-old David did little but curl up and stare for the two weeks after his father left. The only time he responded to anything was when his mother tried to leave his side. "Don't leave me, Mommy. Don't leave me," he would scream in terror,

grabbing her with all his strength. In the third week, David's anger let loose. He kicked everything in sight, including his mother and other children. He tossed books, broke toys, and knocked down the blocks other children were building. One minute he would be the classroom bully, the next he would dissolve in tears, begging his teacher to hold him. His mother, who had all she could do to deal with her own emotions, alternated between pushing him away, yelling at him, and soothing him. Bedtime was a battle of wills for over two months. Exhausted and wanting some peace and quiet, she would repeatedly put him into bed, scolding him to stay put and go to sleep. Just as persistently, he would repeatedly come downstairs crying, with one fist stuffed in his mouth and the other securely clutching his teddy.

Interestingly, in her 10-year follow-up of her study group, Judith Wallerstein found that this group seemed to be the best adjusted a decade after the divorce, despite their greater vulnerability at the time of separation. They had little memory of either the intact family or the trauma of their parents' split. However, this did *not* seem to be the critical factor in their good long-term adjustment. Instead, the critical factor seemed to be that these children tended to receive better care and more love throughout the years following the divorce than did their older siblings.

Six- to Eight-Year-Old Children

Generally, children at this age, particularly boys, are the most openly grief-stricken, feel the most loss and despair, and yearn the most intensely for their absent parent. Six- to eight-year-old children believe that their intact family is vital to their survival. This perception is epitomized by one panic-stricken six-year-old in the California Children of Divorce Study who sobbed inconsolably, "I don't have a daddy! I'll need a daddy!" Their despair is so deep that they can't concentrate in school or relate to playmates. In fact, they can't seem to find any way to distract themselves from their grief.

These youngsters also are very susceptible to feelings of abandonment and rejection and worry that they will be replaced ("Will my daddy get a new little girl?"). They also have a very rough time with parental conflict; they so desperately want to be loyal to *both* parents that they feel they are literally being pulled apart. Those who experience anger most usually express it indirectly rather than directing it at their parents (for example, they may clobber their peers or they may refuse to do homework, to go to bed, or to do routine chores).

Nine- to Twelve-Year-Old Children

A shaken sense of identity and of right and wrong plagues these children. This is the age of grappling with these issues, and children usually rely heavily on their parents' identity and values in defining their own. The nine- to twelve-year-old's distress is frequently expressed in physical complaints, such as head-aches and stomachaches. Many immerse themselves in vigorous activity that helps offset the strong feelings of powerlessness they feel.

The most distinguishing reaction for a significant percentage of 9- to 12-year-olds, however, is their intense anger that they direct at one or both parents, usually whomever they blame for the divorce. Children at this age reason that parents could reconcile their differences if they tried hard enough and bitterly accuse their parents of selfishness and indifference to their children's needs.

Some children this age are easily swept into a bitter and open alliance with one parent (usually the one who was hurt) against the other. Divorce researchers Wallerstein and Kelly hypothesize that the reason these children are willing to join such an alliance is because they so often get lost in the shuffle after sep-aration, which leaves them feeling hurt, rejected, and powerless. Forming an alliance with one parent changes all this—they become needed, important, and powerful. Generally these alignments do not last longer than a year, and when they do, they are fueled by very angry parents who are making poor progress toward closing the door on the divorce.

Don't fall into the trap of drawing your child into an alliance with you against your ex-spouse, no matter how angry you are. Many youngsters grow up feeling guilt, anguish, and regret at the part they played, and they deeply resent the parent with whom they had been aligned for using them as weapons to hurt the other parent. If you are a parent who is the victim of one of these alliances, hang in there. Many a parent has given up too quickly and has need-lessly lost the relationship with his or her offspring.

When 12-year-old Courtney's father left home, her mother was enraged. Courtney too was angry at her dad for his unconscionable behavior. Having always lectured her on the importance of sticking things out, she was furious at him for being such a hypocrite. Each time her dad called, Courtney's mom would stand by the phone and tell her what to say. "Tell him if he loved you, he would come back. Tell him you hate him for leaving you." The few times Courtney visited her dad's apartment, her mother coached her on how to act, what to say, and how to spy on him. "Are there any women's clothes in the apartment? "What does he do with his spare time?" Things went from bad to worse. Courtney's mother filled her with damaging stories about her dad, and Courtney's open hostility toward him caused their relationship to deteriorate to such an extent that he stopped calling altogether. This seemed to confirm what her mother had said all along: He had left *both* of them because he no longer loved either of them. Five years later, her dad called out of the blue. Feeling guilt-ridden over her earlier behavior, Courtney took the opportunity to meet him secretly. The two spent considerable time together over the following months. When her still-bitter mother found out about their meetings, she was furious, calling Courtney a traitor and forbidding her to see him again. Now angry at her mother for using her when she was so vulnerable, Courtney defiantly packed her things and went to her father.

Adolescents

Many parents are surprised to find how deeply their teens are affected by divorce. Adolescents tend to react with a deep sense of loss, grief, anger, feelings of emptiness, difficulty concentrating, and chronic fatigue. Teens also become acutely concerned about their own futures. Does their parents' divorce foreshadow their own future relationships?

Why are teens affected this much when they are so involved with their own lives? After all, they are already becoming independent of their parents anyway. The answer lies in the way adolescents move away from their families and achieve independence. Progress toward independence does not follow a steady course. Teens take several steps forward and then a step backward; they move toward independence and then temporarily move back to the security of the family to refuel and regroup. The family is their safe haven to which they can retreat.

What happens when parents divorce before teens have achieved independence? If homes are disorganized and parents themselves are rapidly changing and less available, adolescents lose their safe haven and feel as if they have been left adrift or thrown out into the world before they are ready.

When adolescents are ready to be thrust ahead in their development, they do well; some even thrive. Many become mature, insightful, and empathetic. They assume additional family responsibilities while achieving a good balance in their own lives. But when teens are not ready to be thrust ahead, their development can get derailed in one of several ways. Many abandon friends, interests, and adolescent activities. Some regress into younger ways of behaving, while others become far older than their years, frequently becoming immersed in the role of family protector and supporter at the expense of their own lives. Some take a third path, and it is the most alarming. They express their distress, anger, and internal conflicts in potentially dangerous ways, not available to their younger siblings: precocious sexual activity (especially girls), alcohol, drugs, or delinquent activities. What makes a teen take this last path? Usually it is some combination of several circumstances, including anger, lax supervision and rules, poorly developed internal controls, poor coping skills, feelings of abandonment, loss of their safe haven, and exposure to parents' sexual behavior. Sometimes these troublesome behavior problems are transient, but sometimes they become permanent patterns if the postdivorce environment is a poor one.

> Holly's parents divorced three years ago when she was 13. Deserted by her father and ignored by her mother who had an active social and sexual life, Holly turned to the liquor cabinet at age 14. Drinking allowed her to bury her feelings, she confided. "It was the only way to make the pain go away." At about the same time, she became sexually active. Feeling abandoned and alone, she thought that sex might be a way to have someone of her own who would care. "But I just seem to go from guy to guy," she admits. "I think I'd rather reject them before they reject me like my parents did."

Many adolescents cope with their parents' divorces by distancing themselves from the crisis at home and looking for support on the outside—from peers, parents of friends, teachers, and so forth. Unless this outside support is detrimental (for example, delinquent peers), this distancing usually helps teens cope successfully with the divorce, and most become reinvolved with the family once the turmoil is ended.

HOW LONG DO CHILDREN'S DIVORCE-RELATED PROBLEMS CONTINUE?

Frequently the duration of children's transient problems roughly coincide with the duration of acute turmoil and disruption in the family. Youngsters' problems fade as parents begin to regain their own emotional equilibrium and are able to provide more nurturance and support, as parental conflict subsides, as parenting schedules become stabilized, and as new routines, rules, and discipline become established. A substantial number of families regain their equilibrium enough so that children are back functioning on course sometime within the first year after their parents separate, although very young children tend to take longer to recover. Problem behavior of younger children is likely to continue for at least the first year and a half after separation.

In general, recovery is easier for children who were well adjusted before the divorce and who have had successes in many areas. These children have a wide repertoire of resources they can call upon, and their resiliency often allows them to resume good functioning at an even faster pace than that at which their families regain equilibrium.

However, the prognosis is not rosy for all children. When Judith Wallerstein and Joan Kelly reassessed their study group 18 months following separation, they were shocked to find that 25 percent of the children (all ages) still had symptoms that had developed in response to the divorce, such as depression, withdrawal, acute anxiety, poor self-esteem, poor school performance, sexual promiscuity, and delinquent behavior. Boys were more likely to be doing poorly than were girls. What surprised these researchers even more was that many children had *worse* problems at this point than they had had early after the separation. Would these problems gradually fade? Or would they become long-term patterns?

ARE THERE LONG-TERM EFFECTS OF DIVORCE FOR CHILDREN?

Three and a half years later (five years after the parents separated), Wallerstein and Kelly assessed their study group once again. Thirty-seven percent of the children were now functioning poorly, many of whom had been functioning adequately when previously assessed. In fact, one-third of the children who previously had been functioning *very well* were now doing poorly. So much for their resiliency pulling them through! Common problems for these poorly functioning children were moderate to severe depression; acute unhappiness; poor learning; intense anger; sexual promiscuity; and delinquent behavior such as drug abuse, alcoholism, and petty stealing.

Based on many studies, most experts now agree that *most* children do adjust successfully to their parents' divorce, but a statistically significant minority develop long-term problems. When compared with children from intact homes, statistically more children from divorced homes perform poorer academically and have more behavioral problems such as aggressiveness, poor self-control, defiance, delinquent behavior, and sexual promiscuity. Except for sexual promiscuity, the problems show up more often in boys. There are a handful of studies reporting that young adults from divorced homes have a better-than-average chance of getting divorced themselves. And another handful of studies have found that a small but statistically significant minority of adolescent girls and young women have problems involving long-term heterosexual relationships. (Since these latter problems are most often found in girls who have had little contact with their fathers in many years, this topic is discussed more fully in Chapter 18.)

What is happening here? Why do a significant minority of children from divorced homes develop long-term problems? Why are problems sometimes worse several years after divorce than they were during the divorce crisis itself?

The answer is that some families do not regain their equilibrium after divorce but become stalled in a chronic state of stress, instability, and transition. Children in these families are continuously subjected to any number of debilitating conditions: bitter battles between their parents over custody, visitation, or child rearing; unavailable and uninvolved parents; overwhelmed or emotionally unstable parents; outright abandonment or rejection; poor supervision and discipline; a chaotic, out-of-control home life; overwhelming responsibilities and worries; multiple moves with changes in neighborhoods, schools, and friends; new adults moving in and out of the home; second divorces; severe economic hardships; and so forth. These children are in a chronic state of stress, and the continuous demands made on them to adapt and readapt far exceed their capacity. Even highly resilient children with startling psychological strength can stand only so much stress and adversity before their resources are overtaxed. Dr. Neil Kalter of the Department of Psychology and Psychiatry at the University of Michigan suggests that the conditions some children experience during the years after divorce are like multiple land mines to be encountered along the path to adulthood. It is important to realize that it is *current life circumstances* that play the critical role in children's long-term problems.

If relationships with parents are close, nurturant, supportive, and dependable, these relationships can buffer children from many (though not all) of the blows inflicted by prolonged stress, just as the British parents buffered their children during the wartime bombings. But, sadly, a sizable minority of parents and children never achieve this kind of relationship after divorce, robbing children of this powerful buffer. Life fell apart for Kevin, a 12-year-old in the California Children of Divorce Study, when he lost his relationships with both parents after their divorce.

> Kevin was an intelligent child and model student when his parents separated. Overnight, his life changed. His dad, whom he worshipped, rarely saw him and constantly broke promises without so much as an apology. At the same time, Kevin's mother began a permanent pattern of burying herself completely in her professional job and rarely spending time at home. The model student turned into a problem child. Kevin became restless, irresponsible, and destructive. He beat up other children and antagonized students and teachers alike. When his teacher was interviewed 18 months after his parents' separation, she reported that Kevin was the most irresponsible child she had ever had. Kevin continued on a downward course, moving on to drinking, smoking pot, and getting into trouble with the law. By the time Wallerstein traced him for her 10-year follow-up, Kevin had already been in jail three times—for drunk driving, dealing drugs, and physically abusing his girlfriend.

What happens to children like Kevin? Why the aggressiveness, defiance, poor self-control, delinquent behavior? Dr. Kalter points out that an important role is played by the anger some children harbor, which often stems from their perceptions of parental rejection. Sometimes children's anger is taken out at school, sometimes at home, sometimes on society. A second contributor is the lack of rules and consistent discipline in many divorced homes. Children have a more difficult time with self-control during times of stress and need clear limits and a more structured environment. Said one 14-year-old girl:

> The worst thing about divorce was that my mom wasn't home. There was no discipline, no rules—just an empty feeling. That's how I got into drugs and sex.[10]

Clear limits and consistently enforced rules will help children eventually develop the internal controls necessary to manage their behavior independently. A third and equally important contributor to many children's aggressiveness and lack of self-control is open conflict between their parents. Why? Because when parents battle with each other, they are unwittingly modeling hostile, aggressive, and impulsive ways to handle problems. It does not take long for children to learn the lessons.

Why poor school performance? The behavior problems that some children like Kevin develop also interfere with learning because of their disruptive effect in the classroom. Dwindling parental supervision and involvement also take their toll academically, as does the excessive home responsibilities piled on some children from divorced single-parent homes.

Why do boys more frequently develop behavior problems and poor school performance than girls? Interestingly, parents battle more frequently in the presence of sons than daughters, which may help to explain why aggressive behavior is more common in boys. But another reason boys' behavior is more troublesome is that they have a particularly difficult time with parental divorce. Studies find that boys generally adjust to divorce slower than girls do and develop more emotional, social, and intellectual problems in the process. At the same time, studies find that boys generally receive less nurturance, less support, and less sensitivity from parents, teachers, and peers. It is no wonder that boys' behavior becomes more problematic!

SHOULD WE STAY TOGETHER FOR THE CHILDREN'S SAKE?

Research suggests that the majority of divorcing men and women have thoughts of reconciliation at one time or another. In one study, 23 percent of the study group actually withdrew their divorce petition and reconciled. Some couples go through a number of separations and reconciliations, and some remain separated for an extended period before filing for divorce. A question predominant in the minds of many parents is, "Should we stay together for the children's sake?"

What is the answer to this often-asked question? The following compelling findings may help you with your decision.

- Children from conflict-ridden homes have more adjustment and behavior problems than do children from conflict-free homes. Problems are particularly pronounced for boys.
- Parental conflict is more damaging to children the longer it continues, the more it is openly hostile, and the more it focuses on the child (for example, child-rearing differences, child-related financial issues, visitation, custody).
- Children from conflict-free single-parent families are usually *better* adjusted than children from discordant intact families.
- Continued parental conflict is more damaging to children who have gone through parental divorce than for children who remain in their intact families.

These findings have led a large number of researchers and mental health professionals to conclude that divorce may provide a better environment for children when their alternative is living in a conflict-ridden intact family. The catch, however, is that the *conflict must end* with the divorce, or children are likely to be worse off. This conclusion also assumes that the postdivorce family will not continue in a chronic state of stress and tension.

From children's perspectives, divorce casts its shadow for a large fraction of their young lives. Unlike their parents, who have a lifetime of experience to fall back on, children have no map or experience to lead them out of this mire. And unlike their parents who made the decision, they have no vision of a better life because of the divorce. And indeed, many children never *do* experience a better life after divorce.

After reading this chapter, you are probably better able to understand divorce from a child's perspective and why divorce *can* have very negative repercussions on children. But at this point, you probably feel that you have been bombarded with a confusing array of information. What do you do with it? How do you use it so that your child will be among those who successfully adjust, in both the short- and long-term?

Chapters 8, 9, and 10 will directly address these concerns and provide you with very concrete guidance. Chapter 8 will guide you through the steps of telling your children about your divorce. It will show you how to ease your children's distress and how best to handle common problems so they will be short-lived. Chapter 9 will identify the *specific* conditions found to be critical to children's long-term divorce adjustment. Chapter 10 is a step-by-step guide to show you *how* to make those critical conditions favorable for your children. If you follow this guide, you will create the kinds of conditions that will allow your children to bounce back from divorce rather than become casualties of divorce.

8

HELPING CHILDREN THROUGH THE CRISIS

"A broken home" is a phrase routinely used to "explain" children's long-term troubled behavior. The good news is that recent studies show that divorced homes *can* provide an environment that enables children to thrive. If parents can provide certain critical ingredients, children can usually bounce back from divorce with amazing resilience.

This chapter will help you set the stage for your children's successful divorce adjustment. It is not going to be a "one-minute guide to kids' successful adjustment," for there are no one-minute steps to success. Divorce is painful for kids and is likely to affect your children adversely for a period of time. If you've read Chapter 7, which looked at divorce through a child's eyes, you understand why. This chapter will guide you in helping your children through the crisis. It takes you through the steps of telling your children about your pending divorce, helping them cope with their confusing and intense emotions, and helping them rebuild their self-esteem, which is likely to have taken a plunge in the wake of your family's rupture. You will also find out how best to handle some of the more common reactions children have—denial, withdrawal, anger, immature behavior, and behavior problems such as aggressiveness and rebelliousness.

Starting children off right will make your children's long-term divorce adjustment more likely, but it will not guarantee it. As you learned in Chapter 7, adjustment isn't resolved in the early months after separation and divorce. Divorce isn't a single event. It sets into motion a chain of events that spans an extended time. It is not only what happens now, but what happens in the coming months and years that will influence how well your children bounce back and whether they develop delayed adjustment problems. Fortunately, research has been able to identify a number of critical conditions that impact children's *long-term* divorce adjustment. They are discussed in the following chapter; don't put off reading it. But right now, let's start at the beginning: how to prepare your children.

110

STARTING OUT RIGHT: HOW TO TELL CHILDREN ABOUT DIVORCE

There is strong agreement about how children should be told about their parents' pending divorce. Generally, the more preparation and support parents provide, the better children adjust to the separation. So prepare your children carefully; think through what you are going to say and how you will say it. How you tell them will help set the stage for the difficult months ahead.

I'll describe the ideal situation. You may be unable to carry out all these recommendations, but use them as guidelines to create as favorable a situation as you can.

Who Should Tell Children?

You and your spouse should break the news *together*. There are several good reasons for this. Your children are less likely to deny the reality of the decision if they hear it from both of you. They are likely to feel more reassured when they see you are willing to work together for their welfare, despite your conflict. And each of you will know for a fact exactly *what* your children have been told.

It is usually a good idea to tell all the children together. This is more likely to create feelings of cohesiveness and closeness among your youngsters. It can be an invaluable asset to them over the difficult months ahead to have siblings to parent (or to parent them), to cry with, and to talk with.

Of course, if your children are of markedly different ages, you will have to put more thought into your wording and have a lengthier discussion later with your older children. Or you may feel that the age span is just too great to warrant a joint discussion. However, don't neglect providing some simple explanation to a very young child, even a two- or three-year-old. Most parents believe that a child of this age is too young to understand what is happening, but these youngsters have a very difficult time adjusting when one parent simply disappears without any explanation. Their active imaginations can concoct frightening reasons for a parent's disappearance. One three-year-old who was given no explanation for his mother's sudden departure was terrified that she had "been burned up in a fire."

The Timing, Setting, and Tone

Wait until your decision is *definite*. Prolonged periods of uncertainty intensify children's adjustment difficulties. Telling them roughly two weeks before one of you moves out is a broad guideline. Basically, youngsters need enough time to adjust to the idea, but not enough time to fuel their natural hopes of your reconciliation. If your children are all older, you may wish to tell them even sooner than this, so you can adequately deal with the many questions they are likely to have.

Choose a setting that will allow a lengthy open discussion, plenty of tears, and freedom to show your affection. You may want to hold a distraught pre-schooler on your lap or to put your arm around an older child. Your home is likely to be the best setting.

Several considerations should influence the tone of your discussion.

- Youngsters should feel free to ask questions and talk about their feelings without fear of hurting or angering you.
- Ideally they should hear the decision in a warm, loving, and calm manner. (Right after a fight would be a poor time.)
- Children would benefit if you could honestly tell them that the divorce has been carefully considered and is necessary to solve a serious problem. Children have a more difficult time coping with a divorce that appears to them to be impulsive or irrational. They would also benefit from hearing that you are sorry to cause them this hurt.
- Do not offer false hopes of reconciliation. In the long run it will add to and prolong their tension and turmoil.

Be Honest

To deal with their parents' divorce, children need to find *some* reason for it. Without sufficient explanation, children's imaginations run rampant with reasons and fears that are usually far worse than the truth. Frequently the most frightened children are those who receive the least information.

Be honest with your kids and tell them the basic reason(s) for your decision. But use caution here. This does not mean that you should bombard them with all your grievances or that you should give them specific details or embarrassing information. And *never*, even indirectly, hold a youngster responsible for your marital difficulties. Even if child-rearing differences have been a major source of your conflict, don't lay this on a child.

Give children a general and well-thought-out explanation that they can understand. "Mom and Dad are very unhappy living together, and we feel we can't go on living like this any longer." "Dad loves someone else and wants to live with this other person." (Children do not need to be told that a parent has been involved in a sexual relationship, but it is better they hear about a new person on the scene from you rather than discover it on their own or hear it from someone else.)

Keep explanations simple. If you bombard youngsters with information, they may feel overwhelmed. Also be sensitive to their reactions. Don't insist that a child listen to an explanation at this time if he or she obviously does not want one. You can give one later when your child is ready. Sometimes the only way children can handle their parents' impending divorce is by denial. I'll talk about this later.

Provide Reassurance

Parents Don't Divorce Children

The anxiety created in most children by the news of their family's rupture provides a fertile ground in which misconceptions and fears can breed. "If Dad and Mom don't love each other anymore, maybe they'll stop loving me too." "Mommy wouldn't leave me if she still loved me." "If Daddy leaves, we won't have any more money for food."

Children need an abundance of reassurance, *both now and in the months ahead*, about your continued love and concern for them. You'll need to make it clear that divorce is just between parents, not between parents and children. They need to know that they will still have two parents, that both of you still love them, and that both of you still want to take care of them. And they need to know that it is all right for them to still love both of you. Children do not want to choose between their parents.

If your spouse has disappeared or is adamant about not being involved with the children any longer, reassurances of your love and concern will be even more critical. Try to make it very clear that their other parent left because of you, not because of them. Also try to help your children see that their other parent's indifference reflects a problem within the *parent*; it does not mean that the children are unlovable and does not reflect any shortcomings in them. (Chapter 10 has additional guidelines to help you.)

They Are Not Responsible

Youngsters need reassurance that the divorce is *in no way* their fault. Although this may never have occurred to you, it is a fear among many children—particularly younger ones, but sometimes older ones too. Children will sometimes sob, "What did I do wrong?" They will often beg their parents to stay together, promising they'll be good from now on. Some become model children after the announcement, hoping they can now alter the decision for which they think they are responsible. Some won't verbalize their fears but will agonize over their past misdeeds.

Children's feelings of guilt can be very deep and very pervasive. One child blamed herself for her parents' divorce for five years, believing that its cause was her failure to deliver a message from one parent to the other.

Give Details About the Future

Children need concrete information about how the divorce will affect them personally. How will their lives be different? How will they be the same?

Most important are details about the departing parent. When will the parent move out? Where will he or she live? How, where, and when will they see the parent in the future? These details will make the future less frightening to them. Of course, you may not yet know all these specifics, but assure youngsters you will keep them informed.

If major changes are close at hand (moving, a new school, mother taking a full-time job, a serious need to cut back on expenses, and so forth), children should be prepared. If there will be no other dramatic changes in the family's life, let them know that too.

Exactly how many details you cover in this single session should depend on how well your kids are absorbing the information and how receptive they are. You don't want to overwhelm them. It is wise to have several discussions before one of you actually moves out.

Encourage Discussion: Both Now and in the Future

Your decision to divorce will probably throw your children's once well-ordered lives into a tailspin. It is almost inevitable that it will stir up a myriad of questions and a well of strong emotions within them, both now and in the months ahead.

Encourage your children to ask questions, and let them know you will always answer them the best you can. Children who bring questions to their parents generally are found to adjust earlier than those who do not. But many youngsters will not ask questions unless they are given a great deal of encouragement.

Encourage them to share their thoughts and feelings about the divorce, whenever they would like. A study reported by British researcher Yvette Walczak found that good communication around the time of separation was vitally important to children's successful coping. Children become emotionally stronger when their feelings are understood. On the other hand, children who do not express or talk about their feelings may harbor those feelings for many years, and this is likely to impair their ability to close the door on the divorce and get on with their lives. Your children's residual feelings may also put a wedge in their relationship with you or with your ex-spouse.

Allowing children to freely express their feelings and emotions may be exceedingly uncomfortable for you. It's natural to want to stop tears with admonitions to "be brave" or to try to talk youngsters out of it when they tell you that you are ruining their lives. It's natural for you to get angry at their angry outbursts. But try not to. Instead, allow them their feelings, remember that they are hurting, and communicate your understanding to them as best you can. Keep in mind that life as they know it has just fallen apart. It will help you to know that these initial feelings and outbursts are not indicative of their future adjustment. They are merely your children's way of temporarily dealing with their pain.

HELPING CHILDREN COPE

Children's initial responses to the announcement of their parents' divorce vary widely, from seeming indifference to running out of the house screaming for help. Parents are often puzzled at their children's unpredictable responses and are not sure what to make of them. Sometimes they really aren't sure how their kids feel. Although children's overt reactions vary greatly, studies find that most kids in divorcing families share similar *feelings*. Generally, children are intensely sad and anxious. They feel rejected, vulnerable, and powerless to stop their world from crumbling to pieces. Many feel angry and betrayed. Some feel guilty, afraid they are responsible for the rupture in some way. Children's self-esteem commonly tumbles. Most fear that they will lose their departing parent, and some worry about complete abandonment. You may wish to refer back to Chapter 7 for a more detailed discussion of children's reactions, as well as for the typical feelings and behavior of children at specific ages.

Your children are likely to show some kind of changed behavior in the months after separation. Their changed behavior is a symptom of distress and reflects their anxiety and fears about what is happening in their lives. Although each of your children may exhibit very different behavioral changes (for example, withdrawal, aggressiveness, rebelliousness, a drop in school grades), each is likely to benefit from the suggestions that follow.

By the way, if you notice *no* behavior changes, do not assume your children are doing just fine. Research suggests that the majority of divorcing parents are not aware of the extent of their children's difficulties. One reason is that parents need to feel that their kids are coping well. Another is that parents are self-involved because of their own distress. Parents are also less apt to recognize some of the more subtle signs of distress in children, such as a lower tolerance for frustration, a drop in self-confidence, increased dependency, refusals to complete tasks, a lack of self-direction, poor impulse control, and so forth. One recent University of Michigan study found that parents automatically assumed that their children were fine if the youngsters' reactions were subdued rather than dramatic. However, in doing so, the parents greatly underestimated the extent of their youngsters' distress (as described by the children themselves). When journalist Linda Bird Francke was writing an article on divorce for *Newsweek* many years after her own divorce, she interviewed her two daughters about their reactions at the time. She was shocked at each child's revelations. Said Francke after interviewing the first of her two daughters,

> I was struck dumb by my maternal ignorance. How could I have failed to pick up the distress signals that she must have been sending out? I could have comforted her, reassured her, at least listened to her. And why hadn't she told me all this before? "Because you never asked," she said.[1]

The following suggestions will be useful in helping *any* child cope with divorce, whether you notice problem behavior or not.

- Try to allay at least some of your children's fears as quickly as you can. Once youngsters realize their fears are unwarranted, their distress and problem behavior often begin to diminish. How do you allay their fears? First, reassure them frequently of your love and concern. Second, strive to get family life stabilized and back to some semblance of normalcy so children can feel safe in the new family situation. (Chapter 10 discusses specific steps you can take.) Third, immediately set up a schedule with their absent parent so they can see that parent *frequently* and *regularly*. The quicker you can do these, the quicker children are likely to respond.
- Children's changed or problem behavior is an *indirect* way for them to express their distress. They may be confused about how they feel and why they are acting as they are. Help them to understand their confused feelings and fears and express them more directly. How do you do this? Chapter 7 discussed the typical fears, feelings, and reactions most children have. Discuss them with your child and see if you can form hunches together about how he or she is feeling. ("Lots of kids feel angry when their parents divorce, even though they still love their parents. They're upset that they can't live with both their parents anymore, and they think it's really unfair that their life is such a mess. It's really frustrating to them because they can't do anything to change it.") Talks such as this may help your child sort out his or her own feelings and see that they are natural and do not threaten you. If your youngster denies feelings of anger, sadness, anxiety, and so on, don't push it. Keep your discussions centered on the way that most children feel. Discussions such as these are still helpful to your child even if you never get any direct feedback from him or her.
- If you have preschoolers, you may need to encourage them to express their feelings in indirect ways. Even if they could put their feelings and fears into words, sometimes young children's fears are so scary to them that they cannot accept them as their own. However, these little ones often thinly disguise their fears and feelings in the stories they tell, in the pictures they draw, and in their play. For example, preschoolers whose parents are divorcing commonly draw pictures of children who are looking

for their homes and for their parents. They commonly tell stories about disasters occurring to people and about animals or people who are very needy. Five-year-old Jennifer expressed how overwhelmed she felt with a story of a child who was adrift in the ocean and was then swallowed up by a whale. Four-year-old Robbie expressed his fears of abandonment in a story about a baby bear cub that was left in the woods by both its mother and father without the skills to find shelter or food. You can use any seemingly relevant play, story, or drawing as a jumping-off point for talks. Talk about the feelings and fears that *most* little children have rather than ask them to face their own fears head-on. Chapter 7 discussed the fears and feelings that preschoolers commonly have. Be sure to let your youngster know that these feelings are natural. Try to allay his or her fears by correcting the common misconceptions that preschoolers have, which were discussed in Chapter 7. (For example, "Many little children feel that something they did caused their mommy and daddy to get a divorce. But divorces are just between mommies and daddies. Children don't cause them." Or, "Some little children wonder if their daddy (mommy) will come back if they are very good. But little children can't fix a divorce just like they can't cause a divorce." Or, "Some little boys and girls are very afraid that their other parent might go away now too, but. . . ." Or, "Some little children think their daddies (mommies) left because they didn't love them anymore, but. . . .")

- Older children may benefit from expressing their feelings on paper, and this is something you can encourage. Some kids find that this is less threatening than verbalizing their feelings out loud, and they find that it is good therapy too. Angela found it very comforting to write her thoughts in a diary each day. Jimmy wrote many letters to his father who never visited him. Even though he never mailed them, he felt better "telling" his father how he felt. Pauline found that writing poetry was a good release from her sadness. "They are terribly depressing morbid poems," she says, "but I often think this is how I got the sadness out of me."[2]
- Allowing children to talk about their feelings is very important, but if you find that a child is expressing the same feelings *over and over* again, be understanding but try to redirect his or her focus into some interesting activities. Sometimes talking about the situation and feelings can become addictive and after a point can become counterproductive.
- Help children get involved with as many outside activities and people as you can. This will help to get their minds off the divorce and to distance themselves from the turmoil at home. It will also give them things to look forward to and other sources of support.
- There are children's books on divorce listed in Appendix C. Either make them available to or read them with your children. Children sometimes read books over and over again. Each time, they gain a little more un-

derstanding, and each time their own pain becomes a little more tolerable. One preschooler's parents wrote their own book for him. Illustrated with photographs and written in very simple language, it told the story of their meeting, marriage, happiness at the birth of their child, and why they came to the decision to separate. It also related how they would always be his parents and would always love him. The youngster wanted the story read to him every night for years. He read it by himself as well. Even now at the age of 11, he sometimes still finds comfort in reading it.

- You might consider getting a child a pet to love and care for. It could be very therapeutic at this time when your child feels lonely, rejected, and distressed, as it was for eight-year-old Billy.

> Billy was despondent for weeks after his mother left. One day as he left school, he found a stray kitten, which he brought home. "It's what turned him around," his father reported. "He cuddled it, loved it, talked to it, slept with it, trained it, and protected it. It got him interested in life again. Pretty soon, he had some friends over so he could show it to them."

Be careful, however, not to get a pet that will create more havoc in your already-hectic life.

- Enlist the help of family, teachers, and adult friends to provide your children with extra support (more on this in Chapter 10).
- Children benefit from talking things out with a counselor at this time, as did 12-year-old Lisa:

> When Lisa's dad left, she was overcome with anger, hating him and hating the world. She got into fights, let her grades drop, and befriended a wild group of kids. One of her teachers talked with her mother and recommended a counselor for her to talk to. "It really helped a lot," Lisa recalls, "having someone to help me figure out how I was feeling and why I was acting the way I was."

Occasionally parents are reluctant to use a counselor in the early stages of separation, but if you feel that a child's reactions are severe or if one of your children is not showing any improvement month after month, try to get some help for that youngster. Many agencies provide counseling on a sliding fee scale, according to income. Call a local child guidance clinic or family service agency for a referral.

- An effective way to help children cope is to help them rebuild their feelings of self-worth.

REBUILDING CHILDREN'S SELF-ESTEEM

Children's self-esteem generally suffers when parents divorce. Youngsters feel rejected, lonely, and powerless to influence a very critical situation in their lives. Following are ways to rebuild a child's self-esteem.

- Show respect for your child, as well as for his or her feelings and rights.
- Don't let children's accomplishments, contributions, efforts, and good behavior go unnoticed. Take every chance to praise their deeds and show that you appreciate them. ("That was a great job you did." "I liked the way you waited so patiently." "You were such a wonderful help today." "That was such a thoughtful thing you did for Johnny." "Thank you for doing your chores without being asked.")
- Offer encouragement; avoid criticism or put-downs.
- Accentuate your children's positives, not the negatives.
- Children often feel that they are no longer as important to their parents after the divorce, especially as parents begin to create new lives for themselves. Reassure them of your commitment, and show them you are interested in them. Spend time talking with them and learning more about them as individuals. What are their feelings, opinions, interests, dislikes? Spend some time each day with each of your children individually. Your interest and individual attention will make them feel special, worthy, and loved.
- Help youngsters to feel competent and successful in some areas in their lives. Think about the things each does well, and give them plenty of opportunities to do those things.
- Try getting them involved in learning something new that they can take pride in doing well.
- Help children set realistic goals that are mildly challenging but certainly achievable. When you want to increase a challenge, do so in *very* small increments. You want to build their confidence, not discourage them.

Checklist for Building Your Child's Self-Esteem

✓ Show your child respect.
✓ Offer praise, encouragement, and appreciation liberally.
✓ Avoid criticisms and put-downs.
✓ Accentuate your child's positives, not the negatives.
✓ Make a child feel special with your interest and time.
✓ Provide opportunities to do things your child does well.
✓ Encourage learning a new skill in which your child can take pride.
✓ Help your child set realistic goals.
✓ Increase challenges in small, achievable steps.
✓ Avoid taking over when your child is trying something on his or her own.
✓ Assign age-appropriate chores and show appreciation for your youngster's contribution to the family.
✓ Involve your child in helping someone else.
✓ Distinguish between a child and his behavior; the behavior is unacceptable, not the child.
✓ Examine whether your expectations are *realistic*.

- Support your children's efforts to do things for themselves. Often, parents take over for children to get things done quickly or "right." In doing so, they undermine their children's confidence and rob them of feelings of accomplishment. Offer children encouragement and assistance if needed, but don't take over. Few things in this world *must* be done perfectly.
- Assign your children some chores that are appropriate for their ages, and let them know that their contribution is important to the family.
- See if you can involve a child in helping someone else—a teacher at school, a younger child, a grandparent, an elderly neighbor. Helping someone else helps children feel good about themselves.
- When disciplining, make the distinction between your child and his or her behavior. Never say, "You're a bad boy." It is the behavior that is unacceptable, not the child. Better to say, "You're a good boy, but what you did was unacceptable" (not good, bad, or whatever).
- Think about the standards you have for your children. Do you find that you are always communicating that you want them to do better? You may have unreasonably high expectations that your youngsters cannot meet, particularly at this stressful period in their lives. When they can't meet your expectations, they feel negative about themselves and may even give up trying ("What's the use, I'm just not good enough").

We'll turn now to some common reactions children have to parental divorce and how to deal with them.

DEALING WITH CHILDREN'S DENIAL

When David's parents told him of their impending divorce, they were bewildered when his only response was, "Oh, can I go out and skateboard?" David's casual response to his parents' announcement did not reflect his lack of caring. His way of dealing with his pain and distress was denying the reality of the news.

Many children will use some form of denial to ease their distress, just as many adults do when a spouse leaves. Their anxiety is so overwhelming that they block out reality. One child may "forget" about the divorce again and again. A second may adamantly refuse to talk about anything related to the separation. Others, seemingly unaffected, may continue with their lives as if nothing has changed. A young child may fantasize that the parent returns home late at night after the child is asleep. One preschooler, who hadn't seen her father in weeks, smilingly told a researcher that he slept in her bed every night. Each finds a way to delay facing the reality of his or her family's rupture because once it is acknowledged, each will have to experience the inevitable pain.

Many parents unwittingly encourage their child's use of denial because they would just as soon not talk about the absent spouse or the separation. They often tell others that "she's taking it so well" or that "he's not fazed a bit." What should you do if your child is using denial?

Try some of the following suggestions, but *go easy* and don't push.

- Talk realistically about the divorce during the course of natural conversation. Mention how life has changed, not only in major ways but in any number of minor ways (an empty place at dinner, less elaborate meals, sadder and less talkative family members, lonelier evenings, quieter without the fighting, new chores that need to be done now that Dad (Mom) isn't here, different T.V. station tuned in, and so forth).
- Gently encourage your child to talk about the divorce and how he or she feels, but don't push if the child resists. Give it time. The children's books on divorce listed in Appendix C may be helpful.
- Share *some* of your own feelings and tears. In this way you can demonstrate how feelings can be expressed and that it is okay to do so. A child is more likely to open up eventually if you are open. But be careful here. Don't overwhelm your youngster with your sorrow, problems, or uncontrollable crying, or an already stressful situation will become worse.
- Provide plenty of reassurances of your love, spend extra time with your youngster, and encourage the other parent to do so too. These will help to relieve your child's underlying fears of losing either of you.

WHAT ABOUT WITHDRAWAL?

Children in a divorcing family commonly lose their lust for life and often withdraw from their normal activities and friends. Many stay close to home. Most are moody, worried, and disheartened. Usually they spend a good deal of time and emotional energy thinking about their absent parent. Their teachers describe them as inattentive, restless, irritable, and preoccupied. Very young children may withdraw into fantasy. These various forms of withdrawal reflect the intense sadness, anxiety, and grief children usually feel when parents separate.

Your children's sadness and withdrawal are likely to continue for some time. The California Children of Divorce Study found that children generally were unable to resume their usual level of involvement with any kind of enthusiasm as long as home problems dominated their concerns. The younger children are, the more difficult it is to distance themselves from what is happening at home. Most families, you may remember from Chapter 7, are in a state of flux and chaos during the first year after separation, and sometimes longer. Children in the California study generally resumed their previous involvements and enthusiasms within this same time frame—usually sometime within the first year after their parents' separation.

What can you do to help your children?

- Realize that they need time to mourn their losses, just as adults do. They have many losses, too—their family, continual contact with a parent, and life as they know it. Give them extra doses of love, support, and sensitivity. Let them talk about their feelings, and don't try to minimize their pain by telling them not to cry, not to think about it, or that everything is okay. Instead, accept their feelings ("I know you're feeling very sad"). They need the freedom to talk. Young children will work out a lot of their grief through play. Allow them lots of playtime and the freedom to be creative.
- Work on creating stability in their home life so they feel safe in their new family situation (Chapter 10 provides specific guidelines).
- Although your children need time to grieve, don't let them skip school because they are upset. School will help distance them from home problems and will impose some external order and stability on their lives. Encourage them to continue in their normal activities as well, even if their participation is halfhearted.

HELPING CHILDREN WITH THEIR ANGER

Anger is fairly common and normal in children whose parents are divorcing. Youngsters generally feel as if their lives are in a shambles, yet they are powerless to stop the painful events that are happening to them. To make matters worse, their pain is being caused by a voluntary decision on the part of one or both parents. It seems so unfair to them. "After all," they say, "this is my life too!" The most intense anger is likely to be expressed by older children (age nine and over), and it is most often directed at one or both parents, usually whomever they blame for the divorce.

Not all children, even older ones, express their anger openly and directly. Some aren't even aware that anger is part of their confused feelings. Some who are aware of their anger hide it, either because they feel guilty about it or because they worry that it will further damage relationships with their parents, which already seem tenuous after one parent has left. Others *act out* their anger. Anger can be acted out in any number of ways: noncompliance, temper tantrums, a drop in school grades, rebelliousness, destructive behavior, bullying, fighting, drinking, taking drugs, or sexual promiscuity.

Some children are found to harbor their anger for many years. When they do, it can alienate them from their parents and prevent them from putting the divorce behind them. However—and this is very important because it is one of the keys to dealing with your child's anger—the intensity of children's anger has been found to diminish when parents are able to show them understanding. How, specifically, can you show your children understanding and help them deal with their anger?

- Once again, help them talk about their anger without trying to talk them out of it or minimizing the intensity of their feelings. Be empathetic and let them know their anger is natural. ("You seem to be very angry. I can understand why. This divorce business must be pretty rough on you. Most children are pretty angry when their parents divorce.") Children are usually relieved and grateful when they feel that parents are "with them."
- As children talk about their feelings, you may discover ways to relieve some of their anger. It may turn out that it is not only the divorce that they are angry about. They may be angry because you are too preoccupied to spend time with them, you are overburdening them with new responsibilities, they resent not seeing friends from their former school, or they do not see their absent parent enough. Knowing this, you can take steps together to change some of these situations. Now, instead of their anger compounding, some of it will dissipate. They can learn a very valuable lesson too: When anger is talked about, solutions can often be found for the problems that caused it.
- Be more tolerant of children's angry outbursts than you might ordinarily be. Does this mean you have to stand by and allow your child to swear at you, punch a younger sibling, or break your favorite glassware? Absolutely not. You need to make the distinction with children between *feelings* and *behavior*. Children can't choose or control the emotions and feelings that well up inside them. Whatever their feelings, they are not bad, and children should not be ashamed of them. How they *express* those feelings, on the other hand, is another matter. In most cases children *can* control their behavior, and they need to know that some behavior is not acceptable. Children both need and want some limits placed on them.
- Help them find acceptable outlets for their anger (in addition to talking about their feelings). Experiment to see what works for them. Some children find it helpful to act out their feelings through drawing, working with clay, or finger painting. Some find that being alone and listening to music or taking a warm bath helps dissipate their anger. Usually vigorous physical activity or sports (running, climbing, throwing balls, hammering, chopping wood) is a good release for anger. Sixteen-year-old Barry recalls how he responded to his parents' divorce decision three years earlier:

> It took maybe a week to settle in. After that I had very destructive feelings. I wanted to hurt somebody and I guess I had to get out my aggressions by physical labor. I joined cross-country running and just ran my guts out.[3]

WHAT TO DO ABOUT TROUBLESOME BEHAVIOR PROBLEMS

Of all the behavior changes children show after parental separation and divorce, perhaps the most alarming to parents are the serious and chronic behavior problems their children (particularly boys) so often develop. Many youngsters become disobedient, rebellious, impulsive, and aggressive (bullying, hitting, destroying things, and so forth). Some older children turn to delinquent activities or precocious sexual activity.

It appears that several circumstances contribute to this very problematic behavior. The first is the culprit we just spoke of—children's intense anger. Behavior problems are a way that children act out their anger. The second is the poor discipline and lax rules typical in so many families for at least the first year or two after separation and divorce. The third is the open conflict that many parents engage in with each other. During these battles, parents unwittingly display angry, hostile, and uncooperative behavior that children too easily adopt.

Why are boys more likely to develop behavior problems? You may recall from Chapter 7 that parents battle more frequently in the presence of sons than daughters, which may help to explain boys' aggressive behavior. Boys also generally adjust to divorce slower than girls, and boys develop more emotional, social, and academic problems in the process. At the same time, boys generally receive less nurturance, support, and sensitivity from parents, teachers, and peers. It is no wonder they have more problematic behavior.

These troublesome behavior problems need timely parental response. Here are steps you can take to reduce them.

- Because a major cause of behavior problems is children's anger, follow the guidelines suggested on page 123 for dealing with anger.
- Help children see why they are acting as they are. ("Lots of kids feel angry when their parents divorce and start to feel angry at the whole world. Sometimes they take their anger out on other people and things, like fighting with people and kicking the dog.")
- Distinguish between *feelings* and *behavior*. Their feelings are okay. Acting out those feelings in destructive ways is not okay.
- Provide them with clear expectations and limits for their behavior. Clearly defined rules and limits are particularly important during divorce because children have a more difficult time exercising self-control during times of stress. Rules and limits provide them with external controls to compensate for their lapses in self-control.
- Be clear about the consequences that will follow when rules and limits are ignored. Do *not* use physical punishment. To do so is modeling aggressive behavior for children; you are teaching them that it is okay to hit people when we get angry. This is exactly what you do *not* want to teach a child who is already behaving aggressively! Effective discipline is discussed in Chapter 16. The effort you put forth to set and enforce limits will be well worth your while; life will become much easier for both of you.
- Give them some coping tools. Teach them to remove themselves from the situation, if they can, when they feel themselves losing control (leave peers and play by themselves, go to their rooms, watch TV, and so on). Also

---

Checklist for Handling Children's Behavior Problems

✓ Help children talk about their feelings, accept them and be understanding.
✓ Can you relieve some of their anger at its source?
✓ Help them to see *why* they are behaving as they are.
✓ Distinguish between feelings (okay) and acting out those feelings in destructive behavior (not okay).
✓ Set clearly defined rules and limits for behavior.
✓ Consistently enforce consequences if rules are broken (do not use physical punishment).
✓ Teach children to remove themselves from the situation when losing control.
✓ Help them find acceptable outlets for their anger.
✓ End conflict with your spouse in your child's presence.
✓ Be supportive; reassure children of your love, and work on building their self-esteem.
✓ Realize that behavior problems are symptoms of children's pain and distress.
✓ Remember boys' special difficulties with parental divorce.

---

help them find an acceptable outlet for their intense feelings, as discussed in the section on anger.

- Make every effort to end open conflict with your ex, at least in front of your children. Could this conflict *really* contribute to your child's problematic behavior, you wonder? Absolutely! In fact, psychologist William Hodges of the University of Colorado reports that children's behavior problems are often *eliminated* once their parents reduce their conflict with one another. Steps you can take to reduce conflict with your former spouse are discussed in Chapter 11.

- Be very supportive of your children. Reassure them of your love, provide them with opportunities to feel good about themselves, and work on building their self-esteem. Keep in mind that as aversive as problem behavior is to you, it is a symptom of a child's divorce-related pain and distress. Finally, try to remember the special difficulties boys have with parental divorce. It is natural to respond to your son's aggressiveness and rebelliousness with anger and withdrawal of your love. But your son needs just the opposite—sensitivity, understanding, extra time spent with him, and *reassurance* of your love.

HOW TO HANDLE IMMATURE BEHAVIOR

Parents of young children (primarily preschoolers) usually find their youngsters regressing to inappropriately immature behavior, such as bed wetting, whining, clinging, thumb sucking, masturbation, temper tantrums, and relying on security blankets. Generally, these regressions to earlier behavior are transient and last several weeks or months, although they can last longer if the home situation continues in a state of crisis. How are regressions to earlier behavior best handled?

The first step, of course, is dealing with their cause. Give your preschooler plenty of sensitivity, warmth, love, and reassurance. Should you overindulge very young children because of the stress they are under? Many divorcing parents take this approach, making no demands on little ones and enforcing no limits. Contrary to parents' instincts, well-known child psychologist E. Mavis Hetherington of the University of Virginia reports that preschoolers adjust better when parents make appropriate maturity demands of them. Parents should do this lovingly but firmly. Very young children, especially, have difficulty with self-control during times of stress, and they *need* external controls placed on them.

It will really help your young child if his or her life, both at home and at school, is very structured with regular and predictable routines—regular time with their nonresident parent, consistent sitters, regular school attendance, and a consistent schedule from day to day (meals, snacks, naps, bedtime, and so forth). When young children are under stress, they generally function much better in highly structured, organized, and predictable environments.

How do you deal with temper tantrums? *Ignore them.* It is difficult, but it is the only way to stop them with a young child. Giving in, sweet-talking, bribing, yelling, or spanking are usually highly ineffective strategies in the long run. Each is a different way of giving youngsters attention, and each will encourage future attention-getting tantrums. Give kids attention when they are behaving, not when they are misbehaving.

Helping your children through the crisis of your divorce will pave the way for their long-term adjustment and make it more likely, but will not guarantee it. The following chapter discusses specific postdivorce conditions that are so critical that they sometimes overshadow what happens at the time of divorce.

CHILDREN'S LONG-TERM ADJUSTMENT: What Is Critical?

*H*ow your children adjust in the months following separation and divorce will set the stage for the future, but it will not firmly forecast their eventual divorce adjustment. In the well-known California Children of Divorce Study, about one-third of the children who adjusted well at first developed problems after a lapse of time. Some youngsters who had serious initial difficulties showed marked improvement over time. Of the children who were doing moderately well initially, some were doing very well and others very poorly five years later.

You may wonder how much children's eventual adjustment is determined by their adjustment before the divorce or by some inner qualities, such as temperament or resourcefulness. These certainly play a role. However, studies find that they are only a part of the complete picture.

We now know that youngsters' *long-term* divorce adjustment is influenced not only by their inner strength, by how well parents prepare them, or by how well they cope in the early postdivorce months, but also by the circumstances they encounter in the years *following* divorce. We've learned that the long-term problems children sometimes develop are not caused by the divorce itself but by events set into motion by the divorce. Because of a large-scale research effort across the country, researchers have been able to identify a number of conditions following divorce that prove to be so critical for children that they may even overshadow what occurred at the time of divorce or immediately afterward.

You and your children can now benefit from this research, and with it, you can engineer these critical conditions to be favorable for your children. The quicker you do so, the better, and Chapter 10 will give you specific help in doing it. All these critical conditions will not be in your control, so you will not be able to create completely favorable circumstances for your kids. However, you can compensate by working harder at those you can control. Let's take a look at these conditions after divorce that will be so important to your children's long-term adjustment.

AMOUNT OF CONFLICT BETWEEN PARENTS

Perhaps one of the most startling discoveries divorce researchers have learned is the devastating consequences that prolonged parental conflict can have for children. Most children can cope well with short-term conflict. However, children who are exposed to long-term parental conflict are more likely to be emotionally troubled children with problems such as depression, withdrawal, poor self-esteem, poor grades, aggressiveness, rebelliousness, or delinquency. A study conducted by researchers at New York University Medical Center found that the negative effects of prolonged parental conflict continue into adulthood. This very ambitious study, known as the New York Longitudinal Study, tracked the same group of children from infancy to young adulthood. It found that the more parental conflict children had experienced during childhood, the poorer their adjustment in young adulthood.

Research findings on the effects of prolonged conflict are so damning that most experts now agree that it is preferable for children to live in a conflict-free single-parent home than in a conflict-ridden two-parent home.

Unfortunately for many children, however, their parents' conflict does not end with their divorce. Judith Wallerstein and Joan Kelly found that nearly one-third of the children in their study group were still exposed to intense parental bitterness five years after the divorce. For these children, not only was their parents' marriage a failure, but so was their divorce. Escaping from parental conflict is one of the few benefits children can derive from their family's rupture. But when the battles continue, report Wallerstein and Kelly, children are bewildered and angry and can't begin to justify the suffering they've experienced.

One of the most frequent subjects of parental fights is when and where nonresident parents will see children. Unfortunately, battles over this topic, as well as over other child-related issues (custody, child rearing, child-related expenses) are more detrimental to children than fights over other issues. The reason is probably that children feel directly responsible for the conflict.

Parents' bickering and fighting are not the only forms of conflict children experience after divorce. Without realizing it, many parents create an environment in which their children routinely feel torn apart by conflicting loyalties. Here are some examples.

- Placing children "in the middle." ("Make sure you get the child-support check before you come home.")
- Enlisting children as "spies" or pumping them for information. ("So tell me about your mother's new boyfriend.")
- Bad-mouthing the other parent in front of youngsters. ("I see your father's still as shiftless and irresponsible as ever.")
- Needling, belittling, or openly insulting the other parent in the child's

presence. ("If you weren't involved in all those crazy women's lib groups, you might have time to better yourself so you could find a decent job.")
- Pressuring children (even subtly) either to take sides or to form an alliance with one parent against the other. The result of such subtle pressure is wistfully remembered by this 25-year-old woman, whose parents divorced when she was 13:

> I wanted to see my father, but pretended not to because of loyalty to my mother. I knew how she felt and I didn't want to hurt her.[1]

Most children want a relationship with both parents and have a very difficult time when they must deal with conflicting loyalties. No matter what they do, they feel guilty and torn. They want to be fair to both, but how? Any move toward one parent is a move away from the other. And if you try to remain neutral, then both are hurt. It's a lose-lose situation for kids. One 17-year-old boy compared his parents' conflict to a spider's web that ensnares you. A 12-year-old said he felt like a tug-of-war rope being yanked at both ends. A 10-year-old said she felt split down the middle. One 14-year-old described feeling like a rubber band being stretched so hard it was about to snap.

CHILDREN'S RELATIONSHIPS WITH *BOTH* PARENTS

A reliable and good relationship with both mother and father plays an important role in how successfully children adjust to their parents' divorce. Close and reliable relationships with both parents provide a child with most of the emotional benefits an intact family can provide and significantly softens the impact of divorce.

If you have read Chapter 7, this finding may not surprise you because you have already become very attuned to the critical role that parents play in their children's lives. But what may surprise you is a look at the typical child years after divorce. In a large national study of children from disrupted families, University of Pennsylvania sociologist Frank Furstenberg and his research team found that only 17 percent of the parents without custody saw their children on the average of at least once a week. Even more surprising is that 49 percent of the children had not even *seen* their parent without custody during the preceding *year*. These are not anomalous findings. A number of other studies have reported that fathers without custody become less available to their children as time goes on. Even many fathers who had good relationships with their children withdraw from them after divorce. (Mothers without custody tend to see their children far more regularly.)

Though it may be tempting to place the blame for the limited contact fathers have with their children entirely on fathers' shoulders, studies find that the situation is more complex. Following divorce, the majority of fathers are found to miss their children intensely. Even many previously uninvolved fathers are troubled with feelings of loss and feeling "shut out." Then why don't more dads stay involved?

Keeping involved in children's lives is easier said than done. Parents without custody find themselves in a new role that is ill-defined and complicated by restrictions on time and flexibility. In fact, the term "visitation" highlights the inherent artificiality of this new and strange situation. Fathers and children often find it difficult to pick up their relationship where they left off when they lived with one another. They often report having the awkward feeling of not knowing what to say, how to act, what to do, or where to go during their allotted "visitation" time. Many find that their time together is simply too short to ever get in sync with each other. There just isn't any time for things to happen naturally. Limited "visitation" is not conducive to meaningful communication or relationships. Instead, it is conducive to fathers becoming peripheral players in their children's lives and relegating children to a peripheral part of their lives. Problems are compounded when moms with custody make it difficult for their ex-husbands to see their children, which is not an uncommon occurrence.

Although it certainly is not the explanation for *all* noncustody parents who drop out of their children's lives, studies find that a significant percentage *do* drop out in frustration, often experiencing depression and a sense of loss afterward. We now know that the relationship between children and their noncustody parent is a fragile one after divorce, placed at risk by the constraints and artificiality of visitation. Experts agree that this relationship needs all the support and encouragement it can get from the parent with custody to help it survive. And it *can* survive. In fact, some fathers who were poor fathers during the marriage develop very good relationships with their children after divorce!

If the relationship does not survive, however, children are the losers. A parent's abandonment is a trauma from which many children do not easily recover. The California Children of Divorce Study dramatically demonstrated the plight of children whose noncustody fathers were indifferent. Even after five years, many of these children still felt anguished, rejected, and depressed. They felt both unloved and unlovable, and they had low self-esteem. Some children are troubled with feelings of loss, rejection, and abandonment throughout their childhoods. Some are angered over their parents' abandonment and act out their anger in behavior problems such as noncompliance, aggressiveness, rebelliousness, or drug abuse.

A good relationship with the parent who has primary custody is even more critical to children's adjustment because of the amount of time they spend together. This relationship is found to be a key to good adjustment for children at all ages, and for younger children, it is vital. A close relationship with a resident parent who is nurturant, supportive, and dependable can go a long way in compensating for an indifferent noncustody parent. It can also buffer children from a good deal of divorce-related stress.

What are the ingredients of a good relationship? British researcher Yvette Walczak asked this question of young people who were doing exceptionally well many years after their parents' divorce. According to them, parents with custody should have the following qualities:

- Be loving and enjoy their children rather than feel burdened by them.
- Be reliable and predictable.
- Have appropriate expectations for their children, expecting them neither to behave as grown-ups nor to be substitutes for a former spouse or for adult friends.
- Appear able to cope with problems and turn to other adults rather than to children when they cannot cope.
- Be detached from their children's relationship with their other parent, neither trying to influence their children's feelings for the other parent nor making it difficult to see their other parent.

THE QUALITY OF PARENTING AND STABILITY IN THE PRIMARY HOME

Parents with custody or who share custody somewhat equally play a powerful role in influencing children's divorce adjustment. Not only are their relationships with children critically important, but so are their parenting skills.

Unfortunately, studies find that most children are parented poorly during the first year after separation and often longer. Children generally receive less attention, less affection, less support, poor communication, and erratic discipline during this time. Most postdivorce homes are in a state of chaos, and children are frequently the target of parents' angry outbursts. Children who are already overwhelmed by their family's rupture feel devastated by the lack of support they receive just at the time they need it so much.

Youngsters anxiously look to their resident parent to see if he or she will be able to take control of the crisis and chaos that have taken over their lives. That parent's ability to function effectively, independent of the other parent, is usually an unknown. When youngsters perceive that the parent has little control over his or her own world, children's anxiety and distress escalate still further. Youngsters can't get back on their feet while their home lives are unduly troublesome and their futures precarious. A resident parent's poor adjustment usually forecasts children's poor adjustment.

The quicker that resident parents begin to get their own lives together, create some stability for the family, and resume good parenting practices, the quicker children are able to get back on their feet. Much of this book is devoted to helping resident parents do just that.

But a word of caution here. Parents with custody are sometimes advised that if they focus on their own adjustment, their children's will automatically follow. This is not necessarily the case. A good example was provided in a well-known University of Virginia study conducted by E. Mavis Hetherington and her research team. These researchers found a number of women who adjusted to divorce exceptionally well. Within a year, they preferred their new lives; were very involved with work, social life, and community activities; and felt self-fulfilled. However, their children's emotional problems were among the *worst* found by the researchers! Why? It turned out that these parents were so involved with their own lives that they had little time left for their children. In the brief time they spent together, the parents were hurried, preoccupied, emotionally distant, and unresponsive to their kids' needs and distress. Parents had achieved their own divorce adjustment but had done nothing for their children's adjustment. Other studies, conducted at Virginia Commonwealth University by psychologist Arnold Stolberg and his research team, confirmed that a parent's good adjustment does not benefit children *unless* that good adjustment increases the parent's availability to children and leads to good parenting practices.

Just what is "good parenting," you ask? Several researchers have been able to identify parenting practices that help children adjust better both to the immediate crisis of divorce and to life in a single-parent home. These are as follows:

- Parental warmth, sensitivity, nurturance, support, and availability
- Open communication between parents and children in which there is a good deal of give and take on both sides
- Clearly defined rules and limits
- Consistent discipline
- Well-organized and maintained routines (because they offer stability and predictability at an otherwise unstable time)
- Allowing children to function as children rather than burdening them with adult roles, problems, and responsibilities

AMOUNT OF ADDITIONAL STRESS IN CHILDREN'S LIVES

How much stress children experience during the years following divorce is another major contributor to their eventual divorce adjustment. Virtually all youngsters find their parents' divorces highly stressful. But ground breaking research in the field of stress has demonstrated that children can usually overcome a *single* source of stress, such as their parents' divorce, quite well. However, if the divorce is compounded by other sources of stress, the risk of long-term problems multiplies. Each additional source of stress compounds youngsters' already-difficult task of reconstructing their lives. A good analogy would be a person receiving a second punch while still dazed and weakened from the first. Although the second punch may not have been very hard, it makes his recovery more difficult. If a third punch immediately follows, it may very well do him in. After all, how much can he take?

What would be considered additional sources of stress? Several have already been discussed: poor parent-child relationships, parental conflict, and poor parenting. When experienced for prolonged periods, each compounds the stress children already feel from the divorce itself. Two other sources of stress are also likely to have an impact on children's adjustment.

The first is numerous other changes in children's lives while they are trying to cope with the divorce. A series of studies also conducted by Stolberg and his colleagues found that the more changes children experience during the post-divorce period, the more likely they are to develop problems such as depression, social withdrawal, low self-esteem, and aggressiveness. Having to cope with many other changes at the same time they are trying to cope with the divorce itself causes children to believe they, as well as their parents, have little control over their world.

Markedly reduced economic resources that leave the new family in financial duress are also likely to take a toll on youngsters' long-term adjustment. You may recall from Chapter 1 that the standard of living for mothers and children usually declines markedly after divorce while that for fathers rises, a situation made worse when child support payments are not made. Some children suddenly find themselves in low-cost housing and going to inferior schools. Some live under a cloud of anxiety about their daily financial survival. Even many who are able to remain in their middle class neighborhoods *perceive* their economic situation as tenuous due to the marked discrepancy between their pre- and postdivorce standard of living, made more evident by the relative affluence of their communities. Sometimes economics becomes a pervasive and long-term source of family conflict and bitterness when fathers live in luxury, in sharp contrast to their struggling families. This was the case in nine-year-old Jeremy's family.

> Every time Jeremy goes to his dad's, his mom packs his old and torn clothes, telling him that his dad is so rich, he should be buying the clothes instead of her. Yet, Jeremy reports, when his dad does buy things, his mother accuses him of playing big shot, buying things that she can't afford. "When you think of it," Jeremy says reflectively, "Mom's right—it's really not fair." Jeremy goes on to talk about the big house and expensive cars that his dad and stepmother have while his mom has to "work her tail off" just to make ends meet. "If Dad really loved us," he wonders, "wouldn't he help out more? Doesn't he see the difference in the way he lives and the way we live?" Jeremy confides that his older brothers are really angry about the money situation, saying it "stinks" the way their dad gets to live and the way they have to live.

Checklist for Guiding Your Children's Long-Term Divorce Adjustment

✓ Am I building *good* relationships with my children?
✓ Am I supporting my child's relationship with my ex-spouse?
✓ Have we stopped our conflict when our child is within earshot?
✓ Am I refraining from:
   • Bad-mouthing my children's other parent?
   • Putting my children in the middle?
   • Pumping them for information about their other parent?
   • Subtly pressuring them to side with me?
✓ Am I returning stability to our home and following routines?
✓ Am I being warm, supportive, and available?
✓ Do my children and I communicate openly?
✓ Am I providing clear rules and consistent discipline?
✓ Am I keeping as many details of their lives the same as I can?
✓ Do I avoid burdening them with adult responsibilities, roles, and worries?
✓ Do I avoid making our reduced financial resources an issue of bitterness and resentment?
✓ Am I making my child support payments to minimize financial problems for my children (for noncustody parents)?
✓ Am I seeking out sources of social support for my children?

If your standard of living *has* markedly decreased, don't assume that your children have automatically been sentenced to a fate of long-term problems. Apparently, close, loving relationships between the resident parent and children can buffer youngsters from a good deal of the stress caused by reduced economic resources. Not surprisingly, however, family economics *are* likely to have negative repercussions for children when a parent is so busy trying to survive financially that children are neglected and poorly parented or when the lack of money becomes a focal point of conflict, bitterness, and resentment in the family.

SOCIAL SUPPORT

Frequent contact with supportive adults outside the family (grandparents, teachers, parents of friends,' therapists, and so on) can be an invaluable asset for children when they are in stressful circumstances. Kids need extra doses of time, support, sensitivity, and understanding during the lengthy period of upheaval after separation and divorce. But because parents themselves are distressed and depressed, they are seldom able to satisfy these extra needs. Outside supportive adults can fill in for parents and provide supplementary support and understanding. These supportive relationships can buffer children from some of the negative impact of the stress in their lives.

Social support is important to children not only at the time of divorce. Even after parents are back on their feet, they are sometimes so stressed from single-handedly juggling the mechanics of home, work, kids, and a social life that youngsters still don't receive the nurturance they need. Continued good relationships with supportive adults plays a role in children's immediate and long-term divorce adjustment.

IS ONE TYPE OF CUSTODY BETTER THAN ANOTHER?

You are undoubtedly wondering whether one form of custody is better for your children's long-term divorce adjustment than another. For those who are unfamiliar with different forms of custody, I'll explain them briefly before looking at their benefits or shortcomings.

The two most common forms of custody in this country are joint custody and sole custody. When thinking about custody, most people think of *physical* custody—that is, where the children will live. The courts, however, distinguish between physical custody and legal custody.

Legal custody refers to who has the right to make the important decisions about children's upbringing, religious training, education, medical care, and so forth. When there is sole legal custody, one parent has the autonomy to make all decisions without input from the other. Gaining in popularity is joint legal custody, in which both parents share in important decisions, rights, and responsibilities for the children.

Physical custody can also be sole or joint. In joint physical custody, children divide their time between two homes. How time is divided is up to the individual family. Children in joint custody split their days, weeks, months, or sometimes even years between their parents' homes. In rare cases, children remain in the family home and parents take turns living with them in the home. Joint custody does not mean that children have to divide their time evenly between parents, and in fact they rarely do. In practice, joint custody frequently resembles sole custody with liberal visitation, with most time spent with the mother. How finances are divided when custody is joint also varies. For example, when children divide their time fairly evenly, couples often provide for their children while youngsters are with them and share major expenses in some way, such as proportional to their incomes.

In sole physical custody, a child lives with one parent and the other has "visitation"; its specifics are often determined by parents themselves, sometimes by a judge. There is another form of custody—split custody, which is less common. In this case, parents *each* have custody of one or more of their children. The reluctance of parents to separate siblings accounts for the relative infrequency of this option. Regardless of the type of custody arrangement, there is unanimous agreement among experts that both parents should keep a strong psychological presence in their children's lives.

Is one form of custody better than another? Although this is becoming a popular subject for study, there seems to be no simple answer. Deborah Luepnitz, a clinical psychologist at the Philadelphia Child Guidance Clinic and a researcher in the custody area, concluded that joint custody *at its best* is better than sole custody at its best. Joint custody maximizes the opportunities for children to continue relationships with both their parents, which is important to children's well-being. And joint-custody parents return to court less frequently over child support, visitation, and requests for custody change than do sole-custody families. But how well joint physical custody works depends on the actual parenting schedule, the age of the children and how adaptable they are, how well parents protect children from their conflict, how close parents live to each other, and how well children can maintain normal school activities and social lives despite having two homes.

Studies generally report that the majority of children seem able to switch homes and lives without too much difficulty, and many have high self-esteem as a result of parents' determination to keep involved in their lives, despite the hassles involved. Some children, however, become anxious and confused. *Frequent* transitions or changeovers between homes (for example, every other day) seem to be particularly difficult and should be avoided. Each changeover causes a disruption in children's lives and requires a number of adjustments. Splitting their time between two homes is likely to pose problems for very young children who have a strong need for stability and a poor grasp of time. Teens also frequently prefer to have a single home base because of busy social lives. (See Arranging Parenting Schedules to Meet Your Children's Developmental Needs in Chapter 10.)

The biggest problem with joint custody, however, occurs when parents are in severe conflict with each other. Joint custody places youngsters right in the middle of the battlefield. A good example was provided by a recent study of high conflict families, which was conducted at the Center for the Family in Transition in Corte Madera, California, by psychologist Janet Johnston and her research team. When children of these highly conflictive parents were in joint custody arrangements, the youngsters were more withdrawn, depressed, aggressive, or otherwise disturbed than were their counterparts living in sole-custody arrangements. At the risk of being overly repetitive, I stress again that it is *critical* for children's well-being that parents minimize their conflict. If they cannot, they at least need to protect their children from it. Chapter 11 is devoted to measures you can take to do this.

To date, the evidence suggests, and most experts on custody agree, that it is not so much the type of custody that is important. Rather, it is the absence of parental conflict and the quality of children's relationships with *both* parents that are important to children's well-being. If custody is sole, it is important that the noncustody parent and children have a good deal of time together to develop and nurture their relationships with one another and that the parent with custody encourages and supports those relationships. Often alternate weekends or one day each weekend is insufficient time to nurture quality relationships. Ideally, noncustody parents should have some extended time with their children and become involved in their school lives. Some noncustody parents and their children find it works well to extend their usual alternate weekends to include Thursday evening and/or Monday morning and to have a midweek contact as well during the intervening week.

Now that you know the circumstances after divorce that are so important for your children's long-term well-being, you are left with the job of making those conditions a reality for them. The following chapter will help you. It is a step-by-step guide to help you create the kinds of conditions that will enable your children to thrive.

10

FOSTERING CHILDREN'S LONG-TERM ADJUSTMENT: A Step-By-Step Guide

*T*here is convincing evidence that, with effort, parents can create conditions that allow children to come through divorce unharmed. Chapter 8 focused on how to help your youngster through the crisis and set the stage for his or her divorce adjustment. It also discussed how to handle problems that commonly arise. Chapter 9 focused on the long-term picture and identified a number of conditions that play a powerful role in children's *long-term* divorce adjustment—whether children will bounce back and get on with their childhoods, be left with lasting problems, or develop delayed problems.

If you read these chapters, you know what your children *need*. However, as you well know, there is sometimes a large gap between knowing what you *should* do and knowing *how* to go about doing it. How do you get your children to talk openly with you? How can you create a stable home environment for them when the entire family's world is upside-down? How do you stop your conflict with your ex when you are both so angry? How can you limit the amount of stress and change in your children's lives when divorce, by its very nature, inevitably causes so much of both? These may seem to be pretty tall orders. But perhaps not. This chapter will develop specific steps you can take to create the kinds of postdivorce conditions that enable kids to bounce back from divorce. Notably missing from this chapter is a guide to ending your conflict with your former spouse. Ending conflict is so critical to your children's long-term adjustment that it warrants a separate chapter, which follows.

Of course, your child's environment after divorce will not be completely in your control. But *every* condition discussed in Chapter 9 does not have to be ideal for your child to adjust well. You can compensate for those beyond your control by working harder at those you *can* control. If you are a custodial or shared-custody parent, you play a critical role in your youngster's postdivorce adjustment. If you are a noncustody parent, your role is far more important than you might imagine; Chapters 18 and 19 are geared specifically to your role and your problems.

If it is already several years after your divorce and your youngster's adjustment is not going well, it is never too late to turn things around. But it will take effort, and the quicker you begin, the better. Don't skip Chapters 8 and 9. Much of their information can be important to you.

BUILDING GOOD RELATIONSHIPS WITH YOUR CHILDREN

The quality of the relationships children have with their mothers and fathers after divorce is a powerful determinant of whether youngsters adjust well to their family's rupture. With close relationships with both parents, children can have most of the benefits and security that an intact family could provide.

Although good relationships with parents are important to all children, they are more important for children of divorce. This is because nurturant and dependable relationships with parents act as a sort of cushion for children that softens the blows inflicted by stress. Children with a poor relationship with one or both parents are more vulnerable to the stress of divorce and its aftermath. A child's relationship with the parent with primary custody is particularly important.

However, because parents are so involved with their own crises at the time of divorce and with rebuilding their lives in the following years, their relationships with their children frequently deteriorate. Make your relationships with your children a high priority. It is critical to their well-being. Here are some suggestions that will help you build them.

- Set time aside every day that your children are with you to spend time with them individually. It doesn't have to be long, it just needs to be consistent. Do something with each child that you both enjoy—talking about your respective days, reading a book together, playing a game, working on a school project, and so forth. You can't possibly find the time, you say? Then enlist a child's help to do a chore with you (making dinner, doing dishes, etc.), and use this time to talk.
- Show your children empathy; let them know you understand their pain and struggles. When children feel that a parent understands them, they become closer to that parent.
- Show children respect and have respect for their feelings and personal rights. Mutual respect is the foundation of a good relationship.
- Give youngsters plenty of reassurance that you love them. Let them know how important they are to you and that they will always be an important part of your life, no matter what the future brings.

- Show an interest in their activities, friends, school lives, and current interests.
- Don't erect barriers to make it more difficult for them to spend time with their other parent. Don't make them feel guilty about loving their other parent, and don't bad-mouth their other parent in their presence. They are likely to resent you for it.
- Reach out to other people. Studies report that single parents who have social support generally relate better with their children and are closer to them.
- Create an atmosphere in which children can openly communicate with you, and make good communication a high priority. Good communication around the time of divorce is important. It can draw parents and children closer together, even when relationships had been poor previously.
- If you are a noncustody parent, you have special challenges in building a good relationship with your child. Specific steps you can take to build your relationship despite the limited time you have together are discussed in Chapter 18.

HOW TO CREATE AN ATMOSPHERE OF OPEN COMMUNICATION

Open communication is important not only during the crisis of divorce; it needs to be an ongoing concern for a number of years. This is because children's understanding of people and relationships matures with time, and with this maturity comes new questions and concerns that would not have occurred to them at a younger age. A five-year-old might be satisfied with the explanation that Mommy and Daddy don't love each other anymore, but at eight, he or she might want to know why they stopped loving each other. At this point the child might be satisfied with a simple answer to that question, but as a teen, he or she is likely to want to explore what happened in greater depth.

There are some concrete steps you can take to open up the lines of communication in your home. Don't try to tackle all of them at once. Try working on a few at a time.

- The first step to good communication is good listening. *Really listen* to your child; don't just act like you're listening. Resist distractions, ask questions, and give feedback ("I see." "Go on." "What else?"). Paraphrase what your youngster has said in your own words.
- Try putting yourself in your child's place so you can understand the feelings that lie *beneath* the words. Then reflect these feelings back ("You seem to feel really scared about what's going to happen."). This will not only

confirm how accurate your perceptions are, but it will show that you understand. It will also encourage your child to *continue* talking.

- Tune into any questions that are divorce-related. This is your time to remind youngsters that you are always willing to answer their questions and talk about their concerns. Make every effort to answer their questions patiently, straightforwardly, and honestly. When you are curt, dishonest, or evasive, you help to break down the lines of communication. If a child asks a very personal question that is inappropriate to answer, say straightforwardly that it is too personal to discuss.

- Permit your children to have their own feelings, thoughts, and opinions. When they express them, be accepting ("It sounds as if you're pretty angry."). Do not be judgmental or defensive ("There's no reason to feel that way." "Don't be angry at *me*. This wasn't *my* idea!"). With acceptance, children become free to share their feelings and problems, points out Dr. Thomas Gordon, the father of Parent Effectiveness Training. When their feelings are not accepted, they close up and become defensive.

- Use what Dr. Gordon calls "door-openers" to encourage children's talk. Examples are, "Tell me about it." "I'd be interested in your point of view." "Shoot, I'm listening." "Sounds like you've got something to say about this."

- Is your child usually too guarded to share his or her feelings? Take the attention off the fact that you are looking for meaningful communication. Get involved together in an activity that is engrossing but doesn't take all your child's concentration, such as doing a puzzle or baking cookies. Then, while attention is focused on the activity and defenses are down, subtly sneak in a probing question.

- Be aware that children may not be ready to share their feelings with you. If your attempts are met with anger or avoidance, don't pry and don't push, but don't give up, either. Stay available.

- Share some of your own feelings with your children, without overwhelming them or bad-mouthing their other parent. When you are open with them, they are more likely to be open with you.

- Be aware that children may feel very mixed-up and not understand *what* they feel or why they are acting the way they are. They need help identifying their feelings before they can talk about them. How you can help them sort through their feelings and express them is discussed in Chapter 8 under "Helping Children Cope." (pages 116–117).

- Work on building your relationship with each of your children. As your one-on-one relationship improves, you will find that your communication about important issues will improve too.

- If you have a tendency to lecture, interrogate, or criticize your kids, work on changing these habits. They break down the lines of communication.

- Are you unsure about how to initiate a divorce-related discussion? Try using a children's book about divorce as a springboard. Some excellent ones are listed in Appendix C.

HOW TO CREATE A STABLE HOME ENVIRONMENT

If your children live with you a significant share of the time, you play a vital role in their adjustment because of the amount of time they are in your care, and this section is addressed specifically to you. How quickly you can get back on your feet, resume good parenting practices, and create a stable home life in which your kids feel safe will dramatically influence their adjustment. In fact, a parent with custody can go a long way in compensating for a noncustody parent who is indifferent.

A good deal of this book is designed to help you get back on your feet, rebuild your life as a single adult, and successfully parent your children solo. Each of these is an ongoing task that you need to work on simultaneously, so don't focus on any one at the expense of the others. To help your children's adjustment, you need to work on your own. A poorly adjusted parent with custody often means poorly adjusted children. However, if you focus exclusively on your own adjustment, your children's adjustment will suffer, and so will your home life.

Adjustment to divorce takes time, so be patient with yourself and reach out to other people for help and support. Don't hesitate to seek out counseling to help you and your children through this difficult time. Here are some specific steps you can take to create a stable and secure home for your children despite the turmoil all around you.

1. Provide your children with nurturance and support. Set aside a time each day they are with you to spend with each of them individually in an activity you will both enjoy. Make it a daily routine, and let them know they have your undivided attention during this special time.
2. Set up regular and organized routines and schedules, and make every effort to stick to them. These include bedtimes, mealtimes, children's after-school schedules, chore lists, and so forth. Children need to know that the chaos in their lives will not be permanent, and routines provide some stability and predictability that they find reassuring. In fact, sometimes they are the only source of stability and predictability on which children can depend. Routines are particularly important for infants, toddlers, and preschoolers. When under stress, these very young children function far better in highly structured environments.
3. Establish rules and limits for your children, and use consistent discipline. (Good discipline is discussed in Chapter 16). Rules, limits, and discipline typically fall by the wayside in divorcing homes, but their absence only

compounds the chaos and confusion children feel because of the family's rupture. At a time when the entire world seems to be falling apart, some rules and limits provide children with the reassurance that some order remains in the world after all.

Divorcing parents are especially hesitant to impose rules and limits on very young children, because they already have so much stress in their lives. However, these very little ones need rules and limits even more than older children do. Under times of stress, children, and especially very young children, have a difficult time with self-control. They *need* external controls to help them.

Generally, divorcing mothers are also more reluctant to impose rules and limits on their sons than on their daughters—another mistake. Studies find that boys who have clear rules and firm limits, which are enforced, function far better on a day-to-day basis and adjust better to divorce than boys with lax discipline. Though clear rules and limits help both boys and girls, boys seem to be in greater need of them. Chapter 16 will help you with rules, limits, and consistent discipline.

4. As quickly and as amicably as you can, resolve the issue of custody and set up a parenting schedule that your children can rely on. If you cannot reach agreement on custody and a parenting schedule yourselves, get the help of a family mediator (Chapter 2).

There is no greater instability for children than not knowing where they will live and when they will see each of their parents. Mark the parenting schedule on a calendar and post it so that children will know when they can expect to see their other parent and where they will be at any given time. Guidelines for parenting schedules that meet children's developmental needs are discussed in the section beginning on page 146.

Many sole-custody parents use their children's needs for stability as an excuse to limit the time they spend with their noncustody parent. They couldn't be more off-base. The stability and continuity of the relationship with their nonresident parent is a critical ingredient of a stable environment for children. It should be given a high priority. If you are a parent with sole custody, the section beginning on page 149 will give you help in handling visitation issues.

If each of you is playing an active parenting role, avoid frequent changeovers between homes. Each changeover is disruptive and requires children to shift gears and adapt to different circumstances. When changeovers are very frequent (for example, some children change homes every other day), children are burdened with having to make many adjustments within a short period of time. You will probably have to experiment with a number of schedules before finding one that works well for your family. Joint custody was discussed in Chapter 9.

5. Make every effort to end your conflict with your spouse. Prolonged parental conflict is not only unsettling, it is destructive for children's well-being. (How to end your conflict is discussed in Chapter 11.)

   Minimizing parental conflict is even more critical for parents with joint physical custody, since joint custody thrusts children right into the middle of the battlefield. If you are a joint-custody parent, be sure to develop a detailed parenting plan. The issues you might want to consider can be found in Chapter 11 on page 159.

6. Support your children's relationships with their other parent's extended family. If they lose these relationships too, it will only compound their feelings of loss and confusion. Your former in-laws can be an invaluable source of continuity, stability, and support for your children. Encourage their involvement.

7. Don't lean on a child to fulfill your needs for emotional support or adult companionship, no matter how mature he or she appears to be. Children feel overwhelmed when faced with adult problems and decisions that they cannot possibly have the capacity to solve, either intellectually or emotionally. Children who fill adult roles of confidant, companion, or absent spouse often become troubled youngsters, overwhelmed with anxiety and insecurity. (These children are discussed further in Chapter 14.) Sharing *some* of your concerns is fine and may lead to a warm and companionate relationship. But find a friend to be your confidant and companion, and let your children have their childhoods and adolescence.

8. Encourage children to assume some additional responsibilities to relieve your burden. Children who contribute to the family grow in self-reliance and self-esteem. However, be sure their responsibilities are *appropriate* for their ages. Children and adolescents should be helpers, *not* stand-ins. Many children in divorced families become overburdened with responsibilities for housework, cooking, and caring for younger siblings. Twelve-year-old Andrea is such an overburdened child.

   > Andrea rushed out of class without saying good-bye to her friends. She never lingered after school and had dropped out of drama and choir long ago. She didn't have time for such kid stuff anymore. Her mom really needed her. Timmy had to be picked up from kindergarten and Tommy from the day care center. She had her hands full until seven when her mom got home, taking care of her two brothers who had become so ornery during the past two years since her dad left. She also made them dinner, got them ready for bed, and had her mom's dinner ready when she got home. "You're amazing," her tired and appreciative mother said each night. Most evenings, Andrea helped her mother wash the dishes and straighten the house before beginning her own homework and school projects at about nine.

Many children who become stand-ins for parents are overwhelmed and resentful. Even children who are not resentful at the time may become so later in life, when they realize their parents' divorce not only robbed them of their intact family but of their childhoods as well. In Chapter 15 you can learn how to tell if you are overburdening your children. It will also give you help with juggling work, home, kids, and your personal life.

9. If there may be a chance of reconciling with your spouse, try to resolve your indecision; marriage counseling may be helpful. Both long separations and repeated separations are hard on children, placing them in a state of limbo—hoping for a reconciliation, fearing a divorce, and unable to get on with their lives. Both place stumbling blocks in the path of children's adjustment.

Clinical psychologist Stephen Johnson, of the University of Oregon, suggests that you think carefully about reconciliation and decide under what specific terms, if any, you would consider reconciling with your former partner. Having this clear in your own mind will help prevent an impulsive reconciliation that is likely to end in another separation.

10. Seek out other people who can provide your children with support, sensitivity, and caring. There will be more on this shortly.
11. If you've created a stable and loving environment and your child continues to have problems, get some counseling for him or her. It is very

---

Checklist for a Stable Home Environment

✓ Spend time with each child individually each day.
✓ Be nurturant, supportive, and available.
✓ Create routines and schedules.
✓ Provide clear rules and limits and use consistent discipline.
✓ Settle custody as quickly and as amicably as you can; try mediation if you cannot agree.
✓ Develop a firm parenting schedule quickly that provides frequent, regular, and reliable contact with the nonresident parent.
✓ Avoid very frequent changeovers between homes if custody is joint.
✓ Take children's developmental needs into account when determining a parenting schedule.
✓ End parental conflict, at least within the child's earshot.
✓ Support children's relationships with their other parent and that parent's extended family.
✓ Do not burden children with adult responsibilities.
✓ Do not rely on children to be your confidants or companions.
✓ Seek out other sources of social support for your children.
✓ Try to resolve indecisions about reconciliation.

---

common for children to receive some professional help at this time, and those who do feel it is very helpful. Counseling is usually available on a sliding fee scale based on your income. If you are a member of Parents Without Partners or a divorce support group, you may be able to get some leads on good children's therapists. Otherwise, get a referral from a local mental health or family service agency or a child guidance clinic.

ARRANGING PARENTING SCHEDULES TO MEET YOUR CHILDREN'S DEVELOPMENTAL NEEDS

Children of all ages need stable and frequent contact with both their parents. However, children of different ages have different developmental needs, and for this reason, a parenting schedule that is appropriate for a six-year-old is inappropriate for either a one-year-old or a teen. Various experts have offered guidelines based on our best knowledge of children's needs at different ages. I'll give you some guidelines so you can take your children's needs into account when working out a parenting schedule.

Infants

Parenting schedules for infants are the most difficult to arrange. Infants need a very stable environment, including stable caregivers and a regular schedule. And when they are separated from their primary source of comfort and nurturance, how can they know if he or she will return? For these reasons, experts now agree that infants should have one primary home and not be separated from a primary caregiver for long stretches of time.

At the same time, babies should have *frequent* contact with the nonresident parent so they will get to know the parent well. Infants' memory is limited, so it is widely recommended that for optimum bonding, a nonresident parent spend a few hours with an infant every two or three days, engaging in lots of cuddling, rocking, talking, and playing. It is this type of interaction on a regular basis, as well as the parent's general responsiveness to the baby's needs, that will determine how securely the baby is attached to the less-seen parent. Ideally, their time together can be spent in the familiar setting of either the primary home or day care setting.

What if a nonresident parent wishes *more* involvement with an infant? If an infant is in day care for long hours, it is difficult for both parents to get extensive quality time with their baby. If parents begin to divide up their infant's limited time too much, there is a danger that he or she will not develop a secure attachment to either parent, which is likely to be detrimental to a youngster's emotional and social development. On the other hand, if the infant does not have to deal with long hours in day care away from a parent, the baby can probably handle longer hours with the nonresident parent at that parent's home—providing their time together is regular and reliable. Consistency and stability are important.

Overnights are usually stressful for infants and are not recommended. For example, a study reported by Tiffany Field of the University of Miami School of Medicine found that older infants smiled less, became fussy and aggressive, and woke up more often crying during the night while their mothers were hospitalized for a few days. It is noteworthy that the infants were being cared for in their own homes by their fathers. Do you have a baby who is already accustomed to overnights away and does not display any symptoms of distress? Your baby may be particularly adaptable, and an occasional overnight at the nonresident parent's home should be okay, too.

If you are a nonresident parent and cannot see your infant frequently, don't try to make up the time with very long visits. The baby is likely to find it distressing to be away from a familiar setting and a familiar caregiver for long periods of time.

One- to Three-Year Olds

As babies grow, they continue to need the stability of a primary home but can gradually handle both longer stays away from their primary source of comfort and longer times between seeing their nonresident parent.

By the time your baby is approaching a year old, he or she may be ready to spend a long day with a nonresident parent each week, but there should be at least one shorter contact in-between.

By the time toddlers are 18 months old, the more liberal guidelines suggest they may benefit from a two day–one night stay with a nonresident parent, providing they know the parent well. Longer stays on a regular basis can still be very distressing because toddlers' conception of time is so poor—they cannot grasp when they will return to their more familiar parent and environment. Try these two day–one night stays on alternate weeks to see how your toddler handles them. Have at least one contact in-between, as well as some brief phone contact so your child can hear his or her parent's voice.

During overnight stays, watch for signs of stress—increased fussiness, aggressiveness, masturbation, or tantrums; pronounced fears about separation; a lack of smiling; or waking up crying through the night. If your toddler shows signs of stress, don't push it. Return to a daytime schedule.

If, at some point, your child is thriving with these two day–one night stays, you might want to work up gradually to have them once each week. Don't forget phone contact in between.

Preschoolers

By the time children are three, the more liberal guidelines suggest that time with the nonresident parent can extend to two-night stretches. If they take place on alternate weeks, there should be contact in between, both in person and by phone. Preschoolers should not go for more than seven to ten days (and preferably less) without seeing a parent. As with younger children, predictable, frequent, and regular time with a nonresident parent is important.

Preschoolers still have a poor concept of time and can't grasp the meaning of next week or three days from now. It is helpful for them to visualize on a calendar when they will see an absent parent again. If they have a television program they watch everyday, they can use that as a reference point. "You will see Dad (Mom) again after three more Sesame Streets."

School-Age Children

Once children are six, they are ready and usually eager to spend extensive time with the less-seen parent. If an equal sharing of the parenting is the goal, this is a good age to begin.

As youngsters become older and their peer group and outside activities assume increasingly greater importance in their lives, they usually spend more time with peers and less time with both parents. Their activities and social lives need to be accommodated in parenting schedules.

Teens

By the time children reach their teen years, they often prefer one home base (and one phone number) because of their active social lives. Many thrive on spontaneous meetings with a nonresident parent that last a few hours. If parents live in close proximity, some teens are comfortable with moving back and forth informally, leaving messages on each parent's answering machine indicating where they are at any given time so friends can reach them.

Flexibility in Parenting Schedules

Obviously, the parenting schedule you first arrange will have to be modified over the years. If you are unable to work out changing schedules, a family mediator can help you. Some parents who don't wish to renegotiate agree on one parenting schedule until children are three, another until they are five, and so on.

The above are guidelines, not hard and fast rules. There are other considerations that should be taken into account. For example, if a nonresident parent has been a very involved parent in a child's life before parents separated, the youngster is likely to benefit from spending more time with the parent than guidelines suggest. A young child who is close to older siblings is likely to be able to handle longer stays away from home if siblings are along, too. And obviously, if parents live a great distance from one another, a parenting schedule in keeping with children's developmental needs is difficult if not impossible to arrange. Some guidelines for parenting long-distance can be found in Chapter 18.

DEALING WITH VISITATION: DON'T MINIMIZE ITS IMPORTANCE

It is not unusual for parents with custody to discourage visitation and children's involvement with their other parent, and most feel they have very valid reasons for doing so. "My kids are always upset before and after visits. Those visits have got to be bad for them." "My ex continually disappoints the kids. They would be better off without him (her)." "My kids always return home from a visit hyper from too much junk food, too little sleep, and no rules. It takes me days to get them back to normal." "My ex has such different values than I want my kids to have. It's just too confusing for them to be taught one thing by me and hear something else from him (her)."

When custody-retaining parents discourage contact between their children and the noncustody parent, the biggest losers are their children, and their loss is usually profound (Chapter 9). Any harm caused to children from junk food, loss of sleep, lax discipline, exposure to different values, or even repeated disappointment pales in comparison to the loss they experience by not seeing their other parent.

There is wide agreement among experts that the relationship between a child and the noncustody parent should always be fostered unless there is clear evidence that the parent is either seriously disturbed, physically abusive, or clearly psychologically abusive. Even then, supervised visitation is often recommended. There is also wide agreement that children's access to their noncustody parent be very liberal, if not free, providing conflict between parents is under control.

In the heat of divorce, it is often difficult for a parent to distinguish between what is in the children's best interests and what is motivated by the parent's own needs and hurts. Here are some suggestions that will help you handle the visitation issue in your children's best interest.

1. Support a good deal of contact, both in person and by phone, between your children and their other parent. Their time together should be not only frequent and regular but of sufficient duration to allow them to build and maintain meaningful relationships.

Honor parenting schedules, but don't be rigid about them. Reevaluate them occasionally to see how they are working out for everyone. Keep in mind that sometimes changes will be necessary because of conflicting demands, and try to work out another time for your children to see their other parent.

2. Don't mistake your children's upset or problematic behavior before or after spending time with their other parent as signals that their time together is harmful. Making the transition from one parent to the other is difficult for children. Each transition requires them to shift gears and loyalty and to say good-bye to a person they love. Transitions are even more troublesome when parents are in conflict. Parental conflict creates enormous loyalty conflicts for children, and transitions force them to wrestle with guilt about leaving one parent for the other or about wanting to be with a parent who causes the other parent so much pain.

   Sometimes children become withdrawn before they leave home to spend time with their other parent. Sometimes they act up. (It is easier to say good-bye when a parent is angry.) Try to make the time before their departure as relaxed and as calm as possible. Give children some space, and don't nag about uncompleted homework or chores. Most important, give them permission to have a good time with their other parent. Don't lay a guilt trip on them about wanting to go.

   When children return home after seeing their other parent, the atmosphere is usually strained. Children often become withdrawn, hyperactive, discipline problems, or sassy. Most parents with custody attribute their children's behavior to either a bad experience with the other parent or the other parent's lack of rules. However, behavior changes are to be expected. Leaving the noncustody parent requires children to switch gears once again and to say good-bye again, this time for a longer time. It is a painful reminder of what is no longer theirs—their intact family. Most children need some space and time to themselves when returning home so they can deal with their feelings and conflicts and adjust to the transition. Rather than greeting them at the door with questions, conversation, or planned activities, allow them some time for themselves.

3. Encourage your former spouse to continue as a full-fledged parent in your children's lives. The constraints of visitation make it difficult for noncustody parents to continue in a parenting role, especially without the support of their former spouses. However, if noncustody parents begin to feel like useless peripheral players in their children's lives, they are more likely to both drop out of children's lives and fall behind in child support payments. This is particularly true for fathers, even previously involved fathers. This paints a stark contrast to fathers who are given the opportunity to continue parenting their children. Many develop closer relationships with their youngsters after divorce than they had

before. Some develop an appreciation for their parental role for the first time. Fathers who keep involved are more likely to pay child support, and many become a valuable source of relief to custody-retaining parents who are carrying the burdens of single parenting.

How parents without custody can keep involved in a parenting role is discussed in Chapter 18.

4. Respect your former spouse's right to develop his or her own relationship with the children and to parent them. Do not interfere when it is their time together. Think of your ex-spouse as your children's other family who they live with part-time, suggests Isolina Ricci, statewide coordinator of California Family Court Services and author of *Mom's House, Dad's House.*

Hopefully, the two of you can agree on some basic rules for your children (for example, about bedtimes, discipline, homework, and television). If you cannot reach some compromises, be clear about what your rules are. Explain to your children that there are different ways of raising children and that your rules reflect what *you* feel is best for them. Be firm that at your home, they should follow your house rules and when they are with their other parent, they should follow that parent's rules. Children can follow different rules in different settings as long as expectations are clear.

5. Never use visits as rewards or punishments, and, as tempting as it may be, mental health professionals unanimously recommend against canceling visits because of missed child support. Visits are not privileges, but *necessities* for your youngsters' well-being. The issue of unpaid child support is discussed in Chapter 17.

6. If you have *good* reason to believe that your former spouse is abusing your children, contact your local Child Protective Services so they can investigate. However, be aware that in the heat of divorce, many former spouses are willing to think the worst of each other, and many jump to rash conclusions that are not indicated by the facts.

IF THEIR OTHER PARENT IS INDIFFERENT

There are some parents, of course, who withdraw from their children's lives, even if the other parent encourages involvement. How can you buffer children from the rejection they are likely to feel?

If your former partner hasn't completely dropped out of the picture, see if you can get him or her reinvolved. Share the information in Chapter 18 about the importance of noncustody parents in children's lives. Ask if there is something you can do to help, and take an honest look at your past behavior as well. Have you supported or thwarted your children's relationships with their other parent? Some studies have reported that up to one-half the custody-retaining parents studied made visitation difficult, even though many did not realize they were doing so. (Common examples were "forgetting" about scheduled visits, refusing to reschedule a canceled visit, and refusing to allow a visit if the other parent brought a date along.)

If your former spouse has completely withdrawn from your children's lives or if you find there is nothing you can do to increase his or her involvement, there are steps you can take to help your children deal with feelings of rejection.

- Help them see that the indifference reflects a problem going on inside their missing parent and that it does not reflect any shortcomings in them. They did not do anything wrong and they are not unlovable, uninteresting, or unworthy. As much as you would like to, try not to disparage your former partner. Children identify with their parents, even an indifferent one. "If my dad's no good, will I grow up to be no good too?" Hearing disparaging remarks about their parent will make them feel worse about themselves. What they need now is help in feeling better about themselves.
- Work on your relationships with them and reassure them frequently of your commitment and love. Remember that a good relationship with you can go a long way in buffering them from stress. Let them talk out their feelings and problems with you, and let them know that you will always be there for them.
- Work on building your children's self-esteem with the methods discussed in Chapter 8.
- Seek out other sources of social support for your children—the more the better. Other people can become caring adults in your youngsters' lives, make them feel good about themselves, help buffer them from feelings of rejection, and give them experience with adults and the opposite sex. Grandparents, aunts, uncles, family friends, parents of their friends, or a special teacher are good candidates. Or you might try to get them involved with organizations like Big Brothers, Big Sisters, or Parents Without Partners where they can have positive relationships with other adults.
- Counseling is an excellent way to help children deal with feelings of abandonment and rejection and come to terms with an indifferent or rejecting parent.

LIMITING THE AMOUNT OF CHANGE IN YOUR CHILDREN'S LIVES

You may remember from Chapter 9 that children are usually able to handle one source of stress (your divorce) quite well. However, when they are exposed to *additional* stresses, their difficulties in reconstructing their lives are multiplied and so are their risks for developing long-term problems. Examples of additional stresses that multiply children's risks are prolonged parental conflict, prolonged poor parenting, chronically poor parent-child relationships, and a marked drop in economic resources that leaves the family in duress. So is having to cope with considerable change and instability. When children must cope with many other changes at the same time they are trying to cope with the divorce, they receive a double whammy. How do you limit the amount of change in their lives?

- Strive for continuity, and, as much as you can, keep details of your children's lives the same after divorce as they were before.
- Ideally, there should be continuity in children's relationships with their absent parent. Contact between them should be *frequent, regular,* and *reliable,* and it should start *immediately* after the parent leaves the home. Preferably the absent parent will continue in a parenting role and continue doing things with the children that he or she always did. Daily phone contact is also a good idea during the early months after separation.
- If at all possible, temporarily delay any major changes such as moving, a new school, and a new job that demands more of your time away from home. In a perfect world, these changes could be delayed until children are back on their feet emotionally. However, the world is seldom perfect.
- When major changes *must* be made, make them as gradually as your situation allows. If you must move, try to keep your children in the same school, at least for a year. Try to continue with familiar routines in your new home. Incorporate as many things as you can from the family home into your new home. (Now is not the time to toss out all your furniture and "get a fresh start.") If you must return to work, can you get along on a part-time job for a while? Children whose at-home parents suddenly return to full-time employment experience a double loss—both father and mother. If a full-time job is necessary, try to make up for your lost time with your youngsters by giving them some undivided attention each night and on weekends.
- If many negative changes in your children's lives are unavoidable, work to offset them. Give your youngsters extra love, time, support, and sensitivity. Remember that a good relationship with you can soften the impact stress has on them. Also introduce some *positive* events and experiences into their lives. Negative changes are more detrimental to children during the divorce crisis if there are few positive events in their lives to offset them.

ARRANGING SOCIAL SUPPORT FOR YOUR CHILDREN

You may be able to give your children's adjustment a considerable boost by arranging for adults outside the family to provide them with some of the extra support and nurturance they need, not only during the divorce crisis but throughout the time you are rebuilding your life. Outside social support can also act as a buffer for stress (though it is a less powerful buffer than is a good relationship with you).

You will probably have to ask for help. In the California Children of Divorce Study, only 25 percent of the youngsters were given support from anyone in the extended family, and only 10 percent received support from someone outside the extended family. People were simply hesitant to intrude.

Who can you ask to give a child support? Grandparents and other extended family members are likely candidates. So are teachers. Many a child has pulled through the rough postseparation months because of the support offered by a sensitive teacher. Additionally, a teacher who is aware of the situation is likely to respond with sensitivity rather than impatience if your child acts out his or her distress in the classroom, as many children do. You might also ask a teacher to keep you informed about any changes in your child's classroom behavior, grades, or friends.

Family friends, neighbors, school counselors, coaches, scout leaders, youth group leaders, or the parents of friends are also good candidates to show your children some extra caring. So is a mature baby-sitter who is nurturing and sensitive. And don't forget your former spouse's family. A word of caution: Don't bounce your kids from person to person and from place to place each day so they feel like they are caught in a revolving door. Although they need social support, they also need consistency, stability, and predictability.

An organization such as Parents Without Partners (PWP) is a good source of social support for both you and your children. PWP has family, teen, and children's activities that allow kids to interact with and receive support from other divorced families. It helps children to have contact with peers who are either going through divorce or who have already survived their parents' divorce. If you cannot locate your local chapter, contact PWP's national headquarters at 8807 Colesville Road, Silver Spring, MD 20910.

Investigate whether your community has a divorce adjustment program for children. Kids usually benefit from these programs, now offered by many schools, universities, family service agencies, and community mental health centers. Some focus on rap sessions where children can share their concerns and feelings with other youngsters in divorcing families. Others not only have discussions but also help children identify and express their feelings, deal with their anger, and resolve their conflicts. Of course, all programs haven't been evaluated, and undoubtedly some are more effective in enhancing adjustment than others. However, youngsters are likely to gain benefits from any of them, if only from the social support they offer. Your school district, physician, or local chapter of PWP may know if any are available in your community. Other sources to check are a local university and a community mental health center.

A professional counselor or therapist can be a very effective source of support, providing children strength, helping them talk about their feelings and conflicts, and helping them to feel better about themselves.

DIVORCE AND "THE STEELING EFFECT"

Guilt is not an uncommon feeling in divorcing parents. Most parents want to do well by their kids and experience anxiety about the repercussions their divorce may have. The fact that you are taking the time to read these chapters suggests that you are a conscientious parent. As such, you are likely to do a good job bringing your children through this stressful time. But as a conscientious parent, you may feel lingering guilt and uncertainty ("Did my divorce have some negative consequences after all? Had I not gotten divorced, would my child be better adjusted? More successful in school? Chosen a different mate?").

It may comfort you to know that sometimes children emerge from their parents' divorce with *greater* psychological strength. How can this be, you say? As a result of extensive research, it is now widely believed that the most effective way to foster resilience in children is not to shield them from stress and adversity, as many parents assume. Rather, it is to allow them to encounter stress in doses that are moderate enough for them to handle. In this way, the stress does not overwhelm them. Instead, it challenges them to learn how to cope with a difficult situation and to master it. If they are successful, they are likely to emerge from the experience with new self-confidence, an increased sense of competence, and the ability to successfully handle a greater amount of stress in the future. Psychologists call this phenomenon "the steeling effect."

The key, of course, is for the stress to be moderate enough so a child can handle it rather than be overwhelmed by it. How do you know how much stress is moderate enough? Remember that children can usually cope with a single stress, such as parental divorce, as long as it is not compounded by other stresses, such as prolonged conflict, chronically poor relationships with parents, infrequent and unreliable visitation, poor parenting, severe financial hardships (especially when they become a source of pervasive conflict and resentment), or overwhelming change.

Carol's parents divorced when she was 8. She is now 16 and appears to be convinced that the steeling effect actually does occur. About the divorce, she says,

> I've gained, I'm more aware, independent and a stronger person because of the divorce. . . . I've learned a lot.[1]

11

HOW TO END CONFLICT WITH YOUR EX-SPOUSE:
A Must *for Your Children's Sake*

*A*ny divorcing person, whether a parent or childless, will benefit from ending the conflict with his or her spouse. Anger and conflict keep former spouses tied to each other, preventing them from closing the doors on their marriages and sapping the energy they need to build their new lives. And when ex-spouses are in conflict with each other, the quality of life after divorce is found to suffer—not only for parents, but also for childless couples, who have less need for contact. For this reason, a chapter on ending conflict could have been placed along with chapters on adult coping. However, prolonged parental conflict is so destructive to children's well-being that it is imperative for parents to end conflict for their children's sake. Hence, this chapter is placed in the section focused on children's needs.

Children whose parents are in prolonged conflict generally become emotionally troubled, expressing their distress in the form of any number of problems, including withdrawal, depression, poor self-esteem, poor grades, aggressiveness, rebelliousness, and delinquency. Generally, the more protracted and hostile the conflict, the more detrimental it is to children. Chapter 9 discussed parental conflict and its repercussions in greater detail.

The *ideal* situation for your child is for you to develop a good relationship with your former spouse. You say a "good" relationship is out of the question? Then strive for a *workable* relationship. A workable relationship is one in which parents keep unresolved spousal issues and conflict compartmentalized so they do not intrude into the business of parenting. Many couples who establish a workable relationship do not have a personal relationship, and some don't even like each other. However, they have learned to separate their personal feelings for each other from their roles as parents. *Spousal issues are kept separate from parenting issues.* This and their shared dedication to their children are the keys to their ability to cooperate with each other as co-parents. For many of these couples, co-parenting does not come easily; it requires considerable effort, ad-

156

aptation, and ongoing resolution. But it is well worth it, these couples say, to see their children thrive despite the divorce. Well-known divorce researchers Constance Ahrons of the University of Southern California and Roy H. Rodgers of the University of British Columbia who study relationships between former spouses, report that approximately 50 percent of divorced couples achieve a relationship that is free of destructive conflict. If you follow the guidelines in this chapter, you are likely to be among that successful 50 percent.

EARLY STEPS

Right now, you may think it is a pretty tall order to separate spousal issues from parenting issues so that you can cooperate in the business of raising your children. It may help to keep two facts foremost in your mind: First, your children *need* a relationship with *both* of you, and second, prolonged conflict is likely to leave its scars on your children for many years.

The very first thing you need to do is work out some details of your future parenting, preferably before you see an attorney. Researchers at the University of Toronto report that once the legal system is involved, conflict usually *escalates*. This is not meant as a criticism of divorce attorneys. Connecticut Superior Court Judge Joseph Steinberg points out that the real problem is the community at large, which believes that adversarial divorces are inevitable. The typical advice from family and friends, points out Steinberg, is "Hire the toughest lawyer you can find." The attorney, in turn, takes steps to do what he or she was hired to do—be tough (which usually translates into "winning" at the expense of the other spouse). Divorce should not be a win-lose situation.

The kinds of parenting details that it would be helpful to work out will be discussed shortly. All parenting decisions do not have to be decided immediately, but the more child-related issues that you can settle, the better chance you will have of keeping your children out of your conflict. Parents' arguments about child-related issues is the form of conflict that is most distressing to children.

The one decision that you should not delay is creating a firm parenting schedule that guarantees your youngsters frequent, regular, and reliable contact with the parent leaving the home; this is critical for your children! Having a set schedule, and sticking to it, will also eliminate the need for contact between you and your ex-partner to arrange each future visit. As you undoubtedly know, each contact can invite new fights, misunderstandings, and power plays. Once conflict is in control, parenting schedules can become more flexible.

Consider trying to resolve some or all of your divorce-related decisions with the help of a divorce mediator. A mediator will work with you to hammer out *mutually* acceptable agreements on any divorce-related issues you choose—custody, visitation, a detailed parenting plan, child support, spousal support, property division, and so on. Please read about this alternative to an adversarial divorce, discussed in Chapter 2. Not only may it reduce your conflict now, it may teach you how to communicate, negotiate, and solve problems together in the future—useful skills to have while you are both still parenting your children.

HOW TO BUILD A DIFFERENT KIND OF RELATIONSHIP

Even if you avoid an adversarial divorce, it may be difficult to separate parenting issues from spousal issues as long as you continue to relate to each other as you always have. What you need to do is restructure your relationship with your spouse so you have a *different* kind of relationship. There are specific steps you can take that will help you end the old relationship and build a different one.

Establish Clear Boundaries for the New Relationship

The idea behind restructuring your relationship is to break with the way you customarily interact with each other and reconnect *on a new basis*. The first step is to define clear boundaries for the new relationship so you do not fall back into the old one, in which your lives were completely intertwined. There are two primary steps you can take to clarify the new boundaries.

1. Eliminate your involvement with each other in *all* but your parenting roles. Here are some specific steps to follow; more can be found in Chapter 6.
   - Do not rely on each other for any of the tasks (other than parenting) previously assumed in the marriage (home-cooked meals, laundry, bill paying, car or house repairs, and so on).
   - Formalize how and when you will contact each other, to discourage unnecessary calls or unannounced visits. Keep a notepad for jotting down things you need to discuss so that everything can be taken care of at designated meetings (when your children are neither present nor within earshot).
   - Stick to your parenting schedule. Once everyone has adjusted, schedules can become more flexible.
   - Send support payments through the mail and think of them as a business arrangement.
2. The second step is formalizing the parenting roles and responsibilities that each of you will assume. If you are in conflict, the more clearly parental roles and responsibilities can be formulated, the better. Everyone's expectations will be the same, and there will be less cause for future conflicts. See how many of the issues you can resolve, either by yourselves or with a mediator. Then write down your agreements in a *parenting plan*.

Details of a Parenting Plan

✓ How will communication be handled? (e.g., mail, phone, meetings)?

✓ What decisions will be shared? How will they be made?

✓ Will you both agree to the other parent's autonomy when children are with that parent?

✓ When will the children be with each of you?

✓ What will be the logistics of transfering children? Be specific. What time? Who will transport? Will children have eaten first? Who will oversee homework? What things are expected to return with them?

✓ What will be done if a scheduled visit cannot take place?

✓ How will each holiday and school vacation be divided? Be specific about times.

✓ When will the child and nonresident parent talk on the phone?

✓ How long can each parent take children away on vacation? How much notice should be given the other parent? Should the vacationing parent provide an itinerary and emergency phone numbers?

✓ Try to agree on some basic rules for both homes (for example about discipline, bedtimes, homework, and television).

✓ How will children continue their relationships with the noncustody parent's family?

✓ Who will go to teacher conferences, and how will information about school progress be shared?

✓ What activities will children continue (e.g. lessons, summer camp)? How will they be paid for?

✓ How will the children be supported?

✓ How will medical, dental, child care, and college bills be paid?

✓ How will future disputes be resolved?

Assume a Business Demeanor

Agreeing on such details will, of course, require talking and negotiating, and this is when your resolve to form a different kind of relationship can break down. While restructuring your relationship, it usually works best to establish a businesslike atmosphere during face-to-face discussions. Follow these guidelines.

- Try to meet in a public place so there will be less temptation to raise your voices.
- Discuss only practical matters. Keep away from personal or controversial topics—the marriage, personal problems related to the separation, spending habits, dating, new relationships, gossip, and so forth. At some point in the future, you may be able to discuss personal topics again, but most people do better if they refrain from doing so during the first year, reports Dr. Marla Beth Isaacs, who directed the Families of Divorce Study in Philadelphia.
- Give respect and expect it in return. Refrain from sarcasm or digs, even

if your ex-spouse uses them (and reward yourself liberally for pulling it off).

- Pretend that a third person is present, suggests Dr. Zev Wanderer of the Center for Behavior Therapy in Beverly Hills, California, and co-author Tracy Cabot in their book *Letting Go*. It should be a person you greatly respect and one whom you wish to convince that you are the epitome of rationality. Don't say or do anything that you would not want to do in front of this observer.
- When you reach agreements on issues, write them down so there are no misunderstandings later.
- If there is still a good deal of anger in the relationship, use the negotiating strategies discussed later in this chapter. Also follow the suggestions in Chapter 5 to deal with your anger.

Redefining the Relationship in Your Own Mind

It may surprise you to learn that an important step in restructuring your relationship is deciding what to call your former spouse from now on. End the negative labels (jerk, witch, bastard, gold digger). Also get away from the term "my ex"; it focuses on your past relationship when you need to focus on the present one. When you are not using your former spouse's name, try "my co-parent" or "my children's mother (father)."

To redefine your relationship in your own mind, you will also have to force yourself to both think about and talk to your co-parent as a *co-parent* and *business partner* rather than as your ex-spouse. This will take some self-control and determination on your part, but you can do it, just as others have.

Focus on the Present

Accept your co-parent's past failures as a *spouse* and try to put them behind you. Focusing on them will deter you from moving on to a workable co-parenting relationship, which is so important for your children. It is this ability that distinguishes well-functioning postdivorce families from conflict-ridden ones, report Ahrons and Rodgers. Chapter 6 can help you with laying the past to rest.

Build a New Independent Life

Usually as people feel better about themselves and are successful at rebuilding a new life, they are better able to establish more comfortable relationships with their children's other parent. Work on rebuilding your self-esteem, creating an

---

Key Steps In Restructuring the Relationship with Your Spouse

✓ Create clear boundaries for the new relationship.
  • Disengage in *all* areas except parenting.
  • Formalize parenting roles and responsibilities, and stick to a firm parenting schedule.
✓ Communicate as business associates would.
✓ Redefine the relationship in your own thinking.
  • Quit using negative labels.
  • Think of your ex in terms of a business partner.
✓ Focus on the present, not the past.
✓ Work on building a new independent life.
✓ Reconnect later on a new basis.

---

identity separate from that of your ex-spouse, developing new interests, and building a wide network of friendships. Chapters 12 and 13 will help you.

Reconnect on a New Basis

After the old ways of relating and feeling have been eliminated, you can reconnect on a new basis. Remember that it is the strength of your feelings about your children's other parent, not whether they are positive or negative, that determines how much you are allowing your former spouse to influence your present life. Your progress in restructuring your relationship may not be steady. Don't get discouraged; relapses are common. Feelings of attachment, sexual attraction, love, and anger often hang on , and don't be surprised if they resurface when your co-parent remarries.

KEEPING YOUR CHILDREN OUT OF YOUR CONFLICT

Ending your conflict and separating spousal and parenting issues may seem an impossible task if you are entangled in an escalating cycle of emotional self-defense and retaliation. If this cycle is already in motion, it will take time to break it. Until you succeed, try to keep your conflict away from your kids. When children are not exposed to their parents' conflict, *they are usually not harmed by it.* Here are some things you can do.

• When children are being picked up or dropped off, don't raise any issues that might cause an argument. Arrange a time and place when the children will not be present or within hearing range to discuss anything controversial, especially if it relates in any way to them.

- If their other parent insists on raising issues at these times, don't get dragged into a confrontation. Cut the conversation off politely. "Thank you for sharing that. We'll discuss it later. I have to go now." Then remove yourself from the situation. If you are the nonresident parent, consider honking the horn for your children instead of going to the door.
- When you want to get your complaints about your ex off your chest, talk to a friend, relative, or counselor. Don't talk to your kids.
- If your children are angry with their other parent, don't add fuel to the fire. Let them talk about their feelings and be empathetic, but try to take a neutral stance. "You sound pretty disappointed Dad hasn't been by in a while," not "It's terrible the way he's just walked out on you. He's a rotten father."
- Avoid bad-mouthing their other parent in front of your children. Children of divorced parents report that this is one of the most distressing behaviors in parents. Bad-mouthing their other parent is not only a form of parental conflict, but it creates painful conflicting loyalties. Many children feel guilty when they hear one parent belittle the other because they feel they are being disloyal to the parent being degraded. Some feel they should come to the defense of the parent who is not there, but they don't want to hurt their other parent either. Asked what she would tell parents who were getting a divorce, eight-year-old Shauna replied:

> I would tell them never to say anything about their kid's other parent. I try not to listen when my mommy says bad things about my daddy. Sometimes I hold my hands over my ears. But she yells so loud, I hear it anyway. It gets me so confused. Sometimes I wonder if the things she says are true. Sometimes I don't even understand what she's saying, but they sound bad. My daddy doesn't seem bad, and I don't think I'm bad. But I don't think my mommy would lie either. I don't know what to think. Tell other parents not to do that.

There is another reason children find bad-mouthing so distressing. Children identify closely with their parents and often see themselves as composites of them. A disparaging remark about a parent is, therefore, often interpreted as a disparaging remark about the child as well. "If my father is no good, how can I be good?" "If he is so despicable, what does that say about me?" "If my mother is a tramp, will I become a tramp too?" Notice how Shauna said, "My daddy doesn't seem bad, and I don't think I'm bad." She was identifying with her father. No matter how bad a parent is, a child needs to know some good things about him or her. It is okay to let your kids know that you are angry and disappointed, but it's not okay to degrade their other parent in front of them.

- If your former spouse is the one degrading you, don't get caught up in his or her game. *Calmly* correct any lies told about you, and explain that people often say things they don't mean when they are upset. Don't dwell on the issue. Your children will appreciate not having to choose between their parents when they are in your home, and as children become older they can see through these games. In the long run, you will be the one they respect.

- Don't ask your children to "spy" on your ex. And don't use them to be a "go-between" to deliver messages; use the mail if you do not want to use the phone. Jill's distress at being a go-between is evident:

> Whenever my dad is late with the child support check, my mom makes *me* ask him for it. I just hate it! It's so humiliating, and I never know what he'll say. Sometimes he really acts embarrassed and says he just doesn't have it this month. Or sometimes he gets mad and asks me what she does with all the money. If I mention things like the rent, he acts like I'm taking my mom's side, and he gets hurt. Sometimes he starts ranting that she's probably spending it on new boyfriends and wants to know whether she's had anyone over to dinner. What do I say? If I say yes, I feel like a rat to Mom. If I say no, then I lie to Dad. It's bad enough they got a divorce. Why can't they just leave me out of it?

- Realize that your children want to be able to love *both* their parents. Don't interpret their love for your former spouse as a threat to you. Don't pressure them to form an alliance with you, to take your side, or to prefer you.
- If your child volunteers to play the role of mediator between you and your former partner, don't allow it. Thank your child for wanting to help, but let him or her know that it is not a child's responsibility.
- Be aware that most children keep the hope of their parents' reconciliation alive for many years, and some try to maneuver parental contact in any way they can. At times, the only feasible way is instigating a situation that sets parents battling. "They'll never get back together if they never even talk to each other," commented one child. Be careful not to get drawn into these situations. Talk with your child about what he or she is doing. If a reconciliation is out of the question, be very clear to your child that you and the other parent will not be getting back together again.

IF YOUR CONFLICT CONTINUES

As long as you are embroiled in conflict with your former spouse, continue to minimize your involvement. Continue to restrict your relationship to the children and discuss only practical matters. Also stick to the parenting schedule you set. Usually children who have battling parents not only prefer a set schedule to be with each parent but adjust better with one too. As mentioned before, each change in the schedule requires contact and invites another round of conflict.

If your conflict continues, it may still be possible for the both of you to parent your children without causing them harm. Some parents who are angry and hostile toward each other can successfully parent their children, according to a study conducted by Judith Greif of Albert Einstein College of Medicine in New York City. How do they do it? Not only are parenting schedules set and adhered to, but children are picked up and dropped off on neutral ground, such as school or a friend's house. Each parent also accepts that children will abide by the rules and values of the parent they are with at the time. Thus, parents need very little contact with each other. When older children are involved, many parents allow the children to make all the arrangements. This allows for flexibility in schedules, and the parents still don't have to deal with each other. These arrangements work for many divorced families. In fact, in a nationally conducted study, University of Pennsylvania sociologist Frank Furstenberg and his research team found that when both parents continue involvement with their children, they most likely engage in what Furstenberg calls "parallel parenting"; they parent independently and rarely discuss child-rearing matters. For children, parallel parenting is a far better choice than either continued conflict or the loss of a relationship with a parent. However, it is *critical* that both parents protect children from their conflict. Here are some suggestions for helping you deal with continued conflict with your ex-spouse so you can protect your children from it.

- Are you full of leftover anger and resentment about your spouse? How to deal with your anger and resentments and let them go were discussed in Chapter 5. So were ways to constructively deal with anger about present conflicts.
- Is your children's other parent very hostile? Humor can help you deal with the hostility so you do not get drawn into an escalating cycle, which is bound to affect your kids. If his or her constant barrage of criticism is a problem, try a technique suggested by Dr. Marian Mowatt, a clinical psychologist and divorce therapist in Seattle, Washington. Try keeping a scorecard handy (out of sight, of course). Divide it into two columns (negative and positive comments) and keep a tally for each "conversation" you and your former partner have together. The ratios of negatives to positives are usually rather lopsided. "Sixteen to one," reported one divorcing spouse. "A complete shutout," reported another. Some people get so caught up in the "game" that they no longer dread each encounter or get drawn into defending themselves. Instead, they sit back and tally away to see if old records will be broken. (Of course, your former partner won't find it nearly as satisfying to criticize you if you don't react, so don't be disappointed if the criticism gradually declines.)
- If your co-parent is so angry and emotional that battles seem to be inevitable, Dr. Mowatt suggests you try another humor technique developed

by psychologist Albert Bernstein of Vancouver, Washington. Dr. Bernstein points out that our thinking brain retreats when we become emotional, and our more primitive lower brain centers—which he calls our "lizard brain"—take over. Any guesses as to how you might add some humor the next time your ex flies off the handle? You've got it: Picture him or her as a lizard brain. You will be surprised at how this will help you keep your cool. The technique may be so effective that you'll use it even when your kids aren't around.

- Humor might lighten the load of your conflict, but it is not a cure-all for it. There will be times when you have to communicate and negotiate with each other, even though you are still enmeshed in conflict, and you will have to do so effectively. Later in this chapter, I'll talk about techniques for negotiating successfully in an emotionally charged atmosphere.

CUSTODY BATTLES: THE MOST DAMAGING OF CONFLICTS

The evidence against the advisability of prolonged custody litigation is striking. Conflict over the issues of custody and visitation is the most destructive kind of conflict for children, probably because they feel responsible for it. Custody battles are usually very prolonged and very bitter, and children who are thrust in the middle of this kind of conflict between the two people they love most in the world often find their plight emotionally intolerable.

Although it is usually beneficial for children to spend a good deal of time with both their parents, this is not the case when parents are entrenched in intense ongoing custody disputes, according to studies conducted at the Center for the Family in Transition in Corte Madera, California, by psychologist Janet Johnston and her research team. These researchers found consistent evidence that the more contact children had with their two warring parents, the more emotionally troubled the youngsters were and the more behavior problems they had. These youngsters were living in a state of chronic anxiety and tension, constantly moving between two enemy camps. Many were taxed beyond the limits of their coping abilities. It is ironic, points out Johnston, that in the process of fighting *for* their children, parents can inflict so much emotional suffering on them. Mental health professionals are unanimous in their advice to avoid custody litigation if at all possible.

Mental health professionals do not stand alone. Those who have been through custody litigation warn others about the nightmare ahead if they take that route. Listen to this woman's account.

As much as I feared the trial and thought I was prepared for it, I never imagined anything could be so terrible. There were our lives dangling out in public for all to see; only it was distorted. It seemed as if every foible of either of us was exposed and exaggerated. . . . I wouldn't wish a custody suit on anyone.[1]

Attorneys also issue warnings to divorcing parents. Listen to the warning given by attorney Elliot Samuelson in his book *The Divorce Law Handbook*:

Be forewarned: Custody litigation is not for the fainthearted and should, where ever possible, be avoided. It is destructive to all persons who participate in the process. It can have a profound effect upon children. It further exacerbates raw wounds of both father and mother. It is frightfully expensive. . . .[2]

Usually conflict does not end when custody is finally settled by the court. Most custody disputes are so bitter that new wounds are piled on old ones, and conflict continues for many years. And if the parent who has lost custody has the money and stomach to continue the fight, the parent who has supposedly "won" can find herself or himself back in court, with its accompanying costs and traumas.

Do everything you can to reach a decision with your spouse about parenting arrangements rather than resorting to a court battle. If you cannot reach an agreement by using the negotiating strategies discussed later in the chapter, get the help of a divorce mediator (Chapter 2). You are the best ones to determine your own and your children's futures, not a judge who has his or her own personal biases and who knows very little either about your children's needs or you.

The whole idea of custody is an unfortunate one. Custody is a term that implies ownership. It is also a term used with prisoners. Your children are neither property nor prisoners. Rather than getting hung up on the issue of who will "get" the children, think of the custody issue from a different perspective: "When will the children be with each of us so that we can each continue to parent them in a meaningful way?" This is, after all, what *they* need for their emotional well-being.

HOW TO COMMUNICATE AND NEGOTIATE EFFECTIVELY IN AN ANGER-LADEN ATMOSPHERE

There are a great many things that you need to settle with your former partner, especially if you have children. The more child-related decisions that you can quickly make yourselves, the better chance you will have of keeping your children out of your conflict. The more that you can learn to talk and negotiate with each other calmly, the less likelihood there is that your future interactions will be dominated by conflict.

Earlier I talked about ways to handle face-to-face encounters, but these strategies won't be sufficient to help you negotiate if there is a good deal of anger and hostility between you and your co-parent. However, there *are* negotiating skills that will help you, even in this emotionally charged atmosphere. The strategies discussed here are a combination of strategies suggested by a number of mental health professionals, mediators, and negotiators. The more complex the issues, the more of the following strategies you will need to use. Don't expect to be able to apply all the face-to-face strategies at once. Choose several that you feel will work the best, and focus on those until you get the hang of them.

Strategies to Prepare Yourself

- Decide what your goal is—reaching an agreement or winning a battle. If it is "winning," realize that you may win the battle but lose the war because losers often retaliate in one way or another (late child support payments, erecting barriers to visitation, and so forth).
- Practice using negotiation skills in your imagination ahead of time. Imagine as vividly as you can a number of possible scenarios, varying your responses as well as your co-parent's reactions. The more situations you anticipate and the more you practice, the better you will be prepared. Use relaxation techniques (Appendix B) while you are practicing to keep yourself calm. Practice until you can run through the scenarios without getting upset.
- Give thought to and clarify your own preferences and interests, and determine your priorities. Don't try to negotiate if you have no direction.
- Prepare several reasonable and well-thought-out proposals in advance. The best way to come up with several good proposals is by brainstorming. Focus on your problem, and let your imagination run wild with *any* possible solution. Approach the problem from every possible angle. Write each idea down without worrying about whether it is good, bad, or even feasible. One idea will lead to another. Afterward, mark those ideas that are most promising and work on improving them.
- Pick a good time and place where you can discuss the problem(s) comfortably and won't be distracted. Make sure your children are neither present nor within hearing range.
- Use some techniques to help you deal with your anger (Chapter 5). Doing so is the first step in creating an atmosphere that is conducive to negotiation.
- If you have learned a deep relaxation technique (Appendix B), use it before the face-to-face meeting.

Face-to-Face Strategies

- Throughout your meeting, breathe deeply and speak slowly and calmly. This will be especially important if your ex becomes excited and raises his or her voice. Keeping calm is an effective way of taking charge of the situation.
- There are some symbolic gestures you can use that will set a more co-operative tone and soften your former partner, such as a touch on the arm, eating together, or starting with a compliment for something that he or she is doing well ("You are doing a good job with the kids," or "I appreciate your sending the child support checks regularly.").
- Tell your former partner that you are committed to solving the problems at hand and suggest that you both follow two ground rules: (a) each should listen to the other without interrupting, and (b) each should check to make sure he or she has understood the other's proposals ("Let me see if I understand what you are saying"). If he or she won't cooperate, stick to the rules anyway. If it is clear that you are listening with an open mind, your ex is more likely to listen to your proposals.
- Avoid using criticism, blame, and "should" statements. They increase the likelihood of resistance and invite a verbal attack on you. Use "I" statements instead (discussed in Chapter 5).
- Coach yourself each step of the way throughout the meeting by talking to yourself ("Take it easy. Just breathe deeply and keep calm." "I won't let myself get as excited as (s)he is, or we'll get into a shouting match." "Remember some humor. It will help keep me calm.").
- If you have a number of issues to deal with, start with the simplest first—the one on which you are likely to have the least difficulty reaching an agreement. This will set a positive mood and give each of you the confidence that you can agree.
- When offering a proposal, state it calmly and clearly, and *be prepared to compromise.*
- Avoid fixating on a position. If each of you takes a position, negotiations can easily deteriorate into a contest of wills, point out Roger Fisher and William Ury of the Harvard Negotiation Project and the authors of the bestseller *Getting to Yes.* Rather than taking a position, focus on your basic concerns and interests. Identifying each of their interests allowed Vic and Margie to find a solution to the custody of their four-year-old son Richie.

> Vic and Margie were stalled on the issue of custody; each was demanding sole custody and was ready to go to court. Neither wanted the compromise of joint custody; each believed that Richie needed the stability of a consistent home because of his young age and the emotional problems he was having since the separation. As a last resort, they went to a divorce mediator, who

explored their concerns and interests. Vic was mainly concerned about losing his close relationship with his son and felt that he needed to be involved with his daily life. He also wanted to be involved in major decisions in Richie's life. Once they got away from "positions" and focused on interests, Vic and Margie were able to arrive at a mutually agreeable solution. They decided that Margie would live in the family home with Richie because her job was not as demanding of her time as Vic's. Vic would call Richie each evening, and Richie would spend a long weekend (Friday afternoon to Monday morning) every other week at Vic's home. Vic would also spend every Wednesday evening with Richie at Margie's home, as well as Friday evening on the weekends that Richie wasn't with him. Vic could fix Richie dinner, play with him, give him his bath, and put him to bed. Richie would have the stability of a consistent home, Vic could continue to be an involved parent, and Margie liked having free time that she could count on to take a class or spend with friends.

Trying to reconcile interests almost always gives a more satisfying solution than compromising between two extreme positions.

- If your former partner has a proposal that you cannot accept, ask yourself why not. Do you have specific interests or concerns that are not being addressed? If so, state them openly. If not, you may be rejecting a good proposal because you cannot separate the proposal from its source. If *your* proposal is being flatly rejected, try to discover your spouse's concerns that are not being addressed.

- If your co-parent *insists* on his or her position, neither reject nor accept it; treat it as a possible solution. Try to put yourself in your ex's shoes and understand his or her perspective. This is one of the most important negotiating skills you can have, point out Fisher and Ury. Before you can influence a person, you need to grasp how that person feels. Look for the interests that underlie the suggested proposal, and try to reconcile them with your own.

- Many people stubbornly stick to a bad proposal because they do not wish to back down. If you sense that this is what is behind your spouse's rigidity, try to find a way for him or her to save face.

- If your former spouse begins to yell, don't yell back. Look at him or her without saying anything. It will give you time to think and time for both of you to calm down. Use your relaxation techniques here. When you do speak, find some way to offer some support ("You're a good parent and I know you want what's best for Linda"). This should be very disarming and should have a calming effect. Then reclarify the problem, taking one point at a time, focusing on interests and avoiding positions. There is a lot to remember here. Guide yourself through each step with self-talk, such as "Don't yell or say anything." "Breathe deeply and keep calm." "Now look for some way to offer some support to disarm him (her)," and so on.

Checklist for Negotiating Techniques

Preparation Strategies

✓ Make your goal reaching an agreement, not winning.
✓ Practice negotiating skills, anticipating different scenarios.
✓ Clarify your preferences and interests; prioritize them.
✓ Prepare several proposals; use brainstorming.
✓ Choose a favorable time and place.
✓ Keep calm; use anger control and deep relaxation techniques.

Face-to-Face Strategies

✓ Use symbolic gestures to set the tone.
✓ Suggest ground rules.
✓ Use "I" statements; avoid blaming, criticism, and "shoulds."
✓ Coach yourself throughout the meeting with self-talk.
✓ Begin with the simplest problem first.
✓ Offer proposals calmly and clearly; be prepared to compromise.
✓ Avoid taking positions; focus on interests.
✓ Separate your spouse's proposals from their source.
✓ Look at each issue from your spouse's perspective.
✓ Look for face-saving retreats for a stubborn spouse.
✓ Don't yell back. Use calming and disarming techniques.
✓ Try some joint problem solving.
✓ Keep focused on the issues by keeping your goal in mind.
✓ Suggest trying out decisions before casting them in concrete.
✓ Don't try to deal with too many problems during one meeting.
✓ Congratulate yourself for *small* accomplishments.

- Try some joint problem solving to arrive at mutually acceptable solutions. A good problem-solving strategy is discussed in Chapter 15.
- Always keep in mind what it is that you want to get out of the meeting. This will help you to keep focused on the issue at hand rather than become sidetracked into arguing, raising old hurts, or proving who is "right."
- It may help you reach decisions if you suggest trying them for a few months and then reevaluating them. It is less threatening than having to make permanent decisions.
- Don't try to cover too much at one meeting. You will have more success if you take small steps.
- When the meeting is over, congratulate yourself for your efforts and accomplishments, even if it did not turn out as well as you had hoped. These may all be new skills you need to learn, and it will take time. Don't give up, and don't get discouraged. Master a few at a time, and then work on a few more. Look for improvement, not perfection!

PART III

BUILDING A REWARDING SINGLE LIFE

REBUILDING

Most people think of divorce adjustment as coping with the divorce itself—weathering the stormy emotions, dealing with the disruptions and problems, helping children adjust, and learning to let go. But there is a second facet of divorce adjustment: building a rewarding new life. Unfortunately, the importance of building a new life often goes unrecognized. Many people emerge from the stormy crisis still frozen in old patterns. They "get over" their divorce, but they do not grow. For them (both leavers and reluctant partners are represented in this group), life after divorce is no more (and sometimes far less) satisfying than was married life.

Life after divorce *can* be rewarding and satisfying, but you will have to invest the time, energy, and planning to make it so. This chapter and the next focus on the ingredients necessary for building a rewarding single life.

REBUILDING SELF-ESTEEM

During the last 5 years of their 15-year marriage, Bonnie and Dale grew further and further apart. Because of conflicting interests and growing disenchantment, they became increasingly more negative and critical with each other. They never really fought, they criticized. "Nothing I do pleases her. I've given up trying," Dale frequently griped. "I can't do anything right in his book," Bonnie likewise complained. Their daily conversations were generously peppered with put-downs and name-calling—inept, selfish, jerk, shallow, prima donna, immature. What wasn't said directly was communicated by innuendo. Their negativeness carried over into their sex life, where both blamed the other's inadequacy for their general dissatisfaction. Throughout the final year of their marriage, each was taking full advantage of the other's vulnerabilities. By the time they finally separated, both Bonnie and Dale were emotionally drained and their self-esteem was seriously eroded.

Bonnie and Dale are not unique. By the time a marriage ends, each partner's feelings of self-worth have generally taken a plunge. Sometimes, as with Bonnie and Dale, self-esteem is damaged over time because of the steady barrage of negative feedback received from a spouse, some of which is inevitably accepted and internalized. Sometimes it is damaged by feelings of rejection, other times by feelings of failure. Yet this blow to self-esteem comes at the very worst time for divorcing people—when they must go out on their own and build new lives. This is a tall order for anyone, but it is overwhelming when self-esteem is shattered. Feelings of self-worth are critical to you right now. With high self-esteem, your task of building a new life is more likely to be challenging than overwhelming. Psychiatrist David Burns compares self-esteem to faith: both can move mountains!

Don't wait for your self-esteem to miraculously reemerge. It may, but it may not. After interviewing her study group 10 years after divorce, researcher Judith Wallerstein wrote of her constant amazement at how many of these long-divorced people continued to carry around the negative self-images formed during their poor marriages—negative images that impaired their ability to create satisfying lives. Your self-esteem can be shaped, and you can be the shaper. Here are some things that you can do to accomplish this. Choose a few that make the most sense to you.

- Your feelings of self-worth are closely tied to your perceptions and thoughts about yourself. For a few days, keep track of the things you say to yourself and write them down. You may find you are telling yourself a lot of negative things ("God, I'm such a jerk." "I never do anything right." "I'm worthless."). No wonder your self-esteem is low! Once you become tuned into your negative self-talk, you can begin to talk back to yourself and break this self-defeating habit. When you catch yourself in negative self-talk, firmly tell yourself to STOP! Then replace your negative thought with a more positive one. Try, "So I made a mistake. That makes me human, not a jerk." Or, "I may not have done *this* right, but I've certainly done lots of other things right." (Then force yourself to think of some examples as evidence.) How do you know how to talk back to yourself positively? One way is to talk to yourself as you would to a friend. You would not tear down a friend constantly. Don't do it to yourself either. You would help a friend to see the folly of his destructive negative thinking. Do the same for yourself. Another way to talk back to yourself is to remind yourself of your *positive* attributes. More on this shortly.
- Buy a wrist counter at a sporting-goods shop (it's inexpensive and looks like a watch), and keep track of each time you make a negative statement about yourself. Record each day's total in a book. No one really understands why, but when people simply monitor their negative statements in this way, their self-control usually improves and their negative self-talk declines. It takes most people about three weeks to reduce their negative self-talk using this method, says Dr. Burns, who successfully uses this

technique with his clients. For the first few days your negative self-talk may actually increase, but then it should reach a plateau and finally decrease. You will find that you begin to feel better when you stop being so hard on yourself.

- The way you perceive yourself not only influences the way you *feel* about yourself, it automatically influences the way you *behave*. And the way you behave influences the way other people perceive you and respond to you. Your thoughts can create a self-fulfilling prophecy! If you perceive yourself as dumb, shy, and boring, that is the image you will project, and that is how others are likely to perceive you too. It is really important to work on your perceptions of yourself.

  A good way to combat your negative perceptions is to write down everything you like about yourself and everything you have going for you. Include all your good qualities, strengths, skills, talents, hobbies, and goals. Keep a running list until you have *at least* 20 to 25 positive attributes (the more, the better). Write each of your positive attributes on an index card and keep them in a file. Each week, place a few of the cards where you will see them often, perhaps on a bathroom mirror or refrigerator door. Each time you see a card, read it and dwell on it. Also go through your file of positive attributes often, especially before social events, so you will project a positive image. You can use your list of positive attributes to counteract your negative self-talk, too.

- Self-esteem is enhanced by new accomplishments. Develop some new interests or hobbies. Or learn some skills that you will need to live independently. If you are a man, you might learn some additional cooking, child care, or home-decorating skills. If you're a woman, you might need to learn more about investing or home repairs. Your self-esteem will be boosted not only by your new accomplishments but also by the confidence you'll gain in being able to live independently. However, be sure to tackle new pursuits in *small steps* so you feel successful and not discouraged. Follow the program in Appendix A.

- Make a list each day of everything you accomplish. All too often, people focus on all they *haven't* accomplished and never give themselves credit for the things they *have* accomplished.

- Think about the things you do well and make room in your schedule to do them *frequently*.

- Whenever you can, socialize with people who are supportive, who like you, and who make you feel good about yourself. Seek out new people rather than limiting yourself to old relationships. At the same time, limit the time you spend with people who are critical or unaccepting.

- Begin to behave assertively. Allowing others to take advantage of you chips away at your self-esteem. When you are angry, don't bottle it up. Express it by using "I" statements, as discussed in Chapter 5. I statements allow you to express your feelings without putting the other person on the defensive ("I feel like I'm being taken advantage of." "I feel very angry about. . . ." "I feel very frustrated when you do this."). If you don't already do it, speak up for your rights in stores and restaurants. Ask for a different table when you are led to that noisy one wedged between the kitchen and the cash register; send back your meal when it's not prepared the way you ordered it; bring an overcharge to a clerk's attention. If your children are taking advantage of you, establish some rules and limits, and follow through with consequences when rules are broken (Chapter 16). Each time you speak up for your rights, you will feel more like a person worthy of respect. Robert Alberti and Michael Emmons's book *Your Perfect Right*, listed in Appendix C, is a good source of assertive techniques. Also, many classes and workshops teach assertiveness.

- Make a list of five adjectives that best describe you, suggested the late Virginia Satir, a very well-known therapist. Indicate next to each adjective whether you consider it a positive or negative trait. Now take each of your negative traits and see if you can find something positive about it. One man realized that what he defined as "weakness" made him a more sensitive person. Another decided that his "tunnel vision" was also responsible for his determination. When Becky described herself to her divorce adjustment group as "wishy-washy," she was surprised that other members thought of her as flexible. The group helped Frieda realize that her shyness made her a good listener, a trait many people appreciate.

- List the things you would like to change about yourself, but make sure they *are* changeable. (Height, sex, and the past do not count.) Choose *one* thing from your list to work on at a time, and follow the self-change program outlined in Appendix A. You will not only be one step closer to becoming the person you wish to be, you will also feel good when you accomplish what you set out to do.

- Begin to give your needs a higher priority, and pamper yourself a little. Take time to do things for yourself that you will enjoy. Get a new hairstyle. Buy some new clothes. Take off some weight. Get in shape. You will begin to feel better about yourself.

- Pay attention to the compliments others give you, and start to incorporate them into your view of yourself. Stop yourself from automatically assuming that compliments are not sincere.

- Keep a file of the compliments you receive. Write each on an index card and date it. Why not also include a dated card each time you accomplish something or do something well? Be sure to go through your file often.

- It is an interesting fact about people that our behavior affects our feelings. Think about how you would treat a *very* special person who came for a visit. Then begin to treat *yourself* the same way—not for an hour, but all the time. Watch yourself begin to feel better about yourself.

- If you are a single parent and are overwhelmed with parenting, work on improving your parenting skills. A study conducted at the University of Virginia found this to be an effective way of boosting single parents' self-esteem. Be sure to read Chapter 15 on how to solo parent successfully and Chapter 16 on discipline. You might also try taking a parenting class where you can meet other people.
- Join a divorce support group. The caring and empathy usually offered in these groups can do wonders for self-esteem. Check local churches and community agencies for a support group in your area. Alternatively, a therapeutic relationship with a counselor may be just what you need at this time to enhance your self-esteem.

OVERCOMING YOUR IDENTITY CRISIS

Mark Ballinger had been a family man. He and Kate had grown further apart over the past five years, but he loved his two daughters and had spent a good deal of time with them each day. When he wasn't spending time with them, he had kept himself busy with home repairs, gardening, or helping one of his neighbors with a project. Kate had planned their social activities, and he had gone along. Now Mark sat in an unfamiliar and barren one-bedroom apartment 10 miles from his home. He got to see his daughters only on alternate weekends and one evening each week, and he missed them terribly. He had lost his "girls," his home, many of his worldly possessions, his neighbors, his customary social activities. Instead of home repairs, he had to tackle cooking, cleaning, laundry, and ironing shirts—tasks distinctly out of character for him. He had not realized how thoroughly he had become entrenched in the roles of married man, father, handyman, and neighbor. Now, without wife, children, and home, he had no idea what to do with himself. In fact, sometimes he didn't know who he was anymore. What was he like before he married Kate? What did he do? How did he feel? It was all so long ago. That person seemed to be gone. And the person he had become during the last 12 years seemed to be gone as well. What now, he wondered.

An identity crisis almost always accompanies divorce. Over the years of married life, spouses inevitably relinquish some of their individuality and pursuits in the interest of the marriage. And because of their shared years, children, home, commitments, and activities, their lives become interdependent, as if the two are woven into a single fabric. With divorce, couples must disentangle the threads of their lives, and the process is likely to leave each with a shaky identity, in need of reworking before it can stand on its own. The common postdivorce identity crisis is induced by other circumstances as well. Divorcing people generally lose many of the material possessions that have become part of "who they are." They may have to assume a number of new tasks that are out of character for them. They may feel as if they are no longer part of the mainstream of society. And they no longer receive the ongoing feedback about themselves that their mates had provided ("I am an efficient person, a good parent, a no-good so-and-so, sexy, strong, weak, sensible, stupid, stodgy, unpredictable"). The converging of many of these elements creates the sensation, so often felt by the recently divorced, that they have been left adrift without an anchor. Questions they thought were settled long ago now surface once again: "Who am I? What do I want out of life? Where do I go from here?"

Your job now is to forge an identity separate from that of your former partner and from your marriage. You no longer have to be the person your spouse expected you to be. You can create a life-style of your own design. You can speak with your own voice. You can pursue your own interests. But it will take time, and until you decide who you are, what you like, what you want to do, and where you are going, you will be between "selves," in a sense, and this may be uncomfortable for you.

Well-known University of Massachusetts sociologist Robert Weiss reports that many divorcing people become upset because they cannot seem to make decisions. They cannot decide what kind of clothes, furniture, house, neighborhood, or life-style is right for them because they cannot separate their own likes and dislikes from those they developed as a compromise with their former partners. Others behave very impulsively because one option seems just as good as another. Many are suddenly open to behaving in ways that they would have found unacceptable previously. Some, Weiss reports, become highly suggestible—flip-flopping their self-images in response to others' reactions to them. The divorcing commonly feel as if they are different people from one day to the next. To the bewildered people around them, they seem indecisive, inconsistent, unstable, and impulsive.

In your quest for a new identity, you are likely to have a number of false starts. You may follow along one path for a period, only to find it unsatisfying. Then you may switch your focus to a second and to a third. The process of carving out a new identity is not a quick one. According to Weiss, most people seem to need several years before they achieve the stability of a consistent self once again. For some, the identity developed after divorce has little resemblance to the identity he or she had within the marriage. This is particularly true for women, whose identities are usually more closely tied to marriage and family than are men's. Studies find that women frequently use divorce to launch themselves on an entirely new life track—often a more confident, independent, and professional one. Sometimes men also use divorce as an impetus to self-assessment and dramatically change the course of their lives as a consequence.

The following suggestions may be helpful to you in overcoming your identity crisis.

- Instead of focusing on losing your old life-style, focus on the challenge of developing a new and more rewarding one of your own design.

- Rely less on your old sources of fulfillment and develop a variety of new ones to supplement them (new friends, new interests, new hobbies, and new skills).
- Identify your goals and decide on your priorities using the method discussed in the following chapter. Then try to set time aside specifically for personal growth and exploration of new directions.
- Think back and try to reconnect with your old roots to see if they might feel comfortable once again. Who were you before you married? What did you like to do? What types of people attracted you?
- Try not to make major decisions that will lock you in. Flexibility and exploration are more likely to lead to a rewarding single life.
- For a two-week period, write down every wish and desire you have, no matter how trivial or outrageous, suggests Leucadia, California, therapist Lynette Triere in her book *Learning to Leave*. (Carry a small pad of paper with you for the purpose.) At the end of the two weeks your list is likely to provide you with many insights into yourself.
- Work to overcome the mentality that you are somehow incomplete without a partner, and consciously try to break the habit of perceiving the world from the perspective of a married person. This may not come easily.
- Keep a journal, and record your progress and setbacks in developing your new identity. What new directions have you taken? How satisfying has each been? Can you identify what it was that you found satisfying or unsatisfying? Your notes may teach you a good deal about yourself and suggest future directions that may be rewarding. Every few months, reevaluate these questions: "Who am I? What are my strengths and weaknesses? What do I want?"
- "Try out" a new identity or self among people you meet in a new setting, such as a club or organization. For example, you may wish to "try out" being more adventurous, confident, assertive, or sexually liberated. Experimentation will be easier if you do not have to buck the expectations of others. And if you happen to fall on your face, you will do so among people you never have to see again if you so choose.

COPING WITH THE LONELY TIMES

Loneliness, or the longing to feel interconnected with others, is generally a fact of life for the recently divorced. Loneliness is usually accompanied by a long list of negative feelings—sadness, depression, vulnerability, boredom, restlessness, self-pity, and self-deprecation. It is not surprising that recently divorced men and women find it so distressing. When asked what loneliness feels like, people commonly respond: "I feel empty inside." "It feels like a hole in my stomach." "I feel depressed, unwanted, left out."

There seem to be two distinct types of loneliness, and each must be remedied differently. The first, *emotional loneliness*, stems from the absence of a close emotional relationship. Even a very socially active person can suffer from this type of loneliness if his or her social network consists exclusively of superficial acquaintances. Feelings of anxiety and emptiness generally accompany emotional loneliness. The second, *social loneliness*, stems from the absence of a social network. Even a close confidant cannot protect you from social loneliness if you have no other friends or acquaintances. Usually feelings of restlessness, boredom, and not belonging accompany social loneliness.

Many divorced men and women jump to the incorrect conclusion that the only way to cure their loneliness is to remarry. In their haste to end their distress, some make poor choices, only to find themselves in an unhappy second or third marriage. You can cure loneliness by building a new social support network that includes a very close friend or two and a number of people with whom to do things. Chapter 13 will help you do this, but until that time, there are steps you can take to manage your loneliness. Try some of the following.

- Plan ahead for weekends and other potentially lonely times by scheduling some activities you can look forward to—a class, a singles activity, a support group, an interesting lecture, a day trip, a movie.
- Begin to develop some new hobbies or interests, and develop a large repertoire of enjoyable activities that you can do by yourself. Try the things you have always wanted to do but never had time for. Return to some hobbies or talents that you let slide while married, or take a chance with something completely new. Think of your time alone as an opportunity to develop yourself. Becoming more comfortable with being alone is one of the most valuable assets you can develop to help you live a rewarding single life.
- Try doing some things by yourself when there is no one to accompany you. You might find them surprisingly enjoyable.
- Share a few private thoughts and feelings with one or two people with whom you would like to become closer. Self-disclosure is often the first step in beginning a close relationship. But remember that making a habit of talking about all your problems is likely to drive people away.
- Work on increasing your self-esteem. Low self-esteem makes people feel more lonely and marginal.
- Thoroughly mourn your losses (Chapter 3) and let go of your anger (Chapter 5). They can keep you self-absorbed and increase your feelings of isolation and loneliness.
- Join a support group or enter into a therapeutic relationship with a therapist or counselor to help you get through this period.
- Consider sharing your home with another person or moving into another's home. Many people are finding that sharing a home with other singles

provides them with a surrogate family. Help with household chores, cooking, finances, and perhaps emergency child care may be added bonuses. If you wish to pursue this option, be very selective about where you advertise, screen people very carefully, and work out clear arrangements ahead of time so that everyone's expectations, roles, and responsibilities are clear.

- Common methods people use to relieve their loneliness include caring for pets, pampering themselves, calling others on the telephone (even if the conversation is superficial), spending time with other lonely people, and reaching out to others in need (such as volunteering at a nursing home, taking a shut-in shopping, and serving meals to the homeless). You may find these helpful, too.

Some words of caution: Be aware that some activities involving others may increase your feelings of loneliness rather than decrease them. Single people sometimes report that their feelings of loneliness and marginality are increased after they spend the evening with a happily married couple or eat alone at a restaurant surrounded by couples or families. Second, do not rely on your children to reduce your loneliness. Not only is it an unfair burden on them, but most adults find that children do not reduce their feelings of loneliness as do other adults.

Increasing your self-esteem, overcoming your identity crisis, and conquering your loneliness will help you create a solid foundation on which to rebuild. The following chapter will help you further along in building a satisfying, rewarding single life. It will guide you in determining your priorities, working toward your goals, building a new social support system, reentering the job market or pursuing a career change, developing new romantic relationships, and exploring opportunities for personal growth.

13

TRANSITIONS

Georgia's husband left her over three years ago. "She had a rough time," says a close friend, "but she's fine now. The depression and anger seem to be gone, and she's feeling better about herself. They had lots of assets, so she got a great divorce settlement—the house and plenty of money to invest. She doesn't even have to work. She's very involved with the kids, the PTA, and the Girl Scout troop. And her friends are very good. They still have her to dinner from time to time—many couples don't do that, you know. She certainly landed on her feet!"

But life doesn't seem quite so full to Georgia. She feels fortunate to have been able to keep the house and have no money problems. And it is a relief to have life on an even keel after the upheavals of the last 2½ years. But she frequently wonders, "Is this all there is from now on?" She feels an emptiness inside her and a feeling of estrangement from her world that she finds hard to put her finger on. Sometimes she dreams that she is bobbing around in the ocean in the dark, without a compass and with no land in sight, and she awakens in terror.

DETERMINING PRIORITIES
AND REACHING GOALS

Divorce requires more change and adaptation than any other event in our society other than the death of a spouse. Because of this, it is usually a major life crisis, for *both* initiators and reluctant partners. Although people tend to think of life crises as negative events, they have a positive side: They provide a rich opportunity for change, growth, and learning. If you take advantage of this opportunity for growth, you are more likely to have a rewarding single life.

To best take advantage of this opportunity, you need to form some goals and clarify your priorities. Without goals, you will drift aimlessly, getting caught up in external events and the demands of others. Your days may be full, but your life will have little direction.

Take some time to seriously examine what direction you would like to take.

Here is a variation of a strategy suggested by E. A. Charlesworth of Baylor College of Medicine and Robert Nathan of the Department of Psychiatry and Family Medicine at Louisiana State University Medical School. Imagine yourself five years from now. What kind of life would you like to have? What would you like to have achieved? What would you like to be doing? What kind of person would you like to be? Be realistic. Not only should your goals be attainable, but you should believe that you *can* attain them. When you have thought this through, do the following exercise.

a. Write down *all* the goals that you would ideally like to accomplish in the next five years, and label them *long-range goals*.

b. Then think about what you would like to accomplish in the next six months to a year. Write these down in a separate list, and call them *intermediate goals*. Some of these intermediate goals can be steps toward achieving your long-range goals.

c. Then think about what you would like to accomplish in the next few months, and write these down in a third list labeled *short-term goals*. Some of these can also be steps toward your longer-range goals.

d. Not all the goals you wrote down will be of equal importance to you. Your next step is to prioritize them. Put an A next to the goals on each of your three lists that are most critical and that you would like to start working on immediately. Place a C next to the goals on each list that you can put off indefinitely. Mark the remainder with a B.

e. Now, focusing *only* on your A goals, choose the two most important from your long-range list, the two or three most important from your intermediate list, and the two or three most important from your short-term list.

f. Make a separate list of these six to eight goals that you have just chosen. These should be your high-priority concerns right now and should guide you in the way you use your time. Don't throw away your master list; keep it for the future.

When Karen Jacobson did this exercise, these are the goals she finally decided on. (Note that whether goals are defined as long-range, intermediate, or short-term is a matter of individual choice. For example, Karen could have made "get myself organized" a short-term goal.)

Long-range:	1. Develop a good social support network.
	2. Develop a broad range of fulfilling interests and involvements.
Intermediate:	3. Enroll in school.
	4. Get myself organized.

Short-term: 5. Learn a deep relaxation technique.
                6. Take a parenting class.
                7. Lose 10 pounds.

Some words of caution. If you have children, they should automatically be a high priority. If your children are not included in your high-priority goals, either add a goal or replace a goal on your list. If you shortchange them in your pursuit of a rewarding new life, you are asking for trouble in the future. You might make it a goal to help your kids through the divorce, to build your relationship with them, to stop burdening them with all your problems and allow them to be children, to improve your disciplinary practices, to give them more stability, and so on.

Make a conscious effort to achieve some progress toward each of your goals every week. To do this, you may have to break down your goals into small steps. (For example, Karen might break down her goal to enroll in school into small steps such as getting some college catalogs, exploring different courses of study and their usefulness to career enhancement, checking on prerequisites, visiting schools, talking to people in the schools' counseling offices, and so forth.)

At the beginning of each week, make a *realistic* list of the specific things you would like to accomplish that week that will move you closer to each of your goals. (Although you may want to focus more on your short-term goals, try to make some steady progress toward your longer-range goals as well.) Post the list where you can see it. At the end of the week, evaluate whether you succeeded in achieving what you set out to do. Seeing tangible evidence of your progress will be rewarding and will keep you on track. As you reach each goal or as new goals assume more importance to you, you can replace old goals with new ones.

If you have trouble sticking to your intentions each week, evaluate whether you have been realistic. Chances are you will have to lower your sights. If you feel that you have been realistic but simply lack the motivation, follow the self-change program outlined in Appendix A.

You say you are already so busy that you don't have any extra time in your tight schedule? Keep track of exactly how you spend your time for a few typical days. Record it on a chart broken into 30-minute segments. Now that you have determined what your priorities are, you will undoubtedly find that you spend a good deal of time in activities that are low on your list of priorities—that is, activities unrelated to your goals. Can you drop some of those low-priority activities? Can you delegate some to other people? Can you lower your standards on low-priority activities so you can do them quicker? Can you learn to say no when people pressure you to do low-priority activities? Chances are you will find at least *some* time each day that you can channel into achieving your goals.

You say you don't know how to achieve your goals? This was Karen's problem. She wanted to develop a broad range of fulfilling interests and in-

---

Steps to Determining Priorities and Reaching Goals

✓ 1. Make three lists.
   • All goals you'd like to accomplish in the next five years.
   • All goals you'd like to accomplish in the next six months to one year.
   • All goals you'd like to accomplish in the next two to three months.
✓ 2. Prioritize your goals on each list.
   • A = Goals you would like to work on immediately (short-term).
   • C = Goals you can put off indefinitely (long-range).
   • B = All others (intermediate).
✓ 3. Choose your *most* important "A" goals from each list.
   • Choose two from your long-range list.
   • Choose two or three from your intermediate list.
   • Choose two or three from your short-term list.
✓ 4. Make a high-priority goal list with these six to eight goals.
✓ 5. Decide how you can reach each goal; try brainstorming.
✓ 6. Break down each goal into *small* steps.
✓ 7. Try to make *some* progress toward each goal each week.
   • Make out a "things to do" list each week. Try to move a little closer to each goal. Be realistic.
   • Use the self-change program (Appendix A) if needed for motivation.
   • Each week, evaluate the progress you have made.
✓ 8. Replace old goals with new ones when appropriate.

---

volvements, but what? If you find yourself facing this question, try some brainstorming. Let your mind roam and think of all the possible ways that you might be able to achieve your goal. At this point, go for quantity and don't worry about quality. This is not the time for evaluation. Write down each and every idea that comes to you, no matter how impractical or ridiculous it sounds. The point is to free-associate. One idea will lead to another. And often a highly impractical idea will stimulate a more useful one that you might not have thought of otherwise. The more things you come up with, the more likely it is that you will end up with some good, usable ideas. Once you have your ideas, you can evaluate how practical and satisfactory each one is likely to be. Based on your evaluation, select some of them, and develop a step-by-step plan to achieve them.

BUILDING NEW SOCIAL SUPPORT NETWORKS

Jan related that it wasn't until she moved from the suburbs that life began for her. After the divorce she had rented a small house in her familiar suburban neighborhood. She had been comfortable there, so it seemed logical. But it was a bad four years, she later concluded. Initially, her married friends had been very supportive and literally bombarded her with invitations. But after several months, they assumed she was over the worst, and the invitations grew more sparse. For almost four years she felt that she was on the fringe of life, not fitting in anywhere. She felt uncomfortable at the few married social gatherings she attended because she wasn't part of that world anymore, and she had no new world to replace it with. She didn't even know other singles. Feeling close to no one, she became more isolated, emotionally barren, and depressed with each passing month. Then the doctor she worked for invested in a condominium and needed a reliable renter. Since there were so many professional singles in the building, he asked Jan if she would be interested. In less than a year, Jan had found a good support group. She had three very close friends she cared about and could count on, as well as some acquaintances—both men and women—with whom she occasionally did things. Jan's eyes sparkled as she related how the building manager recently remarked to her that he couldn't believe she was the same person who had moved there just 10 months previously. "You always looked so forlorn," he said. "Now you're always smiling!"

If single life is to be rewarding, you need to develop a new social network in which you can feel accepted, receive support, and be socially involved. Your married friends are likely to drift away as your lives diverge.

As soon as you can, get started reaching out to new people. Aim to have at least one or two close confidants. For many singles, the friendships formed after divorce are the closest and most rewarding they have ever had. Some have friends who are basically surrogate families, always there ready to help. Ideally, the social network you build will include many acquaintances as well. The larger your network is, the richer your life is likely to be.

Getting Started

- Make contact with old friends and acquaintances from your past.
- Approach other singles at work and in your community. Use any basis to get an acquaintance started. Take a chance. Ask people to join you for lunch, coffee, or a movie. Most singles are open to new friendships.
- Ask friends and relatives to introduce you to other singles of both sexes.
- Begin entertaining in your home. Ask a few singles over for a casual evening. They are likely to reciprocate.
- Start a monthly group with some other singles, such as a gourmet group, a potluck dinner group, a discussion group, a support group, or a theater group.
- Invite a few singles to a party at your home and have them each invite a few other singles.
- If you can afford it, invest in two subscription tickets for some type of event you enjoy. Use the extra ticket as an excuse to invite someone you think you would like to get to know better.

- Most communities now have numerous interest clubs or groups for singles—theater groups, ski clubs, hiking clubs, gourmet groups, dance groups, professional groups, art groups, and so forth. You are probably more likely to meet kindred spirits in interest groups than at open singles events. Usually singles groups and events are listed in the local newspaper once or twice a week.
- If you have an interest for which there is no existing group in your community, place an ad in a newspaper and see if you can get a group going. If you are hesitant about opening up your home, try to use a room at a local church or community organization, or, if you have access to one, a recreation room in an apartment building. One woman started a French-speaking singles club this way; one man started a bowling club for singles; and another started a group for people from his home state. A simple magazine ad was the genesis of New Beginnings, a Washington, D.C.-based support group. Now over 12 years old and more than a thousand people strong, New Beginnings offers small educational and discussion groups at homes throughout the area, a wide variety of social events, and an environment of friendship and support for its enthusiastic membership.
- Try joining a volunteer organization, community group, political organization, or church group.
- Keep in mind that you are more likely to develop friendships in groups that provide an opportunity to work *with* others on projects over a period of time.
- Take some classes. Here, too, you are more likely to develop friendships in classes that encourage projects and participation—gourmet cooking, photography, drama, laboratory classes, discussion classes, and so forth.
- Join a singles or divorce support group, now sponsored by many churches and community organizations. Many people who have reluctantly joined support groups are now enthusiastic proponents of them.
- Many women find wonderful support networks in women's groups that are available in most communities. You don't have to be a women's lib activist to enjoy a group like this. Many women's groups help women discover their own strengths and create a strong sense of solidarity and friendship.
- Men are less likely to seek out men's groups, but mental health professionals recommend they do so because men are often too dependent on women to satisfy their emotional needs. Softball teams, bowling leagues, political groups, men's community organizations, and singles and divorce support groups are possibilities.
- Take a chance on some singles groups or activities that are *not* based on special interests or support. People often return home frustrated from these events because they attend them for the sole purpose of meeting

someone to date. You are far more likely to enjoy the evening if your goal is to have a good time and to meet *any* new people of either sex.

- If you are a parent, try your local chapter of Parents Without Partners. You need not be a parent with custody to join. Many chapters are very active, offering support groups, discussion groups, lectures, and a variety of social activities for both parents and children. Members usually welcome newcomers warmly. Many people who reluctantly try PWP after a passage of time have only one regret—that they did not join earlier. PWP presently has 120,000 members, and there are chapters in almost every city nationwide.

- Shared housing is becoming an increasingly popular way to solve both social and economic needs. If you would like to learn more about this option, write to Shared Housing Resource Center, 6344 Greene Street, Philadelphia, PA 19144.

- Don't forget your married friends. Some may continue to be good friends for life. Others may become good friends again after a lapse of time if they know that you are still interested in the friendship.

Overcoming Barriers

Forming a social support network takes time. Persistence is the key. The more opportunities you expose yourself to, the more success you are likely to have. If you are having trouble getting started, try some of these suggestions.

- Set a goal each week, and follow the program outlined in Appendix A to help yourself achieve it. Be sure to make each goal small and realistic. Of course, what is realistic differs for each person. A single parent with little time might set as a goal "to investigate a different social group each week and attend one each month." Someone with more time might set as a goal "to attend one or two social functions each week." Check the listings in your local newspaper to discover opportunities offered in your community.

- Work on building your self-esteem (Chapter 12). As it improves, so will your confidence.

- If social situations arouse your anxiety, distract yourself by setting a specific agenda on which to focus. For example, you might decide you will focus your attention on getting to know everything you can about a person you meet. Or you may assign yourself the task of putting another person at ease. By focusing on such a predetermined agenda, you will take your attention off your anxiety.

- If your problem is that you fear rejection, think of people who do not respond to your overtures as *nonresponsive* rather than as rejecting, suggests Mel Krantzler, Director of the Creative Divorce Love and Marriage Counseling Center in San Rafael, California, and author of a number of books on divorce. How can they be rejecting you when they don't even know you? They simply are unresponsive to you for their own reasons or because of their own perceptions.

- Listen to your self-talk before and during social encounters and discover what self-defeating things you are saying to yourself. Perhaps you are telling yourself that you are boring, stupid, unattractive, socially inept, or undesirable. Dr. Jeffrey Young, a cognitive therapist from the University of Pennsylvania, suggests that you treat your statements as hypotheses that need to be tested rather than as truths. Then analyze the relationships you have had in the past. Have there been people in the past who have liked you and who have found you attractive and interesting? Divorced people often generalize from the negative feedback they received from their ex-spouses or from a few incidents of rejection—something *everyone* experiences. Once you identify your own self-defeating talk, talk back to yourself with more positive statements, just as you would respond to a friend.

- Spend time imagining yourself in the social situation that you are about to encounter. Visualize as much detail as you can. Imagine yourself approaching people and responding to them positively and successfully. Try out several openings and conversations; envision a number of responses that others may have and how you might respond to them. Try practicing deep relaxation (Appendix B) during your imagery and again during social encounters.

- Weigh your discomfort in initiating a contact or attending an activity against the possibility of developing a potential friendship, suggests Young.

- Do *not* get discouraged. Unless you are a very rare individual, not every attempt you make will be a success. And if you join an ongoing group, keep in mind that you may have to attend a number of times *consistently* before others begin to recognize you.

NEW BEGINNINGS IN THE JOB MARKET

Because of the small percentage of divorces in which spousal support awards are currently granted, most women find it necessary to earn an independent living after divorce. You may be entering the job market for the first time or moving from part-time to full-time employment, or you may wish to move on from a "job" to a "career." If you have not been working outside the home, employment is likely to bring you advantages beyond financial ones. Women who return to work after divorce generally report a boost in self-esteem and in feelings of competence and independence, too. Working outside the home opens up new social networks, contributes to a new identity, and offers financial independence. In contrast, women who remain home full-time after divorce more often become depressed, develop physical ailments, and feel trapped.

However, many divorcing women sell themselves short. They limit their search to newspaper want ads and take the first job they are "lucky" enough to land—often a poor-paying one with little chance for advancement. Don't limit yourself this way. In the popular job-hunting book *What Color Is Your Parachute?*, Richard Bolles reports that as many as 80 percent of the positions in this country (above entry-level ones) are never advertised through traditional channels.

If you have been primarily a homemaker, you may be thinking that an entry-level position is the best that you can do. But perhaps not.

Evaluating Your Skills

In one study, reports Bolles, major U.S. employers were asked what they look for in potential employees. This is what they said (not necessarily in this order).

- Ability to communicate
- Willingness to accept responsibility
- Initiative
- Interpersonal skills
- Self-direction
- Flexibility
- Energy level (i.e., a hard worker)
- Ability to handle conflict
- Leadership
- Intelligence
- Occupational skills
- Self-confidence
- Competitiveness
- Imagination (new ideas, finding solutions to problems)
- Goals (ability to identify, work toward, and achieve them)
- Self-knowledge (realistic assessment of capabilities)

Interestingly, many of these characteristics are ones that most successful homemakers have had to develop to juggle the logistics of running a home, raising children, scheduling, organizing, entertaining, and providing for their family's emotional, physical, and nutritional needs. If you have been involved in volunteer community service work, you are likely to be further ahead. You may have had the opportunity to develop superior organizational, managerial, administrative, interpersonal, prioritizing, leadership, or fund-raising skills.

This is the time to assess all your strengths, accomplishments, and skills. If you have difficulty identifying the skills you have developed over the years, use the exercises in Richard Bolles's book *What Color Is Your Parachute?* The book is revised every year and is in local libraries and book stores. The exercises should help you identify skills that may lead to a number of different kinds of jobs.

Translating Skills Into Jobs

Once you have identified your skills and assets, you will need to match them up with likely occupations. There are several approaches you can take to do this.

- A wealth of information can be found in your local library. The reference librarian can direct you to sources describing occupations, their requirements, ranges of salaries, present availability, future outlook, and related occupations. Two such sources, published by the U.S. Department of Labor, are *The Dictionary of Occupational Titles* and *The Occupational Outlook Handbook*.
- Visit the counseling office at your local community college. Many provide inexpensive career counseling services that can help you discover the kinds of occupations for which you are suited. You can also learn what occupations offer the most promise in the future.
- If you have not been previously employed, take advantage of the services at a Displaced Homemakers center. These centers are specifically designed for women (usually over 40) who have been displaced from their careers as homemakers. They help women assess their skills and offer them employment information as well as job counseling. Most centers also offer job training and job placement services. What is unique about Displaced Homemakers centers is that they work on building women's confidence and making them *emotionally* "job-ready." They also provide women with a warm and caring support group that has served as a lifeline for countless divorced women over the years. Displaced Homemakers centers are funded by both federal and state funds and are often located in community colleges. According to national headquarters in Washington, D.C., there are presently over a thousand centers across the country. To find one, contact your local community college, YWCA, or state Department of Education; a women's center; or an adult-services department. You can also write the national headquarters, which can direct you to your local center (National Displaced Homemakers Networkers, 1411 K St. NW, Suite 930, Washington, DC 20005).
- Be creative and enterprising. You may have talents that will allow you to

start your own business at minimal cost. Divorced women have started catering, housecleaning, bookkeeping, typing, or word-processing businesses. Some charge a hefty fee to shop and run errands for busy people. Others teach classes in their homes. Some make handcrafted items and sell them at shows and swap meets. Some raise and provide plants to restaurants and offices.

- Explore whether your talents might be suitable for sales. Many high-commission sales jobs now available require limited education and experience. Many women, perhaps because of their good interpersonal skills, are finding exceptional success and a lucrative living in this area.

Going After What You Want

Networking is the way many jobs are filled. How do you network?

- Take every chance you can to tell people the kind of job you are looking for. Critical contacts are sometimes made under the most unlikely circumstances. One high-level San Francisco executive recalls that the contact for his current position was a fellow hiker he met while backpacking. One magazine writer made her contact at a class reunion.
- Working for a temporary agency is a good way to make contacts. Talk to people during breaks and find out about their jobs and the company. Sometimes, temporary jobs will last over a long period, and you may be able to impress someone enough to either be offered a position or get a good letter of recommendation. Working as a temporary is also a good way to get a feel for different organizations and companies and to build your confidence and skills.
- Attend meetings of organizations and clubs that are related to your chosen occupation. Talk to as many people as you can, find out about their fields and their jobs, and tell them what you are looking for. If it is appropriate to have business cards made up, do so, and give them out liberally. If something comes up, a job contact is more likely to remember and contact you if he or she has one of your cards.

Of course, networking may not be sufficient. Consider the possibility of updating your skills or even retraining. Before you invest your time in this manner, be sure you have investigated the availability of jobs in your selected field. Four-year colleges and graduate schools are frequent choices for updating or retraining, but there are many other options. Community colleges provide excellent avenues for retraining, offering many two-year programs in a variety of fields. Private vocational schools are another possibility, although they are a more expensive option. If you choose this route, check out the school's credentials, whether it will provide you with marketable skills, and whether it has a guaranteed job-placement program. You may also find a job training or apprenticeship program in your state employment bureau.

Financing your education may pose a problem. Some women work while going to school. Others take out loans. Some are able to get short-term spousal support until they get on their feet or are able to qualify for public assistance.

If you cannot get a job that you believe you are qualified for, you may be able to arrange what is called a "volunteer contract." This type of contract is used by some Displaced Homemakers centers and other social service programs, but you may be able to arrange your own. In a volunteer contract, you sign a formal agreement with an employer to function in the position as a paid person would; however, you take no pay. In return, the employer provides supervision, references, and perhaps a paid position at a future date. The terms of the contract should be very specific. Many include a specific job title and the salary the position would ordinarily command so there will be formal records for the volunteer's benefit. A volunteer contract is a way to prove yourself and get on-the-job training, letters of recommendation, and the recent work experience many employers desire. Employers likely to be interested in such contracts are government agencies and nonprofit organizations.

Of course, don't neglect more conventional routes in your job search. Read the want ads daily, *thoroughly*, to see if any jobs advertised interest you and match your strengths. Private employment agencies are another possibility, but beware of those that charge you up front.

These suggestions are a beginning. Preparing an effective résumé and giving a good interview will be critical to your success. You can find some excellent books to help you with these topics in Appendix C.

NEW ROMANTIC RELATIONSHIPS

For six months, Mike kept all his relationships strictly platonic. "I didn't want anything more than company," he reported.

When people asked Penny if she would like to date, she told them she just got rid of one man from her life and certainly didn't want another.

Jackie couldn't understand what happened to her after her divorce. She had never thought of herself as the one-night-stand type, but for six months, she had an insatiable appetite for sex. She frequented singles' bars and more often than not would spend the night with someone she met there. Now she is grateful it is in the past. "I still enjoy sex, but now I'm very selective about who I share my bed with," Jackie confided.

After his wife left, Ross felt so empty and lonely that he became determined to remarry. He met Cheryl and they married within months. "I thought that I was

head over heels in love with her, but it turned into a disaster!" Ross is determined
to be very careful next time.

Most people find that divorce seriously impacts their relationships with the
opposite sex. Although its effects are felt in different ways, there are common
patterns; feelings like Mike's, Penny's, Jackie's, and Ross's are quite typical. Part
of the fallout from divorce is a plunge in self-esteem. Fear of trusting another
person is also common. Both these reactions influence relationships and need
to be overcome so that future romantic relationships can be satisfying and
healthy.

If you are like a large number of other divorcing men and women, you may
experience several of the patterns just described as you progress through the
postdivorce months. Immediately after separation you may have no interest in
sex. Or you may not even be interested in dating, proclaiming to all that you
have sworn off men (or women) for life. Divorce counselor Mel Krantzler calls
this the "walking wounded" stage. It is an adaptive reaction because it protects
you from involvements for which you are not ready. However, warns Krantzler,
good adjustment to divorce should open options, not deny them. Your fear of
new relationships should not continue for years. If you hang on to your fear
of new relationships too long, Zev Wanderer and Tracy Cabot's book *Letting
Go*, listed in Appendix C, offers a program that may help you get over it.

Do you have an insatiable appetite for sex? Have you embarked upon a
long series of one-night stands? This is a common experience among divorcing
people and has been referred to as the "sex is everything" stage, the "horny"
stage, or the "running" stage. Many divorcing men and women are completely
baffled by their newly aroused needs and uncharacteristic behavior ("I don't
know what's gotten into me."). However, this stage in postdivorce adjustment
becomes less baffling when some of the major motivating forces behind it are
understood. It seems to be largely an attempt to prove one's attractiveness and
desirability, bolster sagging self-esteem, and test sexual capabilities. Confidence
in these areas is usually wounded during a poor marriage and the trauma of
divorce. The advantage of one-night stands for a person still vulnerable from
divorce is that they do not require commitment or trust.

Therapist Bruce Fisher, Director of the Family Relations Learning Center
in Boulder, Colorado and author of *Rebuilding*, Bruce Fisher, points out that
activities other than direct sexual contact can satisfy many of the needs underlying this compulsive sexual behavior. In this age of AIDS, you may find this
reassuring, since AIDS has become a very real threat in the heterosexual community. Fisher suggests that people can relieve some of the pressure of what he
calls the "horny stage" by turning efforts directly toward building self-esteem,
establishing a new identity, and overcoming loneliness (Chapter 12). People also
have a strong need for physical touching during this period, he points out, and

they frequently try to satisfy this need through sex. However, it can be satisfied by nonsexual touching as well, such as getting and giving lots of hugs. You might also try routinely touching people on the arm or hand while greeting them, talking to them, or saying good-bye. Many relieve their sexual frustration during this time by masturbation.

At some point most people become bored with revolving partners, casual sex, and shallow relationships and look for something deeper. It is at this time that a new permanent relationship becomes very tempting—it would be so much more comfortable than being out there alone, having to forge a new identity and life. By all means, develop deep relationships, *but* resist the temptation to remarry at this time. Relationships that are built when you are feeling very needy and vulnerable are usually built on shaky ground. A relationship that may seem serious at this point in your life may later feel like an albatross around your neck once you are back on your feet. Right now you are likely to need someone who will teach you to trust again, bolster your self-esteem, fend off your loneliness, and distract you from your pain and anxiety. But these would be a poor basis for a *permanent* relationship. Once you are feeling confident and whole again and are ready to try new directions, you may find that you are completely out of sync with the person who once seemed so compatible.

Mental health professionals suggest that you experience a number of relationships after divorce without concerning yourself with permanency. Become a person who is interested in people and aim to get to know as many people as you can. Resist sizing up each new date as a potential marriage partner or comparing him or her against some ideal standard. If you do, you will deny yourself many potentially rewarding relationships. You might also spend much of your life feeling disappointed. Fisher suggests that you make your first priority building your social network and new friendships. Some people in your new network will then become close friends and perhaps lovers.

When will you be ready for a new permanent relationship? Not until you have completed two major tasks of divorce adjustment, mental health professionals agree. The first is resolving the end of your marriage (Chapter 6). A new relationship will suffer if you are still emotionally engaged in the old one or if you have never recognized the role that you played in its end. Your second task is to achieve your own sense of identity, direction, and self-worth. Your contribution to a new relationship will be meager if you are still struggling to feel whole again. You should first feel that you can make it on your own. People who *rapidly* progress through the transition–restructuring phase of divorce and also make better-than-average progress in the recovery–rebuilding phase might be ready to enter a long-term committed relationship about two years after divorce. However, most people would need considerably longer.

OPPORTUNITIES FOR PERSONAL GROWTH

As is true for so many things in life, being single has the potential to be as rewarding as you work to make it. You may not be single by choice, but this isn't germane to whether your life as a single will be satisfying. Many others before you have been devastated by divorce, believing it was the end of their lives. Instead, many have found it was their second chance, providing opportunities they would not have had otherwise. One woman commented,

> I thought I would die, I mean really, literally die, when he told me he was leaving. I just couldn't conceptualize life without him—after 24 years. And then one day I realized, hey, I'm still alive. . . .
>
> That was the turning point. Suddenly I stopped feeling like a victim and I had this wonderful sensation that someone had given me another chance, a chance to experience life in a way I had never expected . . . as the architect for all my choices. . . .
>
> I discovered that the life I wanted to lead on my own was very different from the life I'd been living with him. His leaving was the beginning of my development as a person. In a way, I really thank him.[1]

Too often, single life is treated as a transitory period to be endured until one remarries. *You* are the one who needs to make your life right. Don't wait around hoping for someone else to do it for you. Use your single life as a time to explore and develop the many facets of yourself that have been hidden. Open yourself to new experiences. Develop new interests. Forge a new identity. Learn the skills necessary to live independently as a single. Build a large and varied social support network. Develop goals and keep yourself moving toward them. Learn to become a better person because of your divorce. Don't waste this time as a single. Structure it to be rewarding and growth-promoting.

And what of the ambition of having another committed relationship? Time and again, it has been reported that people are most likely to meet a new partner when they are involved with life and the things that interest them. It is when people are absorbed and enthusiastic about what they are doing that others are most likely to be drawn to them. Don't wait for someone to make you happy. Happiness is an inside job.

14

ABOUT SINGLE-PARENT HOMES

At one time, children were considered "different" if they lived in a single-parent home, but today, 24 percent of the children in this country are living with one parent, a figure that has exactly doubled since 1970 (see Table 14.1). More surprising are projections for the future. Based on current trends, Sandra Hofferth of the Center for Population Research at the National Institute of Child Health and Human Development recently made the startling projection that 70 percent of white children and more than 90 percent of black children born in 1980 will spend some time living in a single-parent home before their 18th birthdays. A more conservative yet still startling estimate was made by well-known demographers Arthur Norton, of the U.S. Bureau of the Census, and Paul Glick, of Arizona State University, who projected that 60 percent of children born in the 80s will spend some part of their childhoods in a single-parent home.

Although people most often talk about single-parent *families*, the term is a misnomer for most children of separation and divorce. The term single-parent families implies that children have only *one* parent after divorce. Wrong. They continue to have *two* parents. Many mental health professionals believe that we would make significant progress toward keeping fathers involved with their chil-

---

TABLE 14.1

About 1 in 5 white families, 1 in 2 black families, and 1 in 3 Hispanic families are headed by a single parent.

Of children living in a single-parent family:
38.3% have divorced parents
24.9% have separated parents
30.5% have a never-married parent
 6.3% have a widowed parent

Source: U.S. Bureau of the Census, Current Population Reports, Series P-23, No.162, *Studies in Marriage and the Family*, U.S. Government Printing Office, Washington, D.C., 1989.

---

dren if we stopped disenfranchising them of their status as parents. Using terms such as "single-parent families" and "visiting rights" subtly contributes to both fathers' *and* mothers' feelings that fathers should no longer play a parental role. The more that fathers are shut out, the less likely they are to behave as fathers, and it is children's divorce adjustment that suffers as a consequence. A more accurate term is *single-parent home* because there is only one parent in the home. I will use this term here, as a reminder that children still have and very much *need* the involvement of *both* their parents in their lives, even if their primary home is headed by only one of those parents.

THE BENEFITS AND PROBLEMS OF PARENTING SOLO

A great deal has been written about the difficulties of single-parenting—enough to alarm even the most optimistic individuals starting out in this new role. But there is a positive side to parenting solo as well. When seasoned single parents are asked, the majority of those interviewed speak of definite benefits that accompany their role. In fact, many say they would be reluctant to trade these blessings for the uncertainties that inevitably accompany remarriage. During the difficult transition period, which is likely to span two years, you may be far more aware of the difficulties than the advantages, but these will come in time.

Most studies have found that single parents treasure their independence and autonomy. They are now in control of their own lives. They can develop their own interests, fulfill their own needs, choose their own friends, and engage in social activities of their choice. Money, even if limited, can be spent as they see fit. They can have their own ideas about child rearing, determine their own schedules and routines, and set their own standards for housekeeping. They are no longer half a couple and no longer must make ongoing compromises and accommodations to please a spouse. Single parents now have only their own and their children's needs to consider. The feeling of many single parents is that they may have less time and money now, but at least they are in control of it, and they seem to like that.

Single parents also report a great deal of personal growth and a sense of satisfaction as a result of meeting the challenges and demands of their new role. Many report that they discovered resources they never suspected they had and developed new dimensions of themselves. Men often marvel at their recently discovered nurturance and women at their new competence and self-reliance. Many women, in particular, experience a surge in self-esteem. Said one single mother,

> I think single parenting makes you really strong, very creative and resourceful. You know the saying, "Necessity is the mother of invention"? Well, you find out how strong you really are and just what you can do. It's amazing.[1]

Because the pervasive discord in the home is ended, single parents often report feeling more relaxed and enjoying their children more. A closer relationship with children, whether from reduced family tension or some other factor, is a benefit mentioned by a large percentage of parents, such as this joint-custody father.

> It's weird, but we are much closer than we would have been if I had stayed married. We just couldn't be tighter. It shows itself in lots of ways. They are able to be more relaxed with me, open with me, tell me about secrets, do things with me that show they are more at ease. And I'm much more open with them, more relaxed with them.[2]

And what about the negative side? Even single parents who had shouldered most of the parenting during their marriages are often surprised at how different single parenting is. Unless single parents are truly co-parenting their children with a former spouse, there is no one to share the responsibilities of raising children. There is no one to help make important decisions or to help discipline. No one is around to provide another perspective when problems arise. (What's happening? What should be done about it?). There are no time-outs from children's care, emotional needs, and demands—not even when parents are tired, sick, or emotionally drained themselves. Sometimes there isn't even anyone to share the financial burdens. Then, of course, there is the unending housework, chores, errands, chauffeuring, maintenance, and repairs that need to be done solo. For most single parents, there never seems to be enough time. Neither is there enough money.

There are other problems as well—too little social and emotional support and too much loneliness and isolation. Many single parents find that overloaded schedules preclude their joining in singles activities, but at the same time, their changed lives make them strangers to married friends. Constraints on dating and sexual relationships is another common complaint. Many miss the emotional intimacy and sharing with another adult.

Of course, there is the matter of finding affordable child care that is both reliable and good. While this is a concern for any working parent, single parents are only too aware of the upheavals their youngsters have been through and their special need for a stable and caring environment.

Single parents have other job-related problems as well. When looking for employment, many must fight an employer's fears that too much work time will be sacrificed for parenting responsibilities. Once hired, many find that parenting responsibilities limit their chances for promotion.

ARE SINGLE-PARENT HOMES REALLY SO DIFFERENT?

Whether a home has one or two parents does not predict how much love, support, or parental involvement a child receives. But there are several ways in which single-parent homes usually *are* different from homes with two parents.

Once a parent leaves the home, the way the remaining parent and children interact typically undergoes change. The remaining parent relies on the children to fill some of the gaps left by the ex-spouse. Overwhelmed with all the new household, family, and perhaps work responsibilities, the parent enlists the children's help. The implicit or explicit message is that "we are all in this together," and a coalition between parent and children generally evolves. With children promoted to the status of "junior partners," so to speak, they are also typically given a larger say in family and household matters. Family decisions and rules, once jointly made by parents, become more open to negotiation. Gradually the authority distinctions that once existed between parent and children become somewhat blurred. So do the distinctions between the parent's and children's rights and responsibilities. The end result of this newly developed family style is often positive—an increase in family communication, closeness, cohesiveness, and companionship. However, this family style can be carried too far, and when it is, it often becomes the source of serious difficulties (discussed shortly) that drive many single parents to seek family counseling.

Having no ongoing feedback from another parent also influences the style of parenting adopted by many single moms and dads. There simply is no one to help put things into perspective. One child absolutely *must* have a new dress for a dance. Another wants his "unreasonable" curfew extended. A third hasn't done his chores for the past three months, yet always pleads one "valid" excuse or another. Which children's requests are legitimate? In two-parent families, when one parent is in doubt, the other is there with his or her feedback. "We have already bought three new dresses for Suzanne this year, and I don't think she needs a fourth." "I think it would be okay to extend Jeff's curfew to 10 on school nights, providing his homework is done before he goes out." "I agree with you that Andy is becoming too creative with his excuses and not developing enough responsibility." Because single parents usually do not have the benefit of this kind of adult feedback, they are often uncertain about the validity of their own positions. This causes many single parents to be too easily swayed by the persuasiveness of older children and too readily compromising on issues that, in the long run, are not in children's best interests. Recognizing their single parents' vulnerability, children from single-parent homes often admit that they "get away with" a lot more than they ever could if they were living with both parents.

Finally, if only one parent is really involved with the children, that parent usually assumes a far more pivotal role in children's lives and development than he or she would if a second parent were regularly present. There is only one parent there on a regular basis to serve as a model, to discipline, to provide a point of view, or to help solve problems. When conflicts arise between single parents and children, there is no second parent to act as a buffer. There may even be only one parent on whom to rely. In these cases, all of children's eggs are likely to be in one basket, so to speak. If a child's single parent cannot cope, the child will be at risk of becoming a casualty of divorce. If, on the other hand, a youngster's single parent functions well, copes well with stress, and parents effectively, the youngster is likely to do well and learn how to cope with stress effectively too.

THE "CHILDREN AS PARTNERS" PHENOMENON: TROUBLE ON THE HORIZON

A family style that evolves in a significant number of single-parent homes is one that you need to avoid. Often, it leads to difficulties that eventually get out of control. In the *typical* single-parent home, children are promoted to "junior partners," and this works just fine. But some single parents go a step further and either explicitly or implicitly grant the role of *equal* partners to their children, effectively (although not intentionally) relinquishing their parental role and authority. This is a mistake and often leads to one of these two related problems.

The "Parent Becomes Peer" Family

Families in which single parents become peers to their children are seen with regularity in child guidance clinics and community mental health centers across the country, report Dr. David Glenwick of Fordham University and Dr. Joel Mowrey of Kent State University. In these families, there is typically a very bright, articulate older child (frequently 9 to 13 years old) who appears to be far more mature than he or she actually is. These children's precociousness lures overwhelmed single parents into treating them as peers, confidants, and companions rather than as the children they are. Parent and child become extremely close, with the parent regularly sharing all or most of his or her personal and financial problems, frustrations, and loneliness with the youngster, as if the child were another adult. In some cases, the child functions as the parent's chum. At other times, youngsters begin to parent their parents, providing nurturance, support, and advice. Sometimes these youngsters are the prime forces holding the household and family together.

Although these children appear to have great inner strength, many are stretching themselves beyond their psychological limits. They marshal all their resources to hold their vulnerable parents together because they are well aware that children cannot make it on their own. In the process, they suppress their own needs, as well as their own fears, concerns, and feelings of loss surrounding their parents' divorce. These children's outward appearance of maturity belies the overwhelming anxiety and insecurity they generally feel. But many eventually express their anxiety and fears indirectly in symptomatic behavior—stomach pains, sleeping and eating problems, academic and school problems, drug use, promiscuous behavior, and so forth.

Eight-year-old Gail, one of the children in the California Children of Divorce Study, was one such child.

> Gail's mother was an attractive fashion model who began drinking heavily after her separation. It was not long before she made eight-year-old Gail her constant companion. Gail was brought to adult parties. When her mother wanted someone to hold, she had Gail sleep with her. When her mother wanted company, she kept Gail up so late into the night that the youngster missed school the following day. On several occasions, Gail had a hangover because she had filled in as her mother's drinking companion. Gail's mother asked the eight-year-old for advice on when to go out, whom to date, and whether to become sexually involved.
>
> Gail was robbed of her rightful role as the child and thrust into the role of parent. She withdrew from her friends and school activities and gradually became a socially isolated, frightened, and depressed child. Her school grades dropped, she suffered from nightmares, and she became preoccupied with fears of abandonment.

Sometimes problems do not become evident until the parent begins to date or develops a new romantic relationship. A new person on the scene threatens the child's special relationship with the parent and the prestigious position he or she has earned in the family. Feeling cast off, youngsters are often filled with jealousy and anger and begin to act out their feelings in problematic behavior.

When Children Compete for Power

A second troublesome pattern commonly develops when a parent promotes children to the role of equal partners in the family. The parent sends children conflicting and confusing messages: They are accepted as equal partners one day but are expected to submit to parental authority the next. What often follows is a subtle struggle for leadership and power in the family. It is often the parent who loses, although he or she is seldom aware of it until the situation gets out of control. The parent drifts into the pattern of deferring to youngsters in areas where parents should be in control, including authority over younger siblings. Children also routinely make their own decisions without guidance or input. However, because of their lack of maturity, their decisions are often poor ones.

Once again, children are functioning in an adult role for which they are not prepared emotionally. The parent has effectively relinquished his or her parental role of providing children with discipline, guidance, and protection, and the situation often goes amiss. Common problems that eventually bring these pseudomature youngsters to therapists' attention include rebelliousness against authority, drug abuse, sexual promiscuity, truancy, or a number of other behavior problems. Their single parents, throwing up their hands in despair, report, "I give up. (S)He doesn't listen to me. I can't do anything with him (her) anymore." The underlying problem is not only that children have insufficient guidance and too much power in the family. They are also under too much stress from functioning in an adultlike role before they have the maturity to handle it.

Francine Wilmington and her 15-year-old son Jeffrey are examples of this type of family pattern gone amiss.

Francine's husband left her when Jeffrey was 11. "You're going to have to take over for your father around here, Jeffrey—I just can't do everything," she told the youngster. Jeffrey assumed the role of "man of the house" very quickly. He also watched his younger brother Charlie after school and many evenings when Francine was gone. Charlie bitterly complained that Jeffrey was a dictator but was told to stop fussing. As Francine relied on Jeffrey more and more, it seemed only natural to consult him about household decisions, problems with Charlie, and her problems at work, much as she used to do with her husband. Jeffrey seemed so mature. Francine never realized that she usually yielded to his opinions, even where Charlie was concerned. By the time Jeffrey was 14, he was going out several evenings a week. He never asked permission; he merely mentioned that he had plans. Jeffrey seemed so responsible that it never occurred to Francine that he needed supervision. She wasn't aware that many of his friends were older or that he was drinking.

In fact, the first time she was aware of trouble was when his end-of-the-year report card came. His grades had dramatically declined, and he received an "unsatisfactory" in citizenship and effort in four classes. Aghast, she confronted her son. "My teachers are jerks this year, Mom. There's nothing to worry about. Next year will be different." But the following year the situation turned from bad to worse. Jeffrey developed a reputation as a troublemaker. It seemed he bucked people in authority. He was barely passing his classes and received a number of referrals to the vice-principle's office.

Finally, realizing that some action needed to be taken, Francine put him on restriction. "Restriction! You've got to be kidding! Come on, Mom, get real," he said as he walked out the door. Trying to give him a curfew resulted in the same response. What had gone wrong? She was at a loss for what to do. Finally, she resorted to nagging and yelling, but their relationship quickly deteriorated to one of conflict and acrimony. It was not until Jeffrey had a run-in with the law that Francine finally sought family counseling.

The Importance of Maintaining "Generational Boundaries"

A recurring theme consistently emerges from studies of single-parent homes— the importance of parents maintaining "generational boundaries" between themselves and their children. It is fine for parents to share *some* of their problems and concerns with their offspring and to enlist children as *junior* partners to *help* with family responsibilities. But it is important that parents not relinquish their roles as parents and that they allow their children and adolescents to *function* as children and adolescents. Many children have already lost one parental figure through divorce. They cannot afford to lose the other as well. Children and adolescents need their single parents to be in charge and to provide them with discipline, limits, and guidelines.

If the generational boundaries have become fuzzy in your home, it is time to clarify them. If you are treating your child as a peer or confidant, find an adult friend to confide in, and encourage your youngster to develop friends and outside interests. Allow your child to worry about childhood or adolescent concerns rather than adult ones. Shift the focus from you, and help your youngster adjust to the many losses he or she has had.

If you have been treating your children as equal partners, begin to exert your authority in areas that naturally separate parents and children, such as allowances, chores, homework, and types of television programs that are acceptable for them to watch. Read chapter 16 on discipline, and begin to set and enforce limits and rules. Be prepared for protests and resistance; it is only natural. But don't back down on your resolve. If your home is out of control and you cannot get it straightened out yourself, see a family counselor who will help you do just that.

SINGLE-PARENT FATHERS: DIFFERENT FROM SINGLE-PARENT MOTHERS?

Despite all the press about the increasing numbers of fathers raising their children, men currently head only 12 percent of single-parent homes. Who are these fathers who parent their children singly? They tend to be men who have achieved a higher-than-average educational, occupational, and income level. (In fact, according to the U.S. Census Bureau statistics, their income is twice that of single-parent mothers.) They are somewhat more likely to have custody of preadolescent and adolescent boys, although a sizable 30 to 40 percent are raising girls of all ages. In a study of more than one thousand single fathers, Geoffrey Greif of the University of Maryland found that 20 percent gained custody through a court-settled dispute, whereas the remaining 80 percent had custody by mutual consent or by default. Fathers who seek custody of their children perceive themselves as more loving and nurturing than the average man. According to University of Colorado divorce expert William Hodges, those who seek custody most aggressively are often men who felt abandoned as children.

Unlike single mothers, single fathers do not seek out one another. (They are far more likely to seek out a single mother for help and companionship.) Generally, fathers with custody have fewer friendships and express more loneliness than do their female counterparts. Other problems they report are not much different from those of single mothers—an overload of responsibilities and demanding tasks, constraints on dating and sexual relationships, and limited time and energy for themselves and their children. Similar to single mothers, single fathers also face career and job problems. They, too, choose jobs to accommodate parenting responsibilities, put careers on back burners, and find they are passed over for promotions.

Contrary to popular media portrayals, single fathers, as a group, do not report difficulty assuming household and child-care tasks, even though most had not been heavily involved in managing the household while married. Typically, single fathers report that they share chores with children, with teenage girls doing a greater share than their siblings. In general, however, their children do not appear to be overburdened with home responsibilities.

How do single fathers fare as parents? Very well, studies report. Fathers who do the best are those who had taken an active role in parenting before divorce and who wanted custody. Those who have custody by default usually have a far more difficult time. However, for the most part, fathers and their children report very good relationships with one another. Most fathers studied seem to put forth a great deal of effort attending to their children's emotional and psychological needs. Do they succeed? Interestingly, several studies have reported that children living in father-headed single-parent homes rated their dads as more nurturant than either fathers *or* mothers were rated by children living in two-parent families.

A Canadian study conducted by Anne-Marie Ambert that tracked single-parent fathers and mothers for a number of years suggests that fathers may have an easier transition to single parenting than mothers. The fathers Ambert studied were more effective disciplinarians than the mothers were and had fewer child behavior problems to contend with. Ambert reported that during the postdivorce period, the parent-child relationships in father-headed homes were strikingly different from those in mother-headed homes. Children in the custody of their fathers were most often obedient, respectful, and very appreciative of their fathers' parenting efforts. In comparison, children in single-mother homes were disobedient and unappreciative and often responded to mothers' discipline attempts with threats to live with their fathers. However, children's behavior and relationships with moms did dramatically improve over time.

Fathers are not always found to be good disciplinarians. In the large-scale University of Maryland study, Dr. Greif found that sometimes fathers develop the same troublesome parenting pattern as do many single mothers—functioning as peers rather than as parents. Other fathers seem to be so intent on fighting the myth that children are better off with their mothers that they overcompensate by becoming *too* strict and setting inappropriately high expectations for their children. Neither of these extremes is good for youngsters.

In case you are left with the impression that, for some reason, single parenting is easier for fathers than for mothers, don't be tempted to change custody of your children yet. Oregon researcher Dr. Shirley Hanson has suggested that single fathers report so *few* problems that one is tempted to question whether they are being completely honest. Are these fathers so intent on proving that men can raise children as well as women can that they put on a false front? Regardless of the honesty factor, there are a few reasons to account for single fathers having a somewhat easier time than many single mothers do. As a group, single fathers are far better off financially than single mothers and do not have to fight the continual uphill economic battle that many single mothers find so draining of their time, energy, and morale. Fathers who are raising their children are also a very select group. Most are well educated, actively chose this non-traditional role, and are eager to make it work. In contrast, there is a very broad range of single-parent mothers. Finally, men who have custody of their children often report feeling appreciated by their offspring, and they certainly receive lots of pats on the back from the community at large. "My, isn't he a wonderful father to raise those children!" This is likely to make a single father's job easier, at least psychologically. How many single mothers are thanked or called wonderful? After all, they are just doing what they are "supposed" to be doing.

GROWING UP IN A SINGLE-PARENT HOME: A CHILD'S PERSPECTIVE

What is it like for a child to grow up in a single-parent home? A number of themes regularly emerge in studies. Compared to youngsters raised in intact families, children raised in single-parent homes typically feel they are more independent and self-sufficient as well as more responsible and mature. They feel they are on their own much of the time with fewer rules to follow. They also feel closer to their single parents, yet are lonely much of the time because of the unavailability of both their parents.

At first glance, many of these considerations appear to be either clear advantages or disadvantages of life in single-parent homes. They are, however, mixed bags of blessings and burdens, which many children, with surprising wisdom for their years, seem to recognize.

Kids are usually proud of their self-reliance, for example, and at first this would seem to be a clear advantage of being raised in a single-parent home. But kids see the negative side of their self-reliance and independence as well. Many admit to becoming self-reliant out of necessity because there seems to be no one else to rely on—a feeling that often breeds insecurity. Many children admit that the degree of independence they have is a bit scary, and they are not sure they are ready to handle it. Others believe that their self-reliance has increased their emotional distance from their families. Commenting on this, a group of teens who wrote their own book, *The Kids' Book About Single-Parent Families*, said,

Often, kids who live in single-parent families for a while can become more independent, and the parent and kid can become too busy for each other. . . . It turns into a vicious cycle. Usually, you end up feeling . . . that your parent doesn't love you, or your parent could think that you don't care.[3]

Children from single-parent homes also have mixed feelings about the increased responsibility they usually shoulder and the maturity they develop. On the one hand, most like feeling competent and needed and are proud to make a significant contribution to their families. On the other hand, many envy the carefree lives of their peers and feel they are missing out on much of their childhoods. A minority feel used by their parents and become resentful.

If you asked a random sampling of youngsters from two-parent homes, most would probably say that life would be idyllic if they were given more freedom and had fewer rules. However, many older teens and young adults raised in single-parent homes see real shortcomings in having too much freedom and too few rules. For example, when divorce researcher Judith Wallerstein interviewed her study group 10 years after their parents' divorces, a recurring theme emerged among the oldest group: There had been "no one in charge" while they were growing up. These young adults felt that they had needed more guidance than they received. No one demanded proper behavior from them and no one upheld rules. Without firm parental guidance and rules, it had been harder for them to control their impulses, resist peer pressure, and make wise choices. Some had failed. Others had just found it difficult.

Even children's closeness with single parents can become a double-edged sword. Although kids usually consider the closeness a plus and enjoy the special trust single parents often place in them, some children begin to feel responsible for their single parents' well-being and happiness. This usually occurs when parents build their entire lives around their children. Though parents in two-parent homes can also center their lives around their children, they at least have each other. Not so for the single parent, and children are well aware of this, especially when it comes time to try their own wings and become independent.

Although the loneliness that children in single-parent homes frequently express could be interpreted as a clear disadvantage, youngsters report it can have positive outcomes. Some feel they have become more resourceful and creative, while others report having developed closer relationships with relatives and friends than they might have otherwise.

A child's loneliness stems not only from the busy schedule of a custodial parent, but also from the absence of a noncustodial parent from the child's daily life. However, if the noncustodial parent is involved, having two homes often helps make up for the loneliness children feel.

THE PSYCHOLOGICAL CONSEQUENCES OF GROWING UP IN A SINGLE-PARENT HOME: FACTS OR MYTHS?

If you are like most single parents, you probably worry about whether being raised in a single-parent home will negatively affect your children. You may have heard that single-parent families are a "cause" of psychological problems, academic difficulties, truancy, and juvenile delinquency. How true is all of this? *Are* your children in jeopardy? How much is fact and how much is myth?

It is true that children from single-parent families are overrepresented in the population of children who are brought to counseling, who have academic problems, who are truant, and who have encounters with the law. But studies have discovered that single-parent homes per se do not create children's problems. It is what happens *within* the home that is important, not whether that home has one parent or two. Is the home happy or unhappy? Is it conflict-free or conflict-ridden? Does it radiate love or does it breed insecurity? Is it stable or unstable? Is an adult in charge to provide guidance, supervision, and discipline, or are children on their own without rules and limits? Can children partake in normal childhood activities and live from day to day without shouldering adult problems and responsibilities?

A single-parent home *can* provide children with as healthy an environment as a two-parent home can provide. The reason that children from single-parent homes are more likely than their counterparts in two parent homes to be in the population of children who develop problems is that, *statistically*, fewer single-parent homes are stable and conflict-free, and fewer single parents provide supervision, rules, and limits. And *statistically*, more single-parent homes are in a chronic state of stress, and more children from single-parent homes are overwhelmed with feelings of abandonment, with adult responsibilities, and with adult worries. (Read Chapter 9 to learn the critical ingredients for children's successful divorce adjustment.)

Parenting is a tough, demanding job, and because single parents must do it on their own, their jobs become even tougher. If you are a single parent, the next chapters will help you. Chapter 15 provides a model for how to parent solo. Chapter 16 discusses discipline. Chapter 17 discusses a number of special problems you may have as a single parent. Through all of this, keep one thought in mind: Children *can* thrive just as well in a single parent home as they can in a two-parent family.

15

HOW TO SINGLE PARENT SUCCESSFULLY

*T*he transition to single parenting is seldom easy. When one parent leaves the home, other family members must assume new responsibilities and roles. New routines are needed. Everyone must learn new skills. A new sense of family needs to be created. Reduced financial resources complicate the picture, and if the family must move, problems are compounded still further.

Change always causes stress. But in this case, stress is intensified by the feelings of loss, upset, and confusion that usually accompany separation and divorce. Each person simply has fewer emotional resources to cope with the seemingly unending new demands.

New single parents talk of feeling estranged, displaced, fearful, and in shock. They have lost their familiar role of "married parent" and now must assume the unknown role of "single parent." But how does a person parent children alone? Despite the increasing number of single parents today, there is still no widely accepted model for how to parent singly. Neither society (through education or public media) nor your own experiences will have provided you with many clues about how to forge ahead. You must carve your own path without guidelines during this emotionally troubling time.

This chapter will give you a rough model of how to parent solo. You will learn the following:

- Coping strategies that have been found to be effective for single parents
- How to create a new family situation in which your children can thrive
- How to juggle the demands of work, family, and home while building your own personal life
- How to create an atmosphere in which all family members work together in a team effort
- How to keep from overburdening your children
- How to solve family problems effectively

These, of course, are not foolproof rules, but rather guidelines that are generally found to be effective.

PARENTING SUCCESSFULLY ALONE:
EFFECTIVE COPING STRATEGIES

Successful single parents have many of the same problems as their struggling counterparts—dealing with divorce-related emotional stress, financial pressures, and time pressures; coping with ex-spouses; dealing with children's divorce-related emotional problems; and, of course, the responsibilities of child rearing alone. What distinguishes successful parents from less successful ones is the way they learn to handle these problems.

A number of researchers have been able to identify coping strategies developed by successful single parents that set them apart from their less successful counterparts. Here are some effective strategies that are well worth developing.

1. Firmly establish yourself in the leadership role in the family. Enlist your children as *junior* partners, but under no circumstances make them *equal* partners or peers, either explicitly or implicitly. If you recall from the previous chapter, this is a fairly common mistake that single parents make and often leads to problems that get out of control. If the boundaries between generations have been erased in your home, read about reestablishing them in Chapter 14.

2. Make creating a stable and nurturing home for your children a high-priority goal in your life. With all your other demands, it will take a conscious effort to create the stability they need. However, if you do so, it will in turn provide you a more stable life.

3. Don't create unrealistic expectations for yourself. Remind yourself that you are only one person and you can't do all that two people can. No matter how competent you are, you are only a human being! Consciously look for your successes rather than your failures. If you get in the habit of making a mental list of your accomplishments each day, you will be less tempted to berate yourself for all you did not accomplish and more likely to remain upbeat.

4. Work to end the conflict with your former spouse. (Chapter 11 will help you.) Studies find that an acrimonious relationship with a former spouse takes a toll on single parents' health and well-being and is destructive to children's well-being.

5. Restructure your relationship with your former spouse. You need to break your old patterns of relating and learn to interact on a different basis— as co-parents of your children. Wouldn't it be easier to drive your ex-spouse from your life, you ask? Not in the long run. It is important for your children's well-being to continue their relationships with *both* their parents (Chapter 9). Besides this, you may find, as have many other single parents, that once you restructure your relationship with your ex, you

may have a new resource to call on in a pinch. Specific steps you can take to restructure your relationship can be found in Chapter 11.

6. Your own well-being is basic to your children's well-being. A poorly functioning single parent usually forecasts poorly functioning children. Have you let go of your marriage and your old life (Chapter 6)? Have you let go of your divorce-related anger (Chapter 5)? Have you rebuilt your self-esteem (Chapter 12)? Are you building a new identity and finding new outlets for personal fulfillment (Chapters 12 and 13)?

7. Develop a new social support system. It may surprise you to learn that social support plays an important role in your being able to parent successfully alone. Single parents with good social support systems are more likely to have good parenting practices, good relationships with their children, good morale, and better mental and physical health. Strive to develop a wide network of people who can provide you with many different types of support—emotional support, companionship, relief child care, help in emergencies, practical help, financial help, and so forth. Social support is not likely to fall at your doorstep. Most likely you will have to seek it out actively. I provided suggestions in Chapter 13. Once you have restructured your relationship with your former partner, you may find that he or she becomes part of your support network.

8. Develop the skills you need to live independently. Take a survival skills class and learn to do the tasks that your ex-spouse used to do, unless you can hire them out or exchange services with someone.

   A skill that is often an invaluable help to single parents is assertiveness (and that *is* a skill you can learn). Learn to ask others for help when you need it. Learn to locate resources that you or your children may need in the aftermath of divorce—perhaps counseling, child care, job training programs, public assistance, paid help, a parenting class, a divorce adjustment group, singles groups, or social support for your children. You might also have to learn to "fight the system" to get the help you need, such as temporary public assistance or collection of delinquent child support payments. Robert Alberti and Michael Emmons's book *Your Perfect Right*, listed in Appendix C, will help you develop assertiveness. There are also many classes available now in assertiveness training.

9. Try to find a way to provide yourself with a stable income that is sufficient to provide for your family's needs. Then find creative ways to live within it. Studies find that once income is at a level that meets basic necessities and allows independence, its stability is more important than its size. Successful single parents do not necessarily have large incomes. Chapter 17 discusses your financial pinch.

HOW TO CREATE A HOME ENVIRONMENT IN WHICH YOUR CHILDREN CAN THRIVE

Your children have lost their family as they knew it. It is now up to you to replace it with a new family unit.

Here are the ingredients for an environment in which children can thrive.

1. Adopt an authoritative parenting style. Both boys and girls in single-parent homes are found to be generally better adjusted and to function more successfully on a day-to-day basis when their single parents use an authoritative parenting style. An authoritative style is one in which parents are warm, nurturing, and respectful of their children. They encourage open communication, seek their children's input, and are sensitive to their children's needs and opinions. At the same time, the parent is clearly in charge of the family, providing children with clear expectations and rules. Let me give you an example.

> Fifteen-year-old Mike and 16-year-old Debbie complain to their single mother Janice that they no longer want or need a curfew. Janice discusses the issue with them. *Why* don't they want a curfew anymore? What is their reasoning? What do they propose instead? What curfews do their friends Jack, Andy, Bill, Jeannie, and Marcia have? Janice feels they have some valid points. Perhaps their curfew is too strict. However, she feels that not having a curfew is unreasonable for teenagers and shares her concerns with her kids. She raises other possibilities, and they discuss them. Janice compromises, saying that she can live with extending their 11 o'clock curfew to midnight on the weekend, but their 10 o'clock curfew on school nights stays. They exert additional pressure on her, hoping she'll give in further. Janice remains firm, reminding them that as the adult and parent, her judgment has to be the one to prevail.

Generally, single-parent moms are better at using an authoritative parenting style with their daughters than with their sons. With sons, they tend to use very lax discipline. However, studies find that boys in single-parent homes actually need *firmer* controls than girls do. A significant number of boys who are parented singly by their mothers develop behavior problems, and many researchers believe that the reason is the lack of clear rules and limits they generally receive.

If boys need firmer control, you might wonder whether you should use an authorit*arian* style, in which you make all the decisions and your word is law. This style also creates problems, particularly with adolescent sons who frequently perceive their mothers' dictates as threats to their emerging masculinity. An authorit*ative* parenting style creates a good balance of conditions in which children are able to thrive.

2. Be sure your kids know that they are important to you and will always

have a place in your new life. Set aside some time every day to spend with each of them individually, and do something that you will both enjoy. It need not take a long time, and it will be a good investment in your relationship with one another. Show an interest in *their* interests, activities, opinions, friends, and lives in general.

3. Make a conscious effort to create a new identity for your family and a bank of good memories. This will help to minimize your children's feelings that your new family is somehow incomplete now that it has only one parent. Here are some ways that you can create a distinct family identity.

   - Arrange frequent family activities that everyone enjoys doing together.
   - Try to discover some new activities and interests that you all enjoy and that can come to symbolize your new family. Brainstorming is a good way to come up with new and creative ideas.
   - Develop some new family traditions and rituals. Examples of new traditions might be weekly family meetings, spending *individual* time each day with children, a weekly family night, outings with the local Parents Without Partners group, and yearly Thanksgiving dinner with other single parents and their children.
   - Consider getting a new pet that will always be associated with your new family.

4. Support your children's relationships with their other parent, and encourage their parent to continue functioning as a parent rather than as a "visitor." Ideally, your children should feel like they have *two* families and two homes now, one with you and one with their other parent.

5. If you cannot end your conflict with your children's other parent, it is critical that you protect them from it. Prolonged conflict between the two people they love most in the world creates serious loyalty conflicts for children, and most youngsters express the distress they feel in some kind of emotional, social, or behavioral problems (Chapter 9). Open conflict is not the only form of conflict children find distressing. Equally upsetting is hearing a parent being bad-mouthed, being pumped for information, feeling pressured to take sides, or being placed in the middle ("Be sure to get the child-support check when you're at your dad's.").

6. Do not treat your child as a peer in whom you confide all your problems, no matter how mature he or she appears to be. You may recall from the previous chapter that children who assume this adult role with their single parents frequently become emotionally overwhelmed, eventually revealing their anxiety in physical symptoms, failing grades, substance abuse, or other problems. Sharing some of your concerns is fine, but don't heap adult problems on a child. Allow your children to be children, and find an adult to be your confidant and companion.

7. Provide your children with consistent discipline. Studies find that good

---

Checklist for a Home Environment in which Children Can Thrive

✓ Use an authoritative parenting style.
  • Be nurturant and warm.
  • Respect your children.
  • Encourage open communication and seek children's input.
  • Be sensitive to their needs and opinions.
  • Set clear expectations and rules.
  • Be clear that you are the one in charge.
✓ Spend time with each child individually; show your interest in your children's lives.
✓ Create a new identity for your new family.
✓ Support your children's relationship with their other parent.
✓ Shield children from *all* forms of parental conflict.
✓ Don't rely on a child to be your confidant.
✓ Use consistent discipline.
✓ Establish schedules and routines children can count on.
✓ Don't overburden a child with adult responsibilities.
✓ Create an atmosphere in which everyone feels needed for the family to work.
✓ Enlist children's help with chores.
✓ Use family meetings.
✓ Use problem solving to solve family problems together.

---

discipline plays a critical role in whether single-parent homes function well or poorly. The following chapter will help you in this area.

8. Establish schedules and predictable routines that your children can depend on. They provide stability and predictability that help children feel safe after they have lost so much of the structure and stability in their lives due to divorce.

9. Recognize that youngsters need to participate in childhood and adolescent activities. Although your children should assume additional responsibilities to lighten your load, they should not be overburdened. Shortly we'll look at how to tell if you are overburdening a child.

10. Create the feeling that everyone in the family needs one another to make the family work. Three effective ways to create this kind of atmosphere will be discussed shortly.

HOW TO JUGGLE THE DEMANDS OF WORK, HOME, AND FAMILY—AND STILL HAVE A PERSONAL LIFE

Single parents often feel as if they are jugglers, trying to keep four balls in the air—their jobs, their kids, the household, and their personal lives. Competing demands steadily vie for their immediate attention, and unless there is an involved co-parent or a willing relative, usually no one shares the burdens or steps in when a single parent is fatigued or in trouble. "Oh, for the luxury of relaxing without a worry in the world," is a common dream. For many, it takes sheer determination to set aside that needed time for themselves, and some single parents even feel guilty about doing it.

Work Demands

For most single parents, a full-time job is a fact of life. Many will trade off the better job for one that is less demanding, is closer to home, or has more flexible hours. Many accept that they will be passed over for promotions because they cannot travel or put in overtime. Often, careers are simply put on the back burner until children are raised.

However, studies find that work is important to most single parents. Both their job satisfaction and job performance are found to be high. Many find work to be an important source of self-esteem, fulfillment, and social contacts.

If you are newly working and finding it difficult to juggle your job with everything else, it may reassure you to know that new single parents who have always worked have a less difficult time juggling all they have to do. You, too, should find it easier with time and experience. Here are a few suggestions to help you balance your work and parenting roles.

- If you have young children, you will feel more comfortable at work if you are satisfied that you have made good child care arrangements. Alison Clarke-Stewart's book *Daycare*, listed in Appendix C, provides guidelines for what to look for.
- If your children will be on their own after school, make sure you set up strict rules to assure their safety. An excellent source to guide you is Bryan Robinson, Bobbie Rowland, and Mick Coleman's book *Latchkey Kids*, listed in Appendix C.
- Ask your children to call you at work when they get in from school or if there is a serious problem they cannot handle themselves. This will give both you and them peace of mind. Or, to help establish a routine, tell them that you will call at a specific time.
- If your children call you incessantly with numerous small problems and quarrels, you may wish to do what one parent did—hire an older high school student (who is generally at home anyway) to be available for your children's calls, and have the student handle all but major problems. (You can provide the guidelines for how you would like things handled.)
- If you return home from work and your young child greets you with anger or tears, don't be alarmed. There is a very good reason for this. Seeing you again reawakens the feelings he or she has about being separated from

you. Acknowledge your youngster's feelings and tell him or her how difficult it is for both of you that you must be away. Reassure the child of your love and that you will always return each evening. Then try to spend some time doing something with your child that you both enjoy.
- Find one or two backup baby-sitters who can stay with a sick child. Some parents place an ad in a local newspaper or on a store bulletin board. Some have a neighbor they can depend on and repay with another type of favor. The key is advance preparation so you do not have the dilemma of losing a day of work, sending a sick child to school to get sicker, or leaving a young child home alone.

The Home Front

Household responsibilities usually offer the most flexibility when something has to slide. In fact, time studies suggest that employed single mothers spend less time on household tasks than do their married counterparts. For example, an Ohio State University study found that single working mothers spent an average of 1⅓ hours less each day on house chores than did married working mothers. A Boston study reported similar findings.

How can you save time on household tasks despite having to shoulder them without a spouse's help? Enlist your children to assume some new responsibilities that are appropriate to their ages. Prepare simpler meals, which also means less time shopping and less time to clean up; meals don't have to be fancy to be balanced and nutritious. Try entertaining simply, too; casual potlucks are favorites for many single parents. Work out arrangements with other single parents to be mutually supportive of one another, such as setting up baby-sitting co-ops or car pools. But most of all, get out of the perfection trap and lower your standards. Some things just aren't worth the time it takes to do them perfectly. Save perfection for the important things. This means consciously evaluating how well a task really needs to be done. While you are at it, decide whether you need to do it yourself or whether you can delegate it to someone else.

Even if you spend less time on household chores than your married counterparts do, you may still experience more strain in juggling your responsibilities, and for good reason. First, you may have no reliable source of backup or steady emotional support. Second, you must assume the responsibility for *all* tasks, even those you are poorly equipped to handle. This is where a good social support network will be particularly valuable. The emotional support and availability of emergency help will be a boon to your morale. And exchanging services, talents, and practical help can relieve you of some of the varied responsibilities you shoulder. You might be able to divide labor (taking turns running errands) or exchange services (some sewing for preparing your income tax returns). Home sharing is another possibility that many single parents enthusiastically recommend. It provides them with an extended family and significantly cuts down on costs and work load.

Children

Single-parent homes usually function best when children are made junior partners on a family team headed by the parent, and each family member feels needed for the family to work. Here are some ways that you can create this kind of team feeling in your home and have it run efficiently.

Family Meetings

Begin to hold weekly family meetings in which problems can be aired and discussed, family decisions made, chores divided, and family activities planned. Make it a rule that every member of the family is listened to with respect.

Involving children in family decisions increases their commitment to carry those decisions out. But remember that *you* are the senior partner. Don't yield to pressure and agree to decisions that go against your better judgment, even if *all* your children form a united front. If you do, things can quickly get out of hand. Children simply don't have the maturity to always make wise decisions. You are the one who is ultimately in charge, and your judgment takes precedence. Of course, you don't have to make joint family decisions in all areas, either. For some issues, an adult is in a better position to make a decision than are children. At these times, you may wish to ask for your children's input, but be clear that the decision will be yours.

Family meetings are also a good time to solve family problems.

How to Solve Family Problems Effectively

If you involve your children in finding solutions to family problems, you will not only have a smoother-functioning family but will also teach your kids valuable skills they can use throughout their lives. A good problem-solving strategy consists of the following steps:

1. Define the problem in concrete terms. For example: "Some members of the family have been slacking off on chores." "Our family expenses have exceeded our means for the past two months. We have to find ways to cut back." "I'm getting too many calls at work about fights and arguments, and my boss is getting upset. We have to find a way for you to handle minor problems yourselves."
2. Use brainstorming to find possible solutions. Encourage everyone to come up with as many suggestions as they can, no matter how foolish they sound. Make a rule that no one can say *anything* about another's

ideas during the brainstorming session. This is the time for creative problem solving, *not* evaluation. One idea will stimulate another, and sometimes a completely impractical idea stimulates a sensible and workable one. Someone should have the job of writing down all the solutions mentioned.

3. This step is evaluation. Go through each potential solution and mark the ones that seem to have strong possibilities. Once you have narrowed down the list, discuss the pros and cons of each alternative selected. How realistic is it? How would it be carried out? How effective is it likely to be? Might it have other consequences, besides the desired ones, that should be considered? Once you have discussed each one, rate its potential usefulness on a three-point scale—okay, good, and excellent.

4. Select the idea or ideas that seem to be the best, and determine how they will be carried out.

> When Ann Duffy and her children used the problem-solving technique to try to cut down on family expenses, these were the solutions they agreed on:
> a. Rent a video movie on family night instead of going to a movie theater.
> b. Limit eating out to twice a month.
> c. Eliminate expensive junk food from the family budget and make popcorn for snacks.
> d. Cut down on each person's spending money. Each person can supplement his or her allowance with odd jobs in the neighborhood.
> e. Family members can make their lunch the night before to avoid having to buy it out.
> f. Be more careful with gas and electricity usage by turning lights out when leaving a room, turning down the heat and wearing sweaters, using the washing machine and dryer only when there is a full load of clothes, and limiting showers to five minutes, which could be timed with a timer left in the bathroom.

5. At future family meetings, evaluate how close you are coming to solving the problem. Are the agreed-upon solutions working? Are people sticking to them? If the problem is improving, everyone involved should be praised

---

Steps to Effective Problem Solving

✓ 1. Define the problem in concrete terms.
✓ 2. Brainstorm to find possible solutions.
✓ 3. Evaluate each potential solution.
✓ 4. Select the best idea(s) and determine how to carry it/them out.
✓ 5. Evaluate how the plan is working, once you have given it a chance; return to step 4 if necessary.

---

and encouraged to continue future efforts. If the agreed-upon solutions are not working, you may have to return to the previous step and try different alternatives.

Enlisting Children's Help

Since every member of the family enjoys the use of the home, eats the food that is bought and prepared, and wears clean clothes, every member should pitch in and share some of the household responsibilities. Enlisting children's help with chores will be a considerable help to you and will benefit them too. Generally, children who do chores become more responsible and have higher self-esteem than children who do not contribute to the family.

If you have not done so already, make a list of everything you believe needs to be done. Then assess, honestly, what you can eliminate or do less frequently. Remember to leave perfection for the important things.

Call a family meeting and discuss what needs to be done. You can then jointly decide how to divide jobs. Be realistic. Chores need to be appropriate for children's ages, as well as for their daily schedules. Make children responsible for themselves as much as possible (picking up after themselves, cleaning their rooms, and, if they are old enough, washing and putting away their laundry).

Children will cooperate more readily if they have a say in the chores they do. If some jobs are either very popular or unpopular, they might be rotated, or children may find it more fun to choose them out of a hat. Some families have a job list with each chore assigned a point value. Then children take turns choosing chores until they total a certain number of points.

If you are skeptical about your ability to enlist your children's cooperation with chores, here are some techniques that will help you.

- Emphasize the importance of everyone working together as a team to make the new family situation work.
- Make chores fun. Set a time aside for the entire family to do chores together, and follow it with an activity everyone will enjoy, such as a trip to the ice cream store, bowling, a movie, a picnic, or an hour playing games the family enjoys. It is a good idea to set a time by which jobs must be completed in order to participate so that one slow child does not deny the others their reward ("Everyone who is finished with their chores by noon gets to go for ice cream.").
- Make up a chart so everyone can remember his or her jobs for the week.
- Make the consequences of *not* completing chores very clear. Talk it over with your kids, and allow them to help determine what the consequences should be. A consequence that makes good sense is that chores must be completed before children are free to do fun activities (go out with friends, watch TV). Some parents tie the completion of chores to receiving an

allowance (although others feel allowance should be given consistently so children can learn how to budget their money). A variation on this theme is fining children if chores are incomplete. Some parents withhold privileges (TV, use of the car) or favors (chauffeuring). A more drastic measure tried by some parents whose children adamantly refuse to do chores is to go on strike themselves. No food is bought or cooked, no laundry done, no chauffeuring, and so forth.

How to Keep from Overburdening Your Children

How do you arrive at a balance between enlisting your children's help and overburdening them? A good rule of thumb is that children should not have so many responsibilities that they do not have time for other age-appropriate involvements (friends, play, some after-school activities). Neither should schoolwork suffer because of home responsibilities.

Placing an older child in charge of siblings requires special precautions. It can create a bad situation for both older and younger children alike. Younger children often resent their older siblings and resist their authority. Those in charge often resent the burdens placed on them and sometimes use their authority arbitrarily or belligerently. To prevent these problems, mental health professionals suggest that you take the following steps if you must place an older child in charge:

- Be sure that your child is mature enough to handle the responsibility. Will your younger children be safe? Will your older child be able to keep control?
- Make it clear to *all* your children exactly what your older child's role is and what his or her responsibilities are. Then support your child in that role.
- Be clear about what is expected of younger children and about what your older child should do if rules are broken.
- Acknowledge the important role your older child is playing in the family and the extra burden he or she is assuming.
- If there are complaints from either your older child or the younger children in his or her care, take them up at a family meeting. Allow each child to air his or her grievances and work out a solution for the problem. Remember, when in doubt, your judgment takes precedence.
- Be sure that all your children have sufficient time that *they can plan on* for friends, activities, and schoolwork. Older children should not be on call at all times.

Some children are overburdened not with work but with worry. Though it is fine to share some of your concerns with your children, do not burden them with adult problems. No matter how mature your child may seem to you, he or she is still a child and cannot be expected to function as an adult without running the risk of future problems, as discussed in the previous chapter. Find another adult to be your confidant, and allow your child to live a child's life. If your youngster has forsaken friends and activities to be with you and help you, it is time to encourage a return to previous interests and friendships. Each of you needs a life independent of each other.

Your Personal Life

With all you have to do, it may be tempting to defer your personal life, but this is not good for you or for your children. Successful single parents generally have learned the importance of taking time to recharge their batteries. They realize the difficulty, if not the impossibility, of effectively tending to children's ongoing needs when their own lives are barren. In the long run, denying your own needs may make you a resentful parent and may inadvertently lay a guilt trip on your children as well. Young adults raised in single-parent homes often report a reluctance to create a life of their own, feeling they are abandoning a parent who has sacrificed so much for them. Strive to do the following.

- Set aside a *minimum* of a half-hour each day and one evening a week to do something you will enjoy. If you need to hire a baby-sitter, try to think of it as an investment in yourself. (Perhaps you can exchange baby-sitting with another single parent.)
- Get involved with at least one or two pursuits that will bring you personal fulfillment. Single parents are generally happier if they have outlets, in addition to parenting, that they find rewarding.
- Develop an adequate social support network. With a good support system, you can receive the emotional support, understanding, acceptance, advice, companionship, and intimacy you need. Generally, single parents are happier when their support systems include friends rather than exclusively family. They are also happier when they have some close friends (in whom they can confide) rather than just acquaintances. Chapter 13 discussed how to build a social support network.
- Aim to have as many other single parents in your support group as you can. If they have children the ages of yours, all the better. You will find it immensely helpful to have people with whom to share ideas and perspectives and from whom to seek advice. You may recall that one reason single parents are so easily swayed by their children is that they have no other adult to give them feedback or another perspective. Parents Without Partners and other single-parent support groups are excellent ways to meet other single parents. So is your children's school. Either your children or

their teachers may know of other single parents you can contact. Subscribing to a single-parent magazine is another way to feel connected to other single parents and is a good source of ideas, too. An excellent one is *The Single Parent*, published by Parents Without Partners. You can order it by writing to Parents Without Partners, 8807 Colesville Road, Silver Spring, MD 20910.

In the next chapter, we'll take a look at discipline, an issue that generally poses a particular problem in single-parent homes. It not only affects the quality of daily life, but it is also an important component of an environment conducive to children's healthy development. Don't underestimate its importance.

HOW TO DISCIPLINE EFFECTIVELY AND STILL BE A "GOOD GUY"

*D*iscipline plays a critical role in single-parent homes. It is a key ingredient that distinguishes well-functioning homes from poorly functioning ones. More importantly, poor discipline is found to be an important cause of many of the problems that appear in a sizable number of children raised by single parents, such as noncompliance, aggression, antisocial behavior, early sexual experimentation, and children wielding too much power in the family.

Compared to married parents, single parents (especially mothers) are generally found to be less-effective disciplinarians. As a group, single parents are very permissive, for many seemingly valid reasons. Some believe their children already have been deprived enough due to the divorce and shouldn't be denied further. Some are afraid that children will prefer their other parent. Others find themselves too easily swayed by children's arguments because there is no other adult available to offer them support or an objective point of view. And some single parents are simply too exhausted from their work load to monitor their children carefully.

Many single parents seesaw back and forth between being permissive and temporarily coming down hard on their kids when things get out of control. However, neither permissiveness nor restrictiveness is in children's best interest, nor is vacillating between the two.

Every parent can become a good disciplinarian with some knowledge and practice. This chapter will provide the knowledge. Discipline is a well-researched area, and we have some good evidence about what is effective and what is not. The practice, of course, will be up to you, but it will be well worth your while. Effective discipline is likely to make your children more responsible and your home a more harmonious place to live—and it will not make you an ogre, either.

Before our discussion of effective discipline, you may find it helpful to learn why it is not in your children's best interest to be raised in *either* a very permissive atmosphere or a very restrictive one.

223

DIFFERENT PARENTING STYLES AND THEIR REPERCUSSIONS

For many years, researchers have studied three clearly different parenting styles to determine whether they have any clear impact on children's development. These styles have been labeled permissive, authoritarian, and authoritative, although not every parent neatly falls under one of these labels. We now know that these parenting styles generally *do* impact children's development in important ways.

Permissive parents generally make few demands on children, impose few rules, and allow children to make their own decisions with little guidance. Children raised by permissive parents are often found to have a poor sense of social responsibility. In general, they are found to be impulsive, immature, and aggressive. The reason seems to be that the absence of parental controls makes it very difficult for these youngsters to develop their own *self*-control.

Authoritarian parents are the opposite extreme. In these households, the power and decision making is clearly in the parents' hands. Parents are very restrictive and controlling. They expect children to obey with no questions asked, and they punish disobedience sternly. Children raised in authoritarian homes generally have low self-esteem; that is not surprising given the little respect they have received from their parents. As a group, these children also require a good deal of monitoring: Not only are they poorly self-motivated, but their internal standards of right and wrong are often poorly developed, for two reasons. First, punitive parents do not inspire children's loyalty to their values, and so their youngsters are less likely to accept those values as their own. And second, because their behavior is rigidly dictated with neither explanation nor opportunity to question, children have little opportunity to work out a value system that makes sense to them—a value system that can guide them when facing new situations requiring moral decisions. Compare this parenting style and its repercussions with an authorita*tive* style.

In an authoritative parenting style, a parent

a. is warm, nurturant, and respectful of his or her children;
b. encourages open discussion and seeks children's input;
c. is responsive to children's needs and opinions;
d. provides clear expectations and guidelines for children's behavior; and
e. is the one who is ultimately in charge in the family.

How do children raised in authoritative households develop? They tend to be socially responsive and altruistic (perhaps modeling their parents' responsiveness to them). Generally, they have high self-esteem and are assertive. (Remember, they have been treated with respect, and their needs and opinions have been considered important.) And they develop good self-control and strong *internal* standards of acceptable behavior. Why the latter? First, they are provided with clear guidelines to follow until they are able to develop their own self-control. Second, warm, nurturant, and respectful parents kindle children's loyalty to parental values, so children are more likely to internalize these values. Finally, the continuing give-and-take exchange between parent and child helps youngsters to work out their own standards of right and wrong.

Learning good disciplinary practices will help you develop an authoritative parenting style.

THE PRINCIPLES OF POSITIVE PARENTING

The reason that so many parents have a hard time with discipline is that many of their natural inclinations are counterproductive. The root of the problem may lie in a misunderstanding of what discipline means. Many parents incorrectly equate discipline with punishment. Discipline is not punishment. It is *teaching* children responsibility, self-control, and how to behave appropriately. If you keep this in mind, discipline will take on a whole new meaning for you.

Because most parents incorrectly equate discipline with punishment, they typically ignore their children when they are good and punish them or yell at them when they are bad. Unfortunately, this is the worst thing a parent can do. Few people, especially children, like to be unnoticed and ignored. Ignored for too long, children will do something to get your attention. If the only time you notice them is when they do something bad or annoying, then that's what most children will do (become noisy, have a temper tantrum, throw something, run into the street, whine, start a fight, dress outrageously, and so forth). Now they've gotten what they wanted. You stopped what you are doing and you're paying attention to them. You are rewarding the very behavior you want to stop. Instead of stopping it, you are increasing the likelihood that it will occur again the next time they are not getting the attention they want! True, yelling or punishment is not the kind of attention children prefer, but at least they no longer feel like nonentities. They *can* have an impact on the world after all.

Reward Good Behavior

The first and foremost principle of effective discipline is this: Reward children's good behavior. This does *not* mean you should bribe them to be good. It means that you need to get into the habit of noticing when your youngsters are behaving as you would like them to, and then reward them with praise, attention, and affection. Give them lots of praise when they are following rules, being helpful, playing quietly, cooperating with one another, doing something nice for someone, and so on. (Younger children love hugs, too.) *The more you reward their good behavior in this way, the more likely they are to repeat that behavior over and over again.* Because your children will come to associate their good behavior with your warmth and approval, they will start to feel good when they are behaving appropriately. Eventually, being good will become rewarding in and of itself. This is the beginning of self-discipline—quite a difference from children who behave only when someone is there to punish their misbehavior!

As good behavior becomes more natural for your children, you will need to praise them less frequently for it. This does not mean you should take your children for granted and pay no attention to them. Children always thrive on your love, attention, and appreciation and are likely to revert to some type of attention-getting behavior once again if ignored. Many single parents find this out when they begin an active dating life at the expense of time with their youngsters (Chapter 17).

Ignore Misbehavior

What do you do about those annoying things your kids do that drive you nuts—bickering, whining, temper tantrums? Forget yelling, and forget nagging. By now you have probably noticed that neither works. Neither do empty threats. How about a good swift smack, you wonder? If you have used this technique, ask *yourself* if it works. Your answer will probably be, "Well, it does for a while." Physical punishment usually turns out to be a poor teaching method. It may stop unacceptable behavior at that time, *but only temporarily.* Generally, disciplinary methods that help children feel good about themselves are far more conducive to learning than methods that make them feel bad about themselves. Besides this, physical punishment often causes fear, anger, resentment, or aggressiveness in youngsters.

Then what do you do? Believe it or not, the most effective way to stop the annoying things your kids do (not the harmful things) is to *ignore* it. The reason is that the behavior is usually designed to get attention. If you don't look, don't talk, don't even react, it will eventually stop. And the more you ignore it, the more likely it is to stop *permanently.*

The best strategy to stop misbehavior, therefore, is to *pay attention to kids when they behave and to ignore them when they misbehave.* Consistency is important!

Use Time-Out

You are probably shaking your head and thinking of a list of things that your kids do that would be ridiculous to ignore. What about behavior that is dangerous? What about destructive behavior? What do you do when your kids are being so obnoxious that you can't stand it?

The solution? When behavior is dangerous, destructive, or so obnoxious that you can't ignore it, immediately send or remove your child to a place where he or she *can* be ignored. It is important that you do it very calmly and without discussion, argument, or "another chance." (Remember that any form of attention will reward the undesirable behavior.) The more boring the place you send your child, the better. You don't want to reward him or her with TV, toys, things to explore, or someone to talk to. This technique is called "time-out," and it is a very effective teaching tool. Examples of effective places for time-outs are a bathroom, a laundry room, or even a chair in a boring kitchen. The youngster must stay for a designated amount of time (about one minute for each year of age is a rough guideline).

You say your kids would never stay? Then they get nothing positive of any kind until they do. Again, no discussion or arguments. Just a short, calm, matter-of-fact statement, "I'm sorry but you can't watch TV (have dinner, play that game, go outside and play, and so on) until you've completed your time-out."

After the time-out, ask your child why it was necessary and what he or she could do differently the next time. Try time-outs with children ranging from preschool age to about 11. It is simple but effective.

Provide Clear Expectations, Limits, and Rules

Children should not be expected to learn by trial and error what behavior is acceptable and what is unacceptable. Yet this is what many parents unwittingly expect their children to do.

> After Margie's parents divorced, she began talking back to her mother, often quite abusively. Knowing her daughter was going through a rough time, Mrs. Hamilton usually bit her tongue and tried to appease Margie when she became abusive. At the same time, the woman became increasingly hurt and resentful. Periodically, when she had had a particularly rough day herself, she would blow up at Margie and put her on restriction. Margie typically responded by becoming sullen and hostile. Over time, both Margie's behavior and her relationship with her mother worsened.

What Mrs. Hamilton did not realize was that Margie needed some clear guidelines about what was and what was not acceptable behavior. When Margie used abusive language, her mother was conciliatory one day and punitive the next. Margie was not being taught how to treat other people with respect. Furthermore, she perceived her mother's behavior as arbitrary, capricious, and unfair. It was this perceived unfairness that aroused Margie's sullenness and hostility. How much better it would have been for Mrs. Hamilton to verbally empathize with Margie's pain and encourage her to talk about her feelings, yet let her know in a loving manner that her abusiveness was not acceptable and would not be tolerated. How much better it would have been if she had abruptly stopped a conversation as soon as her daughter became abusive and told her warmly but firmly that they would continue when Margie could talk in a civil manner.

Telling children clearly when their behavior is unacceptable and *why* is an important facet of discipline. Equally important is providing them with alternatives that *are* acceptable. For example, a child who takes out his anger by fighting or kicking furniture needs to have some alternative ways to handle that anger. You might suggest that he remove himself from the anger-provoking situation and engage in another activity until he calms down enough to talk about the problem. He might find some type of vigorous physical activity helpful, such as running, climbing, throwing balls, or chopping wood. Or he might find some calming activities helpful, such as listening to music, drawing, playing with clay, or taking a warm bath.

Your children will need clear limits from you until they have developed self-control and are mature enough to set their own limits. Being able to set appropriate limits for themselves will become more and more critical as they get older and have fewer people to monitor them. How do you help children get to the point of being able to set their own limits? Basically, follow the principles of an authoritative parenting style. Here are some specifics you can do.

First, remember that if you are warm, nurturant, and respectful of your children, they are more likely to internalize your values and make them their own.

Second, be sure they understand the *reasons* for the limits and any rules you set. You can start this when they are very young. "If you throw sand, it can get in people's eyes and it will hurt." "When you treat people like that, it hurts their feelings." "When you smear your food all over the table, it causes the waitress extra work." Helping children understand the underlying reasons for your expectations, limits, and rules will also make them more willing to follow them.

Third, involve your children in a give-and-take discussion about limits and the rules you set, and allow them to help set some of them. The older that children are, the more important it is that they be involved. However, remember that your children need your guidance and experience and that you, as the parent, *always* have the final say in what limits are appropriate.

You will want to have some *formal* rules for children to follow that are very explicit. Save formal rules for important things. You don't want to get bogged down in so many rules that kids can't keep track of them. What formal rules you make will depend on your children, their ages, what is important to you, and what is currently an issue in your household. Safety, health, and the rights of others are prime areas for formal rules but are not the only ones. Examples of areas in which you may want to have clear rules are the way your children treat other people and property, "off-limits" activities when they are

---

The Principles of Positive Parenting

✓ 1. Discipline is teaching responsibility and self-control.
✓ 2. Use an authoritative parenting style.
   • Be warm, nurturant, and respectful of your children.
   • Encourage open communication and seek children's input.
   • Be sensitive to their needs and opinions.
   • Provide them with clear rules and expectations.
   • Be the person who is ultimately in charge.
✓ 3. Reward good behavior with praise, smiles, and hugs.
✓ 4. Ignore annoying misbehavior.
✓ 5. Use "time-out" for dangerous, destructive, or obnoxious behavior you can't ignore.
✓ 6. Impose consequences when rules or limits are broken.
✓ 7. Tangible rewards can be a powerful teaching tool to change undesirable habits.
✓ 8. With difficult teens, use the "no one loses" problem-solving method or contracting.
✓ 9. The foundation of good discipline is a good relationship and mutual respect between parent and child.

---

home alone, how far from home they can roam on their own, curfews, homework, and chores.

Consequences When Rules and Limits Are Broken

For rules and limits to be effective, there must be some consequences for breaking them. Children almost always test rules and limits and will conclude that they are unimportant if no consequences follow.

Sometimes, of course, children forget and just need a reminder. If a child is testing some limit, a warning glance from you may be all that is necessary to stop him. If a child is about to throw something at a playmate, take it away from her and remind her that it is unacceptable to throw things, especially when it may hurt someone. If children proceed after a single warning, then it is time for consequences. There are some important things to remember about consequences.

1. *Consequences should be consistent.* If children experience consequences one day and not the next, it will take far longer for rules and limits to become a routine part of their lives. Without consistency, they will always be testing your limits. Many parents threaten consequences over and over again ("If you do that one more time, I will _____"). However, empty threats *do not work*. Give children *one* warning. If they continue, follow through with the consequences.

2. *Consequences should be realistic.* Before you threaten consequences, be

sure you are willing to carry them out. Then do so after one warning. Peggy, a participant in a parenting class, learned the value of realistic consequences one day on an excursion with her children.

Peggy set out for a day excursion with her two children and another single friend. All had been excitedly anticipating the outing. After 30 minutes, Peggy's children began to tease and fight with each other. "Quit it or I'll turn the car around and we'll go home," she threatened. The two quieted down for five minutes before starting up again. "You heard me. I'll turn right around and go home if you don't stop," she repeated. This sequence of events repeated itself six times, with Peggy and her friend becoming increasingly more frustrated and tense. Finally Peggy lost her temper, smacked her children, and ranted for five minutes about how bad they were. The kids cried, Peggy felt guilty, and all four arrived at their destination tense and irritable.

Why didn't Peggy's children stop their teasing and fighting, despite her threats? Because the consequences were not realistic. They knew she would not return home when both she and her friend had been looking forward to the trip. What could she have done, Peggy asked at her parenting class. Peggy's instructor reminded her that car trips were boring for kids and that she could avoid much of the problem by eliminating the boredom. She suggested they take along some books and toys and that Peggy initiate some car games, such as how many out-of-state license plates can each child spot? Who can spot the most items beginning with different letters, and do it in alphabetical order? For younger children, who can spot items beginning or ending with specific sounds? How about a simple version of "20 Questions"? How about some word games, like "Ghost" or rhyming words? Peggy's instructor also gave her some pointers about setting rules and *realistic* consequences.

Before the next trip, Peggy talked to her children about acceptable and unacceptable car behavior and made sure they had books and some favorite toys. She told them that if they were noisy, it interfered with her driving and created an unsafe situation. She would therefore have to pull the car off the road and stop until they were ready to read or play quietly. She and her friend would sit and chat, but the longer it took the children to quiet down, the less time they would have to play when they arrived. Things ran smoothly as long as Peggy played car games with them, but shortly after she stopped to talk to her friend, the children began poking each other, and the noise level escalated rapidly. Peggy calmly reminded them of the rules and told them this would be their only warning. When they continued, she stopped in a safe place, and she and her friend had a quiet chat. When the stunned children finally realized that they were taking precious time away from their day's activities, they opened up some books and started to read.

Peggy thought she had hit upon a good thing and tried it when she had errands to run, taking along a book to read if she needed to pull over. The car games worked, but pulling over was a complete failure. Why? In this case, her children were not losing time from an activity they were looking forward to. The errands just took longer to complete, which frustrated Peggy more than her kids. To solve this, Peggy began to plan a fun activity to do after the errands, such as a stop at the ice cream store or playing a game together when they got home—assuming, of course, that there was time.

3. *Consequences should be timely.* The sooner that children experience consequences for breaking a rule, the more likely they are to learn. Peggy's children quickly learned to follow her driving rule because a fun activity that they were about to do would be cut short otherwise. Had she imposed a consequence that would not have taken place for several days, it probably would not have been as effective. The more removed the consequences are from an event, the less effective they are likely to be.

4. *Consequences should be logical.* When children can see a logical connection between their infraction and its consequence, it is a far better learning experience for them. If your son throws a dish and breaks it, he pays for it or does enough chores to work it off. If he roams too far from home, he's grounded the next day. If your daughter refuses to eat her dinner, she goes to bed hungry. If she doesn't do her chores, she can't go out until they are done. If she abuses a privilege, she loses that privilege for a short period. If your youngster is ruining a family gathering with his obnoxious behavior despite a time-out, he must leave the gathering until he can control himself. If a child does an injustice to a playmate, she must do something to make amends with the playmate. If a child dawdles and misses the bus, he finds his own way to school. If your toddler leaves his fenced yard, he must come in the house. If your son deliberately breaks one of his toys, he does without it. If a teen misses curfew, she's grounded for a specified period. In this way children learn that their behavior has consequences, and they must bear those consequences if they choose to engage in the behavior. If consequences have no connection to the misbehavior, they lose much of their effectiveness as a teaching tool.

5. *If you cannot find a logical consequence, discuss consequences with your children and reach a joint decision.* The older that children are, the more important it is to involve them in determining consequences when no logical ones are apparent. Discussing consequences with your children will increase the likelihood that the consequences will make sense to them. If they make no sense, not only do they lose their effectiveness as a teaching tool, but in addition it is easy for children to perceive that you are the "bad guy" who arbitrarily imposes punishment because you are more powerful than they are. This kind of perception is more likely to lead to resentment than to learning.

If consequences can be determined before they are needed, all the better. A child who knows the consequences beforehand and chooses

Are Your Consequences Effective?

✓ Do you use them *consistently?*
✓ Are they *realistic?*
✓ Are they *timely?*
✓ Are they *logical* (or jointly determined with your child)?
✓ Are they *fair?*
✓ Do you impose them *calmly* and *warmly?*

---

to misbehave anyway has only him- or herself to blame. A family meeting is a good place to determine consequences, and brainstorming is a fun and effective way to do it. In brainstorming, you may remember, everyone's ideas are written down without comment or evaluation, no matter how ridiculous they are. One idea leads to another, and an outrageous idea may lead to a very good one that may not have been thought of otherwise. After about 10 minutes of brainstorming, go through all the ideas and find a mutually agreeable one. Common consequences parents use include grounding (use only for a short period or it loses its effectiveness), extra chores, and withholding privileges such as being chauffeured, using the car, or watching TV. With a brainstorming session, you may come up with far better ones.

6. *Consequences should be fair.* If consequences are too severe, they are likely to build resentment. A teen who is five minutes late for curfew should not be grounded for a week. Neither should consequences be too minimal. A teen who is an hour late for curfew (without having telephoned) is not likely to take curfew seriously if the only consequence is a comment about his tardiness. Some words of caution: *Never* deny a child time with his or her nonresident parent as a consequence of misbehavior. Not only will your child resent it, but that relationship is critical and should not be interfered with.

7. *Impose consequences in a calm and warm manner.* The purpose of consequences is *not* to punish. It is to teach responsible behavior. If you impose consequences in a vindictive manner, your children are likely to see you as the villain who dispenses punishment because you are more powerful than they. Imposing consequences in a calm, warm manner reminds children that they were the ones who made the choices, and now they are the ones who must accept the consequences of those choices.

After you have followed through with the consequence, ask your child why the consequences occurred. You will then be sure your youngster understands the connection between the misbehavior and the consequence, and the incident is more likely to become a learning experience.

What to Do If You Are Afraid of Losing Control

There may be times when you are under so much stress that a child's misbehavior may be the last straw. What do you do if you feel you are about to lose control and strike out at your child? The National Committee for the Prevention of Child Abuse suggests you follow these steps:

1. Take a deep breath. And then another. Then remember that *you* are the adult.
2. Continuing to breathe slowly, press your lips together and count to 20.
3. Take or send your child to a time-out place. (If your child is older and you don't use time-outs, send him or her to the bedroom until you can cool off.)
4. Phone a friend.
5. If someone can watch young children for you, take a walk.

If you are afraid of losing control, there is a hotline you can call to talk to a crisis counselor anonymously. It is the CHILD HELP USA National Child Abuse Hotline, 1-800-4-A-CHILD.

How to Handle Noncompliant Behavior

Children's noncompliance is a frequent complaint among single parents. Mom repeatedly asks her son to do something, and he ignores her until she gets so angry she explodes. Finally he gets around to doing what he was supposed to do, but the entire sequence repeats itself again and again. Sound familiar?

Studies have uncovered some interesting things about children's noncompliance. First, the average child does not immediately do what is requested of him or her all the time. In fact, observations of large samples of children reveal that on the average, children comply with their parents' commands 60 to 80 percent of the time. A second interesting finding is that parents of children who are exceptionally noncompliant generally employ an unusually large number of negative tactics with their youngsters, such as threats, nagging, and anger. Apparently the threats and nagging are ineffective; they may even be counterproductive!

What do you do about your child's noncompliant behavior? More than a decade ago, a systematic training program was developed at the University of Oregon Medical School to teach parents how to deal with this very problem. It is often taught to parents whose children are referred to child guidance clinics because of noncompliant behavior, and studies have confirmed its effectiveness. The program was developed for younger children. Following is a variation of the Oregon program so it can be used for any age child. Notice how positive the approach is.

1. Reduce the number of commands, criticisms, and questions you use with your child. Children who are continually bombarded with commands learn to tune them out.
2. Whenever your child complies with a request or is behaving otherwise desirably, reward him or her with smiles, praise, or hugs.
3. When you have a request or command, state it *directly* and *concisely*. For example,

> *Indirect*: "It's time you started thinking about bed."
> *Direct*: "In 15 minutes, it will be time to take your bath. Right now it is time to finish up your play and put your toys away."
> *Indirect*: "The living room needs picking up."
> *Direct*: "Please take all your things out of the living room within the next five minutes and put them where they belong."

> *Too wordy and confusing*: "Get in here, Heather, and clean up this kitchen. How am I supposed to cook in a mess like this? What have you been doing all afternoon, anyway? Have you finished your homework? Did you ever call Mrs. Smith like I told you to? Oh, no, look at the mess in the family room! Haven't you been watching Charlie? You know you're not supposed to let him make a mess like this. Can't I depend on you for anything? Now get busy!" Even if Heather had listened to this long and confusing tirade to its completion (which she probably didn't), it is unlikely that she would know what her mother wanted her to "get busy" doing. Clean the kitchen? The family room? Call Mrs. Smith? Watch Charlie? Do her homework? Ten minutes later, Mom returns and finds Heather still watching TV. Livid, she turns it off and yells at Heather to get in the kitchen and get busy. Heather reluctantly goes in, puts a few of the obvious things away, and retreats to her bedroom.
> *Concise*: "I can't make dinner in this messy kitchen. Please come and load the dishwasher, put the food back in the closet, and take all your school things to your bedroom."

4. Give your child time to comply, but do provide a *specific* deadline.
5. If your child complies within the time limit, praise him or her warmly.

What if your youngster does not comply? For younger children, the most effective method is likely to be time-out. The Oregon researchers recommend that you use time-out after *one* warning. If your child leaves the time-out area, return him or her *firmly*, as often as necessary. After a time-out, do not let your child off the hook; he or she must *still* complete the original task. If your youngster still does not comply, repeat the procedure. Persistence eventually does pay off, say the researchers.

For children eight or older, several other methods are likely to be more effective than time-out. Regardless of which method you choose, the first steps are to talk to your children about their noncompliance and the problems it is causing you and to ask about their perceptions. They may be unaware that a problem exists. Or you may discover that you are contributing to the problem and may even get some helpful suggestions. ("Gee whiz, mom. You yell orders at us all day long and insist that everything be done right away, no matter what we're doing. Half the time it's dumb stuff that could wait. Couldn't you give us a list of the unimportant stuff that we could do when we weren't busy?") After you talk about the noncompliance problem, discuss how you can work on it together. If you consistently follow the five step Oregon Program, you are likely to change whatever you have been doing that may have been contributing to the problem (for example, too many wordy and indirect orders). But of course, the problem is not all yours, and there are several ways that you can help your older children change their noncompliant ways. The simplest is to *jointly* arrive at some appropriate consequences for future noncompliance (use brainstorming). Then be sure to follow through with the agreed-upon consequences. The second is to use the tangible reward method discussed below. Two other methods that are particularly appropriate for teens ("no one loses" problem solving and contracts) can be found in the section on Discipline and Teens.

Using Tangible Rewards to Solve Discipline Problems

Tangible rewards are a powerful tool at your disposal that can be used to solve many discipline problems. An effective way to use them is by following the program outlined in Appendix A—"How to Make Changes in Your Life and Stick to Them." Although this program was designed for adults, you can use the same principles with your youngsters.

First, you need to target a few problems that really upset you. Is your child noncompliant, never doing what you ask until you scream? Do your children bicker constantly? Perhaps they leave their things all over the house and you're tired of the mess. Or one of your youngsters may never get to the school bus on time without a constant battle each morning. Perhaps one of your children is getting into trouble in school or not doing homework. Although there may be many problems that bother you, don't fall into the trap of trying to change too much at one time. It won't work. If the problems are major and occur frequently, limit yourself to one or two at a time. If they are minor or sporadic, you can tackle a *few* at a time (but never more than both you and your child can keep track of and work on *consistently*).

Once you have targeted the troublesome behaviors, discuss them with your children. Tell them these behaviors are causing a problem and you would like to work on them together. And since it will take hard work on their part, you

---

Checklist for Handling Noncompliant Behavior

✓ 1. Reward *all* your child's positive behavior, especially compliance, with praise, smiles, or hugs.
✓ 2. Reduce the number of requests and commands you make.
✓ 3. State all requests you *do* make *concisely* and *directly.*
✓ 4. Give your child a *specific* time in which to comply with the request.
✓ 5. Reward your child with praise if he or she does comply.

If noncompliance continues, do the following:

For young children:
✓ 6. Give one warning.
✓ 7. Use a time-out if he or she doesn't comply within the specified time.
✓ 8. After the time-out, restate your request.
✓ 9. Repeat the procedure if necessary. Be persistent!

For older children:
✓ 6. Discuss the problem and *jointly* arrive at some consequences for noncompliance.
✓ 7. You might want to involve your child in a joint effort to correct it through one of the following methods:
  • A behavior-change program using tangible rewards.
  • The "no one loses" problem-solving method.
  • A contract.

---

would like to reward their successes. Then explain the behavior change program to them. If you have been following the self-change program yourself, share this with them. It will make them feel more mature and cooperative.

Here are the steps for the self-change program in Appendix A modified for children.

Step 1: Target the troublesome behavior.

Step 2: Set a small, realistic goal. It is important to break goals into small, achievable steps. If your kids get discouraged, they will give up. The younger they are, the smaller the steps you need to use. For example, suppose you had two preschoolers who fought continually. If you offered to buy them the toy of their dreams, do you think they could go for a week without fighting? I doubt if there's a preschooler in the world who could. How about a day without fighting, for a lesser reward? That's not likely either. However, they might be able to go two *hours* without fighting, if you set a timer and show them what two hours is on a clock. If they think they can do that, make that their goal. Older children should also set goals in small, achievable steps, but their steps would not have to be as small. For older children who bicker constantly, you might jointly set a goal for them to work out their problems quietly by themselves for an entire day.

Step 3:   Determine an appropriate reward. Your children will be only too happy to offer suggestions for rewards. Examples are special desserts, extra time with you in an activity a child enjoys, a trip to the ice cream store, a few M&Ms, a rented video, bowling, a movie, a trip to the park, a special activity they don't normally get to do (perhaps finger painting or a craft), having a friend spend the night, extra TV (unless you allow unlimited TV), a new book, a new box of crayons, and so forth.

Children, of course, usually find larger rewards more appealing than smaller ones. This poses a bit of a dilemma since they learn better by setting small goals and receiving *frequent* rewards. Obviously, you can't use large rewards if you must use frequent ones. A good way to get around this is to use points for rewards. Each time your children reach a goal, they earn so many points, which they can accumulate until they have enough for a larger reward. Most kids love the point system, and it has another benefit: It helps them learn to delay gratification and work toward a long-term goal.

To use a point system, make up a chart with appealing rewards and determine how many points will be needed for each reward. Have a wide range of rewards— many small ones that can be earned for a few points up through some larger rewards that would take many points. (Rewards don't have to cost money.) Include your children in planning the chart. It will give you a good idea of the relative merits of each of the rewards. Interestingly, kids often suggest making rewards harder to earn than do adults.

What reward (or how many points) a child should receive for reaching a goal should be jointly determined. However, it will be your job to keep the rewards appropriate to the effort expended. A reward should be attractive enough to motivate your children to succeed, but not excessive.

Step 4:   Ask your children to make a commitment to work toward the goals they set. If they have been involved in setting goals and determining rewards, this should not be a problem.

Step 5:   Record on a chart each time your child has reached a goal. A posted chart keeps goals in mind, and children love to see visible evidence of their progress and success.

Step 6:   Reward your child if he or she was successful in meeting the goal. Rewards are more effective if they are given immediately. If you are using points, record them on the chart. Besides tangible rewards, be sure to give lots of praise for successes and encouragement for continued effort.

Step 7:   Once a goal has been reached, recorded, and rewarded, set a new goal. Gradually, goals can be increased in very small increments. The idea is to get to the point where the behavior is natural for them, not to give them tangible rewards forever.

Steps to a Behavior-Change Program for Children

✓ 1. Target the troublesome behavior.
✓ 2. Set a realistic goal with your child.
✓ 3. Jointly determine an appropriate reward.
✓ 4. Ask for a commitment to work toward the goal.
✓ 5. Record on a chart success or failure in meeting the goal.
✓ 6. Reward success immediately. Don't forget praise.
✓ 7. Set a new goal.
  • If successful, increase goals step by step.
  • If unsuccessful, evaluate whether the goal and reward are realistic. Readjust if necessary.

For example, in the case of our preschoolers, you would probably continue making goals in two-hour segments for a while because what they are learning to do is difficult for them. As they begin to catch on to solving their problems without fighting, you would begin to increase their goal. The first increase may be to three hours, then to an entire afternoon, then to a day, then to two days, and so forth.

What if your children object to increasing their goals? Draw the analogy with a game. When a game gets too easy, it gets boring, and you begin to look for ways to make it more challenging.

If your child was unsuccessful in reaching his or her goal, set a new goal and let him or her try again. If a child is having trouble reaching a goal, either break down the goal into smaller steps, or reevaluate whether the reward is motivating enough.

DISCIPLINE AND TEENS

Teenagers in many single-parent homes have an unusual amount of freedom. This is a mistake, warn mental health professionals. Teens need supervision, and they need clearly defined rules and limits. Teens who have experienced parental divorce often need supervision, rules, and limits even more than teens in intact families. Why? Because a significant minority of teens express their distress about the divorce or their parents' continued conflict by experimenting with drugs, alcohol, and sex, and some act out their anger in destructive or antisocial behavior. These teens not only *need* firm boundaries and consequences for breaking them, many are *pleading* for them. Psychologist and divorce expert William Hodges tells the story of a teen client who confided to him that she wished she had been raised a Catholic. When asked why, she responded that the Catholic

Church provided clear guidelines about how to behave. She went on to tell him that whenever she sought guidelines from her parents, they told her to do whatever she thought best. Clearly, she did not know what was "best"! Interviews with teens in single-parent homes often reveal that teens interpret their parents' lack of rules as a lack of caring.

At the same time that they need clear rules, teens are blossoming into young adults and moving toward independence. They want to be their own people and do things their own way. Most important, they want to be treated with the respect that they feel their emerging maturity should command. Though all children thrive on being treated with respect, it assumes monumental importance to a teen. When a parent does not grant that respect to his or her teen, their relationship can become very rocky indeed.

How do you achieve the balance between treating your teens with the respect they need while providing them with the rules and limits they need? An authoritative parenting style provides the right balance. With no other age group is this parenting style more necessary than it is with teens.

Sit down with your teen and *jointly* determine guidelines for acceptable and unacceptable behavior, through discussion and a sharing of ideas and concerns. Treat your teen with the same respect with which you would like to be treated, and respect your teen's personal rights as you want yours respected.

What kinds of rules and limits are appropriate for teens? They should have a curfew. They should be responsible for telling you where they are going, who they will be with, and what they will be doing. Of course, sexual experimentation, drug use, alcohol use, and antisocial behavior are appropriate areas for clear guidelines. So are chores, homework, who can be in the home when a parent is not there, places a teen can go without checking first, and the language used when talking to parents (if abusive language is a problem). Within most of these areas, there is room for parent and teen to negotiate and arrive at guidelines with which they can both agree.

It is a good idea to try to get to know other parents of teens and talk to them for perspective. Without other adult input, it is easy for a convincing teen to sway a single parent over to his or her viewpoint of what is acceptable ("Mom/ Dad, this is the 90s. Where have you been? *Everyone* does it!").

What can you do with a "problem" teen with whom life is one big confrontation and everything else you've tried has been ineffective? Two techniques are found to be particularly effective with teens. They can be used with mature older children as well. One is a problem-solving technique and the other is contracting. Each has the flavor of the adult world about it and treats adolescents with the respect they need and thrive on. This may partially explain their effectiveness.

The "No One Loses" Problem-Solving Approach

This technique is one in which parent and teen use a problem-solving strategy to find a solution to their conflicts. If the solution is truly a jointly determined one, and both sides agree that it is fair, teens usually feel a commitment to stick to the agreement. The atmosphere of the home usually becomes a lot less hostile as well. The technique is basically the same as the problem-solving strategy discussed in the last chapter. Its steps are as follows:

1. Identify the conflict and define it in concrete terms. Each of you should tell the other what you think the problem is and how you feel about it. Set some ground rules: You will each listen to what the other says *with respect* and *without interrupting*. When it's your turn, try to avoid putting your teen on the defensive; it will only increase the chances of failure right from the start. How do you avoid putting a teen on the defensive? State the problem using an "I" message, as discussed in chapter 5—for example, "I'm uncomfortable with you seeing Rod because of his drinking," *not*, "The problem is that you are seeing that no-good Rod." Or, "I feel very frustrated that you are not doing your chores," *not*, "The problem is that you are not doing a damn thing around here." Or, "I'm very upset that we are fighting all the time," *not*, "The problem is that you cause one fight after another."

    Then listen openly and with respect as your teen tells you the problem from his or her perspective. Together, try to arrive at a joint definition of the problem in concrete terms that you can work on solving together.
2. Brainstorm to generate a list of possible alternative solutions. Remember, at this stage every suggestion is written down, no matter how impractical you think it is. A ridiculous idea may set you off on a different train of thought that might yield a good idea. During brainstorming, the rule is that no one evaluates or even *reacts* to any suggested idea.
3. Eliminate ideas that either one of you will not consider.
4. Evaluate the remaining alternatives. Listen with respect to your teen's opinions. Try to offer reasons that alternatives are acceptable or unacceptable to you, such as, "I'm uncomfortable with this one because. . . ."
5. Try to reach some agreement on a solution. No single alternative may solve the problem. You may have to combine several, or you may have to renegotiate some to make them more acceptable to one or the other.
6. If it is not obvious, discuss precisely how you will carry out the solution you have agreed on. Both sides will have to make compromises.
7. Make a commitment to keeping your end of the bargain, and ask your teen if he or she is willing to make a commitment too. Decide on a consequence if one of you fails to follow the agreement.

Steps to the "No One Loses" Problem-solving Strategy

✓ 1. Identify the problem in concrete terms.
✓ 2. Brainstorm to generate a list of possible solutions.
✓ 3. Eliminate solutions either of you won't consider.
✓ 4. Evaluate the remaining solutions.
✓ 5. Try to reach agreement on a solution.
   • Can some ideas be combined?
   • Can some ideas be modified?
✓ 6. Determine how to carry out the agreed-upon solution.
✓ 7. Each of you makes a commitment to carry out your share, and you jointly decide on a consequence if either of you fails.
✓ 8. Evaluate the solution's effectiveness at a predetermined time. If it is not working, renegotiate and readjust.

---

8. Decide on a time to discuss and evaluate how well the plan is working. Does it need readjustment or renegotiation?

> Valerie was "in love" with Rod, and her mother Maggie was upset. She had heard rumors that the boy was "wild" and drank. Deciding she didn't trust him, she forbade Valerie to see him. Valerie was furious about her mother's unfairness. After all, she was basing her judgment on rumors and showed no respect for Valerie's judgment. Valerie began to see Rod behind her mother's back. One night Maggie returned home early and found the two in an embrace. She threw Rod out of the house and put Valerie on restriction for three months. The two argued bitterly that night, and Valerie refused to speak to her mother for the next three weeks.
>
> Valerie's silent treatment filled Maggie with guilt. Perhaps she had been too hard. Yet she couldn't tolerate such deceit. "What choice did you give the kid?" a co-worker asked her when she relayed the story. The co-worker told her about the problem-solving approach she had learned about in a parenting class. Although she had never used it herself, several other class members had and were pleased with the results. Maggie decided to try it.
>
> Valerie was cooperative when she realized that her mother was willing to discuss the problem. First, they had to try to define their *mutual* problem, since each thought it was the other's stubbornness. They finally agreed to define it as "to find a way that Valerie can see Rod that Mom can be comfortable with."
>
> They came up with a number of alternative suggestions during the brainstorming session:
>
> a. Mom will get to know Rod better.
> b. Mom will find out more about Rod and investigate whether the rumors are true.
> c. Valerie and Rod can see each other if they are home by 10 P.M. weeknights and 1 A.M. on weekends.

    d. Valerie can see Rod only at home with Mom present.
    e. Valerie can see Rod as long as Mom approves of the activity.
    f. Valerie cannot ride in Rod's car.
    g. Valerie can see Rod only once a week in an approved activity.
    h. Valerie and Rod can go out together only if they are in a group.
    i. Valerie cannot go to Rod's house.
    j. Mom will get to know Rod's parents.

      Valerie and Maggie discussed the alternatives. They decided that several could be combined and renegotiated. Then they worked on specifics: How could the alternatives that were vague be carried out?

Valerie and her mother's agreed-upon terms appear in the next section under contracts, the second strategy that is often effective with teens.

Contracts

A contract is exactly what it sounds like: a written agreement between parent and child in which each agrees to certain terms. Typically, the teen will agree to adhere to specific terms that a parent feels are important, and in return the teen will get certain privileges. Contracts, of course, involve negotiation and compromise. They can be used in conjunction with the "no one loses" problem-solving approach, although simple problems and simple contracts may not require that degree of negotiation. Contracts will always be more successful if an atmosphere of mutual respect is created.

    Contracts should be written and a copy kept by both parent and child. The contract should be very specific so that each party knows *exactly* what is expected and whether or not the contract is being followed. A contract in which a teen agrees to follow "house rules" is too vague; the rules should be written down. Having everything in writing prevents misunderstandings later on down the road.

    Signing a contract increases a teen's commitment to stick to the agreement. Once it is signed, its terms must be carried out by *both* parties. If your teen behaves in an objectionable manner not covered by the contract, you cannot renege on your contract, although you can insist that it be renegotiated. If Valerie and her mother Maggie had written out a contract for their agreed-upon terms, it may have looked like this:

I, Maggie Jensen, agree to the following:

    a. I will spend time with Rod and get to know him better.
    b. Valerie can see Rod a maximum of twice a week under the following conditions: She can invite him to the house, providing I will be home. They can rent videos, listen to music, and have other friends over. They can go to school

activities together. They may also go out in a group, *if* I approve of both the friends and the activity.

c. I will investigate the rumors I've heard about Rod to determine their accuracy.

Maggie Jensen

I, Valerie Jensen, in return for the above, agree to the following:

a. I agree to see Rod only with Mom's knowledge and approval. I agree to see him only at our house, at school activities, or with a group of friends Mom approves of. I agree to see him a maximum of twice a week (and at school).
b. I agree to a curfew of 10 P.M. on Sunday through Thursday and midnight on Friday and Saturday.
c. I agree not to ride in Rod's car unless Mom learns the rumors are false. If there is no other driver, I will drive Mom's car.
d. Rod agrees not to drink when he is with me.

Valerie Jensen

YOUR RELATIONSHIP WITH YOUR CHILDREN: THE FOUNDATION OF EFFECTIVE DISCIPLINE

The discipline principle most frequently overlooked is the most important of all: a good relationship and mutual respect between parent and child. When a parent and child have a good relationship, a child is motivated to avoid behaving in ways that will displease that parent. When a child is the recipient of consequences imposed by a warm and nurturant parent, those consequences have a greater impact than they would have if they'd come from a cold and distant parent. When they are imposed by a nurturant parent who respects the child, the youngster is likely to respond with remorse and determination to try harder in the future. Moreover, children with warm and nurturant parents are more likely to be loyal to their parents' values and internalize them as their own.

Keep this important but often-neglected principle in mind as you work on each of these discipline techniques. They will be far more effective if your child is motivated to please you.

All relationships must be continually worked at to be successful, including relationships with children. With all that is going on in your life, this may be easy to forget unless you make a conscious effort *not* to forget. Try to spend at least a brief time every day with each of your children individually; show an interest in their activities, friends, school lives, and current interests; and create an atmosphere in which your youngsters can communicate openly with you (Chapter 10). If you let them know they are important to you, you will be important to them too. If things have gotten so out of control with your children that nothing works, visit a family therapist. He or she can help get you back on the right track.

17

DATING AND OTHER COMMON PROBLEMS OF PARENTING SOLO

Every time Phyllis had a date, her two mild-mannered children became so obstreperous and demanding that she eventually stopped going out altogether. "It just isn't worth the hassle," she finally concluded. It took a while for Jan to realize that she was not misplacing her makeup before her dates; her kids were hiding it. Betty's son, William, routinely developed asthma attacks before her evenings out, forcing her to either cancel them or spend the evening at home, a choice her dates quickly tired of. Larry's teenage son insulted every woman he brought home. Peggy found her kids to be uncooperative and uncommunicative whenever she had a man in her life. And one adolescent set off a cherry bomb no more than a foot away from his mother's unsuspecting date.

JUGGLING DATING AND INTIMACY WITH CHILDREN IN THE HOME

When a custodial parent begins to date, it is often a very stressful time for the family. It is easy for parents to become angry and frustrated with children if the feelings underlying their erratic behavior are not understood. A parent's dating usually creates a great deal of anxiety in children. They have already lost much of their parents' attention and availability. Now they must share what little is left with a stranger. Children often equate having less of their parents' time with having less of their love, and they have already watched their parents' love for each other wane. Will they be the next ones to be shut out of a parent's new life? It is not unusual for children to be filled with fear, insecurity, jealousy, and feelings of abandonment, a fact that would amaze most parents if they only knew.

Anger is a common defense children use against these terrifying feelings. Some hold their anger in, afraid their resentment may alienate their parent still further. Some express it indirectly by becoming uncooperative and sullen. Some explode directly at a parent. Others express it by rebelling, as did one boy, Mark. Mark reports that things were fine until a new man came into his mother's life. Afterward he began to run wild, and his mother lost all control over him. Why? Mark relates,

> Before that the kids were everything to her. But when her boyfriend came on the scene, it was different. We took a back seat to him. I was so jealous and angry that I couldn't control it. I figured that if nobody gave a damn, I might as well just get into trouble.[1]

Children's problems with their parents' dating are not limited to insecurity and jealousy. Many are filled with conflicts. They want their single parent to be happy, but they do not want their missing parent replaced. They want to like this new person but worry that to do so will betray their absent parent. Some even worry that if they are nice to this new person that it may be an act of disloyalty. And what about their hopes that their parents will reconcile? Surely dating makes this less likely.

Dating can lead to another problem for children. It forces them to acknowledge their parents' sexuality. Most kids prefer to think of their parents as nonsexual beings, and so youngsters tend to become very uneasy when parents begin to date. It can be particularly troublesome for adolescents, who are trying to deal with their own sexual thoughts and feelings.

Laying the Foundation

You do not have to swear off dating. In her highly recommended book *Sex and the Single Parent*, psychologist Mary Mattis points out that many potential problems can be avoided with some *advance* preparation. Mattis suggests the following:

- Begin *now* to set aside regular time to spend with friends and to build a social network. Convey to your children that adults need a social life with other adults just as children need a social life with friends their own age. Then when you do begin to date, it will seem more natural and be less disruptive of their time with you.
- Evaluate your relationship with your children and begin to make changes now. Are you treating one or more of your children as a confidant or equal partner? Not only may you be creating potential problems for your youngster and family (Chapter 14), but it will also be far more difficult to introduce a dating partner into your life in the future. Understandably, your child is likely to feel replaced and become resentful. Allow your children to be children, and seek out adults for your companions.

- Build a good relationship with your youngsters that can weather future changes in your respective lives. Spend time every day with each child individually. Let your kids know how important they are to you, and convey that they will always retain an important place in your life. A child who feels secure about your love is less likely to feel abandoned when you bring another person into your life. However, even a secure child will need reassurance and attention while you are dating. Many parents incorrectly assume that if they spend lots of time with their children while they are not dating, it should carry them through periods when a dating companion occupies the spotlight. Wrong. Most children feel very threatened when a stranger displaces them in their parents' lives.
- Although it is important for *all* parents to teach their children accurate information and healthy attitudes about sex, it is more important for single parents who may one day be engaging in sexual behavior with their children's knowledge, or at least their suspicion. Start your children's sex education early. Clarify your own values so you can begin to transmit them to your youngsters. There are many books on the market that will help you with your children's sex education, but make sure the ones you use are consistent with your values.
- One day you may have a companion spend the night with you, and you will not want your children barging in on you. Yet to suddenly bar them from your bedroom when they have had free access will fuel their feelings of being shut out of your life. Begin now to teach them to have respect for your privacy. The first step is having respect for theirs. Always knock before entering their rooms, and teach them that when your door is closed, it is your private time.
- Talk to your children about dating *beforehand* so they can get used to the idea before the reality occurs.

Becoming a Troubleshooter

Laying the foundation early will help make the transition to dating and a new relationship a smooth one. But once you are dating, become a troubleshooter: Keep an eye out for sources of trouble and eliminate them. Following are ways to handle common problems encountered by single parents.

Children's Jealousy and Insecurity

Nip your children's jealousy and insecurity in the bud. While you are dating, continue to reassure them of your love, and watch that your behavior toward them does not change dramatically, especially in the presence of your dates. Sometimes a parent changes so much after becoming involved in a new relationship that children feel as if they have now lost *both* their parents. It is important that you continue to spend special time alone with each of your children. Parents often assume that it is sufficient to include their children in activities with their companions, but this sends the message to the child that the parent no longer has time for him or her alone.

In a 1990 article she wrote for *Redbook*, New York writer and single parent Carol Kirschenbaum relates how she dealt with her young child's insecurities by comparing love with an earthworm. Because he understood that cutting an earthworm in half results in two earthworms, he understood her analogy that cutting love in half resulted in twice as much love to give.

Children's Attachment to a New Person

Be alert to the fact that children can become very attached to a parent's companion, only to have the person disappear from their lives. This can be very hard on youngsters who have lost a parent through divorce. If children experience too many such losses, they may become very cynical about relationships and friendships in general, points out Dr. R. Vance Fitzgerald, a clinical associate professor at the Medical College of Ohio in Toledo. Most mental health professionals recommend that you do not make a companion part of your children's lives unless you think there is a strong possibility for a long-term relationship. Simply explain that adults like to spend time alone with their friends just as children like to do with *their* friends.

Don't misunderstand. This does not mean that you should discourage *all* contact between a dating companion and your children. Once you begin to see a person frequently, introduce him or her to your children if they live with you, and involve them in an occasional short outing if you would like. Otherwise you will be splitting your life in two, and your children may feel that you are deliberately shutting them out, points out Dorothy Cantor and Ellen Drake, two New Jersey psychologists who work extensively with divorced parents.

How to Introduce a New Partner to Your Children

The key is to go very slowly. Beginning with a few very short outings—perhaps just for an ice cream—won't put anyone under too much pressure to make conversation. Outings can gradually become longer if it looks as if the relationship will be a long-term one.

Before you introduce them, let your children know the nature of your relationship. Children are usually very anxious about a stepparent entering their lives, and this is usually very much on their minds. They should feel comfortable that they will have plenty of warning ahead of time should this be a possibility.

Take this time to reassure your youngsters again of your love for them. They are less likely to accept someone whom they perceive as a threat. It is important they know that the person is not a replacement for their absent parent. Tell them you are hoping that they will get to know him or her as a friend.

Your New Partner's Authority

Companions or even live-ins should avoid trying to take on any kind of parental role. Children, and especially teens, usually become very resentful when a parent's new partner tries to exert any type of authority toward them (disciplining, giving orders, assigning chores, siding with the parent against them). "You're not my parent and you have no right to tell me what to do," is an often-heard cry. Some express their resentment openly, some become uncooperative, some act out their anger, some simply withdraw—none of which makes for a pleasant atmosphere in the home.

Dr. Neil Kalter of the Department of Psychology and Psychiatry at the University of Michigan suggests that parents' companions limit their interactions with children to the following: taking them on outings, helping them with homework, playing with them, talking with them, and joking with them. Asking for their help with a task is okay, too. How to *gradually* move into a parental role is discussed in Chapter 21.

Children's Troublesome Behavior

Try to prevent children's troublesome behavior before it occurs, or at least before it becomes a pattern or source of family conflict. Try the following:

- Discuss with your children in advance how you expect them to behave with your new companion. Set clear rules and limits, and involve them in deciding what the consequences should be for breaking them. (For example, if they do not behave as agreed, they will have to go straight to their rooms and miss the special dessert you prepared.) Chapter 16 should help you with determining consequences. When youngsters are behaving, reward them with smiles, hugs, and praise. If they misbehave, follow through with the consequences you agreed on.
- If a child has a tantrum before you leave for a date, begging you to stay, go anyway. Otherwise you will reward the negative behavior and it will occur again.
- Allow your children to express their feelings and fears. This does not mean you have to give up your relationship if they object to it. They will feel more loved if you listen to them and show your concern about their feelings. Don't pressure them to like your new person. Explain that relationships take time to develop, and you hope that one day they will like this special person in your life.
- See if you can hammer out some type of specific agreements with your children that will satisfy both your needs and their needs. University of Massachusetts sociologist Robert Weiss reports that this has worked well with the single parents he has worked with. You might try the problem-solving approach discussed in Chapter 15.

When a Relationship Becomes Intimate

Some single parents resent advice about combining sexually intimate relationships with kids in the home. Of course, you will have to be the one to make the ultimate decision in this area, but if you are looking for guidelines, there is rather widespread agreement among mental health professionals. Here are the points on which most agree.

- Do not expose your children to a series of casual intimate relationships. It is very anxiety-arousing and stressful for a child to have a series of men (or women) share his or her parent's bedroom. Many become angry, embarrassed, and withdrawn. (Your ex may also seize it as an excuse to fight for custody.) Have overnight guests when your children are spending the night elsewhere. Otherwise, hire or exchange baby-sitting, and go elsewhere yourself. And please remember to take precautions that your partner has not been exposed to AIDS. Use a condom, too. AIDS has become a very real threat in the heterosexual community.
- Most experts agree that long-term committed relationships are quite a different matter where children are concerned. Most children are more able to accept a parent's sexual intimacy with one special person who the parent cares for (although many still find it anxiety-arousing to acknowledge a parent's sexuality).
- Prepare your children *before* you begin an intimate relationship in your home ("I care about George very much, and we want to spend a lot of time together. He is going to be spending the night here quite frequently."). You do not need to be more explicit. What you do behind closed doors is your private concern. Watch for your children's reactions, and try to address their concerns calmly and warmly. Be prepared that they may be very aware of what is going on. Parents are often startled to learn how aware of sex their elementary-school–age children are and how strict their moral codes are.
- If you have teens, you will have a unique problem that must be addressed. Teens are trying to deal with their own emerging sexuality, and having to acknowledge their parents' sexual behavior complicates their task considerably. Many become stimulated and curious, yet repelled, reports Dr. Kalter. Girls can become particularly troubled, uneasy, and self-conscious. For some, there is a fallout that many single mothers do not consider. They become a role model for their daughters' sexual behavior. Teens find it difficult to understand why there should be a double standard for parents and for them. Girls will sometimes defiantly confront their mothers with, "If you can have your boyfriend spend the night, why can't I have mine?" Some mothers become intimidated and allow their teenage daughters far more freedom than is good for them. Studies report that as a

group, girls from single-parent homes are more sexually active at an earlier age and are more likely to become pregnant before marriage than are girls from two-parent homes.

Mental health professionals strongly advise that you draw clear boundaries between the acceptability of sex for adults and for teens and that you do it with conviction and confidence. A common recommendation is to point out that sex is an adult behavior meant for long-term relationships and has a number of responsibilities tied to it that teens are not mature enough to handle. For example, teens are neither emotionally nor financially ready for parenthood. They may not be emotionally ready to handle the end of a sexual relationship, which can be far more devastating than other breakups. They are also unlikely to have the maturity to either question a partner or adequately assess a partner's risk for exposure to AIDS or other sexually transmitted diseases. Dr. Seymour Schneider, an associate dean of faculty at the Alfred Adler Institute in Chicago, warns that making such distinctions will not necessarily solve the problem. From the perspective of many teens, these arguments just don't hold water. It would be less disconcerting if there were an easy solution to this dilemma, but it is something that each single parent must work out individually.

YOUR FINANCIAL PINCH

According to 1988 Census Bureau statistics, the average family income in single-parent homes headed by mothers was just under $12,000 a year. Single-parent fathers fared better—just under $24,000 a year. But even this is substantially lower than the $40,067 yearly average income of two-parent homes.

It is a well-documented fact that most single parents experience a serious decline in their standard of living. While their income is significantly reduced, their expenses decrease very little. Single parents must provide a home large enough to accommodate their children. The utilities must still be paid. Youngsters still need food and clothing and also have school- and entertainment-related expenses—costs that increase as children get older. There may be significant new expenses too, such as child care and nonsubsidized health insurance premiums.

The situation is tough, but single parents generally find that it is not the end of the world. Once the basic necessities are met, economic *stability* after divorce is found to be more important to well-being than is the level of income. The reason is probably that stability allows for planning. Once you know exactly where you stand, you can plan for the future and adjust to living within your means. Your attitude, of course, will be critical. If you allow yourself to feel cheated, resentful, and helpless, you will create *additional* unhappiness for yourself and your children.

If money will be very tight, it is a good idea to share this fact with your youngsters. Children sometimes equate the money spent on them as a tangible proof of love, and they will need to understand why they can't have many of the things they would like. Some single parents find that it is helpful to include older children in making out the family budget, so they know what the family's spending limits are. Not only does this reduce the likelihood of their asking for things parents cannot afford, but many older children willingly get jobs to help out. They can at least make their own spending money.

A word of caution. When discussing your financial limitations with children, be careful not to overburden them with worry and anxiety. Kids worry about whether their single parent will be able to take care of them, and it is easy for them to interpret a parent's words and anxiety to mean that they may not have a roof over their heads or food on the table. If you need someone to lean on and listen to your problems, seek out an adult, not your children.

If your financial situation is tight but not desperate, include your children in decisions about what can be cut—entertainment, groceries, vacations, utility bills, spending money, and so forth. Decide what is important to you, and decide with your children what is important to the family. Then use these as your guidelines, making cuts in areas that have a low priority. Make it a joint family effort to cut expenses. The problem-solving strategy discussed in Chapter 15 is a good way to do this.

If your financial situation is very bad, talk to your youngsters in a matter-of-fact, confident voice. Let them know what will have to be cut and what you are doing to improve the family's situation in the future, such as looking for a better-paying job, improving your job skills, getting help from a financial counselor, or applying for public assistance. Tips for reentering the job market or changing careers were discussed in Chapter 13.

When you are already feeling vulnerable after a divorce, it is easy to feel overwhelmed in dealing with your reduced financial circumstances. You may be having serious trouble working out a feasible budget. Or perhaps you are heavily in debt and have creditors telephoning you. Don't despair. There is excellent help available to you. Contact your local Consumer Credit Counseling Service. Established in the late 1950s and financed largely by the business community, CCCS is a nonprofit organization with 550 offices nationwide. At little or no cost, it provides people with financial guidance about using their money and managing their credit wisely. If your problem is budgeting, a trained financial counselor will help you work out a realistic budget. If your problem is creditors, CCCS will act as an intermediary, working out an arrangement with your creditors that will allow you to pay off your debts on a manageable timetable. You then send your payments to CCCS, and they disburse it for you. To locate your closest office, check your phone book or call a toll-free number: 1-800-388-

CCCS. Several hundred thousand families take advantage of this service each year. A spokesperson at CCCS relates that no one is turned away.

If you are in serious financial need, investigate whether you are eligible for any government-subsidized programs until you can get back on your feet. Government figures indicate that within any 10-year period, approximately 25 percent of households in this country rely on public assistance at some point, and separation and divorce are common reasons. Almost 90 percent of those receiving Aid to Families with Dependent Children are single parents, and on the average, recipients stay on the program for two years.

Turning Adversity into a Strengthening Experience

Many single parents feel bad because they cannot provide their children with everything their friends have. Rather than focusing on what your children are missing financially, try to turn your financial plight into a long-term advantage for them. Crisis situations are like two-headed coins. They have both a threatening and a challenging side to them. Helping your children shift their focus to this less obvious side of crises, rather than dwelling on their threatening nature, may be one of the most important skills you can teach them in life. Adversity can be a *strengthening* experience.

With your help, your children can also learn to be money-smart—another skill that will be invaluable throughout their adult lives. Teach them how to budget their money, how to comparison shop, and how to make financial choices. Perhaps most important, teach them how to set goals and work toward them. The issue of money is a good place to begin to practice dumping the guilt that is so often a part of single parents' lives. How to dump your guilt will be discussed shortly.

Unpaid Child Support

Is your former spouse lax about making his or her child support payments? Try a strategy that may be diametrically opposed to what you are inclined to do. Try *encouraging* him or her to become *more* involved with the children. Recent studies have found that fathers who have frequent contact with their children (including by phone and mail) are far more likely to pay regular child support. Fathers who spend *extended* time with their children are also more likely to pay child support, according to a large-scale national study reported by Judith Seltzer of the University of Wisconsin.

You may be thinking that your former spouse simply isn't interested in the children. However, studies find that most noncustodial parents miss their kids intensely after divorce, even many fathers who had been uninvolved previously.

Apparently, a major reason that noncustodial parents drop out of children's lives is frustration over the artificial nature of "visitation" and the barriers erected by custodial parents that make it difficult to see youngsters. Studies report that when dads are given the chance to spend extended time with their children and function as parents instead of visitors, many become better fathers after divorce than they had been while living with their children full-time. (Read about non-custodial parents' visitation dilemma in Chapter 18.)

Keep your former spouse informed about the children, their progress, and their activities. Try sharing the material in Chapters 18 and 19. It discusses the importance of noncustodial parents in children's lives, how to build a good relationship with children who are not in your custody, and the significance to children of the child support check. How you approach your former partner will be important. If you do so in a hostile, critical, and blaming manner, he or she is likely to become defensive and resistive. Chapter 11 provided some good negotiating strategies that can be used in an emotionally charged atmosphere. Find out if there is anything you can do to make it easier for your former partner to become more involved with the children. Studies find that many custody-retaining parents create subtle barriers without realizing it.

In the long run, the best way to collect unpaid child support is through your former partner's *cooperation*, because resorting to legal means is costly and likely to create additional animosity. Children need both parents in their lives, and they also need to be protected from their parents' conflict (Chapter 9).

However, if the cooperative route is not productive, there is now federal legislation in place requiring states to take a number of courses of action to collect court-ordered child support. These include deducting payments directly from noncustodial parents' paychecks, intercepting federal and state income tax refunds, and attaching assets.

The *quickest* way to take advantage of this legislation is through an attorney, but be sure to use one who is experienced in child support collection. An initial consultation fee is often minimal. Bring as much information about your former spouse's finances as you can find. Find out what the attorney can do for you, how much it will cost, and how long it will take.

If using an attorney is too costly, go to your state Child Support Enforcement Office. In most states it is associated with either the Family Court or the Welfare Department. In most states there is a long wait because of the sheer number of cases waiting to be processed. You can help your case by taking along as much information about your former partner as you can discover—Social Security number, place of employment, assets, financial institutions paying him or her interest, and so on. And be persistent! The old saying about the squeaky wheel getting the grease has some truth. It may cheer you to know that at some point, all states will be attaching noncustodial parents' salaries *automatically*, as soon as there is a child support order in place. Some states are already doing so.

The ins and outs of child support can be found in *The Child Support Survivor's Guide*, listed in Appendix C.

DUMPING YOUR GUILT

Parenting solo is a life-style very conducive to guilt feelings. Divorced parents feel guilty about many things: having subjected their children to the trauma of divorce, their children having only one parent available, not having enough time for their children, not having the money to buy their kids all the material goodies their friends have, having to assign the kids more chores than they would like to, and not being able to provide picture-perfect holidays with a loving, intact family.

Of course, sometimes guilt is appropriate and has a positive outcome because it motivates people to correct some wrong. For example, if a parent uses children as a weapon to hurt an ex-spouse or dumps the lion's share of responsibilities on children so that he or she can pursue an active social life, guilt is appropriate. In such cases, the remedy for guilt is obvious. The parent can make a conscious effort not to satisfy his or her personal needs at children's expense and to attend more to children's needs. The outcome of his or her guilt will be positive.

A more difficult problem to deal with, however, is inappropriate guilt. Many single parents feel that no matter how good a job they do, it is not good enough— their children are still being "deprived" by living in a single-parent home. Many single parents knock themselves out trying to do more than is humanly possible.

Inappropriate guilt does no one any good, and it often does harm. Parents usually have no idea how to handle their guilt and sometimes choose ways that are contrary to everyone's best interests. Poor discipline is an example. Single parents often feel that because their children have been through so much, they should not impose any more restrictions on them than is absolutely necessary. This is usually a mistake if not a disaster, as you may remember from Chapter 14. Others handle their guilt by buying children luxuries that exceed the family budget. Some forsake their own lives to devote themselves to their children, an approach that is good for neither parent nor child.

Inappropriate guilt is not an easy thing to deal with, but a creative and seemingly effective technique has been suggested by psychologist Fitzhugh Dodson, the author of many popular "how-to" books on parenting (*How to Parent, How to Discipline with Love,* etc.). He calls it *negative thinking.*

Dodson points out that the reason guilt has such a powerful influence over our behavior is that many of the feelings underlying it are never verbalized. They are vague, nagging notions operating silently in the back of our minds. Get them out in the open, Dodson says, and they will lose much of the power to influence our behavior. Here is how to do it.

- Imagine a situation that usually arouses your guilt—perhaps imposing rules and limits on your kids, assigning them chores, saying no to something they want you to buy, or going out for an evening when your child is crying for you to stay home.
- While you have a clear picture of the scene in your mind, verbalize all the nagging thoughts that are silently racing through your mind and *exaggerate them as much as you can*. For example, you might imagine a scene in which you make the long-dreaded announcement to your children that you can no longer handle the amount of work you have, and you need more substantial help from them. You might imagine the following scene.

> *Children:* Oh, Mom. That's not fair. We do plenty around here. We do more than any of our friends. We both have hard courses and school commitments. We can't handle any more than we're doing. How are we supposed to get all our homework done and study for tests if we have to do extra chores? We have to get good grades so we can get into college. And we're just teenagers. We *need* free time and a social life.
>
> *You:* They're right. What am I thinking? Why should they have to take on extra chores? It's not *their* fault we got divorced and I have to work. Why should they have to do any more than their friends? They have a hard enough life already doing everything they do around here. It is an immense burden on them to clean their bedrooms, wash their clothes, do the dishes, and empty the trash. After all, there are only two of them to shoulder *all* that responsibility. I should be grateful instead of asking for more! If they do any more, they will *clearly* be overburdened. Their grades will *certainly* drop and they will not get into college. I will ruin their lives for sure. It is completely unreasonable and selfish of me to even *think* of asking them to do more. After all, I only wanted a little free time for myself. How shameful. No *good* mother would ask her children to do a little more just so she could have a little time for herself. Good mothers are completely at their children's service. They do all the cleaning, all the yard work, and all the shopping. They run all the errands, cook their teenagers' food, wash and iron their teenagers' clothes, and cheerfully chauffeur their teenagers around without asking anything in return. If I were the least bit competent I would be able to be a good mother too. I would have no trouble fitting these chores in with my full-time job. Good mothers make sure they do all the work so their children have time for more important things. I am *truly* a rotten mother. And a *selfish* one, too, to think that I should have a little fun in my life. Only my children have a right to have fun. I am certainly going to have to try harder to be a better mother.

- As you hear your nagging thoughts (albeit very exaggerated) clearly stated again and again, they will begin to sound as ridiculous to you as they really are. Continue to do this exercise until you finally shed your nagging thoughts and consequently your guilt.

WHEN CHILDREN PLAY ONE PARENT
AGAINST THE OTHER

"Dad bought me the stereo I wanted. *He* didn't think I should have to work and save for it."

"I don't have to do any chores at Daddy's. Why should I have to here?"

"Mom lets me do it. Why don't you?"

"I'd rather be at Dad's. He doesn't treat me like this."

Sound familiar? Few single parents have never experienced the devastating blows of at least one of their children playing them against their former spouses. Why do children do it? And how should you handle it?

After divorce, many children play one parent against the other as one way of coping with the feelings of powerlessness they feel. They have been thwarted at every turn. They could not stop a parent from leaving. They could do nothing to prevent their family's rupture. They could not stop their lives from falling apart. But by inducing their parents to compete for their favor, they regain a sense of having some control over their world. And the higher the parents raise their bids for children's approval, the more powerful children feel.

Should you then give in to this tactic? Compete with your spouse? Try to win your children over at the expense of your former partner? Absolutely not. To do so is to teach your children to be manipulative. Perhaps their manipulative behavior has already become a learned habit. To allow it is also likely to create undisciplined young people with unrealistic expectations of how the world operates. And although it may boost a child's sagging self-esteem to have parents bidding for his or her approval, having so much power can also be frightening to a child who has already lost so much of the security and structure in life because of divorce. In the long run, you will do your children no favors and yourself none either.

What do you do? Let the principles of authoritative parenting be your guide. If you recall from Chapters 15 and 16, an authoritative parenting style is one in which you are warm, nurturant, and respectful of your children. You encourage open communication and seek their input. You are sensitive to their needs and opinions. But at the same time, you provide clear limits and expectations, and *you remain in charge.*

First, let your child know, in a loving and confident manner, that you are wise to his or her game and that you will not be lured into a competition with the other parent. Then discuss the issue under question with your youngster on its *own* merits. This might be a good opening for a frank discussion between you. Perhaps you are being rigid or unreasonable. Perhaps there is an underlying problem for which you can find a mutually agreeable solution. (Try the problem-solving strategy in Chapter 15.) Perhaps there is room for compromise. But remember that you are the parent. If you are clear in your own mind about the validity of your position, stick to it. Don't go against your better judgment. If it is a matter of rules, explain that there are different rules at different houses, just as there are different rules at school and at home. If it is a matter of spending money, explain that you and the other parent have different financial resources or different values about money. If it is a matter of major child-rearing differences, explain that people have different ideas about raising children and that you and the other parent are doing what each of you considers best. Try to speak lovingly and matter-of-factly rather than defensively or emotionally. Let your child know that you have to do what you believe is right. Finally, remember the motivation that is likely to be underlying his or her behavior. If you continue to build positive relationships with your children, let them know how much you love them, and refrain from reinforcing their manipulative behavior, they may be less likely to resort to these kinds of tactics. They will also be less likely to use them if you and their other parent are able to take a united stand to discourage them from doing so.

Most single parents feel that the ultimate threat is their children saying they want to go live with their other parent. A Canadian study spanning several years found that threats to move in with noncustodial fathers were common after divorce but diminished with time, as fathers created new lives and became less involved with youngsters.

Realize that children sometimes make empty threats in anger or as "blackmail," so a parent will give in to their demands. Other times, requests for custody changes stem from a real need or problem. Try responding calmly and confidently. A long talk is in order to try to discover what is at the root of the request. (If the exchange has been a heated one, do this after tempers have cooled.) If the request seems to be merely an attempt at blackmail, it is simply a variant on manipulative behavior. If there seems to be a real problem, find out as much as you can about it. Is your child truly unhappy? Is there a real problem at home that needs to be worked out? Is the problem a normal childhood or adolescent problem from which your youngster wants to run away? Take the stance that you will work on problems together and that running away is *not* a good way to solve difficulties. To find workable solutions, try the problem-solving techniques discussed in Chapters 15 and 16. You may also want to work on opening the lines of communication (Chapter 10).

There is another common reason that children ask for a custody change. Some children, especially when they become teens, develop a strong need to get to know their other parent better. This is most common for adolescent boys who have been living with their mothers. Often, fathers have been completely uninvolved with them, and mothers are bewildered with their teens' sudden request. If this seems to be the case, and if your teen mentions repeatedly that he or she would like to live with the other parent, a discussion with your former spouse and perhaps a renegotiation of visitation and custody may be called for—

unless you feel a change would be detrimental to your child. In this latter case, you might want to get an objective evaluation from a mental health professional.

Parents become particularly sensitive to their children playing one parent against the other at holiday times.

HANDLING HOLIDAYS

While other families are looking forward to holidays with excited anticipation, single parents and their children often approach these days with reserve, sadness, or dread. Holidays stir up memories of happier family times. They also create a dilemma with no easy solution—either some family members must be apart on the holiday, or children must be shuttled back and forth between homes, often on a tight schedule that leaves everyone tense and drained.

University of Pennsylvania sociologist Frank Furstenberg points out that the key to how well children handle holidays is the way that their parents handle them. There are two keys to happier holidays: planning and your attitude. Although there are no easy solutions to holiday dilemmas, there are ways to make holidays happier occasions.

- Resist dwelling on past holidays and how happy they were. It is bound to make you even sadder and poison your attitude.
- Create some new traditions for holidays. Have an open house, share the day with another single-parent family, invite friends for a tree-decorating party, bake or make gifts with your children, spend the day in the mountains, go on a trip. Involve your children in creating your new traditions, and be sure to hold on to *some* of the old ones; children need continuity.
- When you are making holiday plans, stop to evaluate whether they are in the best interests of your children. If they are to spend part of the day with you and part with their other parent, will it be difficult for them to shift gears (and perhaps loyalties) at midday? Will they be spending a chunk of their day commuting? Will they also be traveling to one or more extended families? Will it be a relaxing, enjoyable day or a marathon that will leave them exhausted? Frequently the second celebration of the day is a letdown for all involved. Tired youngsters can't muster up their enthusiasm, the parent who has anticipated a joyous celebration all day is disappointed, and youngsters feel guilty about letting their parent down. You know your own children best, but consider the alternative of having two separate celebrations on different days. Few children would turn down *two* days of celebrating, and they would be able to enjoy relaxing and spending quality time with each parent.
- When your children are going to their other parent's for a holiday, let them know that it is okay to want to go and to have a good time. Often

children are reluctant to leave their single parents for a holiday because they are concerned about leaving them alone or hurting their feelings.

- If you will be alone on a holiday, plan something to do in advance that will be fun. Most single parents enjoy holidays more if they are with other people, preferably other singles who are also without children for the day. Often singles groups, such as Parents Without Partners, will have activities on holidays. Or you may consider having an open house or a party. If you can find a co-host, you can have a larger party and get to know some new people. Call your children for a brief chat at a prearranged time, and be very positive so you do not put a damper on their day.

- Try to discuss gifts with your children's other parent so you will not give duplicates. And don't get into a competition of buying expensive gifts you cannot afford. Spend extra time with your kids instead, doing special things that you will all enjoy.

The next chapter is for parents without custody, but if you are a parent with sole custody, you may find it very helpful to gain some insight into the problems visitation creates for your former partner. Children need both parents in their lives, but it is difficult for a nonresidential parent to continue in a parenting role without the support of the parent with custody.

PART IV

PART-TIME PARENTING FOR PARENTS WITHOUT CUSTODY

HOW TO SUCCESSFULLY PARENT PART-TIME:
The Critical Role of the Parent Without Custody

*T*heir new role quickly places parents without custody in a dilemma that is seldom recognized by anyone except other noncustody parents. Unfortunately, many who find no satisfying way to solve their role dilemma allow themselves to drift along a path that has a prolonged negative impact on their children. Most don't realize their impact because they believe they have become rather inconsequential to their youngsters' lives. With very few exceptions, they are wrong. The issue is not whether parents without custody have an impact on their children's lives, but whether their impact is positive or negative.

THE VISITATION DILEMMA

What precisely is a parent's dilemma with the noncustodial role? After separation, the great majority of parents without custody are found to intensely miss being involved with their children's daily lives—the contact, the day-to-day events, the small changes. Parents without custody commonly report overwhelming feelings of loss, rootlessness, and being shut out. Even many fathers who had previously been uninvolved become distressingly aware of all they never did with their children when they had the chance. At a time when so much of their identity has been lost through divorce, it is perhaps not surprising that their identity as parents assumes new importance and meaning for them.

To ward off their feelings of isolation and loneliness, most nonresident parents either bury themselves in work or engage in a frenzied social life after separation, and it appears to the outside world, especially to their former spouses, that they are adjusting quite well without their youngsters. Not so, say parents without custody. They long for a meaningful relationship with their children.

Instead of opportunities for a meaningful relationship, however, parents without custody are restricted to "visitation" during prescribed times. Visitation? With your own children? What are you supposed to *do* during "visitation"? Do you take them to your home? Won't they be bored? Do you try to do something spectacular? Play tour guide? Take them on a shopping spree and shower them with presents? After all, you have so little opportunity to show your love these days, and you want them to look forward to seeing you. Perhaps they might even stop coming if you don't show them a good time. Do they want to see you as much as you want to see them? Parents whose children have a wide age difference or conflicting interests have more complicated problems with how to spend their allotted time. A large national study conducted by University of Pennsylvania sociologist Frank Furstenberg and Christine Nord of Child Trends found that the most common visitation arrangement is for noncustodial fathers to take children on a social outing—restaurants, parks, movies, trips, and so forth—a pattern that seems to develop by default rather than by design.

Few parents without custody are satisfied with the visitation arrangement. They complain that there is so much to compress into such a limited time. There is so much they would like to tell their children and so much they want to know about their youngsters' lives and feelings. But there is simply no time to let things just happen naturally. How do you pass on your values and hard-earned wisdom to your children on Sunday afternoon in an amusement park? How do you get children to share their feelings, fears, and inner lives when you have such a limited time together? The question "How are you feeling about the divorce?" is likely to get a one-word mumbled answer when asked abruptly at the wrong time. Getting children to open up takes time, the right situation, and the right mood—luxuries not often enjoyed by noncustody parents and their youngsters.

It is not only *meaningful* communication that is difficult in this strange new visiting situation, say nonresident parents. They and their children often report an awkwardness they never before experienced with one another; they often have the feeling of not knowing what to say, what to do, or how to act with one another. If communication is good, parents might learn about their children's small crises and feats that occurred since the last time they talked—a fight with the class bully, a lost soccer game, a scolding by a teacher, an A in a math test, a compliment for a report well done. But even if children *do* remember and share them, much of the emotional impact associated with the events has faded. Telling or hearing about them so long after the fact falls far short of the initial enthusiasm.

Too often, the parent without custody becomes a peripheral player in his or her children's lives, and whatever sense of intimacy the parent once had with a child feels tenuous at best. And if a parent and child are fortunate enough to *finally* feel comfortable with each other during a visit—if they finally establish some rhythm between them that feels good—it is usually broken by the inevitable good-byes and lapsed time before they see each other again. The small gains they achieve, many say, only make the impending good-byes that much more painful. Many parents without custody have learned that it is far easier to part when visits go poorly.

At some point, most parents without custody ask themselves the question, "Is visitation worth it?" Yes, most do miss their children, sometimes desperately, but each visit can be a tease, reminding them of what is no longer possible. For many, visits invite pain, frustration, feelings of helplessness, and a giant emotional letdown afterward. They also invite contact with ex-spouses and opportunities for fresh conflict and the reopening of old wounds. If their children seem to be doing okay, nonresident parents wonder how much they are really needed, especially if they are dads. (After all, everyone "knows" that mothers are more important to kids than fathers. Aren't they?) They wonder how much influence they can possibly have on the way their children turn out. To many, visitation seems meaningless and futile, and the role of noncustodial parent feels like a sham.

How do parents without custody resolve the visitation dilemma? The majority of fathers and some mothers resolve it poorly; they begin to distance themselves from their youngsters. As they do so, their children become less central to their lives, and visiting, phoning, and letters gradually drop off with the passage of time. Many of these parents eventually join the swelling ranks of parents who have withdrawn from their children's lives completely, a problem growing with alarming rapidity, at least among fathers. (Moms without custody are more likely to maintain contact and a relationship with their children than are noncustodial dads.) In Furstenberg and Nord's national study, 49 percent of the children had not even seen their noncustodial parent in the previous year!

But withdrawal from children's lives has high emotional costs. Everyone loses. Nonresident parents usually do better adjusting to divorce when they maintain regular contact with their children. Those who withdraw contact sometimes report feeling anger and a continued sense of loss for years afterward—quite a contrast from the uncaring, indifferent parents society assumes them to be. The noncustodial parent may well be the least understood party in divorce.

But children are the real losers when parents withdraw from their lives. For many children, it is traumatic and not without long-term negative repercussions.

THE IMPORTANT ROLE OF NONCUSTODIAL PARENTS IN THEIR CHILDREN'S LIVES

The past decade and a half of research on divorce has found that children's divorce adjustment is markedly improved when they have a good relationship with both their parents (Chapter 9). When children know that *both* parents love them, they are more able to deal with the upheaval in their lives and the loss of their families.

In the aftermath of divorce, youngsters cling to their visits with the parent who has left home, and the visits assume tremendous symbolic importance. To youngsters, these visits are not only evidence of a parent's love, but a gauge of how lovable and worthwhile they are. After all, the absent parent *chooses* to see them regularly, despite the hassles involved. It must prove that the children are loved, lovable, and worthwhile. In fact, when absent parents remain involved in their children's lives, it can go a long way in repairing youngsters' self-esteem, which usually takes a plunge after parental divorce.

When contact with the nonresident parent is infrequent and unreliable, it is also symbolically significant in children's eyes. They feel rejected and abandoned, and they look for some explanation for their parents' seeming indifference. "I'm not lovable enough." "I'm not good enough." "I'm not smart enough." "I've done something wrong." "I'm not worthwhile." "How terrible I must be if my own dad (mom) doesn't even want to see me!" The absence of visits is very distressing to youngsters and is a further blow to their already-dwindling self-esteem.

Most noncustodial parents who withdraw from their children's lives would be shocked to learn of the anguish they cause their youngsters and of the prolonged impact their absence has on their children. Although many realize they will be missed initially, they generally assume that their children will get over it. After all, children are resilient. They have their other parent, and sometimes a stepparent, their friends, activities, and lives. "How important can I be?", they wonder. How important are noncustodial parents? Meet Debby, Kelly, and Billy.

Debby is a teenager who has not seen her father since a very young age. Says Debby, "I sit sometimes for hours and think of what it would be like to have a father hold me, take me places, and tell me he loves me. If only I could have that feeling once more. I always see pictures with him holding me, and I get so mad at myself because I can't remember that feeling."[1]

Kelly, one of the children studied in the California Children of Divorce Study, was only two years old when her parents divorced. It is not surprising that her dad felt he was inconsequential to Kelly's life. But one gets a very different impression from Kelly herself. At age 12, Kelly has had very little contact with her dad over the years (he had spent three hours with her during the previous two years), yet she confides to the interviewer, "Once a couple of years ago . . . he invited me to spend a weekend. I had the best time of my life, because I love him more than anyone in the world. . . . I miss him. I miss him so much."[2] The fact that Kelly has a stepfather with whom she is very close makes her idealization of her father and the intensity of her feelings that much more striking.

Billy is Kelly's older brother. He was five when his parents split up, and over the years his dad became convinced that Billy didn't need him. When Billy was interviewed five years after the divorce, he broke down and cried uncontrollably for 35 minutes when asked how often he saw his dad. By the time Billy was reinterviewed in another five years, he had developed more self-control, as is typical of 15-year-old boys. However, at the mere mention of his father, his eyes immediately filled with tears. Billy was unable to regain his composure for the remainder of the interview and sheepishly apologized afterward for being "so emotional."

Debby, Kelly, and Billy are not unusual. Researchers who interview children of divorce frequently report being stunned at children's fierce attachments to parents who have done little but disappoint them over their lifetimes. The interviewers report being deeply moved by children's anguish and distress at their parents' disinterest. They comment on children's grateful acceptance of whatever little attention they receive from errant parents. They marvel at how important a relationship with an absent parent is to a child when, to the outside world, there appears to be *no* relationship. One writer, after interviewing hundreds of children of divorce, commented that the loyalty these children had for their parents, regardless of circumstances, made man's landing on the moon seem commonplace by comparison.

To children, a parent is a parent forever, not someone who is casually forgotten. Although children are usually quite resilient, a parent's abandonment is a unique trauma from which many do not easily bounce back. Some continue to be troubled with intense feelings of rejection, abandonment, and loss throughout their childhoods. Some continue to feel unlovable and to have poor self-esteem. Some respond with anger and act out that anger in behavior problems such as aggression, drug abuse, or delinquent activities. Some, after having seemingly adapted for years, develop a renewed intense desire for their missing parents when they reach adolescence. Children who had a close relationship with a parent before divorce are the most hard hit. To such a child, the parent's disinterest and abandonment are completely incomprehensible and even more distressing. Unfortunately, the withdrawal of a previously involved father is not an unusual occurrence.

Even those children who are resilient and able to bounce back are likely to be affected by their parents' withdrawal in other ways. Probably most moms would not be surprised to read that mothers influence their children's development in important ways, but many dads may not be aware that fathers also make unique contributions to a child's development. At one time it was thought that a father's impact was minor, but the past two decades of research clearly points to the folly of this belief. As one example, fathers' involvement in their children's lives has been found to be highly beneficial to youngsters' cognitive performance and school achievement, especially for boys. Sons also look to their fathers to provide a prototype of male behavior and to help them develop a stable and valued sense of their own masculinity. Girls also need their dads. Girls from divorced homes are found to be more vulnerable to problems with heterosexual relationships as teens and young adults, and those who are most vulnerable appear to be girls who have had little contact with their fathers over an extended period. Manifestations of problems in heterosexual relationships vary but include a devalued sense of femininity, inappropriately provocative and attention-seeking behavior toward the opposite sex, promiscuous behavior, drifting from one relationship to another, marriage at an early age to a less-than-adequate partner, marital problems, and divorce. Earlier, many of these girls had appeared to be well adjusted to their parents' divorce, points out Dr. Neil Kalter of the Department of Psychology and Psychiatry at the University of Michigan. It is not until their teenage years that problems begin to surface. At this time, interaction with an attentive and loving father can be very important to a girl, giving her confidence in relating to men and a sense that she can be valued as a female. Many of girls' problems with heterosexual adjustment appear to stem from their poor self-esteem as females and their inadequate attempts to deal with it.

SOLUTIONS FOR THE VISITATION DILEMMA

Fortunately, there are solutions to the visitation dilemma; constructive suggestions for nonresident parents can be extrapolated from studies. Nonresident parents *can* maintain good relationships with their children despite constraints on the time they have together. In fact, some parents without custody develop *better* relationships with their children after divorce than they had while living with their children full-time. Once freed from the problems in the marriage, some previously uninvolved parents get to know their children as individuals and form warm and intimate relationships with them. How can you have a close relationship with your children within the constraints of visitation?

Before answering this, let's look at what most children really want from their nonresident parents. Is it a steady diet of entertainment or presents? Not unless a parent defines the postdivorce relationship with his or her children in these terms. Children will come to expect these things if parents make entertainment and presents the focus of their interactions after divorce rather than focusing on spending time together. And, interestingly, children usually say that a steady diet of entertainment and presents is only a poor substitute for what they *really* want. What they really want, say children, is to feel loved and valued. They want to feel like their parents are interested in them and in what they do. They want their parents to be involved in their lives, and they want to be involved in their parents' lives, too. In fact, their needs and their parents' needs are usually quite similar.

The question is, how can these mutual needs of noncustodial parents and children best be fulfilled? It is difficult to fulfill them by becoming what has come to be called a "Disneyland parent"—a parent who packs all his or her allotted time with planned activities. Disneyland parents usually have cordial but distant relationships with their children. They are always busy "doing" and never take time to learn how their children are feeling, developing, and changing. And because it is difficult to continue the nonstop entertainment routine indefinitely, Disneyland parents usually decrease their contact with their children as time goes on.

Then what *is* the solution for the visitation dilemma? Usually the most satisfying relationships between parents without custody and children are found when parents create a second home and family for their children. The idea of noncustodial parents creating a second home for their children was first introduced a decade ago by therapist and family mediator Isolina Ricci in her book *Mom's House, Dad's House* and has been enthusiastically endorsed by mental health professionals ever since. Within this more natural environment, parent and children can continue more genuine relationships. They can spend relaxed time together, which all people need to really know one another. They can continue doing many familiar activities together. Parents can feel like parents rather than aunts and uncles, and children can feel like they still have parents rather than newly acquired social directors. It is also the best way for children to feel that they continue to be a part of their noncustodial parents' new lives. Of course, fun outings can be interspersed with at-home visits.

You say your place is too small to become a home for them? Size doesn't seem to matter to most youngsters, providing their parents do a few simple things (discussed shortly) to make it feel like a home for them, too. All your time together does not have to be spent there, but at least it is a home base. You say you are a long-distance parent and can see your children only a few times a year? This presents a more challenging situation, but not an impossible one. You can instill in your children the feeling that they are a significant part of a distant second home and family, *providing* you have meaningful contact with them between visits. Part-time parenting at a distance is discussed later in this chapter.

You say that creating a second home for your children is simply not feasible, for whatever reason? Don't give up. There are still ways to build good relationships with them and to have a positive impact on their lives. These too will be discussed. The following pages are full of suggestions for how to successfully parent your children part-time in a variety of circumstances.

Handling the Transition When You Leave the Family Home

If you are just separating, you have the advantage of being able to start your postdivorce relationship with your youngsters on the right foot. *Continuity* is the key. The more continuity you provide, the better it will be for your child, the easier it will be to continue your relationship, and the smoother your time together is likely to be.

First, in conjunction with their other parent, develop a *firm* parenting schedule that allows your children to see you *frequently* and *regularly*. Ideally, your children should have the specifics *before* you leave about when, where, and how you will see one another, and they should be able to rely on those specifics. Reassure them that your inability to spend more time with them in no way reflects that you *care* any less about them. You will have to prove that you mean it by continuing to show them lots of affection and a strong interest in their daily lives.

Is it really so important to see them frequently and regularly? Absolutely. Frequent time together early after separation not only helps continuity, but it will relieve your children's anxiety about losing you. Frequent visits have two additional benefits. They show your youngsters that you are giving them a high priority in your new life, and they make it easier for everyone to say good-bye because it is for only a short time. The younger your children, the more frequently you'll need to see them. Please read "Arranging Parenting Schedules to Meet Children's Developmental Needs" in Chapter 10.

In the early months after separation, you should keep in contact with daily phone calls, too. Call even if your children are young and don't talk to you a great deal. It will be comforting for them to hear your voice. If your new home is at a great distance, you will have to rely more heavily on the phone. Sending frequent cards, letters, and *small* gifts will also help.

Regularly seeing them is equally important. When contact is reliable and predictable, children feel that their relationship with you is stable and can be counted on. Before you end a visit, remind them when you will see them next. It saves them the anxiety of wondering, "Might this be the last time I see Dad (Mom)?"

Once you leave the family home, the agreed-upon arrangements should begin *immediately*. Some parents believe that a lapse of time will help children adjust to the separation. In reality, say mental health professionals, a time lapse breaks the continuity in the relationship and may heighten children's fears of abandonment.

Immediately after separation is the best time to begin setting up a second home for your children. The suggestions in the next section will help you. When you see your children, continue to do some of the things together that you did while living with them—have long talks, play games, do some fix-it projects, work on homework, cook breakfast, play ball in the park, and so forth. You will have to be sure that at least some of your visits are long enough that you can share these familiar activities in a relaxed and natural manner. However, not all visits need to be long. Better a short one than none at all.

By the way, if you find that you are so emotionally drained from events surrounding your divorce that you have trouble dealing with your children and their problems, being a Disneyland parent for a while can serve a useful function. It can allow you to spend time with your children without having to give a great deal of yourself emotionally. You can switch to more meaningful interactions at a later date. Doing some very special things can also be a boost for your children, who may not have a lot of positive things happening in their lives right now. Let them know that you will return to more usual activities together in the future.

Creating a Second Home for Your Children

Many divorcing fathers always left the mechanics of home life and child rearing to their ex-wives and are at a loss with a recommendation to create a second home for their children. Here are some suggested guidelines.

- Try to make your home feel like a home to your children, too. If possible, involve them while you are setting it up. Display the things they make or give you (pictures, crafts, gifts). Have some of their favorite foods on hand (or go grocery shopping together).
- Find some niche for them, even if it is only a drawer. Have them leave some of their things, such as a toothbrush, pajamas, and some special toys, books, or games that they will look forward to using when they come. (You might let them pick them out.) Try to keep a few changes of clothing there, too, even if you have to buy them. The less they have to carry back and forth in a suitcase, the more they will feel that they have two functioning homes.
- Don't treat your children as guests. Children and nonresident parents become closer when they are involved in the day-to-day activities of each other's lives. Get involved in some activities that full-time parents do. Ask your kids when they come if there is anything they need to do—homework, school projects, haircuts, picking up school supplies, and so forth. Then help them do it. Enlist their help in fixing meals, grocery shopping, or repairing things. Don't use your kids as cheap labor, however; try to make projects an enjoyable part of your time together.
- Spend overnights together. If you don't have lots of room, buy some sleeping bags and inflatable air mattresses, and have your kids "camp" on your living room floor.
- Establish some routines—mealtimes, bedtimes, a bedtime story or talk, some chores. Children are particularly needful of routines after divorce. They are a source of stability for them in a world that feels very unstable.
- Establish some house rules that are important for their health and safety and that will help you have an enjoyable time together. (For example, if you can't stand clutter, you'd better be clear about where they should

keep their things, or you may find yourself irritated the entire time they are with you.) If your rules are different from their other parent's, never undermine that parent's rules. State matter-of-factly that there are different ways of doing things and that this is the way you do it at your house. However, strive to reach some agreement with their other parent on some basic rules (for example, about bedtimes, discipline, homework, or television).

- Get involved in some fun activities that each of you will enjoy—start a hobby together, build something, cook a special meal, play some games, and so on. Be sure to get your children's ideas. Brainstorming is a fun and effective way to come up with new and creative ideas.

- Explore your neighborhood together. Meet some neighbors and learn if there are children to play with, places that interest them, or activities they might enjoy. Invite neighborhood children to join activities you initiate. Establishing ties to the neighborhood will help your children feel that they belong there.

- Encourage them to invite friends to your home.

- Arrange special outings sometimes, just as you would if you lived with your kids full-time.

- Develop some new traditions that symbolize their second family. Discover some special ways to spend holidays together, even if the holiday is not spent on the official day. Try some brainstorming. How about starting a photo album of your new life together and regularly look at it, while recalling events associated with some of the photos? Some parents start a tradition of having family meetings to discuss plans, house rules, feelings, and problems.

- If it is a possibility, consider living close enough to your kids so they can get to activities from your home. This generally creates a more natural situation and allows longer stretches of time together. It also allows older children to drop in for quick visits between scheduled ones.

- An important ingredient to creating a real second home for your children, points out Isolina Ricci, is a change in your vocabulary. Instead of telling people that your children *visit* with you every other weekend, say they *live* with you every other weekend. Rather than thinking of your visitation agreement, think of your *parenting* agreement. Instead of thinking that you have lost your family, think of yourself as having a family that consists of your children who live with you part of the time.

- Chapter 17 discussed how to combine dating and live-in relationships with children in the home.

How to Build Good Relationships with Your Children and Have Successful "Visits"—At Home or Away

These suggestions will be helpful whether you create a homelike atmosphere for your kids *or* see them away from your home. Even if you cannot create a second home for your children, you can still build a good relationship with them and have a positive impact on their lives.

- The beginnings of visits are usually awkward. It sometimes helps to verbalize the discomfort everyone is feeling ("It sure seems strange at first, after we haven't seen each other for a while."). Sometimes it helps if you begin your time together with some kind of ritual to get everyone past the early awkwardness—a ritualistic hug, some roughhousing, stopping for ice cream, playing a word game in the car, stopping at grandma's. However, watch the appropriateness of these rituals as time passes. As children mature, rituals they once loved (for example, hugging or roughhousing) may become decidedly uncomfortable.
- Involve children in planning your time together so they will have input in what you do. This is especially important to older children. If you run out of ideas, brainstorm.
- Keep abreast of your children's interests, activities, and school progress in whatever ways you can. If possible, go to their plays, music recitals, sports games, and other events. Attend school open houses. See if you can take them to music lessons, scout meetings, and other activities from time to time. Learn the names of their friends and teachers. Ask them about the books they've been reading, their favorite TV programs, new interests they've developed. (You might try some of them yourself.) And, of course, ask them about their activities since the last time you talked.
- Make it a point to remember what your children talk about from one time to the next. If they need to tell you the same things over and over again, it won't take long for the lines of communication to shut down.
- Keep in touch between your scheduled times together with phone calls, and encourage your children to call you too.
- Relationships are a two-way street. Share what has been happening in your life. See if you can get your children interested in some of your interests. Share some of your feelings too (without overwhelming them or badmouthing their other parent).
- See each of your children individually when you can, especially if they are of markedly different ages.
- When children's schedules conflict with your scheduled time together, try to be flexible to accommodate their needs. Can you take them to the activity yourself? It would give you time together and further involve you

in their daily lives. If not, see if you can reschedule some time together at a more convenient time (a shorter time is always a possibility).

- Try to make your time together regular and reliable so your children will perceive their relationship with you as a stable one. Except for early after separation, studies find that regularity and predictability of parent-child contact is more important to children's well-being than frequency is. Exceptions are children under six (who need *both* frequent and predictable contact) and older teens (who need flexibility to accommodate their social lives). Talk to teens about their preferences. The California Children of Divorce Study found that teens thrived on spontaneous meetings for a few hours, and so did their relationships with their nonresident parents. If you can't see your teen frequently, keep in touch by phone.
- Make visits long enough for some quality interaction to take place. Intersperse fun activities with some quiet time for talking and relaxing.
- Create an atmosphere of open communication with your children (suggestions were given in Chapter 10). Many children are particularly reluctant to share their feelings and fears with their nonresident parents. Sometimes they simply don't see each other enough to communicate on that level. Sometimes children worry that to do so might jeopardize the relationship in some way. Sometimes parents just haven't figured out a way to approach sensitive topics. If you want to penetrate your child's inner life, you will have to make a special effort to do so.
- Avoid creating parental loyalty conflicts for your children (for example, never pump them for information about what is happening with their other parent, never put them in the middle of your battles, and never badmouth their other parent in their presence). Not only is it harmful to your children, but you are likely to lose a contest with their other parent. Psychologists Arthur and Elizabeth Seagull of Michigan State University point out that children spend the bulk of their lives with their parent who has custody and are likely to make choices that will enable their day-to-day lives to run more smoothly, even if they do not do so consciously. Please read Chapter 9 about the destructive effects of parental conflict on children.
- Be sure to keep the promises you make about future outings and plans. Children who are repeatedly disappointed by an undependable noncustodial parent usually feel rejected and experience a drop in their self-esteem, as did Andy, whose parents have been divorced for five years.

"My dad didn't show again," said 12-year-old Andy. He kicked an empty Pepsi can clear across the field in frustration as his best friend Seth stood by feeling helpless. "Maybe he got tied up with work again," offered Seth. "Come on, Seth. I used to buy that when I was a kid. But how come he gets tied up so much on the one day a month I'm supposed to see him? I mean, how important can I be to him? Half the time, he can't even remember to call and let me know he's not coming. He doesn't care about me anymore. Maybe he never did. I'm just some dumb obligation."

- If you learn good disciplinary practices, you may find that visits go more smoothly. Children need some rules and limits, or things can quickly get out of hand. How to discipline effectively and not seem like an ogre to your kids was discussed in Chapter 16. Learn to use an authoritative parenting style with your children rather than an authoritarian or permissive style, as discussed in Chapter 16.
- If the relationship with one or more of your children is going poorly, hang in there. Some children are very angry because of the divorce, and although they may not verbalize it, their anger can create some stormy visits. Other children try to cover up their fears with arrogance, while still others continually test the sincerity of their absent parents' love by being obnoxious and ornery. Ways that you can help your children through the divorce crisis were discussed in Chapter 8.
- Your visits may go quite smoothly until the last hour or so, when everything falls apart. A common scenario is this: children act up, parent yells, and visits end on a sour note. It usually reflects the tension everyone is feeling about the impending separation. It is much easier to say good-bye when everyone is angry at one another. Arthur and Elizabeth Seagull suggest talking about what is going on before problems begin: "It's easier to say good-bye to someone when you're angry at them, so many kids begin to act up when a visit is coming to an end. Do you think we can keep this from happening to us?" Sometimes it is helpful to spend the last half hour in an activity that will allow you and your children to get some emotional distance from each other before you have to part physically.
- If your time together is too intense because your child cannot seem to get enough of you, try to make visits either longer or more frequent. Your relationship is likely to take on a more normal flavor.
- Limit the number of times you invite an adult companion on visits. Research conducted at Wright State University in Dayton, Ohio found that children's adjustment is related to the amount of time they spend *alone* with their nonresident parent. Taking along a date or live-in companion denies your child the exclusive time he or she needs with you.

> Eight-year-old Celia used to anticipate her dad's visits with excitement all week long. She never cared what they did; she was just happy being with him, holding his hand, and telling him about her week. Now visits make her angry and sad. Two months ago Jan moved into Celia's dad's apartment and has come along on their days together ever since. Celia can't understand why Jan has to come when she sees her dad so seldom and Jan sees him all the time. She was ruining everything. It was so unfair. Half the time her dad and Jan talked to each other and left her out. One day, in frustration, she blurted out, "Why does *she* always have to come?" But her dad became

angry with her. So now she keeps her frustrations to herself, afraid that he will stop coming at all if he learns how angry she is.

If you are going to bring a companion along, be aware, and warn your companion too, that your children are likely to increase their demands for your attention. They will see your companion as a competitor, and if he or she competes for your attention, their fears will be confirmed. Only when your companion steps back and allows your youngsters to have your attention will they feel secure enough to stop demanding it.

- Sometimes children dread the transition times when they are dropped off or picked up. They are afraid that Mom will be angry if they are sad to leave Dad or that Dad will be angry if they are happy to see Mom. If your children find these transitions stressful, it may be helpful to pick them up and drop them off at a neutral place, such as a grandparent's home or school.
- Experiment with different ways to handle your own letdown after you leave your children. Is it best to be alone, to have prearranged plans with friends, to lose yourself in a movie or in work? Some parents prefer to drop their children at school Monday morning and go straight to work themselves.
- Accept the fact that you will not have as much influence on your children's development as you would have if you were living with them full-time. You may be able to broaden their horizons, but don't spend your limited time together lecturing them or trying to change them.
- Some parents find it enormously helpful to join a support group with other noncustodial parents. Support groups are becoming very popular now and are frequently offered through churches and community agencies.

Part-Time Parenting at a Distance

If you live so far from your children that you can only see them a few times a year or less, there are two excellent books listed in Appendix C that will give you lots of help with keeping a relationship with them, even though you live at a distance: Miriam Galper Cohen's *Long-Distance Parenting* and George Newman's *101 Ways to be a Long-Distance Superdad*. Following are some suggestions to get you started.

- Continuity, once again, is critical, so make frequent and regular phone calls. Try to establish a regular time that is convenient for your children's schedule to be sure they will be home. If they are old enough, encourage them to call you when they need you, and teach them how to reverse the charges. Some parents pay for a separate phone line for a child's room so the resident parent will not be involved in phone calls.

- The more you keep abreast of your children's daily lives, the easier phone conversations will be. Encourage them to keep a list of things they would like to talk to you about, and you do the same, suggests Pennsylvania family therapist Miriam Galper Cohen, herself a long-distance parent.
- Send mail frequently—letters, postcards, small items, pictures—anything to keep a presence in their lives and let them know you are thinking about them. Many long-distance parents don't write to their kids because they don't know what to say in letters. This is such a common problem that a Phoenix-based organization, Positive Parenting, has developed a program called The Write Connection. It consists of kits of materials that include ideas for topics to write about and inexpensive things to send, developmental information about children between ages 4 through 12, calendars so you and your kids can keep apprised of each other's activities and future visits, stationery, and return mailers for your children. It's a great way to get yourself started. Send for information to Positive Parenting, 2633 E. Indian School Road #400, Phoenix, AZ 85016, or call 800-334-3143.
- Let your children know that you want to hear about their activities, interests, and lives in general. Ask your older kids to send you reports they've written for school and ask younger ones to send pictures they've drawn. Be sure to provide your kids with self-addressed stamped envelopes, and write back about their letters and the things they send. Get a real dialogue going.
- Why not make a photo album for your children, suggests Cohen. Include pictures of yourself, your extended family, and your home and neighborhood. Most importantly, include lots of pictures of the two of you together taken during visits. If your children have never seen your home and you have access to a video camera, send a video of it (inside and outside) and your neighborhood too.

If you have young children, be sure to read "Arranging Parenting Schedules to meet Children's Developmental Needs" in chapter 10. You have a special challenge to build and maintain a relationship with young children who you cannot see frequently. Because of their limited cognitive ability, young children have difficulty maintaining both an image of a parent in their minds and an attachment to a parent when their contact with the parent is infrequent. While your children are young, it will be important to keep a very active presence in their lives so they will remember you. Here are some suggestions in addition to those above.

- Make tapes and/or videos of yourself reading stories to them, and add a personal message at the end. If you have a cooperative ex-spouse, encourage preschoolers to make tapes for you too—telling you about their day or telling you a story. (If you provide self-addressed stamped envelopes, their other parent may be more likely to be cooperative.)

- Your toddler or preschooler would be thrilled to have a little book to "read," consisting of pictures of the two of you with a few words underneath each. ("Dad and Jimmy having a picnic at the lake. Remember the big fish we saw that day?") You can easily make the pages of the book out of sturdy colorful poster board and hold them together with yarn.

- Whenever you see your children, give each of them something that they can associate with you, preferably something that each has grown attached to. Tell your youngsters, "Every time you look at this, it will remind you of me and the good times we had together."

- Until children are *at least* two, and preferably older, long-distance parents should go to their children rather than have their children come to a distant location (unless the parent with custody can be close by and stay with youngsters at night). Young children become anxious when they are away from their familiar parent for an extended period. Additionally, because of their poor grasp of time, young children have no understanding about when they will be able to return to their parent and familiar surroundings. It is far preferable for you to get reacquainted with a very young child for a number of hours each day and let the youngster spend nights with his or her primary parent. A two-year-old child who is very adaptable and easy going might be able to handle up to a week's vacation with you *if* you have done a good job keeping close contact with him or her. An adaptable three-year-old may be able to handle as much as a two-week stay.

- In preparation for your young children's visit, ask their other parent about their familiar routines and favorite foods (as well as favorite brands of food). The more you can make their environment feel familiar, the more comfortable they will feel and the more they are likely to enjoy their time with you. Ask their other parent to pack a few things that they are very attached to, such as a stuffed animal, blanket, doll, favorite truck, some favorite clothes, etc. As much as you may not like the idea, it would be comforting for them to have a picture of their other parent with them because of their difficulty in maintaining an image of the parent in their minds. While your children are with you, be sure they have frequent phone contact with their primary parent, and help them keep track of the days on a calendar so they can have some idea when they will be returning home. Before they leave, don't forget to give each of them something they have grown attached to so they will have something to help them remember you.

Contrary to what you may have feared, you need not be a peripheral player in your children's lives, and your influence on them need not be superficial.

Though you see them part-time, your continued involvement as a warm, supportive parent *who keeps them out of your conflict with their other parent* is likely to impact their lives in three ways that may have important repercussions both now and in the future.

The first is their divorce adjustment. Having a second caring parent in their lives will make it increasingly more likely that they will bounce back without scars from your divorce.

The second area is their self-esteem. When nonresident parents keep positively involved in their children's lives despite the hassles entailed, children's self-esteem, damaged from the divorce, often climbs. Self-esteem is one of the most powerful gifts you can give to a child. With high self-esteem, life's obstacles become challenges; with low self-esteem, they become stumbling blocks.

The third important area you are likely to impact is your children's ability to handle stress. If you read Chapter 7, you may recall that good relationships with parents act as a cushion for children that buffers them from many of the blows inflicted by prolonged stress. True, your children have their other parent, but a good relationship with one parent usually does not afford children the same protection from stress as do good relationships with *two* parents.

Divorce adjustment, self-esteem, and protection from stress: Think for a minute how important these things can be to your child's life. Having a positive influence in these areas is like throwing a stone into a pond. The stone makes a ripple that gradually spreads over the entire surface. So, too, will your positive influence in these three areas have a ripple effect in your children's lives. Be sure, however, to protect them from any conflict between you and their other parent. The damage caused them by the conflict could undo the benefits gained from your involvement. (Read Chapter 11 to learn how to reduce that conflict.)

To some degree, you will have to take your contribution to your children's lives on faith. There is no way to keep score to prove to yourself how much better they are doing because you hung in there. But you *will* be able to draw comparisons between them and the other children described in this chapter, who were troubled with lasting feelings of rejection and low self-esteem.

Of course, all the benefits from your involvement in their lives need not be intangible. You will be able to enjoy the relationships you build with them over the course of your lifetime. And you can forge a role for yourself that both you and your kids will find satisfying. It may not be the role you had planned or the role you would have played if you lived with them full-time, but it does not have to be any less meaningful. When asked about their noncustodial parents, some children talk fondly of a caring parent who is always ready to provide a warm and safe haven, to be a sounding board, to offer a fresh perspective, or to simply listen and empathize. Listening to these children, it is obvious that their nonresident parents have become special resources which these youngsters can draw upon. Despite their noncustody status, these parents have added another dimension to their children's lives that has certainly enriched them—and this is something that some parents in intact marriages never accomplish.

19

COMMON PROBLEMS FOR
PARENTS WITHOUT CUSTODY

*T*he role of noncustodial parent is seldom easy, but it *is* important, as the previous chapter made abundantly clear. How to parent successfully part-time and how to have meaningful relationships with your children despite the constraints of "visitation" were discussed in the last chapter. But as a parent without custody, you may have other special problems or questions. What if your former spouse is uncooperative? What if your children reject you? Perhaps you are angry about the amount of child support you pay and wonder what your ex does with all of it. You may be a mom without custody and feel a special anguish about not being with your children full-time. If your ex is about to remarry, you may be concerned about the effect a stepfamily will have on your relationship with your child. Or perhaps you are thinking about remarriage yourself and are unsure how to incorporate your children into your new married life. These special issues are discussed in this chapter.

IF THE OTHER PARENT IS UNCOOPERATIVE

Developing a positive, or at least a neutral, relationship with your former spouse will make your life considerably easier after divorce. To a large extent, you are dependent on your ex's goodwill because he or she is in a powerful position to either support or sabotage your relationship with your children and the time you have to spend together. Perhaps not surprisingly, studies find that when relationships between former spouses are hostile, noncustodial parents are more likely to drop out of children's lives, which, as you learned in the previous chapter, can have negative repercussions for children that last for years.

If your marriage was conflict-ridden, it does not necessarily follow that your postdivorce life must be, too. Many former spouses are able to learn constructive ways of interacting with each other once they are released from the pressures of the marriage. If your ex is uncooperative, you may have to do more than your share of the work, but it is to your distinct advantage to do so, and to your children's, too.

Chapters 5 and 11 focused on specific strategies to help you let go of your anger, end your conflict, and communicate constructively with your former partner. The following suggestions should also help you deal with your former spouse, even if he or she is uncooperative.

- Many potential problems can be avoided if you and your child's other parent work out a parenting plan, spelling out precisely when your children will be with you, how holidays will be divided, how canceled visits will be handled, and so on. Other issues you may want to consider are discussed in Chapter 11. A firm parenting plan significantly decreases the amount of contact you will need to have with each other, as well as opportunities for misunderstandings and power plays. Tell your former partner that studies find it is critical for children to be free of parental conflict and to have regular and reliable contact with their nonresident parent, so you would like to set aside your differences to arrange a plan that will minimize future misunderstandings. Try the negotiation strategies outlined in Chapter 11. If you cannot work out a plan yourselves, enlist the help of a family mediator. Mediation was discussed in Chapter 2.
- If you have not been doing so, talk to your former partner courteously and with respect. You may be surprised at the difference it makes. Sometimes, divorcing spouses who stubbornly refuse to budge on *any* issue finally begin to mellow once their former mates begin to show them respect and understanding. The reason is that divorce is a serious blow to self-esteem, and a partner's obvious disrespect can make divorcing men and women feel dismissed and devalued even more than they already do. Their natural response is to protect themselves, so they do not lose *self*-respect as well. How do they do this? One way is by stubbornly "sticking to their guns" and refusing to budge an inch to the ex-spouse who is treating them with disdain ("I'll show him he can't push *me* around."). However, once treated with respect and understanding, they feel less need to protect themselves, and therefore less need for taking such rigid positions.
- Meet all your obligations, including child support. (The issue of child support is discussed later in this chapter.)
- Make it a top priority to be on time to pick your kids up and deliver them. If you *must* be late, be sure to call. Your punctuality sends a loud and clear message: Your kids are important to you and you are reliable. Habitual lateness sends the opposite message. It also interferes with your ex's plans, and this is bound to create ill will. If you are having a good time with your kids and would like to keep them longer, call and see if

it would be compatible with their other parent's plans. This is a common courtesy you should extend to anyone.

- If it is necessary to change your scheduled time with them, let everyone know well in advance.
- Behave like a guest in your ex's home, even if it had been your home at one time. Don't enter unless invited. Don't use things without asking. Respect your former partner's privacy. And if your kids tell you it's okay because it is their house too, have them check with their other parent anyway.
- Look for things to be positive about for which you can compliment their other parent. Is he or she doing a good job with the kids? Has he or she created a warm home for them? Is he or she instilling positive values in them? Teaching them good habits? Helping them with their homework, going to teacher conferences, getting them involved in activities? Is he or she juggling single parenting and a full-time job? Notice your ex's efforts with your children and show your appreciation.
- If your ex frequently "forgets" about your scheduled time with your children, send a polite, businesslike note beforehand confirming each visit.
- What should you do if your kids are never ready on time? If it is merely annoying but does not significantly impact your plans for the day, let it ride for a while. Their tardiness could reflect their custodial parents' resentment at having to relinquish them to you, and the problem may ease once things between you get on a more even keel. Making it an issue right away may add fuel to the fire. If the problem continues, try calling beforehand to see how things are going. If your kids have any control over the situation, they might be able to speed things along. If you can manage it calmly and with respect, try talking to their other parent about the problem the tardiness causes. Ask if there is something you can do to help. Perhaps you need to renegotiate times. Perhaps you can keep more things at your home so suitcases do not need to be packed each time. Perhaps you can take a child to a lesson, provide lunch, or help a youngster with homework at your home.
- Does your ex start a fight each time you pick up the children? Try honking the horn for them rather than going to the door. Or try responding to provocative statements with completely neutral statements, like "I'm sorry you feel that way" or "Thank you for sharing that with me." *End of discussion!* Once it becomes clear that you will not be enticed into an argument, the provocations are likely to become less frequent.
- Set rules and limits for your kids and stick to them. A common complaint of parents who have custody is that children return home exhausted from too little sleep, wired from too much junk food, and out of control because the other parent has no rules. All children *need* rules and limits, and you do them no favors by having none. If you do provide them, their

other parent may become less negative about your children spending time with you.

- Never undermine the rules in the other parent's home. Parents with custody are understandably resentful when their children become defiant and tell them, "Daddy (Mommy) said I don't have to do that if I don't want to." If your rules are different from those in their other home, tell youngsters that there are different ways of doing things, and it's okay to have different rules in different places, just as they have different rules at school. Be clear that when they are with you they follow your rules, and when they are with their other parent, they follow that parent's rules.
- Never undermine or bad-mouth your former spouse in front of your children.
- Keep a consistent presence in your kids' lives. When noncustodial parents pop in and out of children's lives, parents with custody are usually resentful and feel they must protect youngsters from another round of disappointment.

IF YOUR CHILDREN REJECT YOU

Hearing your child say, "I hate you and never want to see you again" is a traumatic blow to a parent, but it sometimes happens. You may recall from Chapter 7 that older children are more likely to express their anger about the divorce openly and sometimes turn against the parent who they perceive is responsible for it. Sometimes children are turned against a noncustodial parent by the parent with custody. Other times youngsters are placed in an impossible loyalty bind, and the nonresident parent loses out. Children need their resident parent for their survival; it is understandable that this parent usually exerts a greater influence than does the parent without custody.

What should you do if your children reject you? Hang in there and continue to show them, in whatever way you can, that you will always care about them, no matter what happens. If they won't see you, phone them and send notes and cards or small "I'm thinking about you" gifts. Continue to let them know that they are important to you, that you will not give up on them, and that you would like to see them whenever they are ready.

On occasions that you do see them, resist bad-mouthing their other parent, as tempting as it may be. It will increase the severity of their loyalty conflicts, and you will be the loser. If their other parent is turning them against you, take the stance that people often say things they don't mean when they are hurt, and you are sorry their other parent is so hurt. If it is evident that lies are being told about you, calmly correct them but don't dwell on them. You may feel that you have to muster up the patience of a saint to hold your tongue, but it will pay off in the long run.

Your persistence with your children is important for their well-being and self-esteem. But experience also shows that persistence usually does pay off. Children mature and become more independent of their custodial parents' grip. When they do, they are generally very grateful that a parent cared enough to hang in there.

CHILD SUPPORT

The issue of child support often becomes the backdrop for an emotional battle after divorce, and the losers are children—not only economically but psychologically, too. Even among fathers who pay support, and there are many who do not, many feel they are being "taken to the cleaner's" and resent having to send the money. It is not unusual for noncustodial parents to make late payments or partial payments or to interrogate children about "where all the money goes." Mothers, who are usually trying to make ends meet on far lower salaries than their former husbands, often instruct children to ask errant fathers for the check. Or, worse, they deny children visitation with their dads until the check is sent. If you read Chapter 9, you learned how destructive parental conflict is for children's well-being, particularly when children are placed in the middle of the conflict.

In addition to the damage that conflict causes children, nonpayment of child support has other destructive effects on youngsters. Whether or not the support check is sent becomes psychologically important to a child. The check becomes a symbol of the nonresident parent's love and the child's value; its absence comes to symbolize the parent's indifference and the child's worthlessness. If a parent refuses to pay for his or her child's necessities in life, how can a youngster feel valued and loved?

Failure to pay child support has a more tangible negative impact on children. There are, of course, exceptions to the rule, but studies find that the standard of living of custodial mothers and children markedly drops after divorce, even when child support *is* paid. When children's financial well-being takes a plunge after divorce, they receive a double whammy. Their already-difficult task of coping with their other losses and trying to reconstruct their lives is now compounded. Studies find that children can usually handle a single stress in their lives quite well (such as their parents' divorce), but when they must also deal with additional sources of stress, the risks of their developing long-term problems *multiply*. There is little doubt that a drastic drop in financial well-being poses a significant amount of additional stress for children.

Do you think the amount of support you are paying is too much? Although child support awards vary from locality to locality, national studies find that child support payments typically do not reflect, even remotely, the actual costs of raising children. Nor do they usually increase to keep pace with inflation or children's needs as they grow older. Custodial parents must pay more for housing that is large enough to accommodate children's needs than they would have to pay otherwise. Larger utility bills go along with it. Full-time child care is so costly that child support often does not even cover it. Medical and dental expenses climb astronomically each year. The cost of clothing keeps rising, and children outgrow their wardrobes regularly. Youngsters eat greater quantities of food each year, too, and by adolescence many seem to become bottomless pits. These are only the bare essentials. Miscellaneous school expenses, allowances, activities, lessons, vacations, and other nonessentials are added on top. But for many children, these nonessentials that had been a routine part of predivorce life are simply out of reach after divorce.

At the same time that custodial mothers' and children's standard of living drops, noncustodial fathers' standard of living usually increases significantly. Stanford researcher Lenore Weitzman found that men's standard of living increased by 73 percent the first year after divorce. Recently, sociologists Gay Kitson of the University of Akron and Leslie Morgan of the University of Maryland reported that fathers who *pay* child support spend on the average 50 percent more per capita on their own basic expenses than do women who *receive* child support. (The economics of divorce was discussed more thoroughly in Chapter 1.)

If you have problems with the amount of child support you are required to pay, you may find that you feel better if you pencil out your ex-partner's budget, checking into the costs of housing, child care, food, clothes, health care, and so forth. Keep in mind the differential between your salaries. Another strategy you might try is to negotiate with your former spouse to pay some bills directly with your support money, such as paying for day care and buying the clothes. Many nonresident parents find it far more agreeable to pay bills directly than to send a check to a former spouse.

MOTHERS WITHOUT CUSTODY

Although precise statistics are unavailable, the great majority of parents without custody are fathers. If you are a mother without custody, you are likely to feel that you have unique problems and may wonder about other noncustodial mothers. Who are they? Do they feel like you do? Are they able to keep a strong presence in their children's lives?

The national organization Mothers Without Custody estimates that approximately 1.5 million mothers in this country are living apart from at least one of their children under the age of 18.

In studying over 500 noncustodial mothers, Geoffrey Greif of the University of Maryland learned that the reasons the majority of these mothers did not have custody were financial. Common reasons included their inability to afford to raise children, their honoring of youngsters' requests to live with fathers because of the advantages their dads could provide (such as staying in the family home), and their inability to afford attorneys as good as the ones their husbands could. More than 90 percent of the mothers had not engaged in court battles. A large percentage had initially been custodial parents, with custody shifted at some point.

Mothers without custody are a varied group. Some are doing well and are satisfied with their role; others are in anguish and unhappy. Some are involved in a continuing battle to gain custody. Some desperately want custody but have not taken the litigation route, either because they cannot afford it or because they want to spare children the ordeal. Others feel that their children are better off with their fathers. Some noncustodial moms have excellent relationships with their children; some never see them.

A large national study, reported by University of Pennsylvania sociologist Frank Furstenburg and Christine Nord of Child Trends in Washington D.C., found that as a group, mothers without custody keep more actively involved in children's lives than do fathers without custody. They more often create a second home for their children, see them on a regular basis, and keep in touch between visits with phone calls and letters. Geoffrey Greif found that 30 percent of the mothers he studied saw their children once a week or more, and 23 percent rated themselves as *very* involved with their children's lives. Another 22 percent saw their children every other week. Fewer than 10 percent never saw their youngsters.

Nevertheless, the majority (70 percent) of mothers studied by Greif were unsatisfied with many aspects of the custody and "visiting" situation and wished to be more involved with their children's lives. Perhaps not surprisingly, the women who were the most comfortable with their noncustodial status were generally those who had good relationships with their children, felt their children were well taken care of and doing well, and had a satisfactory social life and career.

Mothers without custody have many of the same feelings and problems as fathers without custody. The noncustodial role can be a tough one, no matter who has it. But moms without custody have additional problems that make their role even rougher than it is for dads. Mothers frequently suffer more guilt about not having their children with them, and they are also more likely to experience negative reactions from others. Despite the fact that single-parent fathers are growing in acceptance in our society, mothers without custody are still regarded with some suspicion. People never wonder why a father does not have custody of his children, but they do wonder why a mother doesn't. So in addition to having to cope with missing their children and the daily events in their lives, nonresident mothers must also fight social prejudice. Some are never sure when to reveal their noncustodial status to casual acquaintances, some hide it, and some even hide the fact that they have children. For many mothers, their noncustodial status is always on their minds, intruding itself into all areas of their lives.

As a group, mothers without custody are very vocal advocates of joining a support group. A support group is a true lifeline, they say. Within a group of other nonresident moms, you can receive the empathy and emotional support you can't get anywhere else. Being able to share experiences, socialize, and get practical tips about functioning successfully in the noncustodial role are added benefits. Try a support group. Check your local Parents Without Partners (which has many noncustodial parents as members). Mothers Without Custody may also be able to put you in contact with a local group. Their address is P.O. Box 27418, Houston TX 77256. Community or family service agencies are other sources to try. If you cannot find a support group, try placing a newspaper ad and start your own. Mothers Without Custody also publishes a bimonthly newsletter called *Mother-to-Mother*, which can help you feel connected to the 1.5 million other mothers who are sharing your role. It can be ordered through the Texas address.

If you are a mom without custody and having a hard time with your role, you may need to work especially hard at dealing with your anger (Chapter 5). It is important to forge a new identity for yourself in which being a mother is only *one* aspect. The more pursuits and outlets for fulfillment that you can find, in addition to mothering, the more satisfying your life will be. The fuller you make your new life, the less difficult you will find it to accept that your children are not with you full-time. Rebuilding your self-esteem and building a new social support network will be critical to your happiness. (Chapters 12 and 13 will help you with building a rewarding life.) A supportive therapist may be able to provide you with the extra strength, support, and help you need to work out your feelings and get on with your life.

Does your parenting schedule provide you enough time to build good relationships with your children? If not, can you try to negotiate for longer or more frequent time with them? Can you phone more often, so you can keep abreast of the daily events and ups and downs in their lives? Have you been able to create a *real* second home for them? It is when parents without custody provide an actual second home for their children that their relationships blossom and the status of noncustodial parent becomes less painful (Chapter 18). Rather than focusing on the fact that your children are not with you, try thinking of them as living with you part-time. Instead of telling people you do not have custody, tell them your children live with you on alternate weekends, during the summers, or so on. Think of your children as having *two* homes, and instill this idea in them, too. You may enjoy Isolina Ricci's book *Mom's House, Dad's House*, listed in Appendix C.

WHEN YOUR EX-SPOUSE REMARRIES

When a former spouse remarries, many noncustodial parents relinquish contact with their children, thinking it is in their children's best interest now that they have a stepparent and a "real" family ("They don't need me anymore." "They're probably better off if I let their new stepparent take my place."). Nothing could be further from the truth. To children, a stepparent is someone *in addition to* a parent—*not* a replacement for a parent. Children reserve a special slot in their lives and affections for their real parents and fight any attempts to move a stepparent into that slot. Stepparents must earn a place in children's lives, and that place is usually a *new* slot that is gradually created.

When a parent abandons a child, even a close relationship with a wonderful and supportive stepparent often does not ease the child's pain or yearning for the real parent. Said one 22-year-old who had developed a particularly close relationship with a supportive stepfather but had lost contact with his own father: "My stepfather could be Saint Benedict or Saint Francis. He could walk on water, and it would not change the hurt I feel about my dad."[1]

Despite this reassurance, your ex's remarriage may still cause you a good deal of internal turmoil. Old feelings of ambivalence, rejection, anger, depression, or loss may resurface. You may feel jealous because this stranger will spend more time with your children than you do and may have more influence on them, too. You may worry that your children will call this stranger "Dad" (or "Mom") and will grow more attached to the stepparent than to you. You may worry that he or she will do a better job at parenting than you do. You may be afraid that the new couple might try to shut you out. The situation may make you feel a bit powerless and threatened, but watch yourself. Noncustodial parents often try to deal with these feelings by becoming very controlling in their interactions with their former partners. Conflict between former partners frequently escalates as a result, and this doesn't help anyone.

Try the following:

- Keep in mind that in the eyes of your children, your role has *not* significantly changed.
- Tell your ex that you want to remain involved in your children's lives. If you don't want them to call the new stepparent Dad (Mom), express your wishes calmly. Sometimes younger children wish to call a stepparent Daddy or Mommy but are happy using a name like Daddy John or Mommy Ann.
- If you create a spirit of cooperation from the beginning, it will pay off. Ask your former spouse if he or she would like to make any changes in the parenting schedule to accommodate the new marriage. Sometimes remarried couples are happy to increase visitation so they can have some time together without children. Or they may be very grateful if you

switched the weekends your children were with you so they can coordinate your children and the stepparent's children.

- Read chapter 20 on stepfamilies to learn about the problems and adjustments your children will face. One thing they must deal with are loyalty conflicts between you and their new stepparent. Children worry that their real parent will be upset if they like their stepparent. They also worry that their real parent will drop out of their lives because of the stepparent. You can take an enormous burden off their young shoulders by giving them permission to like their stepparent and to be happy in their new stepfamily. Let them know that you will always be their parent and will always love them, and make it clear that a relationship with a stepparent is completely separate from a relationship with a parent.
- Make an effort to develop a cordial relationship with your children's new stepparent. It will make life easier for everyone.

WHEN YOU REMARRY

Remarriage when one parent has noncustodial children often proves to be more complicated than the new couple had anticipated. Since youngsters won't be living with them full-time, many couples fail to discuss how children will be incorporated into their new married lives. Many new spouses are later astounded at their own naivete. Some are surprised to find their weekends devoted to child-centered activities to the exclusion of the couple activities they would prefer. Some find themselves completely locked out of the close-knit family group that gathers in their homes on visiting weekends. Some wives find themselves saddled with all the extra shopping, cooking, and laundry while receiving few, if any, emotional benefits from children's visits. Some complain that their spouses impose so few rules and limits on their visiting children that children are out of control for the duration of their stay. Others find their spouses always siding with their children when conflicts arise. For many new spouses, visits from noncustodial stepchildren are, at best, ordeals to get through. Many find themselves feeling jealous, threatened, angry, and resentful and report that tension and anxiety in the home begin to mount several days before children are scheduled to come.

The situation can be equally trying for visiting children, particularly if their new stepparent has children living full-time in the home. It is threatening for a youngster to see his or her own parent living with a new family. Every interaction that the parent has with the "new kids" is observed with suspicion and jealousy ("Does my parent love them more than me? Does (s)he give them more than me? Is my parent more theirs now than mine? Do I have a place in this new family or am I an unwanted intruder and a second-class citizen around here?").

Stepsiblings who live in the home full-time can also find it difficult when the "visitors" come. In many homes, visiting children are treated like indulged royalty, while live-in children begrudgingly shoulder the household chores, move out of their rooms to accommodate the "guests," and forgo their own social plans to entertain them.

Don't be discouraged. Remarriage when you have noncustodial children *can* be rewarding for you, your spouse, and all the children, but it is clearly a situation requiring a good deal of information, discussion, and planning. What works best, agree stepfamily experts, is to create a real second home and second family for children. Read Chapters 20, 21, and 22 on stepfamilies; they apply to part-time as well as full-time stepfamilies. The suggestions provided in "Creating a Second Home for Your Children" in the previous chapter are also geared for you. Here are some suggestions you may find particularly helpful.

- Open communication with your spouse is a must. For your marriage and new family to work, you will have to have ongoing discussions, negotiation, and compromises. How can you best incorporate your children into your lives? Are your ideas about child rearing and discipline compatible? What role would each of you ideally like your new spouse to play in your children's lives one day? How can you best divide your time, energy, and finances between your new spouse and your children? If you don't reach some agreement on these important child-related issues, your children can drive a wedge between you. Share your feelings with each other and try to empathize with each other's perspective.
- Your children undoubtedly have strong feelings and fears about your new spouse and the family you've created. Encourage them to express them. Try putting yourself in their shoes and empathize with their feelings. Reassure them, through both your words and behavior, that your relationships with them will not be threatened and that you want to create a second family for them. Do everything you can both to make them feel wanted and to make them feel like full-fledged family members rather than guests. To reduce the loyalty conflicts likely to be raised by your remarriage, let your children know that their stepparent is not a competitor with their real parent but will be another caring adult in their lives. Also let them know that they do not have to choose between their two families.
- If you have stepchildren living with you, learn what problems are created for them when your children are with you. Empathize with their perspectives and share yours with them. Try problem solving with them to find some solutions to conflicts created by your children's presence. (An effective problem-solving method was given in Chapter 15.) They will be more cooperative and open to developing relationships with your children if they know their feelings and concerns are taken seriously.
- Work on changing everyone's vocabulary: Your children *live with you*

part-time; they are not visitors or guests. This puts everyone in the same frame of mind and makes your children's position in the family clear.

- Provide your youngsters a permanent place at the dinner table and a place to leave some of their things that is off-limits to everyone else. If they must share bedrooms with stepsiblings, try to have bunk beds or trundle beds so everyone can have a permanent bed. Display your children's artwork and crafts.

- If you move to a new home and your new spouse has children who live with you, you might try what one couple did—have *all* the children spend your first night in the home with you. It made the noncustodial children feel that they were an integral part of the family and this new family home.

- Including your kids in family routines and a few family chores will help them feel more involved with the family. Agree on house rules with your partner, and expect your children to follow them. The more frequently they live with you, the more they should be expected to fit in with family life. A note about chores: Give them chores that allow them to work together with you or another member of the family—perhaps grocery shopping, repairing something, helping with a meal or the cleanup, and so on.

- When your youngsters first come, help them to catch up on what the family has been doing. Have family meetings when they are with you so everyone can openly discuss problems and feelings.

- Encourage everyone in the family to develop relationships with one another. Get your children and stepchildren involved in projects with each other. Arrange some activities so everyone will have fun together. Encourage your new spouse to get to know your kids as individuals.

- Be sure to spend some individual time with your children yourself. Your relationship will always be the most critical one for them. If your spouse feels left out, encourage him or her to do some things he or she would not otherwise take time to do—develop new interests, spend time with friends, and so forth.

- Rather than forcing your stepchildren to entertain your children for their entire stay, actively help your youngsters become involved with neighborhood children and activities, and/or allow them to bring a friend with them.

- If it is difficult to break the ice when your children first come, try arranging some kind of family activity that gets everyone involved.

- If you are tempted to try to gain custody now that you are remarried, read about custody disputes in Chapter 11. If your children are doing okay where they are, ask yourself if you can try to renegotiate with their other parent about an increase in visitation rather than fight for custody.

The next three chapters are devoted completely to stepfamilies. Chapter 20 discusses common myths about stepfamilies and why believing them leads to trouble. It also looks at paths of action stepfamilies so often take that lead to serious problems. Chapter 21 looks at the other side of the coin—strategies stepfamilies can take instead that generally lead to satisfaction and success. Chapter 23 is a question-and-answer forum dealing with questions stepparents often ask.

PART V

STEPFAMILIES

STEPFAMILIES:
Common Myths and Paths to Serious Problems

True or false?

1. Remarriage is often just what is needed to help people get back on their feet after divorce.
2. When we get married, we will be an instant family.
3. When we get married, the children will be able to have a traditional family once again.
4. Usually, well-adjusted people can adapt to stepfamily life after a brief adjustment period.

If you answered true to any of the preceding statements, you are not alone. Each represents a commonly believed myth. However, if you accept *any* of these myths as valid, you will set yourself up for needless disappointment, discouragement, and spiraling problems, just as so many others have. Each of these myths creates unrealistic expectations, and when reality falls short, most people believe there is something wrong with *them* ("Why do I feel this way instead of the way I *should*?" "Why aren't things working out like they *should*?" "Is my marriage on its way to failure?" "What's *wrong* with me?"). Feeling inadequate, many try to hide their feelings and problems, even from their spouses. Others work harder to make the reality fit the myths, but in so doing frequently set into motion a new cycle of problems that sometimes gets out of control.

Remarriage and a stepfamily (sometimes called a blended or remarried family) *can* be a path to a fulfilling life. Studies report that the majority of remarriers have a high level of satisfaction with their marriages and are as likely as first-time–married men and women to be happy and optimistic about the future. But there is a catch. The divorce rate for remarriages is found to be higher than that for first marriages. (Although figures vary, some recent sources place the redivorce rate as high as 60 percent.) Furthermore, a full 40 percent of those failed remarriages never make it past their fourth year. This suggests that large numbers of unhappy couples are quickly weeded out of the remarried population, leaving a more select group to be interviewed by sporadically conducted national surveys (see Table 20.1).

The early years of your blended family's life are not likely to resemble life on "The Brady Bunch" or other television families. However, knowing what is "normal" will buffer you from the feelings of anxiety, frustration, and guilt that couples so often experience during their stepfamilies' fledgling years. And if you are aware of the problems that so often arise in stepfamilies and the reasons that they occur, you can prevent many of them and minimize others. This chapter focuses on common stepfamily myths and compares them with stepfamily reality. It then discusses paths of action stepfamilies so often take that lead to problems. In the following chapter, we will look at the opposite side of the coin—at strategies that generally lead to success and satisfaction for stepfamilies.

Giving up the myths and replacing them with realistic expectations is a necessary first step toward creating a successful stepfamily, whether it is a full-time stepfamily or a part-time one with noncustodial children.

TABLE 20.1

Although the percentage of people who remarry has been on the decline in recent years, more than 70 percent of divorced men and women are continuing to do so.

The majority of remarriages for divorced men and women take place within the first five years after divorce; the median duration of time between divorce and remarriage is three years.

About 40 percent of remarriages involve stepchildren under age 18 who will live in the home.

1,300 new stepfamilies are formed each day in the United States.

17.4 percent of currently married families with children under 18 in the home are stepfamilies.

Demographers have estimated that 35 percent of the children born during the 1980s will spend some portion of their childhoods in a stepfamily.

STEPFAMILY MYTHS VERSUS STEPFAMILY REALITY

Myth: Remarriage is often just what is needed to help people get back on their feet after divorce.

Although developing new relationships may help you let go of the past and get on with your life, *remarrying* before you are back on your feet is far more likely to create new problems than to solve existing ones. No one can invest the energy and commitment needed to make a remarriage work if he or she is stuck in the past or is still emotionally wounded. The new marriage will begin with a serious handicap—being weighted down by the emotional baggage still carried from the previous one. There are any number of ways in which leftover emotional baggage can seriously impair a new marriage. Some people still feel so vulnerable that they keep their new partners at arm's length, denying them the intimacy they need. Others still feel so needy from a former marriage that they make unrealistic demands of their new spouses, expecting a new marriage to make up for past hurts. Some people invest more emotional energy into fighting with their former partners than into building a life with their new partners. Some, because of lingering attachment or guilt, find so many reasons to have contact with former partners that new partners are left feeling insecure, jealous, and competitive. Others routinely flare up at bewildered new spouses who have done things reminiscent of a predecessor. The list of potential problems is long.

Before you consider remarriage, be sure that you deal with your feelings of loss (Chapter 3) and anger (Chapter 5). Be sure that you let go of your past relationship and old way of life (Chapter 6). And be sure that you feel whole again (Chapters 12 and 13). If you have already remarried without having finished your divorce adjustment, it's not too late to work on it now, so you can finally close the door on your marriage and get on with your life.

Myth: When we get married, we will be an instant family.

The myth of the instant family is perhaps the most widely accepted stepfamily myth. However, a marriage ceremony cannot create an instant family. It merely marks the beginning of a long process from which a family may eventually evolve. Stepfamilies attempt to merge two disparate contingents, each with its own allegiances, its own life-style, its own perspective, its own ways of communicating and doing things, even its own in-jokes. Noticeably lacking from this new "family" is any sense of belonging—of shared history or shared identity. Moreover, the bond uniting a biological parent and child predates and is frequently stronger than the bond uniting a newly remarried couple.

Early in stepfamily life, there are generally two distinct mini-families; they may even distrust one another because their differences threaten each others' way of life. Or there may be one mini-family with its distinct identity and life-style and one outsider who is attempting to carve out a significant niche within that family's well-defined boundaries. Stepparents in this latter situation often compare themselves with immigrants who have been plunked down in a strange country to face an unfamiliar language and culture.

Merging these two disparate contingents and blending them into a single family with its own identity, life-style, traditions, allegiances, and shared trust is no easy matter, nor does it magically occur overnight. Until a family does blend, members of stepfamilies often complain, "This isn't a family. It's just a bunch of people living in the same house."

Hand in hand with the myth of the instant family is the myth of instant love. To most people, families and love go together, and couples commonly assume that stepparents will automatically love their stepchildren and that children will quickly come to love their stepparents. When love doesn't magically appear, stepparents frequently feel guilt and shame because they do not feel as they "should." What's more, they feel hurt, frustrated, and rebuffed when their stepchildren are unresponsive to their overtures.

In reality, love and attachment between stepfamily members cannot be rushed. Neither can they be taken for granted. Bonds of affection generally take 1½ to 2 years to develop in stepfamilies. Generally, they are never as strong between a stepparent and stepchildren as they are between a biological parent and child. And in some stepfamilies, affectional bonds *never* develop.

Myth: When we get married, the children will be able to have a traditional family once again.

Most stepfamilies start out assuming that their family and day-to-day living will closely resemble that of a traditional biological family. However, trying to force a stepfamily to fit the mold of a traditional family is bound to lead to trouble. A stepfamily can be a fine environment in which to raise children; it is neither inferior nor superior to a traditional family. However, it is definitely *different* from a traditional family. One of the first steps in achieving a successful step-family is recognizing these numerous differences:

1. A traditional family has a clear identity, whereas the identity and boundaries of a stepfamily are very ambiguous. Who is in the family and who is not is often a matter of interpretation. This ambiguity was clearly evident in a large national study reported by University of Pennsylvania sociologist Frank Furstenberg and his associates that asked stepfamily members to list the members of their family. Thirty-one percent of the children did not list a stepparent with whom they lived as a family member, and 41 percent excluded stepsiblings with whom they lived. Though it is tempting to assume that it is only *children* who are confused about family membership, this was not the case. Fifteen percent of the parents who had stepchildren living with them failed to include these

live-in children as family members. Perhaps, then, the confusion is limited to newly formed stepfamilies? Wrong again. When the interviews of well-established stepfamilies were analyzed separately, the picture did not change! For many stepfamilies, confusion about who is in the family and who is not persists over time. As you might imagine, stepfamily identity is even more clouded when there are stepchildren living with the family only part-time.

2. Unlike in traditional families, in stepfamilies it is not clear what role stepfamily members should play with one another. Is the stepparent a parent or a nonparent? Is good stepmothering the same as good mothering? Does a stepfather have authority over his wife's children? In most states he doesn't even have legal or financial responsibilities for them. How much of a commitment should be made to a spouse's children? Should stepparents become involved in children's education? Who is really in charge of the children? The situation becomes even more ambiguous when a stepparent and stepchild are very close in age. How should they behave with each other? What should their relationship be? What if there is a sexual attraction between them? And what if there is a sexual attraction between teenage stepsiblings? How are they to behave toward each other? One is not supposed to feel that way about a sibling, but are they really siblings?

3. A traditional family operates pretty much autonomously, whereas stepfamilies frequently do not have this luxury. A stepfamily typically has to coordinate weekend schedules, vacations, holidays, and decisions about children with a parent living outside the home. It must accept that children's attitudes, values, and behavior will be significantly influenced by a former spouse, perhaps in ways that are incompatible with its own values. Many a stepfamily cannot even plan its own financial future because of uncertainty about child support coming in or unforeseen expenses incurred by the first family.

4. The complexity of stepfamily relationships is an obvious distinction that sets them apart from their traditional counterparts. It is not unusual for children in stepfamilies to have four parents, numerous stepsiblings and halfsiblings (some living with them full-time, some part-time), eight grandparents, and an array of aunts, uncles, and cousins who are related to each of their parents and stepparents. To make life even more complicated, stepfamilies are splintered, continually needing to juggle incompatible family contingents.

5. Because loyalties and emotional ties are split across households, a stepfamily is not likely to be as close or as cohesive as a traditional family. Children in blended families need more psychological space than do other children so they can move between families without feeling torn by loyalty conflicts. Parents who have children living with former spouses

also have split loyalties that often prevent their complete emotional investment in their new families.

Many mental health professionals, in fact, feel that loose family relationships are more conducive to smooth stepfamily functioning than are close-knit relationships (with the exception of the couple relationship, which should *always* be very strong). Looser relationships work better in stepfamilies because they must have revolving doors, with children continually going to and coming from another family.

Myth: Usually, well-adjusted people can adapt to stepfamily life after a brief adjustment period.

Remarrying couples are usually optimistic when they plan their marriages, assuming that things will fall into place quickly once everyone becomes a "family." But the reality is that just as there was an adjustment period after divorce, there is an inevitable adjustment period for life in a remarried family. Studies suggest two years or longer. Once you take a closer look at the fledgling stepfamily, you will understand why.

Children's Concerns and Adjustment Problems

A parent's remarriage is usually a time of crisis for children, particularly a resident parent's remarriage. Once again in their relatively short lifetimes, children's worlds are turned topsy-turvy, and they are powerless to influence events that have a profound impact on their lives. Once again, the future is an enormous unknown. Once again, anxiety and questions become familiar companions: "What is it like to live with a stepparent?" "Will Mom (Dad) still have time for me?" "Will we still get to make breakfast together on Saturday morning?" "Where will I fit into this new family?" "Will I get lost in the shuffle?" "Will I have to share my room with stepsiblings?" "Will we have to move to their house?" "Will I have to leave my school and friends?" "What will it be like to have an older sister? *I'm* supposed to be the oldest!" "Will Mom (Dad) like the new kids better than me?" "Suppose they have a new baby? It will be *their* kid. Where will that leave me?"

Additional worries focus on the parent outside the home: "Will I still get to go to Dad's (Mom's) house as much?" "Will I still see Grandma and Grandpa?" "Would it be disloyal to my real parent to be nice to my new stepparent?" "Will Dad (Mom) be angry if I like my stepparent?"

Besides anxiety, most children struggle with feelings of loss. Now the parent's attention, time, and love must be shared all the time. The more intense the parent-child relationship had been, the harder it usually is on the youngster and the more the stepparent is seen as an unwelcome intruder. Children who have been confidants to their single parents or who have played other adult roles in the home are particularly hard hit. In fact, many feel betrayed, believing they have been replaced and insensitively asked to become children once again. For these youngsters, a parent's remarriage feels like a hostile takeover.

Having to share a parent is not the only loss with which children must struggle. Many have never given up the fantasy of resuming their old lives and having their parents back together again. A remarriage makes the futility of this ongoing fantasy glaringly obvious. When a parent remarries, many a youngster feels as if the divorce is happening all over again, and the reality of losing the parent as well as the old, comfortable life must finally be faced. Some stubbornly hang on to the cherished fantasy, hoping if they are indifferent enough or mean enough, this intruder will go away.

Thus, at the same time that parents are thrilled with their forthcoming union, most youngsters feel sad, helpless, ambivalent, and/or angry. Data from a large nationally conducted study, analyzed by Princeton University sociologist Nazli Baydar, revealed that children developed more emotional problems after parental remarriage than they did after parental separation. Common problems surfacing in children at the time of remarriage are withdrawal, fighting, restlessness, unhappiness, poor concentration, and substance abuse. Fortunately, children's problems were generally not long-term ones.

Adjustment in Families with Two Sets of Children

Since there is no quick way to blend two families, there is no quick way to adjust to a remarried family. Each of the two contingents comes to the remarriage with its own well-established ways of doing things—from the very important (such as child rearing and how money is spent) to the mundane (such as eating habits and manners). For example, one contingent may be used to meticulous planning and a scheduled life; the other has always hung loose and made last-minute plans. One group eats a formal dinner together each evening; the other eats in shifts in front of the TV. One may prefer traditional and simple food; the other prefers foreign and gourmet meals. One is neat; the other is sloppy. One parent is a strict disciplinarian; the other is lax. One side buys only name brands in expensive department stores; the other values frugality and shops in discount stores. One set of children is expected to do chores for their modest allowance; the other receives a generous allowance with nothing expected in return. One set of teens likes a quiet environment for studying; the other likes a constant parade of friends and loud rock music.

The rules of day-to-day living, once so automatic, now must be consciously reviewed and renegotiated. The givens in life are no longer givens, and each person feels disoriented. Unlike in a first marriage where there are only two people to negotiate about the way that they will do things, now many people are involved in the negotiations, some of whom are tenaciously clinging to the familiar because it represents security in an otherwise insecure new world. The usual result in the early stages of a stepfamily's life, perhaps after a brief "honeymoon" period, is stress, chaos, and confusion. There seems to be an endless period in which nothing feels "right."

Adjustment in Families with One Set of Children

Though it might seem that stepfamily adjustment should be relatively easy when there is only one set of children involved, this is usually not the case, particularly for the stepparent. Because single parents and their children have shared adversity together, they frequently become close-knit groups, and new spouses tend to feel that breaking into these tightly knit circles is about as easy as breaking into a fortress. Things run smoothly as long as a stepparent adapts to the unwritten "rules" the family lives by and does not rock the boat, but this means feeling like a visitor in what is supposed to be his or her own home. Most of these stepparents feel decidedly uncomfortable but are not quite sure what the problem is, reports Dr. Patricia Papernow, a Cambridge, Massachusetts psychologist, who conducted a lengthy study of stepfamily development. Moreover, most of these stepparents have an additional handicap: Their new spouses usually see *no* problem. Everything seems perfectly normal and comfortable to them. So why is the stepparent having such difficulty?

A significant percentage of stepparents spend this period of time in a haze, reports Papernow. Most go through alternating periods of investing their energies into trying to join the family and then withdrawing in frustration and emotional exhaustion. They are continually on the outside looking in, feeling ignored and unappreciated, watching their spouses and stepchildren share in the warmth and love they would like to partake in themselves. Most often they feel isolated, lonely, and jealous. What is more disturbing, they think the problem is theirs and that something is wrong with *them*.

If the remarriage is going to work, these stepfamilies must also go through a blending process that takes time, patience, negotiation, and compromise. In these families, too, the process is usually one full of conflict, one in which the stepparent is the sole voice for change and the biological parent is torn between the conflicting needs of spouse and children.

LOSING STRATEGIES: EIGHT COMMON PATHS TO SERIOUS STEPFAMILY PROBLEMS

Starting a stepfamily is not easy, and society offers no models or rules to guide stepfamilies along the way. In their efforts to write their own rules, many remarried families rely on stepfamily myths as their guides. The myths not only cause disappointment and discouragement, but also lead many unsuspecting stepfamilies down paths that from the start are bound to end in failure. At best, these losing strategies delay stepfamily adjustment. At worst, they lead to family breakup. Let's take a look at them.

Losing Strategy #1: Trying to Replace the Absent Parent

In their endeavor to quickly create a perfect family, many remarried couples fail to see what is all too obvious to a child: A parent is a parent forever and cannot be replaced. There simply is no such thing as an ex-mother or an ex-father, even if a parent is only minimally involved in a child's life. Either overtly or covertly, a child usually remains loyal to a biological parent, and most children will resist an intruder who tries to encroach on what is perceived to be the absent parent's "rightful" place. Some children respond by withdrawing. Some become torn with guilt and loyalty conflicts. Others become hostile and may openly rebel. The end result is to delay or even prevent the bonding between stepparent and stepchild—a result diametrically opposed to that intended.

Trying to take the place of the absent parent can assume a number of forms. Sometimes couples insist that a child call the new stepparent "Mom" or "Dad," the same name used for the real parent. With few exceptions, children want to reserve a special status for a biological parent, and a name is symbolic of that special status. Youngsters need to be allowed to choose a name they are comfortable using for a stepparent.

Trying to replace the absent parent can also take the form of competition with that parent. It is quite natural for stepparents to feel competitive with their predecessors, but many new stepparents feel they must surpass the predecessor in every way to prove that they are the better spouse and the better parent. They set out to become supermoms and superdads, excelling in all areas. However, their efforts usually arouse steely resistance rather than gratitude. Children usually see their behavior as a bid to take over, and they do not like to see their biological parents on the losing end of a contest. The fallout from the competition is likely to be resentment of the stepparent and a fierce loyalty to the natural parent who is absent from the scene. Once again, the outcome is the opposite of that intended. How, then, should competitive feelings be handled? If you are a stepparent, realize that you have something unique to offer your stepchildren, as does their absent biological parent. Allow yourself to shine in your areas and allow the biological parent to shine in his or hers.

Stepparents also employ a third common strategy to replace an absent parent—taking over some of the rituals that children had shared with their absent parent, such as reading a bedtime story in a favorite chair, going for pizza after a soccer game, or making Saturday morning breakfast. Taking over these activities may seem harmless enough, and a stepparent may even be encouraged to do so by his or her new partner. However, unless youngsters specifically invite a stepparent to join in such a ritual, any attempt to do so is likely to be resented. To youngsters, these rituals represent the special relationship with their real parent who is no longer in the home, and they are likely to be sacred. Dr. Marla Beth Isaacs, who directed the Families of Divorce Project in Philadelphia, reports that the relationship between stepparent and stepchildren is better served if the space formerly shared by the absent parent and child is *protected* rather than filled. A stepparent needs to develop *new* rituals and a unique role with a stepchild, not move in on the absent parent's turf.

Losing Strategy #2: Creating a False Sense of Togetherness

Spurred on by the myths of the instant family and quick stepfamily adjustment, many remarried couples try to force a sense of family togetherness that feels phony and contrived to their children. What these couples are doing is asking their youngsters to deny their own feelings and participate in what children often perceive to be a sham. Once again, the tactic has the opposite effect of that intended, reports Dr. Virginia Goldner of Albert Einstein College of Medicine. Rather than feeling like part of one big, happy family, youngsters feel alienated, angry, or ambivalent. Some withdraw, others openly rebel. Frequently, an unfortunate cycle is set into motion from which families have difficulty extricating themselves: The more that parents implicitly demand that children join their mythical happy family, the more children resist; the more that children resist, the more the parents become insecure and increase their demands. Instead of creating a family basking in togetherness, they create a family steeped in conflict, points out Goldner. The older the children, the more likely this scenario is. Feelings of togetherness may eventually evolve, but they *cannot* be forced.

Losing Strategy #3: Forced Blending

A somewhat related losing strategy is the failure to recognize that blending is a process and must evolve over time. In their eagerness to have an instant family, parents sometimes try to force the blending process. They decide how the family will operate and impose their decisions on children. Or sometimes it is a stepparent alone who forces blending by immediately setting out to change how the home and family will be run henceforth. The older the children, the more likely it is that forced blending or immediate radical change will lead to stepfamily problems.

> Helen and Tony Catano each had three children. Tony thought Helen's kids were poorly disciplined and needed a firm hand. Helen thought Tony's kids were undemonstrative and needed a mother's nurturance. They decided that the new family would work best if they each assumed traditional roles. Tony would be the family head, breadwinner, and disciplinarian, and Helen would be a full-time mom for all six children. Tony, who was intent on establishing ground rules for Helen's children immediately, announced a lengthy list of "house rules" that all children would follow. Helen's children were livid. "Why should we have to follow *their* rules? It's not fair, Mom! Why can't they do things our way?" Tony was adamant. Although Helen's

children followed the new rules, they did so begrudgingly, resenting Tony, his children, and Helen for betraying their way of life. Meanwhile, Helen made no points with Tony's children, either. Her first mistake was to immediately reorganize the kitchen (formerly her teenage stepdaughter's domain), commenting on its inefficiency while her stepdaughter seethed. She took over the shopping and cooking, stocking the house with unfamiliar foods and preparing meals that her stepchildren hated. Feeling the house needed "a woman's touch," she redecorated it without consulting anyone. Tony's children felt like this intruder was taking over their lives, but her worst "crime," they unanimously agreed, were the insufferable hugs she continually gave them and insisted on them returning.

The blending of a stepfamily is a process that *must* evolve over time, and if children are to become a part of the family, their opinions and needs must play a significant role in that blending process. Open and extended give-and-take communication is a must. At best, parents who force blending are likely to create a pseudofamily that doesn't feel like a family to anyone. At worst, they will create resentment and open rebellion.

Losing Strategy #4: Dramatically Changing Parent-Child Relationships

Children entering stepfamilies have been through an inordinate amount of change and upheaval in their relatively short lives, and a key ingredient that helps a child weather those disruptions is a good relationship with his or her parents. A good relationship with a parent functions as sort of a cushion for a child, which softens the blows of stress. It can be an enormous asset for a youngster as he or she is asked to make the adjustment to stepfamily life.

However, when parent-child relationships are dramatically changed in stepfamilies, it compounds children's already-difficult task of dealing with their anxiety and coping with all their other losses. Usually, the outcome is poor for everyone. Understandably, children become angry and resentful and usually adjust poorly to the new family. Generally, the stepparent is poorly accepted or even rejected. And family blending is delayed, or even prevented.

Two common situations in stepfamilies result in dramatically changed parent-child relationships and are likely to lead to stepfamily problems. In the first, couples concentrate on forming a tight couple bond immediately because they are so determined to make this marriage work. In so doing, however, many leave children on the outside looking in, resentful and bitterly missing the relationship they once had with the biological parent.

In the second situation, fathers who have missed having a wife to mother their children are usually delighted at the prospect of having a "traditional" family once again, and they often turn over the role of mother to their new partners immediately. However, the shift is too sudden. Children resent this intruder taking over activities they had previously enjoyed doing with their single father and sorely miss the old relationship with him. How can a child like or appreciate a person who robs them of such an important relationship and their way of life? Usually, children respond with withdrawal, indifference, or hostility. A father's demands for them to appreciate or accept their new stepmother only make a bad situation worse.

Losing Strategy #5: Assuming Authority Too Quickly

This is probably the most common cause of problems in stepfather families, but it can cause havoc in stepmother families, too. Discipline is usually a thorny issue in stepfamilies, particularly with stepfathers. Before marriage, most men try to be popular with children, but afterward they usually try to assume the traditional fatherly role of disciplinarian. Many mothers even encourage them in this role.

To youngsters, however, the stepparent is still a guest in the family, and they perceive any attempts to discipline them as out of line. "You're not my father, and you have no right to tell me what to do!" is a common cry that stepfathers hear all too often. The older the children, the more serious the problems over authority and discipline are likely to become.

The situation worsens if the stepfather's style of disciplining is different from the mother's. In youngsters' perceptions, he is not only "out of line," but he is arbitrarily changing the standards they have lived by and believe are "right."

When mothers stand behind fathers, youngsters often feel betrayed and are likely to be at odds with both stepparent and parent. But it is not unusual for mothers, even those who initially invited their new husbands to become the family disciplinarian, to perceive their new partners as too strict and come to their children's defense. Many mothers essentially form a coalition with their youngsters that undermines their new partners' position in the family—a poor way to start off a marriage. To keep the peace, mothers sometimes overtly agree with new disciplinary rules set by their new husbands but subtly sabotage them. A mother may "agree" that youngsters should be in bed by eight but continually "forget" to enforce it. She may "agree" that a teen's curfew should be earlier but insist on accepting weak excuses when it is broken. When children perceive that their real parent does not agree with new rules (and they sense this easily), they ignore both the rules and their stepparent.

Stepfather and stepchild need to build a relationship with each other before a child will willingly accept discipline from him, point out psychiatrist John Visher and psychologist Emily Visher, nationally recognized stepfamily experts. (The same is true for stepmothers.) Trying to assume authority too quickly, before that relationship develops, only courts disaster. In a long-term study of remarried families, psychologist E. Mavis Hetherington of the University of Virginia found that when stepfathers moved into a disciplinary role before their relationships with children developed, they were generally rejected by the youngsters. Moreover, a significant number of these youngsters developed behavior problems, acting out their anger at home and at school. Sometimes this kind of family conflict continues for years in stepfamilies. Sometimes stepfathers, feeling frustrated and inadequate, retreat into passivity. Some marriages do not make it through the turmoil.

Losing Strategy #6: Resisting Family Blending

Stepfamily problems discussed so far have all had a common denominator. They all stem from remarried couples moving too quickly, denying their stepfamilies the time needed to adapt and blend. Because the couple pushes too hard, they unwittingly set into motion a cycle of problems that stand in the way of their becoming an integrated family.

Some stepfamilies' problems stem from the opposite cause. From the beginning, they make no effort toward blending and, therefore, never move forward. Perhaps part of the problem stems from the couples' unpreparedness for marriage and part from a naive assumption that the new family should develop naturally, without work or conscious effort.

Virginia Goldner of Albert Einstein College of Medicine reports that in most families that resist blending, the married partners have failed to develop a strong couple bond and have never shifted their primary commitment from their children to each other. With no united executive team at its head, the family is left to drift without leadership. Strong coalitions based on old family ties continue, and a new family identity never develops.

When two sets of children are in the family, these stepfamilies sometimes live together for years as two separate families in a boardinghouse atmosphere. When there is only one set of children, the typical scenario is for the stepparent to always play second fiddle to the children, who continue to occupy center stage in the home. Correctly perceiving their overriding importance, children are quite happy to permanently exclude the "intruder" from the family's inner circle. After many years of marriage, many a stepparent has sadly voiced the conviction, "If it ever comes down to me or them, I'll be the loser."

Losing Strategy #7: Trying to Shut Out the Former Spouse from Children's Lives

In their attempts to function like a traditional family and to quickly adjust to stepfamily life, many couples believe that life would be so much simpler if only the former spouse were out of the picture. It is an understandable wish and would solve many day-to-day complications that stepfamilies face—having to coordinate weekend schedules, having to share children on holidays, having to constantly deal with all the unpleasantness that so often accompanies contact with former spouses, and so on.

However, families that try to freeze out a biological parent from their children's lives often trade day-to-day inconveniences for long-term problems. In effect, they are saying to children, "This is your family now, and we are all you need." In doing so, they create enormous loyalty conflicts for their youngsters. They ask their children to deny their own feelings, their pasts, and their roots. And they ask them to relinquish a relationship that is important to their future well-being. Studies find that children need *both* their parents and that they suffer a great deal of psychological distress when a parent is no longer a part of their lives.

A child who is enmeshed in intense loyalty conflicts or who has lost access to a parent is a child in distress, and this distress is likely to take its toll on both the child and the stepfamily. Many children act out their distress in behavior problems at home and at school, which places additional stress on their stepfamilies. Many others respond to a stepfamily's demands for complete allegiance by holding back and refusing to join the stepfamily psychologically. Forced to make a choice between their real parent and a stepparent, they feel they have no choice but to remain loyal to their real parent.

Is Your Stepfamily Following One of These Losing Strategies?

✓ Is the stepparent trying to replace the absent parent?
  • In name? Through competition? By taking over the absent parent's rituals with children?
✓ Are you and your spouse attempting to foist the feeling on everyone that you are just "one big, happy family"?
✓ Are you forcing the blending process rather than allowing it to evolve over time?
  • Are you dictating how the new family will be run without considering children's input?
  • Is the stepparent moving quickly to change things?
✓ Has your stepfamily resulted in a dramatic change in the relationships between children and their natural parent?
✓ Is the stepparent moving into an authority role before building good relationships with the children?
✓ Have you failed to form a strong couple bond or to shift your primary commitment from your children to your spouse?
✓ Are you trying to freeze out children's absent parent from their lives?
✓ Do you have a "Let's not rock the boat" attitude in your family, brushing off problems rather than dealing with them?

Losing Strategy #8: Denying Problems and Conflicts

Stepfamilies can feel so vulnerable because of their first families' collapse that they try to bury problems and conflicts when they arise. The pervasive feeling in the family is, "Let's not rock the boat." Mental health professionals use the term *pseudomutuality* to describe this path of action. What's wrong with pseudomutuality is that problems and conflicts can never be dealt with or solved if they are never brought out into the open and discussed. Problems simply compound and fester under the surface until one day the calm facade erupts. *Every* stepfamily has its problems and conflicts, and the family needs to discuss and work on them as a family, not deny them.

This chapter has mapped common paths stepfamilies take that frequently lead to serious family problems. It is helpful to know what to expect and what *not* to do. However, it is even more helpful if you know what *to do*. What to do is the subject of the next chapter. It discusses eight strategies that generally lead to success in full-time and part-time stepfamilies and how to put those strategies into practice.

21

LEARNING WHAT WORKS: Eight Successful Strategies for Stepfamilies

"If only we had known that before!" This is a common regret of remarried couples who finally seek out professional help because their stepfamilies are in trouble. Don't misunderstand. There is no *single* "right" way in which a stepfamily should be shaped. To some degree, each stepfamily must find its own solutions and write its own rules. But as you discovered in the last chapter, some paths stepfamilies commonly take generally lead to problems. There are other paths, however, that generally lead to success and satisfaction. This chapter discusses those alternative paths. They are organized into eight broad strategies and include many practical suggestions to help you implement them. These eight strategies are guidelines, not black-and-white rules that you must follow to the letter.

If you are just starting out in a remarried family, you can begin on the right foot. Are you already in a stepfamily and having a difficult time? Then begin some serious work right now, using these strategies as guidelines. Additional sources of help and support are discussed at the end of the chapter.

STRATEGY #1: OPEN COMMUNICATION

Make open communication a top priority, both before marriage and after. You will find it helpful to discuss the following areas:

a. *Expectations.* Make a list of the most important expectations you have about your marriage and stepfamily, and have your partner make one, too. Include the role each of you would eventually like the stepparent to play in the family. Once you have read Chapters 20, 21, and 22, evaluate how realistic your respective lists are. Then evaluate whether your expectations are consistent with each other's. If not, can they be negotiated so they are compatible?

> When George and Mara compared expectations, they found some important inconsistencies. Mara assumed that George would share household responsibilities fifty-fifty and envisioned entertaining and dining out frequently, particularly on weekends, since they both had full-time jobs. Although George had not thought much about his household participation, he admitted that he preferred a more traditional male-female split of responsibilities. An even more important area that needed negotiation was the way their weekends would be spent. George had hoped to increase his involvement with his three noncustodial children now that he could provide them a real second home. He envisioned weekends revolving around family activities with them, not, as he put it, "the Yuppie weekends Mara envisioned."

b. *Practical problems.* Here are some problems that are likely to be major issues in your family. The quicker you discuss them, the better.
   - How will finances be handled?
   - How will discipline be handled?
   - How will you deal with ex-spouses and ex-in-laws?
   - What problems are likely to arise?
   - How will you handle problems and conflicts when they *do* arise? (Don't bury problems and hope they will disappear.) Work together as a coalition to find compromises or solutions.

c. *Feelings.* If you discuss feelings on an ongoing basis, you will be able to empathize with each other's unique perspective. Fear, guilt, jealousy, anger, and resentment are common feelings in remarried families. They are natural and to be expected, so don't be ashamed of them or hide them. If you cannot understand how your spouse can feel as he or she does, don't be judgmental ("There's no reason to feel that way."). The feelings are very real to your partner, whether or not they seem logical to you. Empathize with those feelings ("I didn't know you felt that way. It must be pretty hard."). Getting to know as much as you can about each other's feelings will help you to function as a team that searches for solutions as problems arise, points out Patricia Papernow, a Cambridge, Massachusetts, psychologist who studies stepfamily development. Even if you see no way to change a disturbing situation, your support and empathy will help.

   You might also want to talk about the compromises each of you must make. Sacrifices are easier to make when they are recognized and appreciated.

d. *Children's concerns.* If children are to feel that this is really *their* family, they should be involved with solving family problems and making family decisions. The principle of open communication extends to them. It is a good idea to have weekly family meetings. Begin by finding out children's expectations about the new family and the role the stepparent will play in it. If everyone starts off with incompatible or unrealistic expectations, there is likely to be a good deal of dissatisfaction and disappointment. One child may assume the family will continue as usual and a new stepmother will somehow "fit in" inconspicuously, whereas a younger child may assume that the addition of the stepmother will automatically create the close-knit family she has always wanted. A teen may assume his new stepdad will continue to be his pal, whereas his stepdad may assume that he will become the head of the family, setting and enforcing the rules. A preschooler may be excited about finally having a dad like his friends do, but his new stepdad may have no interest in filling a fatherly role. Each of these situations is ripe for problems unless expectations are drawn out in the open, discussed, negotiated, and modified to become more realistic.

Get children's input about what is working in the family and what isn't. Make it a rule at family meetings that each person gets a turn to be heard, and create an atmosphere in which everyone's opinions and feelings are respected regardless of age. If you teach children to use "I" statements when they express their feelings, other members in the family are less likely to feel attacked and become defensive. To use I statements, start a statement with an "I" and follow it with the way you feel—for example, "I feel I don't get any privacy," not "Everybody keeps barging in on me and won't leave me alone." Or, "I feel like I'm always on the short end around here," not "*Her* kids always come first around here." Or, "I'm angry that I have more chores than Philip and Emily," not "It's not fair. Philip and Emily don't do a thing around here, and I get stuck with all the work." I statements were discussed in more detail in Chapter 5.

When there are problems in the family, try using the problem-solving method discussed in Chapter 15 to find mutually acceptable solutions. If everyone is involved in finding solutions, there will be a greater commitment to stick to them.

STRATEGY #2: SET REALISTIC FAMILY GOALS

How would each person in the family like to see this new family take form? Agreeing on some long-term family goals will help you move in positive directions rather than drift down negative paths. With family goals, everyone will be working together as a team toward the same ends.

You and your partner, as the "executive team" in the family, should first formulate some clear ideas about the direction you would like the family to take. Then get the whole family involved. An effective way to get everyone thinking about long-term goals is to have each member fantasize about the kind of family they would like in the future, suggests David Mills, Director of the Montlake Institute Family Therapy Training Program in Seattle. Even young children will be able to do this at some level. Realize that the goals you set will be tentative and may change as the family develops.

Janet and Mark Rothstein and their children originally agreed that she would take little responsibility for his two older sons, who were already quite independent, and that he would take little responsibility for her two young sons, who were very involved with their father. They all decided they would be satisfied if they learned to respect one another, live in harmony, and have some enjoyable times together. Several years later, when the older boys had both moved out of the house, Mark wondered if he could play a more active fatherly role with his stepchildren. Since both the children had come to feel positively toward him and he made it clear that he did not want to replace their real dad, the youngsters were willing. Janet, who would now have to give up some of her influence and time with her children because of Mark's potential new role in their lives, also agreed to work toward this new family goal. All agreed that this new approach may make them feel more like a family.

Your goals, of course, must be realistic, and you might have to offer children guidance here. Don't let yourselves fall into one of the traps created by stepfamily myths (Chapter 20). For example, functioning like a traditional family should not be a goal, unless perhaps all children are very young and former spouses and their kin have long disappeared from the picture of their own accord.

To help you set realistic goals, you should be aware of the following considerations.

Average Adjustment Time for Stepfamilies

Experts' estimations of the time it generally takes for stepfamilies to become comfortably unified and integrated range from a minimum of 1½ years (if children are very young) to more than 5 years. At least during the first 2 years, expect stress. Also expect that relationships and family life will feel awkward and contrived. If you expect to feel like a family during this time, you are likely to be frustrated and disappointed.

Children's Ages

The older that children are (up till the late teens), the more resistant they usually are to the new family and the longer their adjustment is likely to take.

Preschool children have the least difficulty adjusting, and some may even welcome a stepparent in their lives. For children over 10, some experts caution that it is unlikely that a stepparent will ever play a role similar to that of a biological parent (that is, be involved in a great deal of nurturing and limit setting).

The older that children are, the more critical it is that they be allowed a voice in how the new family will take form, advise nationally recognized stepfamily experts Emily and John Visher. The more their input is taken into consideration in family matters, the more likely they are to grow to feel that it is truly *their* family.

Teens have a particularly difficult time in stepfamilies. Entering a stepfamily usually arouses very serious loyalty conflicts for them. Furthermore, because they are in the process of grappling with sexual issues, most teens find the obvious sexual implications of the new marital relationship disturbing. To complicate matters further, the needs of a stepfamily collide with adolescents' needs: While stepfamilies want all family members to make a commitment to the family, adolescents have strong developmental needs to loosen emotional family ties.

It is best to give teens space rather than make strong demands for family participation, the Vishers advise. Without this space, there may be constant friction in your home. Another common source of serious conflict with this age group is the differential treatment of stepchildren. However, the thorniest issue is usually discipline from a stepparent. Teens very much need rules and limits, but the biological parent may have to be the disciplinarian rather than the stepparent. The issue of discipline in stepfamilies will be discussed in detail shortly.

Loosening demands on family participation and giving teens space does not mean that a teen should be allowed to treat a stepmother as a convenient housekeeper or a stepfather as a meal ticket. Parents should lay the ground rules for their teens so they treat stepparents with respect and do not take advantage of them.

It may be reassuring to learn that many young people become closer to their stepfamilies after their stormy teen years are over. In fact, many become friends with a stepparent they disliked while growing up.

Boys Versus Girls

Girls generally have more difficulty making the transition to a stepfamily than boys. (In fact, boys, especially younger ones, sometimes thrive when a stepfather joins the family.) Girls, on the other hand, tend to have more stressful relationships with both stepmothers and stepfathers. Why this is so can only be speculated. Girls generally become close to their single moms, and it would be natural for them to perceive a new stepfather as a competitor and threat to the close mother-daughter bond they've formed. Girls are also more likely to feel threatened and displaced by stepmothers, since daughters are often elevated to the prestigious status of "woman of the house" in their single dads' homes.

Stepmothers Versus Stepfathers

The role of a stepmother is more difficult than that of a stepfather, and stepmothers generally have a more stressful time in stepfamilies. Much of the problem seems to lie in the fact that women in our society generally shoulder the primary responsibility for the care and nurturance of children, as well as for the smooth functioning of the home. Because a woman is a stepmother does not seem to relieve her of these expectations, but her pivotal position in the family provides greater opportunity for disharmony with her stepchildren.

Stepmothers are sensitive to the stereotype of the "wicked stepmother," deeply ingrained in our society by popular fairy tales. Most also accept the stepfamily myths of the instant family, instant love, and instant adjustment. Consequently, as a group, stepmothers are found to create unrealistically high expectations for themselves that they cannot possibly achieve. It is not unusual for a new stepmother to fantasize about the happy, close-knit family she will instantly create, in which she becomes a supermom to appreciative stepchildren who immediately return her love. The harsh reality she encounters instead is a shock. It must be that she is doing something wrong, she assumes, so she tries harder. But the more she pushes, the more resistance she is likely to encounter from children who fear that their acceptance of her will betray their real mother. The more she pushes, the more tension there is.

Stepmothers are more successful when they move into new roles slowly, and they are generally happier when they have interests outside the family that provide them fulfillment and give their self-esteem a boost. Many stepmothers are firm advocates of stepparent support groups, which are now offered in many communities through family or community agencies and community colleges.

STRATEGY #3: BUILD A STRONG COUPLE RELATIONSHIP

The cornerstone of a successful stepfamily is a strong couple relationship, stepfamily experts agree. It is this relationship that holds the stepfamily together and prevents it from splitting into the original family groups. In successful stepfamilies, couples generally assume the role of the "executive team" in the family. The executive team guides the family along in the blending process, provides children with rules and limits, and guides them in the process of growing up. The couple discusses issues and decides on a direction they would like to take before discussing the issues with other members of the family. And if no mutually agreeable family decisions can be made, the executive team's combined judgment takes precedence.

When children see their parent and stepparent working together as an executive team or coalition to make the family successful, it is a signal to them that it is safe to make a commitment to this new family—that it is not likely to end in divorce, too. It is also a clear signal that they cannot divide and conquer the couple or make the stepparent leave by causing havoc in the marriage.

John and Emily Visher report that many couples have trouble shifting their primary commitment from their children to each other because they feel that it is a betrayal of their children. However, in the long run, your youngsters will benefit in a number of ways if you are able to make this shift and join your spouse in the role of executive teammates. The most obvious benefits to your children are a stronger family and less likelihood of experiencing the trauma of a second divorce. There will be future benefits for them, too. They will find it easier to visualize success in their own future relationships if they see you happy in a good relationship. In a sense, you will be giving them a working model of a good marital relationship that they will be able to use one day themselves.

Because of the constant presence of children in your lives, you and your spouse may have to be creative in arranging time alone together to build your relationship. Try setting aside a time each day for yourselves. If you can't find privacy in your home, try taking walks. Meet for breakfast or lunch one day a week or arrange an evening out alone. It is a good idea to have frequent discussions about how your marriage and family life are going, but plan some fun time, too. In your efforts to work on your own relationship, however, don't go overboard and exclude your children from your lives. They very much need your support during the early years of your remarried family. It's one of the challenges of a stepfamily to strike a good balance between adults' needs and children's needs.

STRATEGY #4: MOVE SLOWLY; DO NOT PUSH

You may recall that many of the common problems stepfamilies develop stem from their trying to move too quickly, denying the new family the necessary time it needs to blend and adjust. Moving slowly is a *must*! Here are some important guidelines.

Limit Change in Children's Lives

A stepfamily represents major change for children who have already had more than their share of upset in their relatively short lives. Children are adaptive and can usually adjust to some change quite well. However, the more changes heaped on them, the more difficulty they have coping. For this reason, keep children's lives and environments as consistent as you can.

Identify what things will need to change. Then prioritize them. Which things need to change immediately? What can wait for a short while? What can wait indefinitely? From your "immediate" list, choose a few to work on at a time. However, limit the *rate* at which you introduce those changes, and try to keep other aspects of children's lives the same. As youngsters adjust to initial changes, you can introduce additional changes *gradually*.

The most critical area in which to limit change is in children's relationships with their natural parents (unless, of course, relationships will be improved). A good relationship with a parent provides children a buffer from stress, and there is a good deal of stress in the early years of a stepfamily. Moreover, one of the most threatening aspects of a stepfamily to a child is losing a relationship with a parent. Assure your children of your continued love, and prove it by continuing to spend some time alone with each of them, doing some of the things you did together when you were single. If you are a stepparent without children of your own, allow your spouse and stepchildren the time they need together; it is critical for the success of your family. Children also need to be assured that they can continue their relationships with their absent parent without threat of displeasing you. Here are some other steps you can take to limit the rate of change in your children's lives.

- Retain as many familiar everyday routines as you can. This will be more of a problem when two sets of children with different routines join together, but usually some routines from each family can be retained. One new stepfamily had such different and incompatible daily routines that they had to rotate weeks—one week following one contingent's routines and the next week following the other's.
- Maintain consistency in rules and discipline. This will be discussed in greater detail shortly.
- Think about the status and privileges each of your children had in your single-parent home, and try to maintain as many of them as is feasible. An area easily overlooked is the adult roles and responsibilities your children have been accustomed to. Most parents assume their children will be happy to be relieved of their adult responsibilities without realizing the special status they carry. Even many youngsters who had bitterly complained about their responsibilities feel displaced and resentful when a stepparent takes over their roles. No one feels good about being "fired." It is a good idea to get children's input about how the household responsibilities and roles should now be divided and to continue granting children the status attached to those responsibilities they continue. Some negotiation may be required. For example, a teen who has been preparing the family's meals may feel resentful if a stepmother displaces her from

the kitchen. However, she may be pleased to prepare dinners two evenings a week for an appreciative family, and it would give her stepmother a break, too. Changes in privileges are also common when youngsters lose their positions as oldest, youngest, or only child in the family. It is hard enough for youngsters to lose their special position in the family, but when the accompanying status and benefits are suddenly lost too, they receive a double whammy.

- Although moving is a likely possibility, look for a way that youngsters can remain in the same school for at least a year and continue to see their old friends.

Although limiting changes in children's lives may sound easy in theory, it raises two major problems in stepfamilies. The first arises when a stepfamily unites two sets of children from different homes, with different rules and privileges. It is quite a feat to keep life fairly consistent for each set and still be fair to everyone. Children generally object to differential treatment of stepsiblings. A good approach is to involve children in some constructive problem solving during family meetings, using the method discussed in chapter 15. In this way, you can find compromises and solutions with which everyone can agree. Don't work on too many things at one time or everyone will become confused. Zero in on a few areas that everyone agrees are important to the smooth functioning of the family. You say your children are too young? Even young children should be able to feel that they have a say in at least some of the changes in their lives. With young children, try presenting them with a plan that is fair to each of them. Point out the problems that are being created by having different rules for different children, and ask them whether they think the new plan will work. Their reactions might result in ideas you hadn't considered. Try to get a commitment from them to try a new plan, whether the original one or a modification. They will be more willing to comply with changes they have agreed to than with changes that are forced on them. If they completely balk at anything you suggest, say, "Well, let's try this for a few weeks and see how it works. How about it?" You'll probably get an "Okay."

Limiting change in children's lives also creates problems for stepparents without children who enter a "ready-made" family. These stepparents usually feel like guests or boarders in what is supposed to be their own homes and, therefore, have strong needs to change the status quo. If you are in this situation, it is a good idea to plan to feel like an outsider for a while, cautions Patricia Papernow, a Cambridge, Massachusetts, psychologist and stepfamily researcher. However, try to identify one or two changes that would make a significant difference to you, Papernow suggests. Your spouse should be the one to introduce the changes to the children. As the changes become part of the family routine, one or two more can be introduced. As you build your relationship with your stepchildren and become an insider in the family rather than an outsider, you will also be able to play a more significant role in how the family will function.

Slowly Build Your Relationship with Each of Your Stepchildren

Building a relationship with stepchildren cannot be rushed. *Any* relationship takes time to build, but stepparent-stepchild relationships take longer. This is because a parent's remarriage usually raises issues that children need to work out before they become comfortable with a stepparent. One of these is loyalty conflicts. Most children worry about whether accepting their stepparent is disloyal or upsetting to their absent parent. Your marriage may also raise another painful issue for your stepchildren. They may have to *finally* let go of long-held hopes that their parents will reconcile and that their old comfortable lives will return someday. It takes a child time to resolve loyalty conflicts and to completely relinquish old hopes of having his or her family back together again.

For these reasons, stepparents' early attempts at affection and a relationship are usually met with indifference, passive resistance, or outright hostility. Children need to keep their distance while they resolve their conflicts and losses. Even many stepparents who have previously had a friendly relationship with a child find that the relationship falls apart once the marriage is official. Usually a low-key approach is best. Once again, *do not push*.

The following suggestions may be helpful to stepparents in building relationships with stepchildren.

- Right from the start, let each child know that the relationship he or she has with the absent parent will *always* be very special and that you do not wish to interfere with it. You merely hope that someday you will have a place in their lives *too*. If they understand that they do not have to give up one adult in their lives to accept another, their loyalty conflicts will be reduced, and they will be more likely to accept you.
- Be friendly and available, but let them take the lead. Give them the distance they need.
- Go very slowly with expressing affection, especially physical affection. Let it develop at its own pace. After a while, you might give a child a brief, friendly touch, and watch for a reaction. The older the child, the more cautious you should be.
- Try to find some interest that you have in common with each of your stepchildren, and try to arrange to enjoy your mutual interest together—sports, museums, music, cooking, crafts, movies, shopping.
- Try to spend time with each of your stepchildren without your partner along, so you will get to know each other as individuals.
- Be positive. Elizabeth Einstein, founding editor of *The Stepfamily Bulletin*

and author of many books and articles on stepfamilies, suggests you compliment them when they do something well; show appreciation when they make an effort; respond when they are friendly. If you particularly like something about a child, say so "I love to listen to you play the piano." "I like the way you dress." "I like the way you are so considerate."

- If you discover things your stepchildren enjoy and make them available (their favorite food in the refrigerator, paints or wood in the garage for projects), it will make them feel more valued.
- Develop empathy. Remember the changes and losses they are trying to cope with and the conflicts they are trying to sort out. Try to put yourself in their place, and try to understand how they are feeling.
- Although it is unlikely you will ever *feel* the same way about your stepchildren as you do about your own, aim to treat all the children in the family fairly so your stepchildren do not feel like second-class citizens. This does not mean that you have to treat all the children identically, point out Emily and John Visher. After all, they have different needs, likes, and dislikes. Don't feel that you must include the entire group in everything you do, either. Your own children need some individual time with you (as your stepchildren need with your spouse). It would be preferable to do some things with your own children individually and arrange to spend some time with your stepchildren individually, too. Where will you find the time for all this individual attention? Individual time does not have to be extensive for children to feel special. Invite a child on an errand and stop for an ice cream. Help a child with homework, read a story, or play a favorite game. Ask a youngster to help you bake cookies, cook a special meal, or work on a fun project.
- Even though your stepchildren may be far from your ideal of what children should be like, don't start out by trying to make them over or change the way they do things. They will only resent you and resist your efforts. If you are ever going to change anything about them, it will be *after* you have developed a relationship with them.
- Try not to interpret your stepchildren's negative behavior as a personal attack on you. It has more to do with the fact that you married their parent and are a potential threat to their relationships with both their parents than it has to do with you personally. Their negative behavior is natural and to be expected for a while.
- Try not to become defensive when your stepchildren talk about their missing parent, no matter how much they idealize him or her. Allowing them to talk about their absent parent with you will lessen the intensity of their loyalty conflicts, which in the long run will help them to accept you.
- When your stepchildren are around, try to behave *as if* they like you, suggest the Vishers. You will find that you behave differently and send

out different messages. You may also find that they behave differently toward you. We sometimes create our own self-fulfilling prophecies.

- Try some of the techniques discussed in Chapter 10 to open up the lines of communication.
- Ask your spouse for help. He or she will have to stand back and let you develop your own relationships with your stepchildren. Your spouse will also have to refrain from intervening all the time and allow you and your stepchildren to work out your own difficulties. Many parents keep the bonds with their children so tight that it is difficult for stepparents to form their own relationships with them.
- Work on accepting and respecting your stepchildren (and expect polite and respectful behavior from them). Love *may* follow.

STRATEGY #5: DEVELOP YOUR OWN UNIQUE ROLE WITH YOUR STEPCHILDREN; DO NOT TRY TO REPLACE THEIR ABSENT PARENT

Most stepparents initially assume that they will be a parent to their stepchildren. However, when they try to move into that role too quickly, they are usually rebuffed, and the more they push, the more resistance they encounter.

There are many roles stepparents can play other than a parental one—that of an adult friend, a confidant, an adviser, a role model, a support person who offers encouragement, an aunt (or uncle) or older sister (or brother), a neutral third party who buffers conflict in the home. However, the role a stepparent plays needs to evolve over time.

If you are a stepparent and are trying to work out your role in the family, think about your individual strengths and propensities. What role would you ideally *like* to play one day? Decide what you would *like* to do, what you are *willing* to do, and what you are *not willing* to do. Explore possible roles with your partner, and then explore them with your stepchildren. What kind of a stepparent would they like to have? If you stick to specific behavior, you are likely to have a more productive discussion, point out Margaret Crosbie-Burnett of the University of Wisconsin and Constance Ahrons of the University of Southern California. For example, what kinds of things would they like a stepparent to do and to avoid doing? How do they feel about your doing the kinds of things that you were hoping to do? This kind of open discussion helps everyone feel that they have at least *some* control over what is happening in their lives.

Once you understand the family's feelings, try out a role that seems to be comfortable for everyone, and see how it works. You may try out many roles during the first two years before you find your niche. Many stepparents find that the role of an adult friend is the most comfortable and satisfying for everyone. Here are some things to remember about roles.

- Always be yourself and emphasize *your* strengths. Never try to compete with the absent parent. If children make comparisons between you and their other parent, try not to become defensive. Simply state that each of you is different from the other.
- Keep in mind that you will not play a meaningful role in your stepchildren's lives until you have built relationships with them.
- Your role may evolve differently with different stepchildren. With a young child, you may become another parental figure. For a 12-year-old, you may become a caring and supportive adult. To an older teen, you may become a confidant.
- If you are hoping to play a parental role with your stepchildren, aim to be *another* parent rather than a replacement parent. Even if a parent has completely left the picture, he or she needs to be psychologically dead for a child before you are accepted as a replacement.

STRATEGY #6: LET THE BIOLOGICAL PARENT HANDLE DISCIPLINE WHILE THE STEPPARENT BONDS WITH STEPCHILDREN

How to handle discipline is a dilemma for every remarried family, and it is the most common source of serious stepfamily problems, particularly in stepfather families. The approach that usually works best is for the biological parent to continue to handle the discipline during the first year or longer while the stepparent works on building good relationships with the children. Why? First, children need consistency in their lives during this time of upheaval. Second, until a stepparent is accepted as a member of the family rather than as an outsider, children will perceive his or her attempts at discipline as an arbitrary and illegitimate display of power. Most children will resent and fight such attempts. If the stepparent persists, the only way he or she is likely to obtain compliance is by the use of force. The fallout is usually an atmosphere laden with conflict and resentment.

Admittedly, this slow approach to discipline takes a great deal of patience on the part of stepparents, but it is likely to pay off in the long run. There are a number of common outcomes when stepparents move too quickly to assume authority, and none are good. First, children reject, and often hate, their stepparents. Second, many stepfamilies fail to blend; frequently, stepparents withdraw from the family because they feel ineffectual and frustrated. The third common outcome is for families to become enmeshed in prolonged conflict.

And the fourth is for children to act out their anger and develop behavior problems at school and at home.

Here are some pointers for stepparents about discipline.

- Discipline is a topic that should be discussed in depth with your spouse—the sooner the better. If your family is to run smoothly, you will need to agree on long-term disciplinary policies to work toward, and you will need to support each other in this area. You should both be working toward becoming a strong executive team or coalition who will work together and support each other. Otherwise, your children will adopt a divide-and-conquer strategy. Arriving at a mutually agreeable style of parenting may require *ongoing* frank communication and negotiation. Chapter 16 will help ("How to Discipline Effectively and Still Be a Good Guy"). If you have very different parenting styles, it may help to take a parenting course together.
- If you feel that any changes in discipline, standards, or house rules *must* be made right away, discuss them with your partner. Don't go overboard; focus on a few that are critical. At least for the first year, have your partner introduce changes and enforce them with his or her children, advises Patricia Papernow. Children are likely to respond more positively if they are brought into discussions about new rules and their input is considered than if new policies are merely dictated to them. Sometimes, compromises can be reached that will make everyone happy. Jennifer discovered this principle after she created needless conflict.

> When Jennifer joined the family, she thought that her stepchildren's slovenliness would drive her crazy. Deciding she couldn't take it any longer, she laid down the law about picking up their things and cleaning their rooms. They balked at her new rules and ignored them, making her even angrier. When the problem was finally discussed calmly at a family meeting, some compromises were made fairly easily. The children agreed to keep their things out of the common living areas of the house, and Jennifer agreed that their rooms were their domain, to be kept as they saw fit as long as the doors were kept closed.

- During the first year or longer, concentrate on developing some common ground with your stepchildren. Get to know one another, and build a warm relationship with each child individually. Refrain from lecturing, nagging, scolding, and punishing. Keep any attempts to control their behavior very positive—praise, appreciation, or incentives ("If we all work together to get the chores done, we'll have time to rent a movie.").
- When you are with your stepchildren for long periods when your spouse is away from the home, he or she should specifically tell the children that you are in charge and will enforce the rules and make decisions. Children

should know what the rules are, what their parent expects of them, and the consequences if they do not follow rules or expectations. If these are clear ahead of time, it will be *their* decision whether to incur the consequences, and you will not become the heavy.

- Respect your stepchildren and expect respect in return. Also, set your own *personal* limits with them. Examples of personal limits are setting a policy about their use of your personal property or asking them to turn music down after a certain hour if it interferes with your sleep.
- At least for the first year, try to keep out of battles between your partner and his or her children. Many mental health professionals suggest that stepparents occasionally side with a child if they believe the child is right. This helps to build a child's trust in a stepparent as a fair person. There will be times when your spouse also needs your support, but don't make it a habit to take sides openly.
- As your relationship with your stepchild develops, *slowly* move into a more active disciplinary role. Progress from enforcing your spouse's rules in his or her absence to enforcing rules even though your partner is present, suggests Jamie Keshet, Director of Stepfamily Services at Riverside Family Counseling Inc., in Newtonville, Massachusetts, and author of *Love and Power in the Stepfamily*, then gradually work up to becoming an equal partner with your spouse in a team effort to set and enforce rules. At some point, you may be able to set and enforce rules completely independently. It may take two or three years to get to this point, and you are unlikely to ever get to this point with a teenager. With a teen, your disciplinary role may be limited to actively supporting your spouse in his or her disciplinary actions, point out Emily and John Visher. If discipline is not your spouse's strong suit, Chapter 16 will help. Teens *do* need clear rules and limits.
- When you do assume a disciplinary role, be sure to use an authorita*tive* parenting style, rather than an authorita*rian* one. An authoritative style is one in which you are warm and respectful of children, seek their input, and are sensitive to their needs and opinions. At the same time, it is clear that you are an equal partner of an executive team that is in charge of the family and that you provide clear rules and expectations. Although this approach, discussed in greater detail in Chapter 15, is preferable for *any* parent, it is found to be especially effective for stepparents.
- Be aware that unless your partner supports you, you will make little headway in disciplining your stepchildren. If you find they continually ignore you or buck you on some issue, discuss the problem with your spouse. You may find that he or she does not agree with you, and the children have sensed this. If this is the case, you need to renegotiate the rules with your spouse, not demand compliance from your stepchildren.

If you tried to discipline too early and are already enmeshed in conflict with your stepchildren, here is the standard procedure that mental health professionals recommend: Back off and allow their natural parent to handle *all* discipline while you remain completely neutral. You might also try this approach if your stepchildren have withdrawn or have developed behavioral problems at home or at school. Children often express their anger or distress in these less obvious ways. As the situation improves and you and your stepchild develop a better relationship, you can try to take a more active role once again, but do so *very gradually*. If the situation still does not improve, a mental health professional may be very helpful in getting your family back on track.

What about families with two sets of children who are used to very different rules and discipline? This complicates the discipline problem because children are likely to resent it if stepsiblings live by different rules. It will take a good deal of discussion, negotiation, and compromise to achieve some kind of balance for all the children. Once again, as discussed previously in strategy #4 (limiting change), children should be involved in discussions and decisions about new house rules and new discipline policies. If you are going to have a truly blended family, everyone's needs and input must be considered.

Try to limit the number of areas in which you make new rules to fewer than five. There are only so many things you can work on effectively at one time. Choose the areas that are most important to your family's smooth functioning. Once some ground rules are agreed on, you might try what one couple did. Each partner rewarded his or her *stepchildren* for their compliance with the new family rules and imposed consequences on their *own* children for noncompliance.

STRATEGY #7: BUILD A FAMILY IDENTITY

One of the most important tasks during the first two years of a stepfamily's life is to develop some sense of family identity. Much of it will emerge gradually as a result of the blending process.

Blending

As you work out the mechanics of living together in a mutually agreeable lifestyle, feelings of belonging will grow—*providing* there is a real blending of the two contingents rather than one swallowing up the other's identity.

As the executive team in the family, you and your spouse should first discuss possible ways of combining disparate life-styles and identities. Then seek children's input. Youngsters generally assume that their family's ways of doing things are the "right" way and usually want to stick to those ways. Help them see that there are no right and wrong ways, just *different* ways. Create an atmosphere in which differences are accepted, new ideas are tried, and ongoing negotiation and compromises are par for the course. Gradually, you will all begin to feel like members of the same team working toward a common future.

Many well-functioning stepfamilies report that weekly family meetings were an indispensable part of their lives while trying to blend their two contingents. During these meetings, they discussed problems, tried to find solutions, shared feelings, aired grievances, and congratulated one another for the progress they had made to date. Some stepfamilies have been known to hold *nightly* meetings during the early stages in which they discussed what was working and what wasn't. Emily and John Visher suggest having two containers handy in your home in which family members can leave comments—one container for bothersome issues and the other for things that are appreciated and liked in the family.

If you have trouble breaking down the walls between the two contingents in your stepfamily, a technique therapists often use is having each side of the family share their pre-stepfamily pasts with each other—memories of early childhoods, first families, single-parent homes, and the early months of the stepfamily. It is a great icebreaker, even for stepsiblings who appear to be hopelessly antagonistic toward one another. Twelve-year-old Jeanne opened up to 11-year-old Angela after learning how Angela felt about leaving her home, bedroom, school, and friends and moving into Jeanne's bedroom. Jeanne had been so busy resenting having to share her bedroom with Angela that the two had exchanged only hostilities before.

There are some other steps you can take that will help build a family identity.

Family Traditions and Rituals

Consciously develop some family rituals and traditions. They bind a family together and give it a feeling of "we-ness" and legitimacy. Some can be taken over from each contingent and some completely new ones can be created. Try the following:

- Find things to do or places to go that the entire family enjoys—bicycling, camping, hiking, picnicking, going to the movies, visiting museums, playing softball, and so forth. Be sure to involve children in coming up with ideas. When you find a winner, make it a frequent family activity. It will soon come to symbolize the new family in each member's mind.
- A good way to develop a sense of "home," reports Mary Whiteside, a psychologist at Ann Arbor Center for the Family in Ann Arbor, Michigan, is to set aside a few specific times during the week in which all family members *routinely* do something together—a weekly family meeting, a

family dinner or breakfast, a time for everyone to do chores, renting a video, an evening of cards or board games, going out for pizza or ice cream. When you find something that works well, make it a weekly routine. Don't go overboard. Your children are likely to resist *excessive* attempts at family unity.

- Develop some new family traditions around birthdays, holidays, and your stepfamily's anniversary. One family decided to jointly make their father's favorite dinner on his birthday and had so much fun doing it that it was the start of a tradition for everyone's birthday. Another family made it a tradition to go out to a special restaurant every year on the stepfamily's anniversary. Deciding how to spend holidays is pretty rough for many stepfamilies during their first year or two together because each side understandably feels that their way is best. Discuss both families' traditions and see if you can arrive at some way to combine the two. One family decided they would cook both roast beef with Yorkshire pudding *and* turkey with all the trimmings for their first Christmas dinner. Another had such different ways of decorating their Christmas tree that they decided to buy all new decorations that they chose together.
- Try brainstorming to arrive at creative solutions for new traditions. If a family identity is going to take shape, it is important that both sides of the family agree rather than one foisting their traditions on the other.

Building a Family History

Family identity also evolves from building a history together. Make a conscious effort to make your family more aware of its history. Celebrate your stepfamily anniversary together and reminisce over the wedding, the early months, and the events of the past year. Of course, you don't need anniversaries to recall events that you shared. Reminisce from time to time when you are all together, recalling the bad along with the good. It is *all* part of your history. Keep a scrapbook of the new family in a visible place, and occasionally spend time looking at it together. If you add new pictures to it while everyone "happens" to be present, it will seem less contrived to invite children to go through it. Of course, while you're looking at it, talk about the events surrounding some of the pictures ("Remember the day this was taken? What a disaster!").

STRATEGY #8: DO NOT ATTEMPT TO FREEZE OUT THE OTHER BIOLOGICAL PARENT OR FORCE LOYALTY ISSUES

Contrary to the instincts of many remarried couples, stepfamilies usually work best when children are able to continue relationships with their outside parent. Many remarried couples try to exclude the outside parent from children's lives (either physically or psychologically) and try to replace that parent with the stepparent. However, to a child, a stepparent is someone *in addition to* a natural parent, not a replacement for that parent. Children reserve a special slot in their lives for a natural parent and usually fight any attempt to fill that slot with someone else. At some point, a stepparent may earn a special place in a child's life, but it is usually a *new* slot that a child gradually creates.

The outcome of trying to freeze out the real parent is frequently the opposite of that intended. It is generally the stepparent who loses out when loyalty issues are forced. This is likely to be the case even when biological parents are only minimally involved in children's lives, because youngsters tend to fear that their outside parent will be driven away *completely*.

On the other hand, when the relationship with the absent parent is protected, most children seem better able to accept and relate to stepparents. When they do not have to deal with severe loyalty conflicts or give up a relationship with a parent, they are more likely to be relaxed in the new family and more comfortable with forming a relationship with another adult. Trying to freeze out the other parent is very likely to be detrimental to your stepfamily and even

---

Eight Successful Strategies for Stepfamilies

✓ 1. Open communication.
   - Have you discussed expectations, finances, discipline?
   - Do you discuss feelings, problems, and conflict?
   - Do you seek children's input and involve them in family decisions?
✓ 2. Set realistic family goals.
   - Don't be misguided by the four stepfamily myths.
   - Are you all working on the same team for the same goals?
✓ 3. Build a strong couple relationship; be an executive team.
✓ 4. Move slowly; do not push.
   - Are you limiting the changes in children's lives?
   - Are you protecting parent-child relationships?
   - Are you allowing children space to resolve losses and conflicts and develop relationships at their own pace?
✓ 5. Develop your *own* unique role with stepchildren.
   - Are you allowing your role to evolve over time?
   - Remember: Never try to replace the absent parent.
✓ 6. Let the biological parent handle the discipline while the stepparent bonds with the children.
✓ 7. Build a family identity.
   - Is *everyone* involved in blending the new family?
   - Are you developing new traditions?
   - Are you consciously building a family history?
✓ 8. Support children's relationships with the outside parent.

---

more detrimental to the children. (Read Chapter 18 about the important role parents without custody play in their children's lives.)

The best situation for children is one in which conflict between parents is minimized and children are given permission by each parent to love the other parent. It will help you to be supportive of children's relationships with their outside parent if you model your family after what stepfamily experts call a *linked* family, a term originally coined by Doris Jacobson of the University of California at Los Angeles. A linked family consists of two households—the custodial parent's and the noncustodial parent's, with children representing the link between the two.

Ideally, say mental health professionals, children will be parented by what John and Emily Visher call a *parenting coalition*, consisting of both natural parents and, if either is remarried, the stepparents. This is not a farfetched notion. Many couples carry it off, and their children reap the benefits. Ultimately, the respective stepfamilies reap benefits as well. Here are some pointers to help parents develop a linked family for children.

- Develop a strong couple relationship so that contact with a former spouse does not cause jealousy and suspicion.
- Keep in mind how important it is for children to maintain a relationship with their other parent (Chapter 18). This will help you to become willing to share the power and responsibilities of child rearing with your children's other parent.
- Be sure you have resolved the end of your previous marriage and the relationship with your former spouse. Chapter 6 will help you if you have not.
- If you have not already done so, take steps to restructure your relationship with your children's other parent so you learn to interact on a *different* basis—as co-parents for your children rather than as ex-spouses. Also make every effort to end your conflict with your former spouse, at least in your children's presence. Chapter 11 will help you with both of these.
- If your former spouse is the one who hasn't let go of the marriage or persists in an adversarial relationship, remember that it takes two to fight. Learn to respond with completely neutral statements rather than getting dragged into a battle. "Thank you for sharing that with me. I really must hang up now" is likely to nip a potential fight in the bud. Chapter 11 also provides techniques to help you communicate and negotiate effectively with a hostile ex-spouse. You will also need to limit contact with your ex. If he or she calls continually, set a specific time during the day when it will least interfere with your daily life and accept calls *only* during that time. Learn to keep all conversations focused on the children. When your ex digresses, steer the conversation back on track. Keep conversations short.

- If you feel you cannot deal with your former spouse, see if your new spouse can act as the go-between. In some linked families, it is the two stepparents who make all the arrangements for children.
- Allow your children to come and go freely between your home and your former spouse's home. When they return, always give them time to themselves to make the transition between homes. Don't try to compete with or undermine the other home, and don't pry into what is going on there. If children insist on sharing information about the other home, allow them to, but take what they say with a grain of salt. Sometimes children tell their parents what they think the parents *want* to hear. Sometimes they try to play one parent against the other. (Read about how to handle it in Chapter 17.)
- Although your children should be free to move freely back and forth between your home and their other parent's home, a former spouse should not be free to interject him- or herself into your lives. You and your spouse should feel that you have a separate and private life with each other. Stepparents frequently complain that it feels as if there are three adults in the family—the couple and a former partner. A typical scenario is for a former partner to continually ask for and receive favors, often at the expense of the present partner. Though being at the beck and call of a former mate may ease one's guilt over leaving a marriage, it is usually bad for the new marriage.
- Linked families work best if everyone's roles, responsibilities, and expectations are clear. Read about determining roles and responsibilities and parenting plans in Chapter 11. Some linked families work out their respective roles and responsibilities with the help of a family mediator (Chapter 2).

It may comfort you to know that many couples report that their anger and discomfort diminish over time, once they start working together for their children's sake. Most former spouses in linked families eventually come to feel detached from each other, as if they were acquaintances.

SEEKING OUTSIDE SUPPORT

A decade ago, few resources were available to help stepfamilies during their early difficult years. Not so now. Besides books such as this one, classes for stepfamily couples are available in many communities. Check your local community colleges, educational extension programs, or community agencies for a class in your area.

A lifeline for many stepparents or stepfamily couples is a support group. Some groups consist of couples, others are restricted to stepparents. Many people continue in such groups for years, thriving on the support they receive and learning from the ideas they share. Don't feel you cannot join a support group because you are not new to stepfamiy life. Check your local family and community agencies for a support group in your area. If you cannot find one, consider starting your own by placing a notice in a local school, church, or community newspaper. There are plenty of stepfamilies around, and most of them would like some support just as much as you would.

Subscribing to a stepfamily newsletter is another way to feel connected with other stepfamilies and to learn about new ideas. Three are available: "The Stepfamily Foundation Quarterly," published by The Stepfamily Foundation, 333 West End Avenue, New York, NY 10023; "Stepfamilies Quarterly," published by The Stepfamily Association of America, 215 Centennial Mall S, Suite 212, Lincoln, NE 68508; and "Stepfamilies and Beyond," published by Listening, Inc., 8716 Pine Avenue, Gary, IN 46403.

Does your family feel overwhelmed by the practical problems it faces in becoming a full-fledged family? If you cannot work out the details of family life in a satisfactory way, consider enlisting the help of a family mediator. Some stepfamilies and soon-to-be stepfamilies are choosing this route to help them sort through the complexities of stepfamily living, find creative solutions to their practical problems, and negotiate how they will implement those solutions. Examples of issues stepfamilies can deal with in mediation are financial issues (Chapter 22), the mechanics of living together, setting up house rules, numerous day-to-day problems, and the role the stepparent plays in the family. Depending upon the issue, either the couple or the entire family is involved. As mentioned earlier, some biological parents and their respective spouses meet together with a mediator to work out how they will jointly parent children. Since mediation is a process of rational problem solving and negotiation, it is particularly well suited for stepfamilies to work out many of the complex details of stepfamily life. It may help you avoid a good deal of chaos and stress during your stepfamily's early years. Mediation as it is used in divorce is discussed in Chapter 2.

Is your family enmeshed in serious conflict about emotional and relationship problems (rather than practical problems)? A family therapist may be able to help. Be sure it is one who specializes in stepfamilies. Your family cannot operate like a traditional family, and trying to make it do so will simply compound your problems.

You may still have a long list of questions about your stepfamily and what is best for it. The principles discussed in the previous two chapters can be extrapolated to answer many questions, but not all. The following chapter consists of a question-and-answer forum of such questions that stepparents often ask.

22

A QUESTION-AND-ANSWER FORUM FOR STEPFAMILIES

How much say should my children have in whether I remarry?

There is wide agreement among mental health professionals that children should never be given the power to decide whether or not a parent should remarry. Children simply lack the perspective that is necessary to make a rational decision on this issue. The qualities they look for in an adult are not necessarily the qualities you want in a marriage partner. Additionally, children's decisions are likely to be based on present circumstances and their limited perception of the way your new marriage will impact them. Your children's feelings and concerns should be one factor in your decision, but the choice should not be theirs. While you are considering your youngsters' feelings and concerns, take into account that most children are ambivalent, if not negative, about a parent's remarriage. (Learn why in Chapter 20.)

I would like to remarry but am hesitant to put my children through another major change. Is there some optimum time when children are likely to adjust more easily to a parent's remarriage?

In general, children whose parents remarry between two and four years after the family breakup seem to adjust more easily. If you marry too quickly, your children may not have sufficient time to thoroughly mourn the loss of their family and old way of life. However, the longer they live in a single-parent home, the more likely it is that they will resent a stepparent for intruding in their lives and threatening their relationships with you.

The fact that divorce rates are higher for second marriages discourages me. What are the reasons thought to be responsible for this?

There seem to be two separate reasons. The first is that complications stem from children and former spouses. The second is that remarried people are a select population—those who have come to accept divorce as a viable solution to an unhappy marriage. In fact, in their study of remarried families, Frank Furstenberg of the University of Pennsylvania and Graham Spanier of the State University of New York at Stony Brook found that their remarried study group generally felt that it would take *less* to convince them to divorce a second time than it did the first time. It is perhaps surprising that the redivorce rate is only slightly higher than the divorce rate for first marriages. Perhaps the reason can be found in the reports of remarried couples who generally say their marriage choices are better the second time around and that they have more realistic expectations. They also report better communication with their second spouses and greater self-knowledge as a consequence of their divorces.

Are there any steps I should take to prepare my children for my remarriage and life in a stepfamily?

Absolutely! Remarriage is yet another major change in children's lives and opens the door once again to uncertainty, stress, and anxiety for them. It is important to take steps to prepare them emotionally. Do the following:

- Tell them about your upcoming marriage long before it occurs, and arrange for them to spend a good deal of time with their future stepparent (including some one-on-one time) so they can begin building good relationships with each other.
- Reassure each child that your love for him or her is unshakable and that your relationship will not be threatened.
- Reassure them that their relationships with their other parent and that parent's extended family will be protected. They should know that their new stepparent is not to be a replacement parent. This is critical, so be sure to stick to it!.
- Don't build up their new stepparent and promise them they will love life in their new family. Adjustment will take time, and giving them unrealistic expectations will set them up for disappointment.
- Encourage them to express their concerns and feelings, and try to deal with their concerns as best you can. (Children's usual concerns are discussed in Chapter 20.) Their feelings are likely to be ambivalent or negative. Don't try to minimize their feelings or talk them out of them ("Don't be silly. There's nothing to worry about. Everything will be fine."). Their feelings are very real to them and, if not expressed verbally, may be acted out in troublesome behavior. Accept their feelings and show them empathy ("I can see you're really worried. It must be scary for you not knowing what it will be like living in a new home with a new family."). Suppose they tell you that they don't like their future stepparent? Don't panic. This isn't unusual. Tell them that it takes time for liking and relationships to develop. Then allow them enough time and space for positive feelings to

develop naturally. Don't push them to like your new partner. Be sure to keep the lines of communication open with them (Chapter 10).

- Encourage your children to share their expectations about their new step-family and stepparent, and be sure they are realistic. Chapters 20 and 21 will help you determine this.
- If your children are like most children, they are still hanging onto fantasies of you and their other parent reconciling. Now they must *finally* relinquish these fantasies, but to do so, they may need to talk a great deal about their other parent and the loss of their biological family. Don't be con-cerned that they are losing ground because of this sudden surge in talking. They are moving forward in the adjustment process. Allow them to talk, and empathize with their feelings of loss.
- Your youngsters are probably feeling that they have no control over their lives right now. Allow them to make as many choices as you reasonably can, so they can see that they *do* have control over many aspects of their lives. Of course, the issues on which you allow choices must be suitable for their age. Allowing teens the choice of terminating their curfews or preschoolers the choice of a midnight bedtime are inappropriate. However, even very young preschoolers can make choices about lunchtime meals, clothes to wear (it can be a choice between two outfits), friends to invite for an afternoon, and TV programs (again, it can be a choice between two programs).
- If there will be two sets of children (even if one set will be visiting), provide opportunities for them to get to know one another and have fun times together. Encourage them to share their family histories, routines, and traditions. Acknowledge the differences between the families, and begin to explore ways that everybody's needs can be met. Family meetings (Chapter 21) and problem solving (Chapter 15) are good techniques to use. Be sure everyone realizes that arriving at a mutually satisfying life-style will not happen overnight. It is a process that will happen over time (Chapter 20).
- If your children are trying to thwart your new relationship, discuss it openly with them. If they know you are on to them and you stand firm, it will help them accept the reality of your forthcoming marriage. Be sure to reassure them that you love them and that your relationship with them will not be threatened.
- There are a number of good fiction books available for children that will help them become familiar with the complexities of stepfamily life and good ways of coping with it. Several are listed in Appendix C.

What is the best way to handle our wedding ceremony as far as the children are concerned?

Your wedding ceremony can serve as an opportunity to formally welcome chil-dren to your new family right from the beginning, points out Mary Whiteside, a psychologist who works extensively with stepfamilies at the Ann Arbor Center for the Family in Ann Arbor, Michigan. Try to involve *all* the children in some way, whether they will be living with you full-time or "visiting." If you exclude noncustodial children, they may feel alienated from the rest of the family.

There are any number of ways to involve children: addressing invitations, preparing food, decorating, welcoming and serving guests, taking charge of the guest book. Their names can be included on engagement announcements. Their input can be sought in planning. Children who play musical instruments can be invited to play. Youngsters can be included in the actual ceremony as well. They can stand with you during the ceremony or join you later in the ceremony for a blessing. Your marriage vows could even include a promise to care for stepchildren (by name). One couple each promised to support the new spouse and the children's other parent in parenting decisions.

Although being included in the wedding makes the new marriage more real to children, do not force them to be involved, or even to attend, if they resist. A word of caution: Don't ask them to make promises during the ceremony, such as to love their stepparent. It is a potential guilt-raiser for them, point out leading stepfamily experts Emily and John Visher.

What is the best way to handle finances after remarriage?

The two problems cited most frequently by couples in stepfamilies are children and finances. They are also the most common reasons given for the breakup of second marriages. Ideally, financial issues should be faced squarely and agreement reached *before* your marriage. Learning how to live and blend together as one family will present enough challenges without your having to tackle the thorny issue of finances at the same time.

Financial decisions in a stepfamily are far more complicated than they are in a first marriage. What are each partner's financial responsibilities to the other's children? How will money be allocated among children? Will money be pooled, or will each parent be responsible for his or her own children? How will markedly different spending habits between the two original families be handled? If one child takes music lessons, can the other take karate classes even though his parent contributes less money? If one set of children is overindulged by a noncustodial parent, will more of the family income be spent on the other set? If one set is headed for college and the other isn't, how will college costs be handled? How will you compensate for missed child support payments? How will unexpected expenses in the first family be handled? What assets will become joint? How will insurance be handled? How will your estate be divided in your wills? How will the financial security of each partner and his or her children be protected? Does one partner have debts to repay or financial promises to keep, such as financing college educations for children from a previous marriage or supporting aging parents? Before starting out in a stepfamily, such tough financial issues should be discussed, points out Claire Berman, former president of the Stepfamily Association of America.

To complicate matters, many of these issues are highly emotional ones about which each partner is likely to have strong feelings. It is a good idea to discuss these feelings, too. How resentful will a stepparent feel if family income is spent on unexpected expenses incurred by the previous family? Or if he or she is paying out child support but none is coming in for stepchildren? How resentful will a partner be if stepchildren spend the family's money freely while his or her own children maintain the frugal values they were taught? What if there is not enough money for the couple to have a new child because of a partner's commitment to finance college educations for children from a previous marriage?

There is no right way or wrong way to handle finances after remarriage. Each couple must find what works best for their own family. Usually, remarried families choose either a common-pot or a two-pot approach to finances. In the common-pot approach, partners pool their resources and allocate them according to need. In the two-pot approach, money is kept separate. Most couples using this approach have no joint savings or checking account. Partners contribute to the household and assume the responsibility for themselves and their own children. Each of these approaches has its advantages and its shortcomings. A common-pot approach usually results in a more integrated stepfamily. However, many couples who have been through divorce-related financial crises need the security of knowing that they and their children will be protected in the future. For this reason, they often feel that a two-pot approach is the only feasible option for them. If the financial resources of each family are markedly different, however, a two-pot approach can cause considerable conflict and tension, point out Emily and John Visher. You can wind up with two different families living under the same roof—the "haves" and their "poor relations," who have good reason for the resentment they usually feel. A modified common pot may be one answer in these cases. Some money can be held back for a sense of independence and security while the remainder is pooled for the needs of family members. There are other ways to protect yourself and your children in the future, point out Barton Bernstein, a Texas family law attorney, and Shelia Collins of the Graduate School of Social Work at the University of Texas at Arlington. Some couples set up trusts for their children. Many arrange formal prenuptial agreements. Some make out premarital assets inventories. Some make formal *ante*nuptial agreements once they have settled into marriage for several years and have a better idea of what to do. If you feel overwhelmed with discussing and making decisions about so many financial issues, consider enlisting the help of a family mediator. Mediation (Chapter 2) can be an effective way to work out many of the complexities of stepfamily life.

We are having a disagreement about where to live after our marriage. Their place is big enough for all of us, but I'm uneasy about us moving there.

Most experts agree: Move to "neutral territory" if it is at all financially feasible. Otherwise, the "home team" feels intruded upon and the newcomers feel like intruders. Starting off in a fresh home puts everyone on an equal footing and gets rid of the "ghosts" of the previous marriage that linger in the old residence. It's less stressful, and it's more conducive to the two contingents growing together and blending as one family.

If moving to a new home is not possible, try to change the existing one so that it reflects the new family. Get the whole family involved in redecorating. Discuss different possibilities at family meetings, and try to find some common tastes so that everyone will feel comfortable. Try to use space differently, too. If stepsiblings must now share bedrooms, can the bedrooms be changed so that the new room belongs to *both* children rather than having the new child intrude on the other's territory? Allowing children to decide how to decorate their new rooms will help them feel more at home and is a good icebreaker for new roommates.

Will it help or hinder our stepfamily to have another child after we remarry?

There is no simple answer other than this: Do *not* have another child in hopes that it will cement a shaky marriage and a troubled stepfamily. A new child could cause additional problems if the family is already troubled. With a new child there are increased demands to meet the needs of still another person— needs that will often conflict with the needs of the other children and your couple relationship. If the other children in the family do not feel secure, a new child could make them feel less valued because the newcomer is the child of *both* parents. And a stepparent may become even more estranged from his or her stepchildren because of the thrill of the new baby, especially if it is the stepparent's first child. If so, children are likely to feel more rejected and their parent resentful.

On the other hand, if your marriage is very sound and the children in the family feel secure and loved (and you continue to make them feel so), the birth of a new child can have many positive effects: Everyone may begin to feel that they are finally a real family instead of a temporary arrangement of people living under the same roof. Stepfamily members may feel a new closeness with one another now that there is a common biological link uniting them. Stepchildren may begin to feel that their stepparent has more legitimacy as their parent. In fact, a new excitement and contentment may pervade the entire family.

Ideally, you should discuss the prospect of having a mutual child with your partner *before* you marry. Many a couple learns after marriage that one partner desperately wants a child while the other is against "starting all over again." However, even if you agree, wait until you create a situation in which a new child will have a positive impact on your family.

Ever since I decided to remarry, my former spouse has become impossible to deal with. We're losing ground every day. Is this indicative of what lies ahead?

When people remarry, their former spouses often fall victim to intense and confusing feelings. Old feelings of ambivalence, rejection, anger, depression, and/or loss can be reactivated, and new feelings of competitiveness and jealousy commonly emerge, even in people who initiated the divorce or who have themselves remarried.

When children are involved, former spouses have very real worries. Parents with custody fear that children will want to live with the new stepfamily. Nonresident parents fear they will be replaced by the stepparent. The fear of losing their children often arouses hostility, anger, and feelings of helplessness in former spouses. Quite frequently, they try to cope with feeling powerless by trying to control their former partners who are about to change the status quo. Frequently, conflict escalates and old battles resurface.

It is usually noncustodial parents who feel the *most* threatened and helpless, and with good reason. The new stepparent will have more contact with the children. Won't he or she also have more influence ("Will I be replaced by this stepparent?" "Will I be shut out?" "Will I lose my children?")? Biological parents who are only marginally involved with their children sometimes feel even more threatened than do involved parents, since they have a greater chance of becoming merely a ritual figure in their children's lives. This is an uncomfortable role, and it is often the cause of marginally involved parents retreating still further from their parental role when their ex-spouses remarry.

The new difficulties with your former spouse are likely to be temporary. You can help alleviate them by removing some of their underlying causes. Make it clear to your former partner that his or her relationship with the children will be protected and that your new spouse will not attempt to replace him or her in your children's lives. If conflict continues, Chapter 11 has many suggestions for ways to deal with it.

My former spouse has wanted custody ever since our divorce. I'm recently remarried and life is so chaotic, I wonder if I should give in. My ex is a good parent.

Remarriage is a time when parenting arrangements, ideally, should be reevaluated to accommodate the new family. Perhaps a nonresident parent can take children more often and the new couple can have more time alone. Perhaps different visiting weekends can be arranged so that children from both marriages will be in the home at the same time, leaving some weekends free for the couple. If it is the nonresident parent who remarries, it may no longer be appropriate for children to come all weekend, every weekend.

However, mental health professionals widely recommend that custody should *not* be changed at this time, because children are likely to feel rejected and devalued and suffer a loss in self-esteem. The parent who relinquished them may also come to feel resentful, concluding that the price of remarriage was the loss of the children. Don't make a rash decision. Give everyone time to settle in and adjust, and remember that adjustment will take time—a minimum of a year and a half. Then carefully consider the pros and cons of a custody change. You may be interested in knowing that stepparents usually come to feel more positively toward custodial stepchildren than they do about part-time stepchildren.

Changing custody is likely to be an emotional decision for everyone involved. Make it correctly so you will not be bouncing your children back and forth.

We each brought children into this marriage, and the fighting between them has turned our home into a battlefield. What can we do?

Siblings in all families fight, but stepsiblings are suddenly plunged into a new environment in which they have to compete for space, attention, a place in the new family, and their own parent's time and affection. Suddenly bathrooms, TVs, stereos, friends, pets, and toys are expected to be shared. Many lose their much-prized privacy. Some lose their prestigious status as oldest, youngest, or only child in the family, as well as the privileges that go along with it. When there are large discrepancies in material possessions, rules, and privileges between the two sets of children, there are additional grounds for jealousy and animosity. For a time, there is usually an "us against them" mentality operating. Yet, with time, most stepsiblings do develop harmonious relationships with one another, and some become even closer than they are with their own brothers and sisters.

To put the situation simply, if the benefits of being stepsiblings outweigh the costs, good relationships are more likely to develop. Alternatively, if the costs outweigh the benefits, conflict is more likely to continue. Here are some things you can do to reduce the costs of being stepsiblings:

- Try to make each child in the family feel valued, respected, loved, and secure.
- Although it is natural to love your own children more, *treat* all the children fairly. Differential treatment is a source of strain for stepsiblings. Your respect, expectations, and discipline should be similar for both sets, and the distribution of money, presents, privileges, and attention should be fair to all. This is particularly critical for children of similar ages. Treating all children alike presents more of a problem when children are used to very different rules, privileges, and discipline. Chapter 21 will help you resolve this problem.
- Both you and your spouse should spend some time alone with your own children. Youngsters do not feel that stepsiblings have an equal claim to their parent and usually resent getting no time alone with their own parent. Each of you should also spend some time alone with the other's children to develop your relationships with them. Stepsiblings usually get along better when the relationships between stepparents and stepchildren are good.
- One of the most common problems that older children in stepfamilies complain about is a lack of personal space and no respect for privacy. If

children must now share rooms, try to arrange some space that they can call their own. How about a partition in the room or a curtain that can be pulled? What about a corner in a basement? The easiest solution may be setting aside a scheduled time each day during which each child can have the bedroom *alone*, to talk on the phone, do homework, or just think. Children may also like the idea of having a place for their prized possessions that they can keep locked.

- Plan activities in which everyone can have fun together and get to know each other better.
- Have stepsiblings work together on a shared project that requires some cooperation—baking cookies, preparing a special dinner, going with a parent to select new items for their joint room, decorating their room, building a bookcase, and so forth.
- If one set of children is overindulged by a nonresident parent and it is causing resentment and deprived feelings in the other set, occasionally provide something special for the other set.
- Encourage grandparents to treat all the children similarly.
- Ignore the small confrontations and work on the major problems and issues. Children will never be able to work out their differences with one another if you intervene constantly.
- One set of children moving into the home of the other set creates special problems and resentments. Some ways to deal with this problem were discussed previously under the question pertaining to where the new family should live.

Each of us has a teen of the opposite sex, and we are concerned about what might develop after they are living under the same roof. Do incest taboos extend to stepsiblings?

Sexual attraction between teens is a common problem in stepfamilies. Although the law does not consider sex between stepsiblings to be incestuous, it will be detrimental to your family if your teens become sexually involved, points out sociologist William Beer of Brooklyn College, a leading researcher in stepsibling relationships. Because no clear societal taboos exist, it is up to the individual stepfamily to develop its own incest taboos, says Beer. Be sure you set clear rules for dress codes and privacy. Teens should not be allowed to walk around in sexually stimulating attire and should keep bedroom and bathroom doors closed when inappropriately dressed. Family members should also knock before entering a room with a closed door.

Try not to leave your teens home alone together for long periods, especially overnight. Keep your own passionate displays of affection with your spouse for the bedroom. Teens are often stimulated by the obvious sexual implications of the couple relationship in a stepfamily, report Emily and John Visher. However, your warmth and tenderness for each other is fine for all your children to see.

Don't pressure opposite-sex teens to become close friends. Teenage step-siblings who are sexually attracted to each other are often decidedly uncomfortable with their feelings because they are not sure whether incest taboos extend to stepsiblings. A common way for them to fight against their sexual feelings is through conflict and hostility toward each other.

If you suspect your teens are attracted to each other, talk to each of them separately about how difficult it must be to be living in the same house with someone that he or she could be dating. Sometimes this acknowledgment helps relieve tension and feelings of guilt or embarrassment. Spend some time discussing the difference between feelings (which cannot be controlled) and behavior (which *can* be controlled), suggest the Vishers. And make your expectations for behavior very clear.

My husband is a terrific father with his own children who aren't living with us. I assumed he would be a good stepfather for my children, but he doesn't seem to try with them. They're good kids. I don't understand this.

Many remarried fathers without custody suffer a great deal of guilt when they form a new family. They feel they are denying their own children needed love and time and unconsciously feel that it is unfair to give it to their stepchildren. Their guilt often prevents them from opening up to their stepchildren and developing relationships with them. Some withdraw, some even become resentful. Guilt is one of the most difficult problems stepfathers with noncustodial children have to deal with, although many are not aware of the extent that it is impacting their present relationships. Becoming aware of their guilt is the first step in dealing with it. Chapter 18 has many suggestions for building good relationships with noncustodial children. If a father becomes more comfortable with his relationships with his own children, he may feel free to develop relationships with stepchildren. Reading about "Dumping Your Guilt" in Chapter 17 may also be helpful.

My spouse feels that my children manipulate me and resents them. I think that with all my kids have been through, my spouse should be more tolerant, but it's causing a rift in my marriage. What is the best way to handle this?

Children who become manipulative after divorce and remarriage often do so because they feel powerless and insecure. They have had little or no say in major events that have dramatically changed the course of their lives—the loss of their biological family, the loss of close contact with a parent, perhaps a new home and reduced financial resources, a new stepfamily. Is it so surprising that when they find they *can* have some control, especially over one of the most significant people in their lives, that they exploit it? Sometimes children's manipulative behavior is more an expression of their unhappiness, hurt, and anger: "(S)He caused all these problems, so (s)he should make up for it." Understandably, parents who feel guilty about the losses their children have suffered are vulnerable to these kinds of tactics.

Understanding what is behind children's manipulative behavior may help your spouse be more tolerant. However, knowing that you are doing your children no favors by giving in to their manipulative behavior may help you decide that you cannot allow it to continue. By reinforcing it, you are giving them a poor model of relationships and unrealistic expectations about the way the world functions. You are teaching them how to grow into manipulative adults. (Perhaps their manipulative behavior is already more indicative of learned behavior than anything else.)

If your children are aware of the rift they are causing in your marriage, and they probably are, it may even be frightening to them to have so much power. Why? Because children who have already lost so much security and structure in their lives after divorce do not want to feel that their future security rests on their own shoulders. Children should not have this much power, and they know it.

Provide your children with security and love. Allow them to talk with you about their anger and hurt. But don't let them manipulate you. They need firm limits. Chapter 16 discussed discipline and setting limits. Chapter 17 discussed what to do when children play one parent against the other.

My ex wants to stay involved with our children, but the rules and values are so different over there that I am very concerned. Isn't it harmful to bounce children back and forth between such different home environments?

There is wide agreement among mental health professionals that children can usually adjust to different households, life-styles, values, and rules far easier than they can adjust to losing a parent. You can really help them if you take the following steps:

1. Let them know that there are different ways of doing things rather than a right way and wrong ways. Otherwise, they may always be fighting the ways of one home because they perceive them to be "wrong." You will need to become tolerant of the differences in your former spouse's household. It may help to keep in mind how important your former spouse's involvement is to your children's well-being (Chapter 18).
2. Try to agree on some common rules with their other parent, but if you cannot, be sure that the different rules and ways of doing things in each home are clearly defined for your children so they will know what is expected and what is acceptable in each household: "In this house we do it this way."

3. Give your kids permission to adapt to their other parent's home by your remaining neutral about the other household—its rules, values, and ways of doing things. Remember, other ways of doing things are different, not wrong: "In your dad's home you can leave your things around, but in this house you must put them away," not, "It's disgusting the way your father lets you be a slob and I have to retrain you all over again every time you come home."
4. Give your children some time to themselves as a transition period when they return to your home from their other parent's.

Help! I am sexually attracted to my teenage stepdaughter. Is there something wrong with me? What should I do?

There is nothing wrong with your feelings, but it is good that you are concerned about a situation that could become very explosive. Sexual attraction between a stepparent and a stepchild is not unusual. Both are suddenly thrown together in an intimate living situation without the protection of firm incest taboos. Often a stepparent finds the same qualities in a teen that made him or her so attracted to the teen's parent. At the same time, the sexual nature of the couple's relationship may be overstimulating to teens, provoking them to dress and behave seductively around a stepparent.

Sometimes, stepparents and stepchildren try to handle their uncomfortable feelings of attraction by pushing each other away, not allowing any positive emotion to surface, report Emily and John Visher. It may help to establish clear rules about the manner of dress that is appropriate in your home, about keeping bedroom and bathroom doors closed, and about knocking on closed doors. Be cautious about touching and physical contact, too. If it appears that your stepdaughter shares the attraction, your spouse should help her talk about her feelings. If everyone understands that sexual feelings are not uncommon in stepfamilies, a lot of the tension and guilt that may be pervading your home can be eased.

While there is nothing wrong with feelings of attraction between stepparent and stepchild, *acting* on those feelings is, of course, quite a different matter. It is important that distinctions are clear in everyone's mind between feelings, which cannot be controlled, and acting on those feelings, which *can* be controlled. If you continue to have difficulty in dealing with your feelings, it will probably help to talk with a family therapist who works with stepfamilies.

Should I adopt my stepchildren?

Stepchildren account for about one-third of the adoptions in the United States. However, sometimes stepparents adopt their stepchildren for the wrong reasons. They believe adoption will erase the past, create an immediate bond with a stepchild, and turn the stepfamily into a "real" family. Sometimes it is a subtle way to push the other biological parent out of the child's life.

Adoption is not magic. It does not erase the past. For a child, there is no such thing as an ex-parent, and his or her identity is tied to that parent. (Usually a child's loyalty is, too.) Adoption does not create immediate love and bonding; these must develop over time. Neither does it create an immediate family; this, too, must evolve over time (Chapter 20). Furthermore, pushing a child's biological parent out of the picture is likely to create more problems for both the child and the stepfamily than it will solve (Chapters 20 and 21).

Most experts agree that unless the biological parent has *completely* dropped out of the child's life, adoption is a poor idea. For a child's psychological well-being, the relationship with his or her biological parent should be protected, and adoption by stepparents usually has the effect of driving biological parents further away from their youngsters, whether it was the intention or not. On the other hand, points out University of Colorado psychologist Dr. William Hodges, if the biological parent has completely abandoned his or her children, adoption by the stepparent may help the children loosen their identification with the real parent and look to the stepparent to fulfill their needs. It can be a signal to children of complete acceptance and commitment by their stepparent. Children should always be consulted about adoption. Even if a biological parent has dropped out of the picture, a child must still deal with the feelings of rejection that may accompany this symbol of final abandonment.

The financial implications also need consideration. With adoption, the stepparent assumes financial responsibility for youngsters as if they were his or her biological children, even if the marriage ends.

If the major reason for adoption is for the entire family to have the same surname, children can usually use their stepparents' name without a legal change. Even most schools now allow this. If the major reason is to establish a legal relationship for inheritance or other purposes, you might look for other legal means to accomplish your purposes.

23

CLOSING REMARKS

*D*ivorce is the death of a marriage. With it, you enter a new, changed world, whether you're ready or not. With this transition comes a confusing mix of anxiety, sadness, grief, anger, euphoria, and feelings of worthlessness and failure—all in amounts you never thought possible. These emotions and feelings, so understandable, eventually need to be brought under control, sorted out, dealt with, and let go of. Broadly speaking, there are three levels in this changed world: surviving change, adapting to change, and, finally, growth. You will encounter them again if you remarry and create a stepfamily. Loosely termed, the entire process is the achievement of new beginnings, and it has been the focus of much of this book.

As the old adage says, "It is a wise person who profits from the misfortunes of others." Fortunately, in recent years divorce and family researchers have intensively studied and analyzed countless divorce and stepfamily experiences. From others' misfortunes much has been learned. And much of it is encouraging, offering people valuable help in finding shorter and smoother paths through divorce, rebuilding, and/or creating a stepfamily.

First, however, some hard lessons of divorce must be recognized. A disconcerting surprise for most people is that the aftermath of divorce is not short-lived. Most people expect to have a difficult time for a while, but when the difficult period extends month after month after month, a new stress, this one self-generated, appears: "Why is it *this* bad?" "What's wrong with *me*?"

For divorcing couples with children, stress and problems are compounded. Parents with custody must contend with distressed, bewildered children who are likely to respond to their families' ruptures with at least transient emotional or behavioral problems. Parents without custody must find a way to cope with being shut out of their children's day-to-day lives and to avert the real possibility of being demoted from a parent to a peripheral player in their children's futures.

And what of divorcing men and women who find a new love, remarry, and form a stepfamily? The unsuspecting majority believe that an instant family, abounding in love and happiness, will soon be theirs, but research shows otherwise. Stepfamilies, too, face an extended transitional period of surviving, adapting, and growing before they can experience new beginnings as a full-fledged family.

The years surrounding divorce are likely to be the most challenging ones of your life, and there may be times when you wonder if you will emerge from them with some semblance of happiness and fulfillment. It may encourage you to learn that we human beings have an impressive ability to successfully overcome personal tragedy and serious setbacks of all sorts. If we can take self-reports at face value, studies find that the majority of people eventually manage to emerge from personal tragedy and serious setbacks with a level of satisfaction equal to, if not greater than, that which they had enjoyed prior to their personal misfortunes.

Within these pages have been the maps for what lies ahead, as well as the coping skills divorcing people and couples forming a stepfamily need to survive change, to adapt to change, and, finally, to grow and thrive. With these, you need not forge ahead unguided. You can avoid many of the mistakes others make and the problems others encounter. An enormous amount of territory, information, and coping skills has been covered, and it defies summary in a single chapter. Yet there are key consistent threads running throughout this book that are important whether you are divorcing, learning how to parent solo, or creating a stepfamily. In these final pages, I'd like to pull some of these threads together so you can keep them in mind in the coming years, regardless of what your future brings.

Successful new beginnings can be yours, whether you wanted the divorce or it was forced on you, whether you remain single or remarry. However, unless you have a *successful* divorce, you are likely to get stalled along the way. A successful divorce is the foundation on which the remainder of your life will be built. Don't minimize its importance, even if you are already remarrying; unresolved divorce issues can haunt your new marriage (Chapter 20). Take a careful look at whether your divorce was successful so you will know whether you have more work to do; it is never too late.

What is a successful divorce? There are a number of important ingredients.

- Your anger is spent and you've let it go (Chapter 5).
- You have distanced yourself from your former spouse, so you no longer feel sorrow, longing, dependency, regret, resentment, or hatred—only indifference, concern, or perhaps tenderness (Chapter 6).
- You have let go of your marriage. You've recognized and mourned your losses—and you *do* have losses, no matter how much you wanted the divorce (Chapter 3). And you have arrived at a *balanced* understanding of why your marriage ended and the role you played in it (Chapter 6). Don't avoid this searching analysis. Few divorces are caused solely by one partner, and although it may be tempting to place all the blame elsewhere, you will be the loser if you do. Generally, people who fail to recognize the

role they played feel like helpless victims who have little control over their lives or futures: "What's to stop it from happening again?" If you feel victimized, your ability to cope effectively, close the door on your marriage, and move on will be impaired.

- You have rebuilt your self-esteem (Chapter 12).
- You are consciously moving ahead to forge a new identity, separate from your ex-spouse, and a new life of your own design (Chapters 12 and 13). Many people assume that divorce adjustment involves only surviving the stormy emotions and upheavals. But unless you *consciously* build a *new* life to replace your married one, you may emerge from divorce frozen in old patterns and fail to grow. If so, life after divorce may be less satisfying than married life was.
- If you are a parent, there is another component of a successful divorce: You are providing your children with the support, love, and good parenting they *continue* to need. Unfortunately, what is good for you at this time is not necessarily good for them. You need to be aware of and deal with your own adjustment and theirs simultaneously.

Parents seldom realize just how stressful divorce is for children. It turns children's worlds topsy-turvy, robbing youngsters of their families—their source of stability, security, and continuity. Divorce leaves children feeling vulnerable, overwhelmed with loss, and powerless to influence events that have a profound impact on their lives. Although we tend to think of divorce as a single event, it sets into motion a chain of events that can cast shadows over a large fraction of a youngster's childhood.

For children whose parents drift away from them, either physically or because of their preoccupation with their new lives or new loves, the pain of divorce and feelings of rejection linger throughout childhood and sometimes into young adulthood. For children whose parents continue to battle each other, the pain of divorce is compounded by unrelenting feelings of being pulled apart by the two people they love most in the world. For children who are poorly parented after divorce, there is too much time with no guidance and too many opportunities for life to go awry. For children whose parents remarry, there is another long period of upheaval.

Children's behavior reflects their feelings. And many children act out their anger, distress, anxiety, and fears in troublesome behavior—tantrums, noncompliance, disobedience, poor grades, aggressiveness, delinquency, substance abuse, promiscuity. But their troublesome behavior only compounds their problems. Rather than eliciting the empathy, sensitivity, and support for which they yearn, their behavior is more likely to elicit anger and impatience from parents, teachers, and peers who do not understand its cause.

Yet children *can* emerge from divorce unscathed. They can bounce back and resume their childhoods with amazing resilience if parents can provide them with a few fundamentals, not only at the time of divorce but in the ensuing years (Chapter 9). What happens to a child in the years *after* divorce is at least as important as what happens at the time. These same fundamentals are, therefore, important to children in single-parent homes and in stepfamilies, too.

First on the list of fundamentals for children is an end to your conflict with their other parent. At the very least, protect them from it. One of the most startling things researchers have learned is the devastating consequences that prolonged parental conflict has for children (Chapter 9). It makes no difference whether they are living in an intact home, in a single-parent home, or in a stepfamily. Parental conflict is destructive in *all* settings, and its scars follow children into their adulthood. It is not only overt bickering and fighting that is harmful. So is creating conflicting loyalties (bad-mouthing their other parent, enlisting children as spies, placing them in the middle, pressuring them to take sides). Chapter 11 was devoted to ways to end your conflict.

A stable home and good parenting is a second fundamental your children need. Although these are important to *all* kids, they are particularly important to children who have experienced change and upheaval in their home lives through divorce or remarriage. Chapters 10 and 15 discussed the ingredients of a home life that enables children to adjust well to divorce and flourish in a single-parent home. The same ingredients are important to children in stepfamilies—with the caution that any changes be initiated very slowly and that the biological parent be the disciplinarian until the stepparent has bonded with the children.

Next on the list of fundamentals is a good relationship with *both* parents. Children should not have a "broken" home after divorce; they should have *two* homes. Their parents' love and support buffers children of all ages from a good deal of the stress caused by divorce and remarriage. Your children *need* your love, attention, interest, and reassurance that they will always be an important part of your life. They need your support and empathy just as much. Encourage them to share their feelings, and when they do, be sure to *accept them*. It may be disconcerting to learn that your children are angry about the divorce, yearn for their other parent and intact family, are unhappy about your upcoming marriage, or dislike their new stepfamily. But if you show them empathy and accept their feelings, the love and intimacy between you will grow. If you minimize or discard their feelings, they will harbor them instead, and harbored negative feelings can create stumbling blocks that hinder not only your relationships with one another, but also their adjustment to their changed lives (Chapters 8, 10, and 21).

Good relationships with both you and their other parent will continue to be important to your children's well-being throughout childhood and adolescence. Make your relationships with them a high priority. Just as important, *support their relationships with their other parent.* If you remarry, avoid the mistake that many stepfamily couples make—trying to freeze out the biological parent and substitute the stepparent. It causes problems not only for children but for stepfamilies, too (Chapters 20 and 21).

Limiting additional stress in children's lives is a final fundamental for children's good adjustment. Children can usually handle one stress in their lives quite well, such as parental divorce or becoming part of a stepfamily. However, it is important that additional stress be minimized. The reason is that the negative effects of stress are not simply additive for children; they *multiply*. Each additional source of stress makes it increasingly more difficult for them to reconstruct their lives (Chapter 9). How can you limit additional stress? Keep as much continuity in children's lives as possible, introducing changes gradually as they adapt to initial changes (Chapters 10 and 21). Allow them their childhoods and adolescences; do not saddle them with adult problems and responsibilities, no matter how mature they seem (Chapters 10, 14, and 15). Try to give them enough economic security so at least basic needs will be met (Chapter 15). And find as many sources of social support for them as you can (Chapter 10).

The years surrounding divorce, learning to parent solo, and creating a stepfamily are challenging ones. Many people seek professional counseling during these years for both themselves and their children, and they are rarely disappointed. Don't underestimate the value of having a strong person to support you and/or your children during stressful times, to be a sounding board, to provide an objective perspective, and to guide you in obtaining relevant information and making wise decisions. To many, a therapist or counselor is a lifeline.

Divorce thrusts you into a jungle of emotions and events. The emotions are deep, and the events are fast-moving and not always easy to comprehend. Most likely, you have never experienced anything like it before. Your personal experience, experiences of friends, and society in general provide you with only a few tidbits for survival. At this time, it would be easy to let yourself become overwhelmed, confused, and bogged down with all the problems.

Armed with the knowledge provided by thousands of people who have preceded your venture into divorce, the jungle will change its character from a dark, unknown, and threatening place to one with known but challenging obstacles. This book's goal, its purpose, has been to prepare you for the emotions and events that you are likely to encounter. The challenges center around your own personal problems, the problems of solo parenting, and the challenges of new relationships and possibly stepfamilies. With your new understanding, it is hoped that your venture will consist of a series of challenging obstacles and not a series of paralyzing threats. Focusing on unknown threats leads to feelings of helplessness and the belief that mere surviving is the most you can hope for. Focusing on the challenges will encourage you to mobilize your resources so you can first adapt and then grow in your new, changed world. With the knowledge and suggested coping tools contained in this book, you can discover a shorter and smoother road to new beginnings. With those new beginnings comes the promise of a *stronger* person entering into a *better* life.

Appendix A
How to Make Changes in Your Life and Stick to Them

You may get excited about a number of the coping techniques discussed throughout this book. Filled with a new sense of optimism, you may vow to try some of them and even use them for a time. But then you may find yourself back in your rut, saying to yourself, "I really should get back to those techniques. They worked while I used them." Or you may simply say to yourself initially, "They sound good. But I never stick to those things. So why try?"

How to get people to *start* and to *continue* using effective coping strategies has been a dilemma psychologists have faced for some time. Following is a five-step method that will help you make changes in your life and stick to them. It is not difficult, and it *is* effective.

1. Set a specific *goal* for yourself. Don't get grandiose here. Your goal must be *realistic*. Be sure you can succeed in it or you will be setting yourself up for failure and disappointment. That is not what you need right now! There are three important keys to setting realistic goals:

    - Make your goals *small*.
    - Make your goals *short-term* (divide long-term goals into short-term segments).
    - Be sure you can *realistically* fit your goals into your schedule.

    As you achieve each small, short-term goal, set a new goal for yourself, increasing each new goal gradually, one step at a time.

2. Write a *contract* for yourself and sign it. This may sound insignificant, but it is important. Signing a contract is an effective way to commit yourself to your goal. Your contract should include some positive reward for accomplishing your goal and perhaps some penalty for failing to accomplish it. (More about rewards and penalties later.) One Washington, D.C., man's contract looked like this:

351

I will get up 20 minutes early each day this week and practice my deep relaxation technique. If I practice 20 minutes each day for five days out of the next seven, I will reward myself by going to see the new exhibit at the National Gallery. If I fail in my goal, I will contribute $15 to the Democratic Party (which I despise)!

Each time you complete a contract, write a new one. You may wish to extend the same goal for a similar period of time, or you may wish to increase your goal in some way. You may also wish to alter your rewards or penalties.

3. *Record* each day whether you met your goal for that day (or how close you came to meeting it). Don't skip this step—it keeps you honest. Not only is it a good reminder, but it will boost your commitment as well. Keep a daily record on a calendar.

4. *Reward* yourself for sticking to your contract. The reward you choose should be something you will look forward to (buying a new book, allowing yourself a favorite activity you rarely take time to do, indulging yourself with a special meal or dessert, and so forth). Make your reward appropriate to the amount of effort you put forth. Make it appealing enough to motivate you without going overboard. Save large or costly rewards for goals that take a major effort.

There are two things to remember about rewards: They are far more motivating if they are *frequent* and if they come *soon after* you complete your task. Promising yourself a trip if you exercise three times a week for a year is unlikely to make an exerciser of you. Promising yourself a night out each week is likely to be far more effective. Or you may need a reward immediately after you exercise to get yourself started.

You may find that you are more motivated if you also include a penalty in your contract for not accomplishing your goal (washing windows, organizing a closet, or, as this man did, donating to a cause you despise). Another effective technique is denying yourself TV or some other favorite activity you normally do until you reach your goal for the day.

Besides material rewards and punishments, get into the habit of using positive *self-talk*. Pat yourself on the back and praise yourself for a job well done. If you did not reach your goal, praise yourself for your efforts and encourage yourself for the next time ("I didn't meet my goal every day, but I did stick to it four days. I'll do better next week.").

5. *Reevaluate.* If you accomplished your goal, set another one and sign another contract to keep yourself going. Can you increase your goal this time? Perhaps you are ready to either lengthen the time or the number of days you exercise. Are you ready to tackle two goals? Are you ready to write a contract for two weeks rather than one?

If you did not accomplish what you set out to do, reevaluate your contract. Was your goal realistic? What *would* motivate you to complete it this time? If you find that a particular coping strategy is not working for you, no matter how small you set your goal or how you reward yourself, try a different strategy.

Continue writing contracts in this way until the new behavior becomes a normal part of your life. If you find yourself reverting to old patterns, resume the contracts and rewards.

Appendix B
Learning a Deep Relaxation Technique

Learning a deep relaxation technique is not difficult, but it does require practice, as does learning any new skill. The easiest method that is effective for most people is one developed by Herbert Benson and described in detail in his book *The Relaxation Response*. These are the steps to Benson's relaxation method.

1. Choose a quiet place and time when you will be free of distractions. A little creativity may make this easier than you think. One executive told his secretary that he was in conference each day and was not to be disturbed for 20 minutes. One busy mother plopped her kids in front of their favorite TV program each day and retired to her bedroom for 20 minutes. She disconnected the phone and promised the kids an appealing snack if they stayed put and did not bother her. Other people get up 20 minutes earlier in the morning, use their coffee break at work, or utilize a daily train commute. Preferably you can find a time at least two hours after eating, since the digestive process can interfere with achieving deep relaxation, says Dr. Benson.

2. Find a comfortable and relaxed position that will allow you to relax your muscles (but one in which you are not likely to fall asleep). Close your eyes.

3. Tune into your muscles and try to relax them one by one. Start with your feet, and progress to your legs, torso, arms, shoulders, neck and throat, and finally to your facial muscles (around your mouth, cheeks, nose, temples, eyes, and forehead). Sometimes it helps to imagine the tension flowing from each muscle and leaving your body via your mouth, head, fingers, and toes. Do not worry if this is difficult for you to do; it will get easier with practice.

4. Tune into your breathing. Breathe through your nose easily and naturally.

5. Each time you exhale, silently say the word "one" to yourself. Focus on the word; it will help you to push away other thoughts from your mind.

6. Assuming a *passive* attitude is very important, says Benson. A passive attitude simply means this: Don't try too hard, don't worry about how well you are doing, don't be upset if other thoughts pop into your mind. You cannot relax if you are worried. (When other thoughts do pop into your mind, and it will happen, just shift your focus to the word "one" and let the thoughts fade away slowly on their own.)
7. Continue your breathing, saying the word "one." Relax your muscles for 20 minutes. Don't use a timer or alarm; it will startle you. But you can open your eyes to check the time.
8. When you are finished, don't jump up. Continue to sit quietly for a minute or two, first with your eyes closed and then with them open.

It is important to practice relaxation consistently, preferably each day. Once you have learned the technique, you will be able to relax with little effort. Even better, you will be able to use a shortened method to relax before and during situations that are stressful, anxiety-arousing, or anger-provoking. Think of the tool you will have if you can relax, at will, during times of high tension!

This is how to successfully relax during these stressful times:

1. Start tuning into signs of rising tension within your body, such as a lump in your throat, clenched teeth, your stomach churning, your hands fidgeting, or tension around your eyes or forehead. It is always easier to nip tension in the bud than to reduce it once it is full-blown.
2. Once you notice your tension rising, take some deep, slow breaths and say the word "one" to yourself each time you exhale.
3. Picture yourself in your favorite relaxing spot, and remember the feeling of relaxation you have achieved during practice sessions.

That is all there is to it, *once* you have mastered the technique. You can also use relaxation to help you unwind and sleep at night. However, don't use bedtime as your practice time. The physiological changes you achieve during relaxation are different from those that accompany sleep.

Appendix C
Suggested Readings

FOR ADULTS

Alberti, R.E., and Emmons, M.I. *Your Perfect Right: A Guide to Assertive Living*, 6th edition. San Luis Obispo, Calif.: Impact Publishers, 1990.

Belli, M.M., and Krantzler, M. *Divorcing*. New York: St. Martin's Press, 1988. (Legal issues)

Bolles, R.N. *What Color Is Your Parachute? A Practical Manual for Job Hunters and Career Changers*. Berkeley, Calif.: Ten Speed Press, revised annually.

Burns, D.D. *Feeling Good: The New Mood Therapy*. New York: New American Library, 1980.

Burns, D.D. *The Feeling Good Workbook: Using the New Mood Therapy in Everyday Life*. New York: New American Library, 1990. (Includes "How to Give a Dynamic Interview When You're Scared Stiff")

Burns, D.D. *Intimate Connections*. New York: New American Library, 1985.

Clarke-Stewart, Alison. *Daycare*. Cambridge: Harvard University Press, 1982.

Cohen, M.G. *Long-Distance Parenting: A Guide for Divorced Parenting*. New York: New American Library, 1989.

Cut Your Bills in Half, by the editors of the Rodale Press. Emmaus, Penn.: The Rodale Press, 1989.

Einstein, E. *The Stepfamily: Living and Learning*. New York: Macmillan, 1982.

Ellis, A. *How to Live With—and Without—Anger*. New York: Thomas Y. Crowell Company, 1977.

Ellis, A. *How to Stubbornly Refuse to Make Yourself Miserable About Anything—Yes, Anything*. New York: Carol Publishing Group, 1990.

Fisher, Bruce. *Rebuilding*. San Luis Obispo, Calif.: Impact Publishers, 1981.

Good, C.E. *Does Your Resume Wear Apron Strings?* Charlottesville, Va.: Blue Jeans Press, 1989.

Greif, G. *The Daddy Track and the Single Father*. Lexington, Mass.: Lexington Books, 1990.

Johnson, S.M. *First Person Singular: Living the Good Life Alone*. Philadelphia: Lippincott, 1977.

Koff, G.J. *The Jacoby and Meyers Law Offices Guide to Divorce.* New York: Henry Holt & Co., 1991.

Lewinsohn, P.M., et al. *Control Your Depression.* Englewood Cliffs, N.J.: Prentice Hall Press, 1986.

Mattis, M. *Sex and the Single Parent.* New York: Henry Holt & Co., 1986.

Newman, G. *101 Ways to Be a Long Distance Super-Dad.* Mountain View, Calif.: Blossom Valley Press, 1984.

Ricci, I. *Mom's House, Dad's House.* New York: Macmillan, 1980.

Robinson, B.E., Rowland, B.H., and Coleman, M. *Latchkey Kids.* Lexington, Mass.: Lexington Books, 1986.

Schneider, K., and Schneider, M. *Divorce Mediation: The Constructive New Way to End a Marriage Without Big Legal Bills.* Washington, D.C.: Acropolis, 1984.

Schnell, B.T. *The Child Support Survivor's Guide.* Yorklyn, Del.: The Advocacy Center for Child Support, 1988.

Visher, E., and Visher, J. *How to Win As a Stepfamily.* New York: Dembner Books, 1982.

Ury, W. *Getting Past No.* New York: Bantam Books, 1991. (How to negotiate)

Wanderer, Z., and Cabot, T. *Letting Go.* New York: Dell, 1978.

FOR CHILDREN

Adler, C.S. *Footsteps on the Stairs.* New York: Delacorte, 1982. (Stepfamily fiction—teens)

Berger, T. *How Does It Feel When Your Parents Get Divorced?* New York: Julian Messner, 1977. (Elementary school age)

Berman, C. *What Am I Doing in a Stepfamily?* Secaucus, N.J.: Lyle Stuart, 1982. (Ages 6–10)

Boeckman, C. *Surviving Your Parents' Divorce.* New York: Franklin Watts, 1980. (Teens)

Brown, L.K., and Brown, M. *Dinosaurs Divorce.* Boston: The Atlantic Monthly Press, 1986. (Ages: preschool–early elementary)

Craven, L. *Stepfamilies: New Patterns of Harmony.* New York: Simon & Schuster, 1982. (Ages 11+)

Danziger, P. *The Divorce Express.* New York: Delacorte, 1982. (Fiction—teens)

Dolmetsch, P., and Shih, A., eds. *The Kids' Book About Single-Parent Families.* Garden City, N.Y.: Doubleday & Co., 1985. (Ages 11–15)

Gardner, R.A. *Boys' and Girls' Book About Divorce.* New York: Bantam, 1971. (Ages 8–12)

Gardner, R. *The Boys' and Girls' Book About One-Parent Families.* New York: Bantam, 1978. (Ages 7–12)

Gardner, R. *The Boys' and Girls' Book About Stepfamilies.* New York: Bantam, 1982. (Ages 7–12)

Getzoff, A., and McClenahan, C. *Stepkids: A Survival Guide for Teenagers in Stepfamilies.* New York: Walker, 1984.

Gilbert, S. *How to Live with a Single Parent.* New York: Lothrop, Lee, & Shephard, 1982. (Teens)

Hunter, E. *Me and Mr. Stenner.* Philadelphia: Lippincott, 1976. (Stepfamily fiction—teens)

Hyde, M. *My Friend Has Four Parents.* New York: McGraw Hill, 1981. (Ages 8–12)

Lash, M., Loughridge, S., and Fassler, D. *My Kind of Family: A Book for Kids in Single-Parent Homes.* Burlington, Vt.: Waterfront Books, 1990. (Ages 4–9)

Martin, A. *Bummer Summer.* New York: Holiday House, 1983. (Stepfamily fiction—teens)

Richards, A.K., and Willis, I. *How to Get It Together When Your Parents Are Coming Apart.* New York: David McKay Company, 1976. (Teens)

Rofes, E.E., ed., *The Kids' Book of Divorce: By, For, and About Kids.* Lexington, Mass.: Lexington Books, 1981. (Older children and teens)

Sobol, H.L. *My Other Mother, My Other Father.* New York: MacMillan, 1979. (Stepfamily fiction—ages 9–12)

Notes

CHAPTER 1

1. L. Halem, *Separated and Divorced Women* (Westport, Conn.: Greenwood Press, 1982), p. 166.
2. A. Trafford, *Crazy Time* (New York: Harper & Row, 1982), pp. 66–67.
3. R.S. Weiss, *Marital Separation* (New York: Basic Books, 1975), p. 238.
4. G.B. Spanier, and O. Thompson, *Parting: The Aftermath of Separation and Divorce* (Beverly Hills: Sage, 1984), p. 170.
5. S. Matthew, *Intimate Strangers* (Edinburgh: Mainstream, 1984), pp. 32–33.

CHAPTER 2

1. Weiss, *Marital Separation*, pp. 265–66.
2. K. Kressel, *The Process of Divorce* (New York: Basic Books, 1985), p. 147.
3. Ibid., p. 147.

CHAPTER 3

1. Weiss, *Marital Separation*, p. 46.

CHAPTER 6

1. J. Johnston, and L.G. Campbell, *Impasses of Divorce* (New York: The Free Press, 1988), pp. 61–62.
2. M. Hunt, *The Affair* (Cleveland: World Publications, 1969), pp. 233–34.
3. K. Hallett, *A Guide for Single Parents* (Millbrae, Calif.: Celestial Arts, 1974), p. 8.
4. Halem, *Separated and Divorced Women*, p. 160.

CHAPTER 7

1. J. Krementz, *How It Feels When Parents Divorce* (New York: Alfred A. Knopf, 1984), p. 25.
2. L.B. Francke, *Growing Up Divorced* (New York: Linden Press/Simon & Schuster, 1983), p. 16.
3. Spanier and Thompson, *Parting*, pp. 111–12.
4. Halem, *Separated and Divorced Women*, p. 165.
5. T. Arendell, *Mothers and Divorce: Legal, Economic, and Social Dilemmas* (Berkeley: University of California Press, 1986), p. 84.
6. B. Robson, *My Parents Are Divorced Too* (New York: Everest House, 1980), p. 154.
7. Women in Transition, Inc., *Women in Transition* (New York: Charles Scribner's Sons, 1975), p. 53.
8. Krementz, *How It Feels When Parents Divorce*, p. 40.
9. J.H. Neal, "Children's Understanding of Their Parents' Divorces," in *Children and Divorce*, ed. L. Kurdek (San Francisco: Jossey-Bass, 1983), pp. 7–8.
10. J. Wallerstein, and S. Blakeslee, *Second Chances: Men, Women and Children a Decade After Divorce* (New York: Ticknor & Fields, 1989), p. 169.

CHAPTER 8

1. Francke, *Growing Up Divorced*, p. 16.
2. Y. Walczak, *Divorce: The Child's Point of View* (London: Harper and Row, 1984), p. 64.
3. Robson, *My Parents Are Divorced Too*, p. 24.

CHAPTER 9

1. R. Rosen, "Children of Divorce: What They Feel About Access and Other Aspects of the Divorce Experience," *Journal of Clinical Child Psychology* (1977): p. 26.

CHAPTER 10

1. Rosen, "Children of Divorce," p. 26.

CHAPTER 11

1. Halem, *Separated and Divorced Women*, p. 41.
2. E.D. Samuelson, *The Divorce Law Handbook: A Comprehensive Guide to Matrimonial Practice*, (New York: Human Sciences Press, 1988), p. 71.

CHAPTER 13

1. D.R. Kingma, *Coming Apart: Why Relationships End and How to Live Through the Ending of Yours* (Berkeley, Calif.: Conari Press, 1987), p. 85.

CHAPTER 14

1. Arendell, *Mothers and Divorce*, p. 84.
2. R. Weiss, *Going It Alone* (New York: Basic Books, 1979), pp. 71–72.
3. D. Dolmetsch and A. Shih, eds., *The Kids' Book About Single-Parent Families* (Garden City, N.Y.: Doubleday & Co., 1985), pp. 73–74.

CHAPTER 17

1. Dolmetsch and Shih, *The Kids' Book About Single-Parent Families*, p. 149.

CHAPTER 18

1. Dolmetsch and Shih, *The Kids' Book About Single-Parent Families*, pp. 108–9.
2. Wallerstein and Blakeslee, *Second Chances*, p. 242.

CHAPTER 19

1. Wallerstein and Blakeslee, *Second Chances*, p. 247.

Selected Sources

Ahrons, C.R., and Rodgers, R.H. *Divorced Families: A Multidisciplinary View*. New York: W.W. Norton, 1987.

Ambert, A.M. "Custodial Parents: Review and a Longitudinal Study," in *The One-Parent Family in the 1980s*, ed. B. Schlesinger. Toronto: University of Toronto Press, 1985.

Arendell, T. *Mothers and Divorce: Legal, Economic, and Social Dilemmas*. Berkeley: University of California Press, 1986.

Baydar, N. "Effects of Parental Separation and Reentry into Union on the Emotional Well-Being of Children," *Journal of Marriage and Family* 50, (1988): 967–81.

Beck, A., et al. *Cognitive Therapy of Depression*. New York: Guilford Press, 1979.

Beer, W.R., ed. *Relative Strangers: Studies of Stepfamily Processes*. Totowa, N.J.: Rowman & Littlefield, 1988.

Beer, W.R. *Strangers in the House: The World of Stepsiblings and Half-Siblings*. New Brunswick, N.J.: Transaction Publishers, 1989.

Belovitch, J., ed. *Making Remarriage Work*. Lexington, Mass.: Lexington Books, 1987.

Benson, H. *The Relaxation Response*. New York: Wm. Morrow & Co., 1975.

Bronstein, P., and Cowan, C.P. *Fatherhood Today: Men's Changing Role in the Family*. New York: John Wiley & Sons, 1988.

Burns, D.D. *Feeling Good: The New Mood Therapy*. New York: New American Library, 1980.

Burns, D.D. *The Feeling Good Workbook: Using the New Mood Therapy in Everyday Life*. New York: New American Library, 1990.

Cantor, D., and Drake, E. *Divorced Parents and Their Children*. New York: Springer Publishing Co., 1983.

Charlesworth, E.A., and Nathan, R.G. *Stress Management: A Comprehensive Guide to Wellness*. New York: Atheneum, 1984.

Cohen, M.G. *Long-Distance Parenting*. New York: New American Library, 1989.

Day, R.D., and Bahr, S.J. "Income Changes Following Divorce and Remarriage," *Journal of Divorce* 9 (1986): 75–88.

Dolmetsch, D., and Shih, A., eds. *The Kids' Book About Single-Parent Families.* Garden City, N.Y.: Doubleday & Co, 1985.

Ellis, A., *How to Stubbornly Refuse to Make Yourself Miserable About Anything—Yes, Anything.* New York: Carol Publishing Group, 1990.

Emery, R.E. *Marriage, Divorce and Children's Adjustment.* Beverly Hills, Calif.: Sage Publications, 1988.

Erickson, S.K., and Erickson, M.S. *Family Mediation Casebook: Theory and Process.* New York: Brunner/Mazel, 1988.

Fisher, B. *Rebuilding.* San Luis Obispo, Calif.: Impact Publishers, 1981.

Fisher, R., and Ury, W. *Getting to Yes.* Boston: Houghton-Mifflin, 1981.

Francke, L.B. *Growing Up Divorced.* New York: Linden Press/Simon & Schuster, 1983.

Furstenberg, F.F., Jr., and Cherlin, A.J. *Divided Families.* Cambridge, Mass: Harvard University Press, 1991.

Furstenberg, F.F., Jr., and Nord, C.W. "Parenting Apart: Patterns of Childrearing After Marital Disruption." *Journal of Marriage and the Family* 47 (1985): 893–904.

Furstenberg, F.F., Jr., and Spanier, G.B. *Recycling the Family: Remarriage After Divorce.* Beverly Hills, Calif.: Sage Publications, 1984.

Ganong, L.H., and Coleman, M. "A Comparison of Clinical and Empirical Literature on Children in Stepfamilies." *Journal of Marriage and the Family* 48 (1986): 309–18.

Glenwick, D.S., and Mowrey, J.D. "When Parent Becomes Peer: Loss of Intergenerational Boundaries in Single Parent Families." *Family Relations* 35 (1986): 57–63.

Goetting, A. "The Six Stations of Remarriage," in *Family in Transition* 5th ed., eds. A.S. Skolnick and H.H. Skolnick. Boston: Little, Brown & Co., 1986.

Goldner, V. "Remarriage Family: Structure, System, Future," in *Remarriage Families,* eds. J.C. Hansen and L. Messinger. Rockville, Md.: Aspen System Corp., 1982.

Greif, G. *Mothers Without Custody.* Lexington, Mass.: Lexington Books, 1988.

Greif, G. *Single Fathers.* Lexington, Mass.: Lexington Books, 1985.

Grossman, T.B. *Mothers and Children Facing Divorce.* Ann Arbor: University of Michigan Press, 1986.

Halem, L. *Separated and Divorced Women.* Westport, Conn.: Greenwood Press, 1982.

Hallett, K. *A Guide for Single Parents.* Millbrae, Calif.: Celestial Arts, 1974.

Hanson, S.M.H. "Healthy Single Parent Families." *Family Relations* 35 (1986): 125–32.

Hanson, S.M.H. "Single Fathers with Custody: A Synthesis of the Literature," in *The One-Parent Family in the 1980s,* ed. B. Schlesinger. Toronto: University of Toronto Press, 1985.

Hetherington, E.M., and Arasteh, J., eds. *Impact of Divorce, Single Parenting, and Stepparenting on Children.* Hillsdale, N.J.: Lawrence Erlbaum Associates, 1988.

Hetherington, E.M., Cox, M., and Cox, R. "Effects of Divorce on Parents and Children," in *Nontraditional Families*, ed. M.E. Lamb. Hillsdale, N.J.: Lawrence Erlbaum Associates, 1982.

Hodges, W.F. *Interventions for Children of Divorce.* New York: John Wiley & Sons, second edition, 1991.

Hofferth, S. "Updating Children's Life Course." *Journal of Marriage and the Family* 47 (1985): 93–115.

Hunt, M. *The Affair.* Cleveland: World Publications, 1969.

Hunt, M., and Hunt, B. *The Divorce Experience.* New York: McGraw-Hill, 1977.

Ihinger-Tallman, M., and Pasley, K. *Remarriage.* Beverly Hills, Calif.: Sage Publications, 1987.

Isaacs, M.B. "Facilitating Family Restructuring and Relinkage," in *Therapy with Remarriage Families*, eds. J.C. Hansen and L. Messinger. Rockville, Md.: Aspen Systems Corp., 1982.

Isaacs, M.B., Montalvo, B., and Abelsohn, D. *The Difficult Divorce.* New York: Basic Books, 1986.

Jacobson, D.S. "Family Types, Visiting Patterns, and Children's Behavior in the Stepfamily: A Linked Family System," in *Remarriage and Stepparenting: Current Research and Theory*, eds. K. Pasley and M. Ihinger-Tallman. New York: Guilford Press, 1987.

Johnson, B.H. "Single Mothers Following Separation and Divorce." *Family Relations* 35 (1986): 189–97.

Johnson, S.M. *First Person Singular: Living the Good Life Alone.* Philadelphia: Lippincott, 1977.

Johnston, J., Kline, M., and Tschann, J.M. "Ongoing Postdivorce Conflict: Effects on Children of Joint Custody and Frequent Access." *Journal of Orthopsychiatry*, 59 (1989): 576–92.

Johnston, J.R., and Campbell, L.G. *Impasses of Divorce.* New York: The Free Press, 1988.

Kahn, A.J., and Kamerman, S.B. *Child Support: From Debt Collection to Social Policy.* Beverly Hills, Calif.: Sage Publications, 1988.

Kalter, N. *Growing Up Divorced.* New York: The Free Press, 1990.

Kalter, N. "Long-Term Effects of Divorce on Children." *American Journal of Orthopsychiatry* 57 (1987): 587–600.

Kaslow, F.W., and Schwartz, L.L. *The Dynamics of Divorce. A Life Cycle Perspective.* New York: Brunner/Mazel, 1987.

Kelly, J. "Is Mediation Less Expensive?" *Mediation Quarterly* 8 (1990): 15–26.

Kingma, D.R. *Coming Apart: Why Relationships End and How to Live Through the Ending of Yours.* Berkeley, Calif.: Conari Press, 1987.

Kitson, G.C., and Morgan, L.A. "The Multiple Consequences of Divorce: A Decade Review." *Journal of Marriage and the Family* 52 (1990): 913–24.

Krementz, J. *How It Feels When Parents Divorce.* New York: Alfred A. Knopf, 1984.

Kressel, K. *The Process of Divorce.* New York: Basic Books, 1985.

Lewinsohn, P.M., et al. *Control Your Depression.* New York: Prentice Hall Press, 1986.

Luepnitz, D.A. *Child Custody: A Study of Families After Divorce.* Lexington, Mass.: Lexington Books, 1982.

Matthew, S. *Intimate Strangers.* Edinburgh: Mainstream, 1984.

Mattis, M. *Sex and the Single Parent.* New York: Henry Holt & Co., 1986.

Mills, D. "A Model for Stepfamily Development." *Family Relations* 33 (1984): 365–72.

Mowatt, M.H. *Divorce Counseling: A Practical Guide.* Lexington, Mass.: Lexington Books, 1987.

Mulroy, E.A., ed. *Women as Single Parents.* Dover, Mass.: Auburn House, 1988.

Neal, J.H. "Children's Understanding of Their Parents' Divorces," in *Children and Divorce,* ed. L. Kurdek. San Francisco: Jossey-Bass, 1983.

Neely, R. *The Divorce Decision: The Legal and Human Consequences of Ending a Marriage.* New York: McGraw-Hill, 1984.

Norton, A.J., and Glick, P.C. "One Parent Families: A Social and Economic Profile." *Family Relations* 35 (1986): 9–17.

Papernow, P.L. "Stepparent Role Development: From Outsider to Intimate," in *Relative Strangers: Studies of Stepfamily Processes,* ed. W.R. Beer. Totowa, N.J.: Rowman & Littlefield, 1988.

Pasley, K., and Ihinger-Tallman, M. *Remarriage and Stepparenting: Current Research and Theory.* New York: Guilford Press, 1987.

Peterson, R. *Women, Work, and Divorce.* Albany: State University of New York Press, 1988.

Propst, L.R., et al. "Predictors of Coping in Divorced Single Mothers." *Journal of Divorce* 9 (1986): 33–53.

Ricci, I. *Mom's House, Dad's House.* New York: Macmillan, 1980.

Robson, B. *My Parents Are Divorced Too.* New York: Everest House, 1980.

Rosen, R. "Children of Divorce: What They Feel About Access and Other Aspects of the Divorce Experience" *Journal of Clinical Child Psychology* 6 (1977): 26.

Rubenstein, C., and Shaver, P. "The Experience of Loneliness," in *Loneliness: A Sourcebook of Current Theory, Research, and Therapy,* eds. L.A. Peplau and D. Perlman. New York: John Wiley & Sons, 1985.

Samuelson, E.D. *The Divorce Law Handbook: A Comprehensive Guide to Matrimonial Practice.* New York: Human Sciences Press, 1988.

Seagull, A.A., and Seagull, E.A.W. "The Non-Custodial Father's Relationship to His Child: Conflicts and Solutions" *Journal of Clinical Child Psychology* 6 (1977): 11–15.

Seltzer, J.A. "Relationships Between Fathers and Children Who Are Apart: The Father's Role After Separation." *Journal of Marriage and the Family*, 53 (1991): 79–101.

Spanier, G.B., and Thompson, L. *Parting: The Aftermath of Separation and Divorce.* Beverly Hills, Calif.: Sage Publications, 1984.

Steinberg, J.L. "Rambo and Mother Theresa: A Judge Looks at Divorce." *The American Journal of Family Therapy* 16 (1988): 364–67.

Tavris, C. *Anger: The Misunderstood Emotion.* New York: Simon & Schuster, 1982.

Trafford, A. *Crazy Time.* New York: Harper & Row, 1982.

U.S. Bureau of the Census, Current Population Reports, Series P-23, no. 146. *Women in the American Economy,* by C.M. Taeuber and V. Valdisera. Washington, D.C.: U.S. Government Printing Office, 1986.

U.S. Bureau of the Census, Current Population Reports, Series P-23, no. 162. *Studies of Marriage and the Family.* Washington, D.C.: U.S. Government Printing Office, 1989.

Visher, E.B., and Visher, J.S. *Stepfamilies: A Guide to Working with Stepparents and Stepchildren.* New York: Brunner/Mazel, 1979.

Visher, E.B., and Visher, J.S. *Old Loyalties and New Ties: Therapeutic Strategies with Stepfamilies.* New York: Brunner/Mazel, 1988.

Walczak, Y. *Divorce: The Child's Point of View.* London: Harper & Row, 1984.

Wallerstein, J., and Blakeslee, S. *Second Chances: Men, Women and Children a Decade After Divorce.* New York: Ticknor & Fields, 1989.

Wallerstein, J.S., and Kelly, J.B. *Surviving The Breakup.* New York: Basic Books, 1980.

Wanderer, Z., and Cabot, T. *Letting Go.* New York: Dell, 1978.

Weiss, R.S. *Marital Separation.* New York: Basic Books, 1975.

Weiss, R.S. *Going It Alone.* New York: Basic Books, 1979.

Weitzman, L.J. *The Divorce Revolution.* New York: The Free Press, 1985.

Whiteside, M.F. "Family Rituals as a Key to Kinship Connections in Remarried Families." *Family Relations* 38 (1989): 34–39.

Women in Transition, Inc., *Women in Transition.* New York: Charles Scribner's Sons, 1975.

Young, J.E. "Loneliness, Depression, and Cognitive Therapy: Theory and Application," in *Loneliness: A Sourcebook of Currente Theory, Research, and Therapy,* eds. L.A. Peplau and D. Perlman. New York: John Wiley & Sons, 1982.

Index